SE
I
M
.II

1/12/01

Kiencke · Nielsen, Automotive Control Systems

Springer

Berlin
Heidelberg
New York
Barcelona
Hong Kong
London
Milan
Paris
Singapore
Tokyo

Uwe Kiencke · Lars Nielsen

Automotive Control Systems

With 291 Figures

 Springer

Professor Dr.-Ing. Uwe Kiencke

Institute of Industrial Information Technology
University of Karlsruhe
Hertzstraße 16
76187 Karlsruhe, Germany
e-mail: kiencke@iiit.etec.uni-karlsruhe.de

Professor Dr. Lars Nielsen

Department of Electrical Vehicula Systems, ISY
Linköping University
58183 Linköping, Sweden
e-mail: lars@isy.liu.se

Copyright © 2000

Society of Automotive Engineers, Inc., 400 Commonwealth Drive, Warrendale, PA 15096-0001 U.S.A.
Phone: (724) 776-4841; Fax: (724) 776-5760; E-mail: publications@sae.org; http://www.sae.org
    ISBN 0-7680-0453-5
United States Library of Congress Number: 99-69354

SAE Order No. R-283

ISBN 3-540-66922-1
Springer-Verlag Berlin Heidelberg New York

CIP data applied for

Die Deutsche Bibliothek - CIP-Einheitsaufnahme
Kiencke, Uwe: Automotive control systems / Uwe Kiencke ; Lars Nielsen. -
Berlin ; Heidelberg ; New York ; Hong Kong ; London ; Milan ; Paris ; Singapore ;
Tokyo : Springer, 2000
    ISBN 3-540-66922-1

Springer-Verlag is a company in the specialist publishing group BertelsmannSpringer
© Springer-Verlag Berlin Heidelberg 2000
Printed in Germany

Cover: Medio, Berlin; Typesetting: Camera ready by authors
Printed on acid-free paper   SPIN: 10754562   62/3020 hu - 5 4 3 2 1 0

To Margarete and Ingrid

Preface

Automotive control has become a driving factor in automotive innovation over the last twenty five years. In order to meet the enhanced requirements for lower fuel consumption, lower exhaust emissions, improved safety as well as comfort and convenience functions, automotive control had to be applied.

In any area of technology, control design is an interplay between reality, physics, modeling, and design methods. This is also true in automotive control, and there has been extensive work done in research and development leading to a number of descriptions, models, and design methodologies suited for control.

Goal of the book

Our purpose of writing a book on Automotive Control is to present this interplay between thermodynamics, basics of engine operation, vehicle mechanics as well as parameter estimation and automotive control approaches.

There are several good books available on the separate disciplines (some of the major references are in German). However, up until now there has not been a text available that explores more deeply the connections between reality, measurements, models and control design.

It has been natural for us to treat all the major aspects of automotive control in the same book. This means that we cover engine, driveline, and complete vehicle. One reason is that there are similarities in methodology when analyzing and designing automotive control systems. This includes the point of view of finding models of suitable complexity and expressiveness. Another, perhaps more important, reason is that there is a strong trend that engine control, driveline control, and vehicle control rather than being separate will be more and more integrated, so that overall vehicle optimization is possible.

It has also been important to us to show real measurements. This gives a reader the possibility to see how models are approximations of reality, and to judge the modeling assumptions. A consequence of this approach is that we have selected to treat systems that are close to some of those utilized in actual vehicles, rather than discussing speculative systems or presenting purely theoretical results.

Intended readers

This book should enable control engineers to understand engine and vehicle models necessary for controller design and should introduce mechanical engineers into vehicle-specific signal processing and automatic control.

In fact, our inspiration to write the book came from this. We are both members of the IFAC technical committee on Automotive Control (with the first author being the chairman). We met there and also at SAE meetings, and we saw the potential value of bridging a gap that was obvious to us. However, even more important to us is to share some of the fun and excitement that goes into the area of Automotive Control Systems and thus give it the attention it deserves.

Organization of the book

The outline of the book starts with engines, continues with drivelines, and finally deals with the vehicle.

Chapters 2 to 4 treat engines with regard to basics, thermodynamics, models, control, and advanced concepts. All the major control systems and their design are treated . The thermodynamic models in Chapter 2 deal with parameters that vary under one cycle and the resolution of interest is typically one crank angle degree, whereas the time scales of mean value models are in the order of 1 to several engine cycles, and the variation in variables that are considered are also averaged over one or several cycles. These models form the basis for understanding the complex phenomena that influence the engine operation, efficiency and emissions. They also serve the purpose of describing the properties influencing control design and performance in Chapters 3 and 4.

The driveline (engine, clutch, transmission, shafts, and wheels) which is a fundamental part of a vehicle is the topic in Chapter 5. Since the parts are elastic, mechanical resonances may occur. The handling of such resonances is basic for functionality and driveability, but is also important for reducing mechanical stress and noise. Two important modes of driveline control that are treated are driveline speed control and driveline torque control, having their applications in cruise control and automatic gear shifting control.

Vehicle dynamics control systems help the driver to perform the task of keeping the vehicle on the road in a safe manner. These systems are thus often safety-oriented, which means that they only interact in situations where they can reduce the possibility of an accident, but then they affect the immediate behavior of the vehicle within fractions of a second. Some systems are also used for improving the comfort of the driver. The performance of a vehicle, regarding the motions coming from accelerating, braking, cornering, or ride, is mainly a response to the forces imposed on the vehicle from the tire-road contact. Much of study of vehicle dynamics is a study on why and how these forces are produced and how they can be effectively understood and treated in simplified models.

The basics of these models and some associated control systems are presented in Chapters 6 to 8.

Chapter 9 is the exception from that all the systems and principles in this book is close to some of those utilized in actual vehicles. The reason is that road and driver modeling is part of simulation design rather than part of a vehicle. Nevertheless, it is important to realize that road and driver models are important parts in the design cycle of automotive systems design due to the importance of advanced simulation.

Background and use of the book

The material in this book has been used in courses at the universities of Karlsruhe, Germany and Linköping, Sweden. It is well suited for the later stages (third or fourth year) of the engineering programs at our technical institutes ("Diploma-engineer", "Master of Science").

The book, to a large extent, covers the basic material needed, but of course it is advantageous to have a background from basic undergraduate courses in automatic control, signals and systems, mechanics, and physics.

The course lay-out includes problem-solving sessions and laboratory experiments. The laboratory assignments typically include measurements, building models of the type treated in the book, and finally designing controllers and simulating them. Here students with more background, for example in modern control, can do more elaborate designs. This is also the case when the book is used in an introductory graduate course.

The authors

Dr. Kiencke's experience in this field started in the early nineteen seventies when developing adaptive lambda control and knock control at Robert Bosch Corporation. In the following years more complex approaches for engine modeling [2], [19] and controller design [38] were published. At that time he headed a team that developed the vehicle communication network "Controller Area Network (CAN)" [37]. Networking allowed to combine formerly stand-alone control schemes into an integrated vehicle control system. In the early nineteen nineties he joined the University of Karlsruhe in Germany where he could intensify engine and vehicle control research.

Dr. Nielsen has more than fifteen years background in academic mechatronics research (obtaining a good start at the Department of Automatic Control in Lund, Sweden). He has during that time continuously collaborated with industry, and has lead joint research projects with Scania AB, Mecel AB, Saab Automobile AB, Volvo AB, and DaimlerChrysler. He is since 1992 holder of the chair Sten Gustafsson professor of vehicular systems at Linköping University in Sweden.

Acknowledgments

The control systems presented were mostly developed within a team. Therefore the first author would like to thank especially the following cooperation partners: Dr. Martin Zechall in lambda (air-fuel ratio) control, Dr. Böning in knock control and engine map optimization, Alfred Schutz in engine idle speed control, Heinz Leiber in ABS braking control, Dr. Michael Henn in misfire detection, Dr. Achim Daiss in vehicle modeling and identification and Dr. Rajjid Majjad in road and driver modeling. It was a great pleasure to cooperate with these people and it created many friendships. The second author is especially indebted to Magnus Pettersson for joint work in driveline control, and to Lars Eriksson for joint work in engine modeling and control. Also Lars-Gunnar Hedström, Jan Nytomt, and Jan Dellrud deserves special mentioning as research dedicated industrial partners.

Furthermore we both thank Christopher Riegel, Jochen Schöntaler, Dara Torkzadeh, and Dr. Tracy Dalton for their tremendous effort to translate and revise parts of the book, as well as Dr. Dietrich Merkle as a publisher.

Last but not least we to thank our families and especially our wives Margarete and Ingrid for tolerating that so much weekend and vacation time was dedicated to this book.

Being in November 1999 looking forward to the next millennium, we hope that readers will share some of the excitement that comes along with Automotive Control Systems.

Uwe Kiencke   Lars Nielsen

Contents

1 Introduction

Vehicles are now computerized machines. This fact has had an enormous effect on the possibilities for functionality of vehicles, which together with needs and requirements from customers and from society have created vigorous activities in development.

1.1 Overall demands

The overall demands on a vehicle are that it should provide safe and comfortable transportation together with good environmental protection and good fuel economy. This means that there are three main objectives for automotive control systems:

- Efficiency, which leads to lower fuel consumption.

- Emissions should be low to protect the environment.

- Safety is of course a key issue.

There are a number of additional objectives like comfort, driveability, low wear, availability, and long term functionality.

1.2 Historic remark

Many of the technologies that today are considered advanced, sometimes even new, have been around for a long time. It is therefore interesting to ask ourselves why these technologies are surfacing now as commercial products. Direct injection of gasoline engines is one example. These concepts are not new, even if sometimes presented so, but the novelty is instead that they now with proper **control** can achieve competitive functionality and performance.

It is thus the breakthrough of computer control that is a driving factor. A good example is ABS (Anti-lock Braking Systems) which is an old idea, but it was not functional enough using mechanical solutions or analog electronics. Now these systems are readily available and widely spread.

1.3 Perspectives

Looking at the future, the three overall objectives above will be in focus. The demands of reduced emissions and advanced diagnosis functionality are steadily increased by legislators and customers. The key areas that help meeting the increased demands are the development of control and diagnosis functions in the control units. Further, this functionality will have to be obtained not only when the car is new, but over a sustained period of time. Other examples are improved stability due to handling control, and improved driveability due to driveline torque control, which also can be used to e.g. reduce clutch wear.

Regarding methodology development, mathematical models will play an important role. They will be used for model based control and diagnosis. They will also be the basis for e.g. sensor fusion, adaptive control, and supervision.

Co-design

Automotive control will not only improve existing vehicle designs. It will also to a large extent change the view of vehicular systems design leading to:

- New mechanical designs. These new designs are made possible by, and rely on, the existence of a control system.

Design of vehicles is thus evolving into co-design of mechanics and control. The goals for this development can be set high, and the perspectives on automotive control systems are therefore concluded with an inspiring mind teaser:

A mind teaser

It can not be ruled out that a car can function as an air cleaner for usual town air. In a typical town in the industrial world, the air is typically somewhat polluted from many sources, including cars, but also due to house heating and industries. Existing and upcoming technology lowering exhaust emissions are such that the concentrations in the exhaust after the catalyst can be lower than in town air. This means that the originally available pollutants have been combusted or have been collected in the catalyst.

Since such a perfect combustion produces only water and carbon dioxide, the problem of carbon dioxide is then a matter of less fuel consumption.

If at all possible, such a development will rely heavily on automotive control systems since the car has to function as an air cleaner under all possible circumstances, load variations, and driving styles. This is a mind teaser, but understanding the material in this book is a first step.

2 Thermodynamic Engine Cycles

In this chapter, the thermodynamic characteristics of basic engine cycles are explained. For each concept, the thermal efficiency is derived from thermodynamic equations. An introduction into Thermodynamics can be found in Appendix A.1.

2.1 Ideal Combustion Engines

Commonly used combustion engines in cars are four-stroke engines. They have two intermittent cycles: the gas is compressed, combusted and expanded in the first cycle, and the gas is exchanged in the second cycle. In this section the second (or passive) cycle will not be considered to simplify the mathematical derivations. The processes related to the second cycle will be discussed in Chapter 3.

Two different types of combustion engines have to be distinguished:

1. Spark-ignited Engine: Combustion caused by an electric spark-ignition.

2. Diesel Engine: Combustion caused by self inflammation due to compressional heat.

In most sections, p represents the in-cylinder pressure, V the cylinder volume, ϑ the in-cylinder temperature, S the entropy, q the thermal energy of the gas, u it's internal energy and h it's enthalpy.

2.1.1 Spark-ignited (SI) Engine

The first SI engine was presented by Nikolaus Otto in 1862. The combustion process can be modelled as an **isochoric process** where the gas volume is considered to be constant. The pV-diagram in Figure 2.1 illustrates that the gas

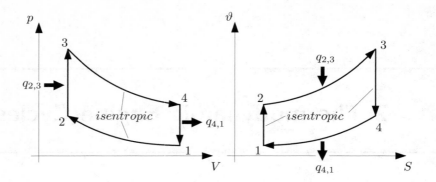

Figure 2.1 pV-diagram (left) and ϑS-diagram (right) of the SI engine process

volume does not change between step 2 and step 3. The ratio of maximum to minimum volume is given by:

$$\varepsilon = \frac{V_1}{V_2} \tag{2.1}$$

This ratio ε is called the **compression ratio** of the engine. The different steps for a complete cycle in the pV-diagram and in the ϑS-diagram can be seen in Figure 2.1. Mathematically they can be described as followed:

$1 \rightarrow 2$: Isentropic compression, $dq = 0$:

$$
\begin{aligned}
dq &= du + dw = 0 \\
q_{1,2} &= 0 \\
dw &= -du = -m\,c_v\,d\vartheta \\
w_{1,2} &= -\int_1^2 m\,c_v\,d\vartheta = -m\,c_v(\vartheta_2 - \vartheta_1)
\end{aligned}
$$

The work $w_{1,2}$ is used to compress the gas and therefore, it is negative.

$2 \rightarrow 3$: Isochoric input of thermal energy, $dV = 0$:

$$
\begin{aligned}
dw &= p\,dV = 0 \\
w_{2,3} &= \int_2^3 p\,dV = 0 \\
dq &= du = m\,c_v\,d\vartheta \\
q_{2,3} &= m\,c_v \int_2^3 d\vartheta = m\,c_v(\vartheta_3 - \vartheta_2)
\end{aligned}
$$

The increased thermal energy $q_{2,3}$ is caused by combustion of the gas.

$3 \rightarrow 4$: Isentropic expansion, $dq = 0$:

$$q_{3,4} = 0$$

$$dw = -du = -m\,c_v\,d\vartheta$$

$$w_{3,4} = -\int_3^4 m\,c_v\,d\vartheta = -m\,c_v(\vartheta_4 - \vartheta_3)$$

This state change describes the power stroke of the engine where $w_{3,4}$ is the output of kinetic energy from the gas, which is positive ($\vartheta_4 < \vartheta_3$).

$4 \rightarrow 1$: Isochoric heat loss, $dV = 0$:

$$dw = p\,dV = 0$$

$$w_{4,1} = \int_4^1 p\,dV = 0$$

$$dq = du + dw = m\,c_v\,d\vartheta$$

$$q_{4,1} = m\,c_v\int_4^1 d\vartheta = m\,c_v(\vartheta_1 - \vartheta_4)$$

The loss of thermal energy $q_{4,1}$ is due to the gas exchange: The burnt hot gas is pumped into the exhaust and the combustion chamber is filled with a cold mixture of unburnt fuel vapour and air ($q_{4,1}$ is negative because of $\vartheta_1 < \vartheta_4$).

The thermal efficiency of the engine is equivalent to the ratio of all the kinetic energies to the input of thermal energy $q_{2,3}$ at the combustion of a complete cycle:

$$\eta_{th} = \frac{w_{1,2} + w_{2,3} + w_{3,4} + w_{4,1}}{q_{2,3}}$$

$$= \frac{m\,c_v(-\vartheta_2 + \vartheta_1 - \vartheta_4 + \vartheta_3)}{m\,c_v(\vartheta_3 - \vartheta_2)}$$

$$= 1 - \frac{\vartheta_4 - \vartheta_1}{\vartheta_3 - \vartheta_2}$$

$$= 1 - \frac{\vartheta_1}{\vartheta_2}\frac{\vartheta_4/\vartheta_1 - 1}{\vartheta_3/\vartheta_2 - 1}$$

The relationship for isentropic changes $1 \rightarrow 2$ and $3 \rightarrow 4$ can be used to simplify the equation:

$$\frac{\vartheta_4}{\vartheta_3} = \left(\frac{V_3}{V_4}\right)^{\kappa-1} = \frac{1}{\varepsilon^{\kappa-1}} = \frac{\vartheta_1}{\vartheta_2} \tag{2.2}$$

This yields:

$$\eta_{th} = 1 - \frac{1}{\varepsilon^{\kappa-1}} \tag{2.3}$$

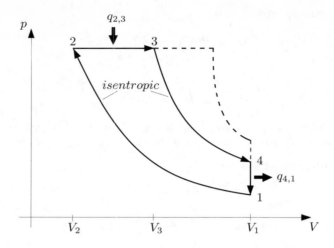

Figure 2.2 pV-diagram for Diesel Engine

Please note that the thermal efficiency η_{th} does not depend on the absolute temperature values. It mainly depends on the compression ratio ε. Example: For a compression ratio of $\varepsilon = 11$ and an adiabatic coefficient of $\kappa = 1.4$ the theoretical thermal efficiency η_{th} is:

$$\eta_{th} = 0.617$$

2.1.2 Diesel Engine

Rudolf Diesel developped this engine from 1893 to 1897. In a diesel engine, the combustion takes place in an **isobaric state change** during the downward movement of the piston. At the beginning of this process the combustion is controlled by the injection of fuel to maintain a constant pressure at the expansion from 2 to 3. The isobaric state change is indicated between steps 2 and 3 in the pV-diagram in Figure 2.2. The more fuel is injected, the longer the distance between steps 2 and 3 and the larger the volume ratio:

$$\rho = \frac{V_3}{V_2} = \frac{\vartheta_3}{\vartheta_2} \quad . \tag{2.4}$$

This ratio is called **injection ratio** or **load**. The injection ratio ρ has an impact on the thermodynamic efficiency which is derived after explaining the different parts of the cycle:

$1 \rightarrow 2$: Isentropic compression, $dq = 0$:

$$
\begin{aligned}
dq &= du + dw = 0 \\
q_{1,2} &= 0 \\
dw &= -du = -m\,c_v\,d\vartheta \\
w_{1,2} &= -m\,c_v(\vartheta_2 - \vartheta_1)
\end{aligned}
$$

The mechanical work $w_{1,2}$ is used to compress the gas (equivalent to the SI engine). It is negative.

$2 \rightarrow 3$: Isobaric gain of thermal energy, $dp = 0$:

$$
\begin{aligned}
dq &= dh - V\,dp = m\,c_p\,d\vartheta \\
q_{2,3} &= m\,c_p(\vartheta_3 - \vartheta_2) \\
dw &= p\,dV = m\,R\,d\vartheta \\
w_{2,3} &= m\,R(\vartheta_3 - \vartheta_2)
\end{aligned}
$$

In this process, the combustion generates the thermal energy $q_{2,3}$ and produces the kinetic energy $w_{2,3}$.

$3 \rightarrow 4$: Isentropic expansion, $dq = 0$:

$$
\begin{aligned}
q_{3,4} &= 0 \\
dw &= -du = -m\,c_v\,d\vartheta \\
w_{3,4} &= -m\,c_v(\vartheta_4 - \vartheta_3)
\end{aligned}
$$

Note that $w_{3,4}$ is positive since $\vartheta_4 < \vartheta_3$.

$4 \rightarrow 1$: Isochoric heat loss, $dV = 0$:

$$
\begin{aligned}
dw &= p\,dV = 0 \\
w_{4,1} &= \int_4^1 p\,dV = 0 \\
dq &= du + dw = m\,c_v\,d\vartheta \\
q_{4,1} &= m\,c_v \int_4^1 d\vartheta = m\,c_v(\vartheta_1 - \vartheta_4)
\end{aligned}
$$

Note that $q_{4,1}$ is negative since $\vartheta_1 < \vartheta_4$.

With $\kappa = \frac{c_p}{c_v}$ and $R = (c_p - c_v)$ the thermodynamic efficiency of the diesel engine can now be calculated:

$$
\begin{aligned}
\eta_{th} &= \frac{w_{1,2} + w_{2,3} + w_{3,4} + w_{4,1}}{q_{2,3}} \\
&= \frac{-m\,c_v(\vartheta_2 - \vartheta_1) + m(c_p - c_v)(\vartheta_3 - \vartheta_2) - m\,c_v(\vartheta_4 - \vartheta_3)}{m\,c_p(\vartheta_3 - \vartheta_2)} \\
&= 1 - \frac{1}{\kappa}\,\frac{\vartheta_1}{\vartheta_2}\,\frac{\vartheta_4/\vartheta_1 - 1}{\vartheta_3/\vartheta_2 - 1}
\end{aligned}
$$

This equation can be simplified by using the relationship for the isentropic process (Eq. 2.2) and the relationship for the isobaric process (Eq. 2.4). Additionally, the following relationship is used for the isochoric heat loss:

$$
\frac{\vartheta_4}{\vartheta_1} = \frac{p_4}{p_1} = \frac{p_4\,p_2}{p_3\,p_1} = \frac{V_3^\kappa\,V_1^\kappa}{V_4^\kappa\,V_2^\kappa}
$$

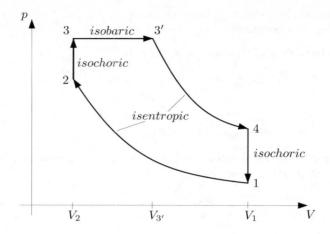

Figure 2.3 pV-diagram of Seiliger process

In that, we have $p_2 = p_3$.

$$\frac{\vartheta_4}{\vartheta_1} = \left(\frac{\vartheta_4}{\vartheta_3}\right)^{\kappa/\kappa-1} \left(\frac{\vartheta_2}{\vartheta_1}\right)^{\kappa/\kappa-1} = \left(\frac{\vartheta_4}{\vartheta_1}\right)^{\kappa/\kappa-1} \left(\frac{\vartheta_2}{\vartheta_3}\right)^{\kappa/\kappa-1}$$

This results in: $\vartheta_4/\vartheta_1 = (\vartheta_3/\vartheta_2)^{\kappa} = \rho^{\kappa}$, which yields the thermodynamic efficiency of the Diesel engine:

$$\eta_{th} = 1 - \frac{1}{\varepsilon^{\kappa-1}}\frac{1}{\kappa}\frac{\rho^{\kappa}-1}{\rho-1} \tag{2.5}$$

It can be seen that the efficiency η_{th} decreases as the load ρ is increased. At high loads, the diesel engine has a lower efficiency compared to the SI engine, supposing the same compression ratio ε for both (see Figure 2.4). The compression ratio for Diesel engines is however much higher than for SI engines to improve the thermodynamic efficiency.

2.1.3   Seiliger Process

The Seiliger process models the thermodynamic process in automotive engines much better than the previously described models of SI and Diesel engines. Figure 2.3 shows that the combustion is now divided into two parts: In the first part, the gas is heated in an **isochoric process** between step 2 and step 3. In the second part the gas is expanded in an **isobaric state change** between step 3 and step 3'. The cycle is characterised by the **compression ratio** $\varepsilon = V_1/V_2$, the **injection ratio** $\rho = V_{3'}/V_3$, and the **pressure ratio**:

$$\chi = \frac{p_3}{p_2} \tag{2.6}$$

The different steps of the cycle are the following:

$1 \rightarrow 2$: Isentropic compression, $dq = 0$:

$$
\begin{aligned}
dq &= du + dw = 0 \\
q_{1,2} &= 0 \\
dw &= -du = -m\,c_v\,d\vartheta \\
w_{1,2} &= -m\,c_v(\vartheta_2 - \vartheta_1)
\end{aligned}
$$

$2 \rightarrow 3$: Isochoric input of thermal energy, $dV = 0$:

$$
\begin{aligned}
dw &= p\,dV = 0 \\
w_{2,3} &= 0 \\
dq &= du = m\,c_v\,d\vartheta \\
q_{2,3} &= m\,c_v(\vartheta_3 - \vartheta_2)
\end{aligned}
$$

$3 \rightarrow 3'$: Isobaric input of thermal energy, $dp = 0$:

$$
\begin{aligned}
dq &= dh - V\,dp = m\,c_p\,d\vartheta \\
q_{3,3'} &= m\,c_p(\vartheta_{3'} - \vartheta_3) \\
dw &= p\,dV = m\,R\,d\vartheta \\
w_{3,3'} &= m\,R(\vartheta_{3'} - \vartheta_3)
\end{aligned}
$$

$3' \rightarrow 4$: Isentropic expansion, $dq = 0$:

$$
\begin{aligned}
q_{3',4} &= 0 \\
dw &= -du = -m\,c_v\,d\vartheta \\
w_{3',4} &= -m\,c_v(\vartheta_4 - \vartheta_{3'})
\end{aligned}
$$

$4 \rightarrow 1$: Isochoric heat loss, $dV = 0$:

$$
\begin{aligned}
dw &= p\,dV = 0 \\
w_{4,1} &= 0 \\
dq &= du + dw = m\,c_v\,d\vartheta \\
q_{4,1} &= m\,c_v(\vartheta_1 - \vartheta_4)
\end{aligned}
$$

The thermodynamic efficiency of the Seliger process is then:

$$
\begin{aligned}
\eta_{th} &= \frac{w_{1,2} + w_{2,3} + w_{3,3'} + w_{3',4} + w_{4,1}}{q_{2,3}} \\
&= 1 - \frac{\vartheta_4/\vartheta_1 - 1}{\vartheta_3/\vartheta_1 - \vartheta_2/\vartheta_1 + \kappa(\vartheta_{3'}/\vartheta_1 - \vartheta_3/\vartheta_1)}
\end{aligned}
$$

The isentropic process is characterised by:

$$
\frac{\vartheta_2}{\vartheta_1} = \varepsilon^{\kappa - 1}
$$

which yields:

$$\frac{\vartheta_4}{\vartheta_{3'}} = \left(\frac{V_{3'}}{V_4}\right)^{\kappa-1}$$

$$= \left(\frac{V_{3'}}{V_3}\frac{V_3}{V_4}\right)^{\kappa-1} = \left(\frac{V_{3'}}{V_3}\frac{V_2}{V_1}\right)^{\kappa-1}$$

$$= \left(\frac{\rho}{\varepsilon}\right)^{\kappa-1}$$

In the isochoric process, the relationship

$$\frac{\vartheta_3}{\vartheta_2} = \frac{p_3}{p_2} = \chi$$

can be used, and the temperature ratio in the isobaric process is given by:

$$\frac{\vartheta_{3'}}{\vartheta_3} = \frac{V_{3'}}{V_3} = \rho \quad .$$

Therefore, the following temperature ratios may be expressed as:

$$\frac{\vartheta_3}{\vartheta_1} = \frac{\vartheta_3}{\vartheta_2}\frac{\vartheta_2}{\vartheta_1} = \chi \, \varepsilon^{\kappa-1}$$

$$\frac{\vartheta_{3'}}{\vartheta_1} = \frac{\vartheta_{3'}}{\vartheta_3}\frac{\vartheta_3}{\vartheta_1} = \rho \, \chi \, \varepsilon^{\kappa-1}$$

$$\frac{\vartheta_4}{\vartheta_1} = \frac{\vartheta_4}{\vartheta_{3'}}\frac{\vartheta_{3'}}{\vartheta_1} = \left(\frac{\rho}{\varepsilon}\right)^{\kappa-1} \rho \, \chi \, \varepsilon^{\kappa-1} = \chi \, \rho^{\kappa}$$

The thermodynamic efficiency of the Seliger process can be simplified to:

$$\eta_{th} = 1 - \frac{1}{\varepsilon^{\kappa-1}}\frac{\chi \, \rho^{\kappa} - 1}{\chi - 1 + \kappa \, \chi \, (\rho - 1)} \tag{2.7}$$

It can be seen that the thermodynamic efficiency of the SI engine is obtained when $\rho = 1$ and that of the Diesel engine when $\chi = 1$ (Fig. 2.4).

2.1.4   Comparison of Different Engine Concepts

The in-cylinder pressure during combustion is plotted over the crankshaft angle in Fig. 2.5. The compression ratio ε for the SI engine is limited by the maximum allowable pressure p_3 during the combustion process. Under part load conditions, the maximum pressure of a cycle is far below this limit, since the SI engine power output is modulated by throttling the air intake thus modulating p_1 (Fig. 2.6). A low compression ratio ε is also helpful to reduce knocking of the engine and to meet material demands. In contrast to SI engines, the maximum pressure for Diesel engines is closer set to the maximum allowable pressure p_3. As the Diesel engine is unthrottled (modulation of ρ), it can afford higher compression ratios $\varepsilon = V_1/V_2$ than the SI engine (Fig. 2.7).

The four-stroke engine works intermittently: A hot combustion cycle is always followed by a cool gas exchange cycle. In the first cycle, peak temperatures

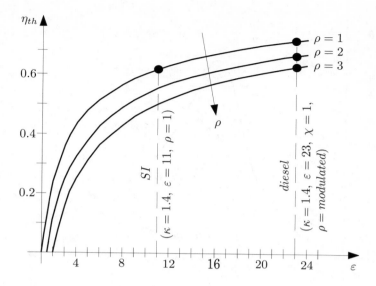

Figure 2.4 Thermodynamic efficiency η_{th} depending on compression ratio ε and load ρ (Eq. 2.7)

of $2500 - 2800\,°C$ occur. Compared to that, the maximum temperature of gas turbines must be kept much lower ($1300\,°C$), since the combustion process is continuous. Diesel engines have a higher thermodynamic efficiency than SI engines at low and medium power (Fig. 2.4). At turbocharged Diesel engines also p_1 is modulated. In order to stay below maximum temperatures, the compression ratio ε is reduced at turbocharged Diesel engines. The absolute effective power output of combustion engines depends on the displacement volume V_d, the specific work output per power-stroke w_e and the number of crankshaft revolutions n:

$$P_e = w_e\, V_d\, \frac{n}{2} \qquad (2.8)$$

where:
P_e is the absolute effective power output
w_e is the specific work referred to the displacement volume V_d
V_d is the displacement volume $V_1 - V_2$ (here, only one cylinder is regarded)
n is the number of crankshaft revolutions per minute

The factor $1/2$ is necessary in determining the power output of four-stroke engines since only every second cycle contributes power. The mean piston velocity $\bar{s}$ depends on the number of crankshaft revolutions per minute n and the maximum piston stroke $2\,r$ from top dead to bottom dead center. The mean piston velocity is:

$$\bar{s} = 4\,n\,r \qquad (2.9)$$

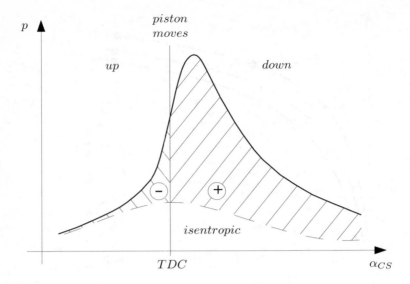

Figure 2.5 In-cylinder pressure over crankshaft angle during combustion process

A typical value in car engines is $\bar{\bar{s}} = 15 \, m/s$ at maximum power output. Equation 2.8 can now be written as:

$$\frac{P_e}{V_d} = w_e \frac{\bar{\bar{s}}}{8\,r} \qquad (2.10)$$

Please note that the specific power P_e/V_d is inversely proportional to the maximum piston stroke $2\,r$ (r is the crankshaft radius). Table 2.1 gives some examples of engine types and their characteristic values. It can be seen that the specific

Table 2.1 Specific power output of various combustion engines

Engine type	$\bar{\bar{s}}$	w_e	$2\,r$	P_e/V_d
	$[m/s]$	$[J/m^3]$	$[cm]$	$[kW/dm^3]$
Car engine	15	13	8	61
Truck engine	10	18	12	38
Big four-stroke diesel	8	20	32	13
Big two-stroke diesel	6	15	60	4

power decreases with increasing dimensions r at large engines. They are mainly used in ships because of their thermodynamic efficiency. When size and weight are major concerns at high power levels, gas turbines are preferred e.g. in aircraft.

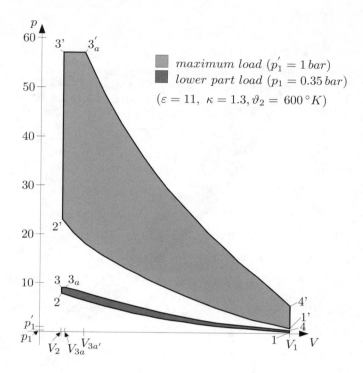

Figure 2.6 Load behaviour of SI engine (Modulation of p_1), $1\,bar = 10^5\,Pa$

2.2 Alternative Combustion Engines

2.2.1 Gas Turbine

In the gas turbine engine fuel is combusted in a continuous process. The air has to be compressed before it flows into the combustion chamber where the fuel is injected and burned. The resulting expansion of the gas is used to turn the turbine shaft. Therefore, the effective power is the power of the turbine minus the power used for the compressor. The process can be modelled as a **Brayton cycle** (or Joule process) which is shown in Figure 2.8. The different steps of the Brayton cycle:

$1 \rightarrow 2$: Isentropic compression, $dq = 0$:

$$
\begin{aligned}
dq &= du + dw = 0 \\
q_{1,2} &= 0 \\
dw &= -dh = -m\,c_p\,d\vartheta \\
w_{1,2} &= -m\,c_p(\vartheta_2 - \vartheta_1)
\end{aligned}
$$

The kinetic energy $w_{1,2}$ is provided by the compressor.

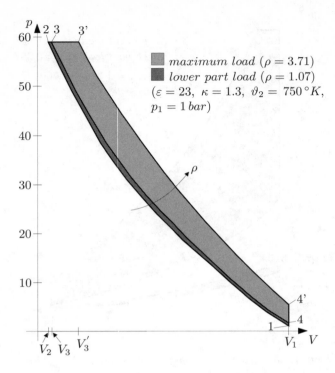

Figure 2.7 Load behaviour of Diesel engine (Modulation of ρ), $1\,bar = 10^5\,Pa$

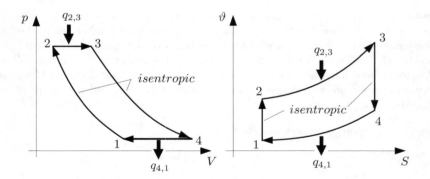

Figure 2.8 pV-diagram (left) and ϑS-diagram (right) of the Brayton cycle

$2 \rightarrow 3$: Isobaric input of thermal energy, $dp = 0$:

$$
\begin{aligned}
dq &= dh - V\,dp = m\,c_p\,d\vartheta \\
q_{2,3} &= m\,c_p(\vartheta_3 - \vartheta_2) \\
dw &= p\,dV = m\,R\,d\vartheta \\
w_{2,3} &= m\,R(\vartheta_3 - \vartheta_2)
\end{aligned}
$$

$3 \rightarrow 4$: Isentropic expansion, $dq = 0$, generation of work:

$$
\begin{aligned}
q_{3,4} &= 0 \\
dw &= -dh = -m\,c_p\,d\vartheta \\
w_{3,4} &= -m\,c_p(\vartheta_4 - \vartheta_3)
\end{aligned}
$$

$4 \rightarrow 1$: Isobaric heat loss, $dp = 0$:

$$
\begin{aligned}
dq &= dh - V\,dp = m\,c_p\,d\vartheta \\
q_{4,1} &= m\,c_p(\vartheta_1 - \vartheta_4) \\
dw &= m\,R\,d\vartheta = 0 \\
w_{4,1} &= m\,R(\vartheta_1 - \vartheta_4)
\end{aligned}
$$

The thermal energy $q_{4,1}$ and mechanical work $w_{4,1}$ are both negative because of $\vartheta_1 < \vartheta_4$.

The thermal efficiency of the gas turbine is:

$$
\begin{aligned}
\eta_{th} &= \frac{q_{2,3} + q_{4,1}}{q_{2,3}} \\
&= \frac{m\,c_p(\vartheta_3 - \vartheta_2) + m\,c_p(\vartheta_1 - \vartheta_4)}{m\,c_p(\vartheta_3 - \vartheta_2)} \\
&= 1 - \frac{\vartheta_4}{\vartheta_3}\frac{1 - \vartheta_1/\vartheta_4}{1 - \vartheta_2/\vartheta_3}
\end{aligned}
$$

As pointed out before, the isentropic process is characterised by:

$$
\frac{\vartheta_1}{\vartheta_2} = \left(\frac{V_2}{V_1}\right)^{\kappa - 1} = \frac{1}{\varepsilon^{\kappa - 1}} = \frac{\vartheta_4}{\vartheta_3}
$$

The relationship $\vartheta_1/\vartheta_4 = \vartheta_2/\vartheta_3$ for the isentropic process and the injection ratio $\rho = \vartheta_3/\vartheta_2$ are used to simplify the thermodynamic efficiency:

$$
\eta_{th} = 1 - \frac{1}{\rho}\frac{\vartheta_4}{\vartheta_2} \tag{2.11}
$$

The efficiency of the gas turbine depends on the temperature ratio ϑ_4/ϑ_2. Reasonably high efficiency levels can only be reached, if the heat of the outgoing air is used to heat up the incoming air in front of the compressor. Figure 2.9 shows

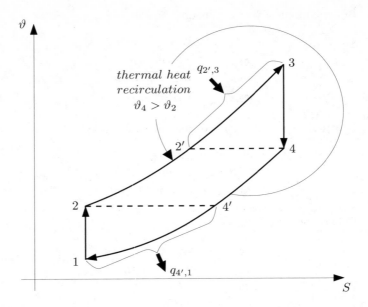

Figure 2.9 ϑS-diagram of the Joule process with heat recirculation

the ϑS-diagram supposing a complete recirculation of thermal heat. Assuming $\vartheta_2 = \vartheta_{4'}$ and $\vartheta_{2'} = \vartheta_4$, the necessary input of thermal energy for each cycle can be reduced to:

$$q_{2',3} = m\,c_p(\vartheta_3 - \vartheta_{2'}) = m\,c_p(\vartheta_3 - \vartheta_4) \tag{2.12}$$

and the heat loss is also reduced to:

$$q_{4',1} = m\,c_p(\vartheta_1 - \vartheta_{4'}) = m\,c_p(\vartheta_1 - \vartheta_2) \tag{2.13}$$

Equation 2.11 can be modified:

$$\eta_{th} \quad = \quad \frac{q_{2',3} + q_{4',1}}{q_{2',3}}$$

$$= \quad 1 - \frac{\vartheta_2}{\vartheta_3}\frac{1 - \vartheta_1/\vartheta_2}{1 - \vartheta_4/\vartheta_3}$$

Finally, by using the same relationships as before, the thermodynamic efficiency of the gas turbine with complete heat recirculation is:

$$\eta_{th} = 1 - \frac{1}{\rho} \tag{2.14}$$

The thermal efficiency depends only on the load $\rho = \vartheta_3/\vartheta_2$. The higher the load the better the efficiency. The maximum temperature ϑ_3 is mainly limited by the material from which the gas turbine is constructed. Equation 2.14 is not valid for extremely small loads as the heat recirculation does not work properly under these conditions. The main advantages of gas turbines are the following:

- Gas turbines are much smaller and lighter compared to four-stroke piston engines: The weight per power output in gas turbines is $1.7 - 2.7 \, kg/kW$ and for four-stroke piston engines it is $2 - 4 \, kg/kW$.

- High torque can be generated even at very low revolutions.

- Different types of fuel can be used for combustion: multi-fuel capability.

- Gas turbines are easy to start even at low temperatures.

- Low vibrations because of a continuous combustion.

- Long service intervals between required maintenance.

- Reduced emissions of noxious exhaust gases. ECE test results: $CO = 20 \, g$, $HC = 0.8 \, g$, $NO_x = 2 - 3 \, g$ per test.

However, there are some disadvantages:

- Low efficiency for low loads.

- Poor dynamic behaviour during transients.

Gas turbines are mainly used in air planes because of their low weight. Their efficiency can be increased by raising the maximum allowable temperature. Ceramics like Al_2O_3 or laminated silicon-carbon materials are used for the construction to allow higher temperatures. An example of temperature values for two different turbines types is given in Table 2.2.

Table 2.2 Temperature values in $°C$ at different locations of a metal and a ceramic gas turbine

Location of measurement	Metal gas turbine	Ceramic gas turbine
Compressor inlet	230	250
Heat exchanger outlet (air)	700	950
Combustion chamber outlet	1000-1100	1250-1350
Heat exchanger inlet (gas)	750	1000
Heat exchanger outlet (gas)	270	300

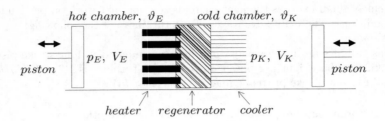

Figure 2.10 Mechanical representation of the Stirling engine

2.2.2 Stirling Engine

The Stirling engine is a piston engine which uses a continuous heat supply. It was invented by Robert Stirling in 1816. The cycle process has a high efficiency, comparable to that of the reference Carnot cycle. Even though the engine was redesigned by Philips Corporation (in 1938) and recently by other companies, some mechanical problems remain unsolved. Figure 2.10 shows the mechanical representation of the Stirling engine. It consists of three main parts:

H	heater	the gas is heated from outside
R	regenerator	the regenerator stores thermal energy
C	cooler	the gas is cooled from outside

The heater, regenerator and cooler are located in the middle. The pistons on the left and right side are linked mechanically. The cycle consists of the following four steps that can be seen in Figure 2.11:

$1 \rightarrow 2$: Isothermal compression: $\vartheta_1 = \vartheta_2$
  The heat is absorbed by the cooler when the two pistons move to the left to compress the gas.

$$w_{1,2} = m R \vartheta_1 \ln \frac{V_2}{V_1}$$
$$q_{1,2} = w_{1,2}$$

The emission of heat $q_{1,2}$ is equivalent to the input of kinetic energy $w_{1,2}$.

$2 \rightarrow 3$: Isochoric input of thermal energy: $V_2 = V_3$
  The two pistons move simultaneously to the left and the gas is heated by the regenerator. Both, pressure and temperature are increased.

$$q_{2,3} = m c_v (\vartheta_3 - \vartheta_2)$$

$3 \rightarrow 4$: Isothermal expansion: $\vartheta_3 = \vartheta_4$
  The thermal energy is supplied by the heater, when the pistons move back

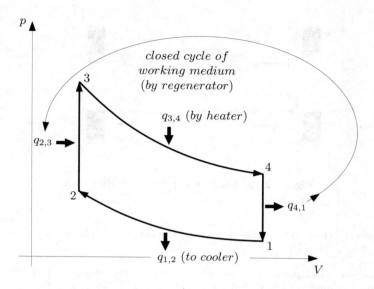

Figure 2.11 pV-diagram of the Stirling cycle

to the right.

$$w_{3,4} = m R \vartheta_3 \, ln\frac{V_4}{V_3}$$
$$q_{3,4} = w_{3,4}$$

The mechanical work $w_{3,4}$ is equivalent to the thermal energy $q_{3,4}$.

$4 \rightarrow 1$: Isochoric heat regeneration: $V_4 = V_1$
   As the pistons move simultaneously to the right, thermal energy is stored
   in the regenerator. The pressure as well as the temperature drop to lower
   levels.

$$q_{4,1} = m \, c_v(\vartheta_1 - \vartheta_4)$$

By exploiting the fact that $\vartheta_1 = \vartheta_2$ and $\vartheta_3 = \vartheta_4$ for the isothermic processes,
and $V_1 = V_4$ and $V_2 = V_3$ for the isochoric processes, the thermal efficiency of
the Stirling engine is:

$$\eta_{th} = \frac{q_{1,2} + q_{3,4}}{q_{3,4}} = 1 - \frac{\vartheta_1}{\vartheta_3} \tag{2.15}$$

Hence, the efficiency depends only on the temperature ratio ϑ_1/ϑ_3. For example,
a temperature ratio of $80\,^{\circ}C/600\,^{\circ}C$ results in a thermodynamic efficiency of:

$$\eta_{th} = 0.87 \tag{2.16}$$

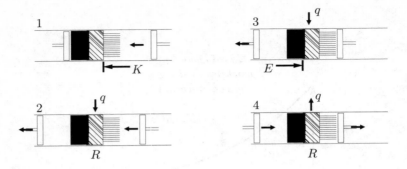

Figure 2.12 The four steps of the Stirling cycle

which is very close to the efficiency of the Carnot cycle. The main advantages of the Stirling engine are:

- Engine is independent of the heat source. Instead of combusting fossil fuels, alternate heat sources such as solar heat could be employed.

- High (theoretical) efficiency.

- Very quiet.

- Reduced emission of noxious exhaust gases. ECE test results: $CO = 4 - 6\,g$, $HC = 0.5 - 2\,g$, $NO_x = 0.6 - 2.0\,g$ per test.

On the other hand, there are some disadvantages:

- Expensive to construct.

- Regenerator: conduction and storage of heat are difficult to combine.

- Heat resistant materials needed.

- A heat exchanger for the cooler is needed to increase the efficiency. It increases however volume and costs.

Experimental Stirling engines with temperatures of $40 - 80\,^\circ C/600 - 650\,^\circ C$ can reach an effective thermodynamic efficiency of

$$\eta_{eff} = 0.35 - 0.40 \qquad (2.17)$$

which is much lower than the theoretical value (Equation 2.16).

2.2.3 Steam Engine

The steam engine introduced by James Watt is the oldest engine using continuous combustion. The steam is transferred from the boiler to the cylinder. The piston is moved by the expanding steam. The linear movement of the piston is translated

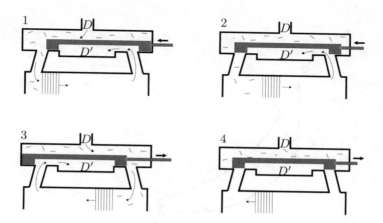

Figure 2.13 Steam engine

into a rotation of the crankshaft by the connecting rod. The different steps are illustrated in Figure 2.13 and Figure 2.14.

The different steps of the steam engine cycle are:

$1 \rightarrow 2$: Isochoric compression, followed by an isothermal expansion:
This process can be divided into two parts: First, hot steam is injected into the cylinder through the open valve at constant volume $(1 \rightarrow 1')$ where $V_{1'} = V_1$. Second, the gas expands at a constant temperature $(1' \rightarrow 2)$ where $\vartheta_{1'} = \vartheta_2$:

$$\begin{aligned}
w_{1,1'} &= 0 \\
q_{1,1'} &= m\, c_v(\vartheta_{1'} - \vartheta_1) = m\, c_v(\vartheta_2 - \vartheta_1) \\
w_{1',2} &= m\, R\, \vartheta_{1'} \ln \frac{V_2}{V_{1'}} = m\, R\, \vartheta_2 \ln \frac{V_2}{V_1} \\
q_{1',2} &= w_{1',2}
\end{aligned}$$

$2 \rightarrow 3$: Isentropic expansion:
After the valve is closed, the expansion is continued until the maximum volume is reached.

$$\begin{aligned}
q_{2,3} &= 0 \\
w_{2,3} &= m\, c_v(\vartheta_2 - \vartheta_3)
\end{aligned}$$

$3 \rightarrow 4$: Isochoric heat regeneration and isothermal compression:
This process can be divided into two steps: The pressure drops at constant volume after the valve is opened at $3 \rightarrow 3'$ where $V_3 = V_{3'}$. Second, the

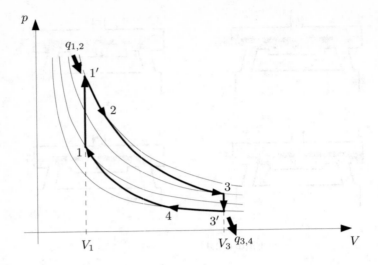

Figure 2.14 pV-diagram of the steam engine

steam is compressed isothermally at $3' \rightarrow 4$ where $\vartheta_{3'} = \vartheta_4$.

$$
\begin{aligned}
w_{3,3'} &= 0 \\
q_{3,3'} &= m\,c_v(\vartheta_{3'} - \vartheta_3) = m\,c_v(\vartheta_4 - \vartheta_3) \\
w_{3',4} &= m\,R\,\vartheta_{3'} \ln \frac{V_4}{V_{3'}} = m\,R\,\vartheta_4 \ln \frac{V_4}{V_3} \\
q_{3',4} &= w_{3',4}
\end{aligned}
$$

$4 \rightarrow 1$: Isentropic compression: After the valve is closed, the gas is compressed mechanically:

$$
\begin{aligned}
q_{4,1} &= 0 \\
w_{4,1} &= m\,c_v(\vartheta_4 - \vartheta_1)
\end{aligned}
$$

The mechanical work $w_{4,1}$ is negative.

The thermal efficiency of the steam engine is expressed by:

$$
\begin{aligned}
\eta_{th} &= \frac{w_{1',2} + w_{2,3} + w_{3',4} + w_{4,1}}{q_{1,1'} + q_{1',2}} \\
&= 1 - \frac{\vartheta_3 - \vartheta_4 + (\kappa - 1)\vartheta_4 \ln(V_3/V_4)}{\vartheta_2 - \vartheta_1 + (\kappa - 1)\vartheta_2 \ln(V_2/V_1)}
\end{aligned}
$$

By inserting the compression ratio $\varepsilon = V_3/V_1$, the partial compression ratio $\rho = V_2/V_1 = V_3/V_4$ and the pressure ratio $\chi = p_{1'}/p_1$, this leads to:

$$
\eta_{th} = 1 - \frac{1}{\varepsilon^{\kappa-1}} \frac{\rho^{\kappa-1}(\kappa - 1)(1 + \ln \rho)}{(\chi - 1) + (\kappa - 1)\chi \ln \rho} \tag{2.18}
$$

Table 2.3 Typical storage volumes and weights of different energy sources with an energy of $1000\,kWh$.

Source	Volume V in $[l]$	Mass m_1 in $[kg]$	Tank m_2 in $[kg]$	Mass+Tank $m_1 + m_2$ in $[kg]$
Fuel	117	83	21	104
Diesel	102	85	17	102
Methanol	224	180	41	221
Liquid gas	153	78	90	168
Methane	259	72	500	570
H_2, liquid	426	30	142	172
H_2, hydride buffer	200	30	970	1000
Battery (lead)	5000	0	10000	10000

An example is given for $\rho = 2$ and $\chi = 10$:

$$\eta_{th} = 1 - \frac{1.065}{\varepsilon^{\kappa - 1}} \qquad (2.19)$$

which is $\eta_{th} = 0.31$ for a $\kappa = 1.4$ and $\varepsilon = 3$.

Advantages of the steam engine:

- Engine is independent of the heat source: multi-fuel capability.
- Noxious exhaust emissions are low because of continuous combustion.
- High torque at low revolutions.

Disadvantages of the steam engine:

- Heavy weight.
- Poor thermodynamic efficiency.
- The water in the boiler needs to be heated before the engine can be started.

2.2.4 Potential of Different Fuels and Propulsion Systems

Table 2.3 illustrates that a constant amount of stored energy varies considerably in its volume and weight. Standard *lead batteries* are much too heavy. Other types of batteries are lighter, but they are still not comparable to the weight of ordinary fuel. Power is dissipated in the charging and discharging process of the battery, reducing the overall efficiency. Eventually, battery driven vehicles

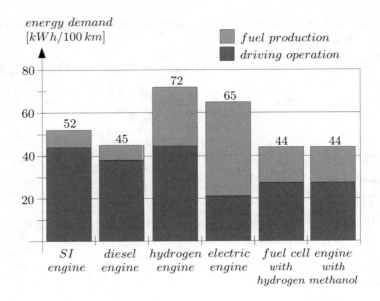

Figure 2.15 Energy demand of different engine concepts [45]

with a reduced buffer size may be used in special applications at short distances. Another promising approach are hybrid vehicles, where an internal combustion engine is combined with an electrical motor. The electrical motor may be activated to smooth out transients of the combustion engine and the driveline, contributing to reduced noxious emissions. Under part load conditions the combustion engine can also load the battery, so that battery volume and weight are significantly reduced.

Hydrogen H_2 gas is too voluminous to be used as adequate energy source. It can be stored either at an extremely cold temperature of $20\,K$ or at relatively high pressure at room temperature. Over long time periods, H_2 leaks through even thick walled steel tanks. In hydride buffers, H_2 is chemically bound. Since hydrogen burns at high combustion temperatures, emissions of nitrogen oxide (NO_x) become a problem.

Fuel cells produce electrical energy directly at low temperatures. Thermal efficiencies of $70\,\%$ are reached for the synthesis of H_2 and O_2. The storage of hydrogen is again the problem. If H_2 must be however generated from natural gas or from methanol, efficiencies become much lower. The task is to generate the exact amount of hydrogen from e.g. methanol even under realtime transient engine conditions. For this the fuel conversion process can be modelled, and the actual masses reacting in the conversion process be estimated in realtime, as a basis for state space control. *Fuel cells* appear to be a promising alternative to combustion engines. In Figure 2.15, the relative energy requirements to move a vehicle by $100\,km$ are shown for different propulsion systems.

3 Engine Management Systems

3.1 Basic Engine Operation

3.1.1 Effective Work

Four-stroke engines are characterised by two alternate cycles: In the first cycle, equivalent to the first and second strokes, the gas is compressed, combusted and expanded. In the second cycle, equivalent to the third and fourth strokes, the gas is transferred to the exhaust pipe and the cylinder is filled with fresh air from the intake manifold. Figure 3.1 shows the two cycles. The crankshaft is turned $360°$ per cycle. SI and diesel engines are controlled differently: In diesel engines, fuel is directly injected into the combustion chamber. The amount of injected fuel per stroke is then proportional to engine torque. The amount of air is almost constant at a given speed. In SI engines, the amount of fuel as well as air is controlled. When the fuel is injected into the intake manifold, a homogeneous air-fuel mixture is sucked into the cylinders. The mechanical work generated in the combustion cycle can be obtained by an integration in the pV-diagram. The mechanical work can be normalised by dividing by the displacement volume V_d:

$$ w_i = \frac{1}{V_d} \sum_{j=1}^{CYL} \oint \Big(p_j(V_j) - p_0 \Big) dV_j \quad , \tag{3.1} $$

where:

$$ V_d = CYL \cdot (V_1 - V_2) \quad \text{is the displacement volume of all cylinders} $$
$$ CYL \qquad\qquad\qquad\quad \text{is the number of cylinders} $$
$$ w_i \qquad\qquad\qquad\qquad \text{is the (normalised) \textbf{indicated specific work}.} $$

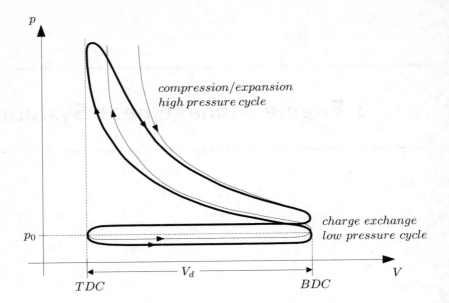

Figure 3.1 pV-diagram of four-stroke combustion engine

The value of w_i can be determined by measuring the in-cylinder pressure during a cycle. An indicated specific work of $1\,J/cm^3$ is equivalent to a mean pressure of $\bar{p} = 10\,bar$ $(= 10^6\,Pa)$. Dealing with a four-stroke engine, the measurement has to last for two cycles. The transfer of the combustion torque to the engine torque available at the crankshaft can be calculated from the following motion equations.

The piston stroke from Top Dead Center (TDC) is

$$s(\alpha_{CS}) = l(1 - \cos\beta) + r(1 - cos\alpha_{CS}) \quad .$$

From Figure 3.2 we get

$$
\begin{aligned}
l\sin\beta &= r\sin\alpha_{CS} \quad , \\
\cos\beta &= \sqrt{1 - \frac{r^2}{l^2}\sin^2\alpha_{CS}} \quad ,
\end{aligned}
\tag{3.2}
$$

which yields the piston stroke as

$$s(\alpha_{CS}) = r\left(1 - cos\alpha_{CS} + \frac{l}{r}\left(1 - \sqrt{1 - \frac{r^2}{l^2}\sin^2\alpha_{CS}}\right)\right) \quad . \tag{3.3}$$

At Top Dead Center, we have $\alpha_{CS} = 0$, $s(\alpha_{CS}) = 0$, and at Bottom Dead Center

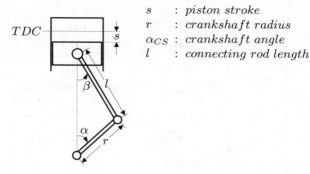

s : *piston stroke*
r : *crankshaft radius*
α_{CS} : *crankshaft angle*
l : *connecting rod length*

Figure 3.2 Piston and crankshaft motion

$\alpha_{CS} = \pi$, $s(\alpha_{CS}) = 2r$ respectively. The derivatives of the piston stroke are

$$\frac{ds}{d\alpha_{CS}} = r\left(\sin\alpha_{CS} + \frac{r}{l}\cdot\frac{\sin\alpha_{CS}\cos\alpha_{CS}}{\sqrt{1 - \frac{r^2}{l^2}\sin^2\alpha_{CS}}}\right)$$

and

$$\frac{d^2 s}{d\alpha_{CS}^2} = r\left(\cos\alpha_{CS} + \frac{\frac{r}{l}(\cos^2\alpha_{CS} - \sin^2\alpha_{CS}) + \frac{r^2}{l^2}\sin^4\alpha_{CS}}{\left(\sqrt{1 - \frac{r^2}{l^2}\sin^2\alpha_{CS}}\right)^3}\right) \qquad . (3.4)$$

These derivatives over crankshaft angle can be related to the derivatives over time as follows:

$$\dot{s} = \frac{ds}{dt} = \frac{ds}{d\alpha_{CS}}\cdot\frac{d\alpha_{CS}}{dt} = \frac{ds}{d\alpha_{CS}}\cdot\dot{\alpha}_{CS}$$

$$\ddot{s} = \frac{d^2 s}{dt^2} = \frac{d}{dt}\left(\frac{ds}{d\alpha_{CS}}\cdot\frac{d\alpha_{CS}}{dt}\right) = \frac{d}{dt}\left(\frac{ds}{d\alpha_{CS}}\right)\cdot\frac{d\alpha_{CS}}{dt} + \frac{ds}{d\alpha_{CS}}\cdot\frac{d^2\alpha_{CS}}{dt^2}$$

$$= \frac{d^2 s}{d\alpha_{CS}^2}\cdot\dot{\alpha}_{CS}^2 + \frac{ds}{d\alpha_{CS}}\cdot\ddot{\alpha}_{CS} \qquad (3.5)$$

The indicated specific work can be written as

$$w_i = \frac{1}{V_d}\oint\sum_{j=1}^{CYL}(p_j(\alpha_{CS}) - p_0)\,A_p\,\frac{ds_j(\alpha_{CS})}{d\alpha_{CS}}\,d\alpha_{CS}$$

$$= \frac{1}{V_d}\oint T_{comb}(\alpha_{CS})\,d\alpha_{CS} \qquad . (3.6)$$

The combustion torque at the crankshaft is thus defined as

$$T_{comb}(\alpha_{CS}) = \sum_{j=1}^{CYL}(p_j(\alpha_{CS}) - p_0)\,A_p\,\frac{ds_j}{d\alpha_{CS}} \qquad . (3.7)$$

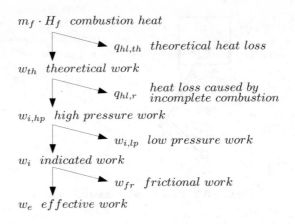

$m_f \cdot H_f$ *combustion heat*

$q_{hl,th}$ *theoretical heat loss*

w_{th} *theoretical work*

$q_{hl,r}$ *heat loss caused by incomplete combustion*

$w_{i,hp}$ *high pressure work*

$w_{i,lp}$ *low pressure work*

w_i *indicated work*

w_{fr} *frictional work*

w_e *effective work*

Figure 3.3 The effective work delivered by the engine is much lower than the thermal energy caused by combustion.

The piston strokes in different cylinders are shifted by phase.

$$s_j(\alpha_{CS}) = s\left(\alpha_{CS} - (j-1) \cdot \frac{4\pi}{CYL}\right) \quad , \quad j = 1, ..., CYL \qquad (3.8)$$

The average combustion torque is

$$\begin{aligned} \bar{T}_{comb} &= \frac{1}{4\pi} \oint T_{comb}(\alpha_{CS}) d\alpha_{CS} \\ &= \frac{P_i}{\dot{\alpha}_{CS}} \quad , \end{aligned} \qquad (3.9)$$

where P_i is the mean indicated power. The total indicated work $w_i V_d$ can now be written at stationary engine operation as

$$w_i V_d = 4\pi \bar{T}_{comb} = 4\pi \frac{P_i}{\dot{\alpha}_{CS}} = \frac{4\pi P_i}{2\pi n} = \frac{2P_i}{n} \quad ,$$

and the normalised work

$$w_i = \frac{2P_i}{V_d n} \quad , \qquad (3.10)$$

where $n = \dot{\alpha}_{CS}/(2\pi)$ is the engine speed. In reality, the effective work w_e per volume is much lower than the indicated work w_i (see Figure 3.3). The effective thermodynamic efficiency η_e is at constant fuel flow

$$\eta_e = \frac{P_e}{\dot{m}_f H_f} = \frac{w_e V_d n}{2 m_f n H_f} \cdot \frac{2}{CYL} = \frac{w_e}{m_f H_f} \cdot \frac{V_d}{CYL} \quad . \qquad (3.11)$$

where:

P_e is the effective power in W

w_e is the effective specific work per cycle in J/m^3

m_f is the mass of fuel measured per cylinder in kg

$\dot{m}_f$ is the fuel flow in kg/s

H_f is the specific energy of the fuel released in the combustion J/kg

V_d is the total displacement volume in m^3

      (V_d/CYL displacement volume per cylinder)

The indicated thermodynamic efficiency (friction not considered) is:

$$\eta_i = \frac{w_i}{2m_f H_f} \cdot \frac{V_d}{CYL} \tag{3.12}$$

Some examples of typical values for the indicated efficiency are given in table 3.1.

Table 3.1 Indicated specific work w_i, theoretical heat loss $q_{hl,th}$, and realistic heat loss $q_{hl,r}$ for different engine types, related to fuel combustion heat.

Engine Type	SI	Diesel	Big Diesel
w_i	33-35 %	40-43 %	45-48 %
$q_{hl,th}$	23-28 %	22-25 %	12-14 %
$q_{hl,r}$	37-44 %	35-40 %	26-33 %

3.1.2 Air-Fuel Ratio

The ratio of air to fuel is very important for the combustion process of internal combustion engines. There are several effects that have an impact on the amount of air m_a transferred to the cylinder: Throttling of the air flow by the throttle butterfly, aerodynamic resistance and resonances in the intake manifold, rebounding of already burned gases from the cylinder into the inlet pipes and other effects. The amount of air which would theoretically fit into a displacement volume V_d under the normalised pressure $p_0 = 1.013\,bar$ and the normalised air density $\rho_0 = 1.29\,kg/m^3$ is expressed by $m_{a,th} = \rho_0 V_d$. The ratio of real to theoretical value is equivalent to the relative air supply:

$$\lambda_a = \frac{m_a}{m_{a,th}} \tag{3.13}$$

Similarly, the ratio of measured fuel mass m_f to theoretical fuel mass $m_{f,th}$ is equivalent to the relative fuel supply:

$$\lambda_f = \frac{m_f}{m_{f,th}} \tag{3.14}$$

The theoretical fuel mass $m_{f,th}$ is equivalent to the mass of fuel needed for an ideal stochiometric combustion with the oxygen. Under normal conditions the stoichiometric ratio for gasoline is:

$$L_{st} = \frac{m_{a,th}}{m_{f,th}} = 14.66 \qquad (3.15)$$

The air-fuel ratio lambda is defined as:

$$\lambda = \frac{\lambda_a}{\lambda_f} \qquad (3.16)$$

It can be extended:

$$\lambda = \frac{m_a}{m_f} \frac{m_{f,th}}{m_{a,th}} = \frac{1}{L_{st}} \cdot \frac{m_a}{m_f} \qquad (3.17)$$

For an ideal stochiometric combustion, this ratio is equivalent to one: $\lambda = 1$. The air-fuel ratio has an impact on the effective work w_e and the effective thermodynamic efficiency η_e. The air-fuel ratio can be influenced in two different ways, by variation of λ_a or of λ_f:

1. **Variation of λ_f at a given λ_a:**
   Typical applications are SI engines operating around a stochiometric air-fuel ratio. The relative air supply λ_a is determined by the driver.

   Lean operation ($\lambda > 1$): Less fuel is injected than needed for stochiometric combustion (reduced λ_f). Due to a reduced high pressure work $w_{i,hp}$ the effective work $w_{i,hp}$ decreases. In the range of $1 < \lambda < 1.1$, the thermodynamic efficiency η_e increases however, caused by higher combustion peak temperatures. This results in high emissions of nitrogen oxides NO_x. If λ is further increased, η_e will decrease because of an even lower high pressure work $w_{i,hp}$ at a given low pressure work $w_{i,lp}$.

   Rich operation ($\lambda < 1$): More fuel is injected than needed for stochiometric combustion (higher λ_f). The fuel surplus increases both high pressure work $w_{i,hp}$ and effective work w_e. Below $\lambda < 0.9$ incomplete combustion results in high emissions of hydrocarbon HC in the exhaust gases and in a decreasing effective work w_e. At $\lambda < 1$ the thermodynamic efficiency η_e is always decreased.

2. **Variation of λ_a at a given λ_f:**
   Typical applications are lean-burn SI-engines at part load and Diesel engines. The relative fuel supply λ_f is determined by the driver.

   Lean operation ($\lambda > 1$): More air is admitted than needed for stochiometric combustion (increased λ_a). Therefore, high pressure work $w_{i,hp}$ is increased while low pressure work $w_{i,lp}$ remains constant. Both effective work w_e and thermodynamic efficiency η_e are increased. It should be mentioned that lean gas mixtures are less flammable. In Si-engines delays between spark ignition and complete combustion increase.

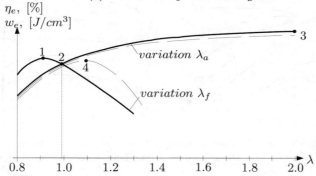

(1)   *SI engines at maximum power output*
(2)   *Stochiometric SI engines*
(3)   *Diesel and lean − burn engines*
(4)   *Moderately lean SI engines*

Figure 3.4 Effective work w_e and thermodynamic efficiency η_e of combustion engines depending on variation of λ_a or λ_f.

Misfiring at SI engines must be avoided by e.g. direct injection of a fuel stratified charge into the cylinder, which forms an enriched mixture around the spark plug. This operation is quite similar to that of Diesel engines. Combustion is either triggered by a spark or by self-inflammation due to high compression ratios. The engine can only operate up to its maximum gas load (maximum λ_a). Due to lean operation its maximum power according to the displacement volume is, however, not reached.

Rich operation ($\lambda < 1$): Less air is admitted than needed for stochiometric combustion (decreased λ_a). This leads to a decrease in both efficiency η_e and effective work w_e. Incomplete combustion results in higher hydrocarbon HC emissions and in a reduction in high pressure work $w_{i,hp}$.

Figure 3.4 shows the dependency of the effective work and effective thermodynamic efficiency over λ, assuming an optimal control of fuel injection and ignition timing.

Engines may use recirculated exhaust gas instead of fresh air to increase the relative air supply λ_a. As long as sufficient air is available for the combustion this is similar to a higher air-fuel ratio λ. Exhaust gas recirculation reduces the emission of NO_x due to lower combustion peak temperatures.

3.1.3   Engine Concepts

The **SI engine** is controlled by the air supply λ_a. This is done by throttling the air flow into the engine. The fuel supply λ_f is subsequently regulated to maintain a given air-fuel ratio λ. The range of λ is limited by the ability to inflame air-fuel

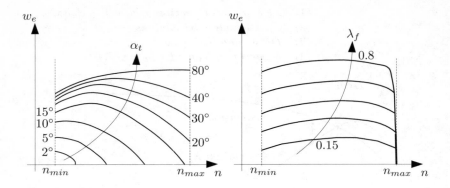

Figure 3.5 Effective work w_e over engine speed for SI engines (left figure) depending on the throttle angle α_t and Diesel engines (right figure) depending on relative fuel supply λ_f .

mixtures by spark ignition. Conventional SI engines operate on approximately homogeneous mixtures ($0.9 < \lambda < 1.3$). Lean-burn engines operate at very lean mixtures equivalent to Diesel engines. Combustion is ensured by directly injecting a stratified charge of rich air-fuel ratio around the spark plug.

The **Diesel engine** is controlled by the fuel supply λ_f. The intake manifold is not throttled. The air supply λ_a is always at its maximum. Therefore, the air-fuel ratio λ changes within a large range. The inflammation of extremely lean mixtures is still possible because of the non-homogeneous fuel distribution in the combustion chamber. Such inhomogeneous mixtures burn with a yellow flame. The average air-fuel ratio should not be below $\lambda = 1.3$ to avoid the generation of soot. Since the effective work w_e is given by the amount of injected fuel, the fuel supply must be cut-off when reaching the maximum engine speed. Otherwise the engine power would continue to increase with speed resulting in a self-destruction of the engine. Fuel may be injected in two steps. A first small amount of fuel starts the combustion process more smoothly. The second main injection then results in lower peak pressures and temperatures, yielding lower NO_x emissions and less combustion noise. Eventually the injection may be decomposed into more than two injection steps.

Lean-burn SI engines are a compromise between diesel and stochiometric SI engines. Driving at part load, the air-fuel ratio is very lean. By properly designing injection pressure, spray cone and air turbulance, an enriched stratified charge is assembled around the spark plug. The resulting combustion is equivalent to that of Diesel engines (inhomogeneous mixture, yellow flame). Lower noxious emissions can be achieved by separating into two injections. First, about 1/4 of all fuel is injected, which forms a lean homogeneous mixture in the combustion chamber. This lean mixture is also less sensitive to knocking. Second, 3/4 of fuel is injected as a stratified charge. After burning this rich mixture, the homogeneous lean mixture burns in a blue flame, resulting in a reduction of noxious emissions. At high loads, the operating conditions are shifted from very lean to stochiometric mixture. At a given engine displacement volume, more fuel can be combusted from stochiometric mixtures, increasing power output.

Figure 3.5 shows the dependency of the effective work w_e over engine speed for SI and Diesel engines. The displacement volume of a naturally aspirated diesel or lean-burn SI engine must be 60 % higher than that of a stochiometric SI engine to obtain the same maximum power output. Therefore diesel and lean-burn SI engines are often turbocharged which increases the relative air supply λ_a at a given displacement volume V_d.

3.1.4 Inflammation of Air-Fuel Mixtures

The kinetic gas theory describes gases as a cloud of molecules with a given velocity distribution according to their temperature. The collision of different molecules will start a chemical chain reaction if their kinetic energy is over a certain activation energy E. The relative amount of effective collisions A is expressed by the Arrhenius law

$$A = e^{-E/R\vartheta} \quad . \tag{3.18}$$

The activation energy E is low for radicals (not saturated molecules). The probability for a collision is increased by the concentration of molecules and by the temperature. A chemical reaction must be started by a high temperature. During the chain reaction, more radicals are generated than destroyed. Under appropriate conditions, a spontaneous spark ignition is sufficient to start the combustion process at the location of the spark plug. The air-fuel mixture must be within a certain range $(0.9 < \lambda < 1.3)$ and its pressure (or respective temperature) must be over a threshold for a certain period of time. The gas is compressed isentropicly, neglecting heat conduction. Figure 3.6 shows how pressure and temperature courses over time influence self inflammation under different conditions.

1. In curve a, pressure and temperature rise immediately. In curve b, inflammation starts only when reaching a higher pressure level than in curve (a). In the case of (b), the increase in pressure and temperature was first delayed until t_0.

2. In curve c, temperature and pressure rise immediately, but level off at a lower level. Inflammation occurs after a longer time delay. In the case of (d) the rise is first delayed until time t_0. Self inflammation happens later than in (c).

It can be seen, that self inflammation depends on something like the integral of pressure or temperature over time. Many parameters have an impact on the time delay of self inflammation, like location of the spark plug within the combustion chamber, etc. Woschni [80] gives an empirical formula of the inflammation delay time, depending only on mean temperature ϑ and mean pressure p, without any integral portion.

$$\tau_d = 0.44 \, e^{4650° K/\vartheta} \left(\frac{p}{p_0} \right)^{-1.19} \tag{3.19}$$

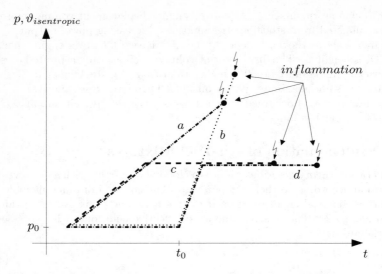

Figure 3.6 Isentropic temperature $\vartheta_{isentropic}$ and pressure p over time. The conditions for self inflammation (a, b, c ,d) are explained in the text below.

The inflammation lag τ_d over temperature ϑ with the pressure p as parameter can be seen in Figure 3.7. The time delay τ_d is reduced for high temperatures and high pressures. This is why e.g. turbo-charged Diesel engines operate with a start-of-injection angle which is approximately $10°$ (crankshaft angle) later than that of naturally aspirated Diesel engines.

3.1.5   Flame Propagation

The velocity v_{fl} of flame propagation depends on two components:

1. **Combustion velocity:**   The combustion propagates through the gas mixture, for example with a velocity of $1\,m/s$.

2. **Transport velocity:**   The burning gas itself is swirled as the rising piston generates turbulance in the combustion chamber. The transport velocity is approximately proportional to the piston velocity $\dot{s}$ which depends on the engine speed n. At low engine speeds, the transport velocity can be increased by a swirl inlet port generating a turbulent gas flow. The turbulences accelerate the combustion speed proportional to engine speed.

Figure 3.8 shows the flame propagation velocity v_{fl} depending on piston velocity $\dot{s}$ (left) and air-fuel ratio λ (right). The inflammation delay time τ_d must be considered in the engine control to position the combustion process right over the downward moving piston. The time lag τ_d must be convoluted to a crankshaft angle lag, increasing with the engine speed. The ignition angle α_i must therefore be advanced over engine speed.

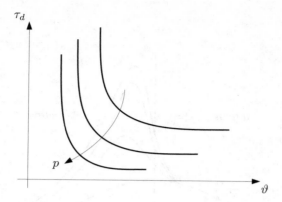

Figure 3.7 lag of self inflammation τ_d over temperature ϑ for different pressure values p.

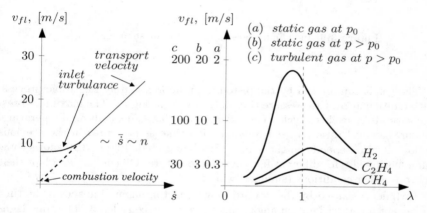

Figure 3.8 Flame propagation velocity v_{fl} over average piston velocity $\bar{\bar{s}}$ (left) and over air-fuel ratio λ (right).

Contrary to that, the position of the combustion process over the crankshaft angle is almost constant. This is due to the fact, that the flame propagation velocity at combustion is mostly determined by the transport velocity. Thus the angle position of the combustion process is independent of the engine speed. With higher engine speeds, flame transport velocity is increasing, speeding up combustion over time, leaving it however constant over engine speed.

3.1.6 Energy Conversion

The in-cylinder pressure can be plotted over time or over crankshaft angle α_{CS}. The angle of 360° is equivalent to a complete high pressure cycle. Figure 3.9 shows the in-cylinder pressure over crankshaft angle.

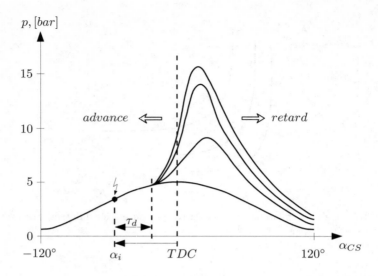

Figure 3.9 In-cylinder pressure p over crankshaft angle α_{CS}.

The gas is compressed by the piston in an approximately isentropic process. With ignition at α_i, the pressure rises only after time lag τ_d. The maximum pressure varies from cycle to cycle. The inflammation lag τ_d depends on temperature, pressure, air-fuel ratio and self inflammation time as described in the previous section. It also depends on the type of fuel being used. Figure 3.10 shows some inflammation lags for different fuels over temperature. Oil companies adapt their fuel to weather conditions (summer, winter).

Turbulence caused by the upward moving piston has no impact on the time lag τ_d. For a correct ignition angle, this lag must be considered. The time lag is convoluted to an angle lag, increasing proportional to engine speed. Contrary to that, the engine speed has almost no impact on the position of energy conversion as turbulences increase the transport velocity with higher engine speeds.

The energy conversion caused by combustion is shown in Figure 3.11 for different air-fuel ratios λ. In these curves, the isentropic pressure curves are suppressed. The differential output of thermal energy per angle $dE/d\alpha_{CS}$ (its gradient) is normalised to the total thermal energy E_0. The shape of the relative energy conversion is therefore almost constant.

If the air-fuel ratio is increased e.g. to $\lambda = 1.2$ as shown in Figure 3.11, the ignition lag τ_d will rise. At a constant ignition angle α_{i1} the energy conversion is then retarded. Therefore, the ignition angle must be advanced to α_{i2}, to compensate for the increased delay. The energy conversion returns to its previous position. It should be mentioned that a high air-fuel ratio λ increases the variance of the time lag τ_d.

The ignition angle α_i depends on λ which can be seen in Figure 3.12. The angle is computed by averaging the energy conversion over 0.1 %, 1 %, 10 %, 50 %,

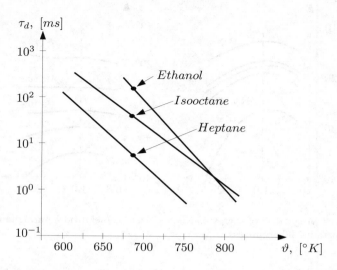

Figure 3.10 Inflammation lag τ_d over temperature for different fuels.

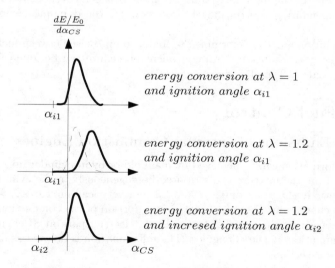

Figure 3.11 Normalised energy conversion caused by combustion for different air-fuel ratios λ.

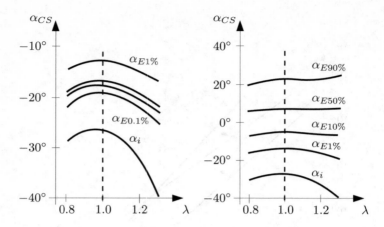

Figure 3.12 Angle α_{CS} of energy conversion over air-fuel ratio λ during ignition (left) and combustion (right) process.

90 % points. The angles for $\alpha_{E1\%}$ and higher are almost independent of the air-fuel ratio λ. In-cylinder pressure measurements can be used to control the ignition angle in a closed loop to maintain a constant position of energy conversion as shown in Figure 3.13. The angle of maximum pressure gradient $max(dp/d\alpha_{CS})$ may be used as a control variable. The controller time constant must be relatively large because of the high delay time variances between consecutive cycles. Thus closed loop ignition control may be too slow for the dynamic response of the engine.

The ignition angle is determined to find a compromise between fuel consumption, emissions or knocking. An equivalent procedure can be found for the fuel injection angle at Diesel engines.

3.2 Fuel Control

3.2.1 Emissions of Internal Combustion Engines

Mixture formation can be achieved by manifold or by in-cylinder injection. With sufficient time the mixture is distributed homogeneously in the cylinder with an air-fuel ratio in the range of $0.9 < \lambda < 1.3$. For very lean mixtures $\lambda > 1.3$, a rich stratified charge must be concentrated in a portion of the combustion chamber.

The combustion process is started by an electric spark at SI engines and by self-inflammation at Diesel engines. The inflammation is delayed as described in the previous section.

- Homogeneous mixture, stochiometric air-fuel ratio: The flame has a characteristic blue color. Almost no soot (carbon particulates) is produced.

- Stratified charge, lean air-fuel ratio: The flame has a characteristic yellow color. Soot is produced.

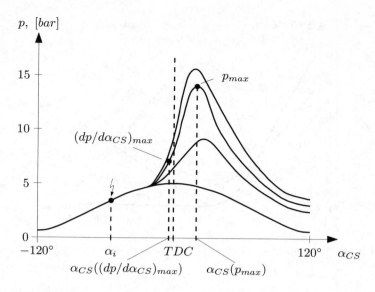

Figure 3.13 Closed-loop control of ignition angle α_i to maintain a constant position of energy conversion.

- Inflammation starts combustion from one location.

The inflammation process depends on pressure p, temperature ϑ, air-fuel ratio λ and activation energy E of the fuel. For $\lambda < 1$ the exhaust gases are generated according to the concentration ratio

$$k = \frac{n_{CO} \cdot n_{H_2O}}{n_{CO_2} \cdot n_{H_2}} \quad . \tag{3.20}$$

This ratio is temperature dependant. A typical value for $\vartheta = 1850\,^\circ K$ is $k = 3.6$.

The pollutant emissions like CO, HC, NO_x depend strongly on the air-fuel ratio which is shown in Figure 3.14

$\lambda < 1$: Increased emission of hydrocarbon HC and carbon monoxide CO.

$\lambda = 1$: Stochiometric combustion. Very low emissions after three way catalytic converter.

$\lambda \approx 1.1$: Highest nitrogen oxide NO_x emissions due to highest combustion peak temperatures.

$\lambda > 1.1$: Decreasing nitrogen oxide NO_x concentration and lower combustion temperatures. Increasing hydrocarbon HC emissions at eventual misfires.

$\lambda > 1.5$: Lean operation. For very low emissions, a NO_x reducing catalytic converter is required.

The concentration of oxygen O_2 in the exhaust gas can be used to determine the air-fuel ratio λ for $\lambda \geq 1$ using a lambda-sensor.

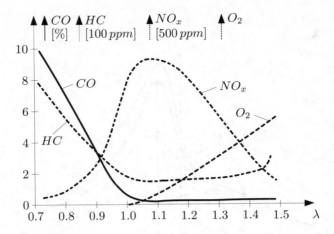

Figure 3.14 Raw emissions of CO, HC, NO_x and O_2 over air-fuel ratio λ for SI engines.

3.2.2 Fuel Measurement

The air-fuel ratio λ is an important variable for fuel control which is based on different control concepts:

rich mixture $\lambda < 1$: Maximum power per displacement volume because of increased relative fuel supply λ_f. It was used at high engine loads until 1970. Nowadays it is only used for cold engines during the warm-up phase. High emission rates.

stochiometric mixture $\lambda = 1$: Acceptable power output. This ratio is required for proper operation of three-way catalytic converters. At high engine loads, a good compromise between power output and exhaust emissions is achieved.

moderately lean mixture $1 < \lambda < 1.5$: Good efficiency because of increased air supply λ_a, but high emissions of NO_x. This method was used at part loads until 1980.

lean mixture $\lambda > 1.5$: High efficiency because of high λ_a. NO_x emissions are still high, so that catalytic converters for NO_x reduction are required. This method is used in lean-burn engines at part loads and in Diesel engines. Maximum engine power cannot be reached.

The reference torque desired by the driver controls either the relative air supply λ_a via the throttle angle α_t at SI engines or the relative fuel supply λ_f at Diesel engines. The amount of fuel being mixed with the air is regulated by the fuel control system to obtain a predefined air-fuel ratio λ. There are two different injection systems:

1. **Manifold injection:** The fuel is injected into the individual inlet pipes in front of the inlet ports. There is at least one inlet valve for each cylinder. Problems may occur at idling because of incomplete fuel evaporation due to a low air flow velocity into the cylinders. Additionally, the distribution of air flow into the different inlet pipes may vary. The amount of injected fuel is less accurate at idling because electromagnetic injection valves are time controlled: Errors due to different rise and fall times have a larger impact on the amount of fuel injected at small injection times. The advantage of manifold injection is the creation of a homogeneous fuel distribution in the cylinder at $\lambda = 1$. This burns with a blue flame. There are few restrictions for the design of the inlet pipes. The exchange of gas can be optimised without major effects on the injection system as it is located at the inlet valves. The inlet pipes are designed to produce acoustic resonances at low engine speed. This increases the relative air supply λ_a and the effective work w_e without turbo charging. The inlet valves are cooled by the evaporating fuel. The reduced gas temperature lowers knocking and allows higher compression ratios to increase efficiency. The injection timing is phase-shifted for each cylinder. It is aimed to terminate the injection just before the inlet valve is opened to avoid the emission of soot. The injection can be controlled individually and fuel supply can be individually cut off for each cylinder: limitation of engine speed and vehicle speed, fuel cut-off at coasting or cylinder switch-off at multi-cylinder engines.

2. **In-cylinder injection:** The fuel is injected directly into the cylinders. The aim is to assemble a sufficiently rich mixture (e.g. stochiometric) in a limited portion of the combustion chamber, e.g. at SI engines around the spark plug at the time of ignition. The amount of fuel, the injection pressure (thus fuel atomisation), the injector spray angle (width and depth of injection) and the injection timing are adjusted in each engine operation point. The swirl is controlled by special geometry of the piston head.

   The aim is to burn very lean air-fuel mixtures. This can be done by multiple injection. By an early injection, a homogeneous lean mixture is developing throughout the combustion chamber until the time of ignition, due to the swirl. The follow-up injection creates the richer stratified charge, which is burning fast with reduced cycle-to-cycle variations. Due to the reduced amount of the fuel in the stratified charge, peak temperatures are also reduced. The early generated lean homogeneous mixture is burned afterwards. Since the mixture is very lean, it takes significant time, limiting maximum allowable engine speeds. In the combustion of the stratified charge, soot was generated. In the blue flame of the homogeneous mixture, this can be effectively reduced.

The total amount of injected fuel depends on the following parameters:

- aspirated air flow per time $\dot{m}_a$

- intake manifold pressure p_m at SI engines

- throttle angle α_t and it's derivative at SI engines

- engine speed n

- crankshaft angle α_{CS} and TDC signal of a reference cylinder

- engine temperature ϑ_e

- ambient air temperature ϑ_a

- battery voltage U_b (indirectly)

Major functions of the fuel control:

- Control of injected fuel per time $\dot{m}_f$, following the aspirated air per time $\dot{m}_a$, depending on the desired air-fuel ratio λ.

- Enriched fuel injection in warm-up phase of the engine after cold start at SI engines.

- Increased relative air supply λ_a or relative fuel supply λ_f for the cold engine because of higher friction.

- Compensation of intake manifold dynamics at SI engines.

- Compensation of fuel film dynamics at manifold injection. This phenomenon is also temperature dependant.

- Fuel cutoff at coasting. This reduces overall fuel consumption by around 5 %.

- The measured air flow is eventually corrected for ambient air temperature ϑ_a and barometric pressure p_0 changes.

- Engine idle speed control.

- Maximum engine speed limitation by fuel cutoff.

- Lambda control of the air-fuel ratio.

- Exhaust gas recirculation control.

3.2.3   Intermittent Fuel Injection

Intermittent fuel injection has turned out to be more economical than continuous fuel injection, due to the different accuracies required in those systems. The power output of an engine varies within a wide range. Between idling P_{min} and maximum power P_{max}, the ratio is about $1 : 100$.

$$\frac{P_{max}}{P_{min}} = 100 \tag{3.21}$$

The engine speed varies in the range of:

$$\frac{n_{max}}{n_{min}} = 10 \tag{3.22}$$

At stationary engine operation, the amount of injected fuel per time $\dot{m}_f$ is proportional to the effective power output P_e of the engine which is expressed in Equation 3.11. In this consideration air pulsation in the intake pipes are neglected.

Supposing a **continuous fuel supply** $\dot{m}_f$, the relative error of the open loop fuel measurement at low loads should be

$$\frac{\Delta \dot{m}}{\dot{m}_{min}} < 3\% \quad . \tag{3.23}$$

This will cause an absolute error related to maximum fuel flow

$$\frac{\Delta \dot{m}}{\dot{m}_{max}} = \frac{\dot{m}_{min}}{\dot{m}_{max}} \frac{\Delta \dot{m}}{\dot{m}_{min}} = \frac{P_{min}}{P_{max}} \frac{\Delta \dot{m}}{\dot{m}_{min}} < 3 \cdot 10^{-4} \quad . \tag{3.24}$$

Hence, the absolute error at idle is 100 times smaller than the relative error. A continuous fuel injection system should be designed for the absolute error. It must be extremely accurate. High production costs are the consequence.

Fuel measurement can alternatively be achieved by **intermittent fuel injection**. For each combustion cycle, a certain amount of fuel m_f is injected. The number of injections per second are proportional to the engine speed n. The amount of injected fuel per cylinder and combustion cycle is

$$m_f = \int\limits_0^{\frac{2}{n \cdot CYL}} \dot{m}_f \, dt \quad , \tag{3.25}$$

where CYL is the number of cylinders of the engine. The factor 2 is due to the fact that air is combusted only every second cycle in the four-stroke process. Supposing a constant fuel flow $\dot{m}_f$ at stationary operation, the integration leads to:

$$m_f = \frac{\dot{m}_f}{n} \cdot \frac{2}{CYL} \tag{3.26}$$

The ratio of maximum to minimum amount of injected fuel per cycle is given by Equation 3.11:

$$\frac{m_{max}}{m_{min}} = \frac{P_{max}}{P_{min}} \frac{n_{min}}{n_{max}} = 10 \tag{3.27}$$

Supposing again a relative error at minimum load of

$$\frac{\Delta m}{m_{min}} < 3\% \quad , \tag{3.28}$$

the absolute error related to maximum fuel per cycle is now

$$\frac{\Delta m}{m_{max}} < 3 \cdot 10^{-3} \quad , \tag{3.29}$$

i.e. 10 times larger. Compared to a continuous fuel supply, intermittent fuel injection systems can be implemented with significantly lower accuracy requirements and therefore can be produced at lower costs.

3.2.4 Injection Time Calculation

The fuel supply is controlled by the **injection time** t_{inj} during which the injector valve is open. Therefore, the amount of fuel per injection into a cylinder can be calculated using the following relationship for constant air flow $\dot{m}_a = const.$

$$m_f = \frac{m_a}{L_{st}\,\lambda} = \frac{1}{L_{st}\,\lambda}\,\frac{\dot{m}_a}{n}\,\frac{2}{CYL} \quad , \tag{3.30}$$

where $L_{st} = 14.66$ (see Equation 3.15). The amount of injected fuel m_f is proportional to the injection time t_{inj} and the square root of the pressure difference Δp between fuel rail and manifold at manifold injection or between fuel rail and combustion chamber at direct in-cylinder injection [43]. The fuel density ϱ_f and the effective opening area of the valve A_{eff} are assumed to be constant.

$$m_f \sim \varrho_f \cdot A_{eff} \cdot \sqrt{2\frac{\Delta p}{\varrho_f}} \cdot t_{inj} \tag{3.31}$$

At manifold injection, the pressure difference Δp is around $5\,bar$. At direct in-cylinder injection, the pressure difference Δp is $400\,bar$ for SI and $2000\,bar$ for Diesel engines.

The injection time at stationary engine operation is proportional to

$$t_{inj} \sim \frac{1}{\lambda}\,\frac{\dot{m}_a}{n}\,\frac{2}{CYL} \quad , \tag{3.32}$$

and for a reference air-fuel ratio λ_0 a reference injection time t_0 is proportional to

$$t_0 \sim \frac{1}{\lambda_0}\,\frac{\dot{m}_a}{n}\,\frac{2}{CYL} \quad . \tag{3.33}$$

For arbitrary air-fuel ratios λ we get

$$t_{inj} \approx \frac{\lambda_0}{\lambda}\,t_0 \quad . \tag{3.34}$$

The injection time t_{inj} per combustion cycle depends on the following values:

Mass air flow $\dot{m}_a$**:** Must be measured. Systematic measurement errors at some sensors can be reduced by taking air density and temperature into account.

Air mass per stroke m_a**:** is computed by implementation of Equation 3.38.

Reference air-fuel ratio λ_0**:** Must be determined, e.g. stochiometric. A look-up table can be implemented to compensate for possible errors of sensors and actuators: $\lambda_0 = \lambda_0(\dot{m}_a, n)$.

Actual air-fuel ratio λ**:** Depends on several factors such as temperature depending enrichment during warm-up and correction for dynamic transients. At Diesel engines, lambda is always $\lambda > 1.3$.

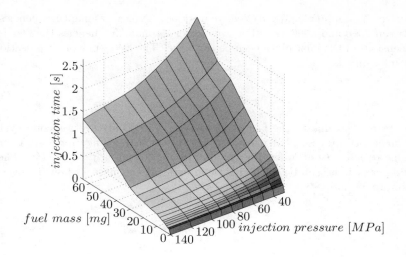

Figure 3.15 Piezoelectric injector map ($10MPa = 10bar$)

Battery voltage U_b: It has an impact on the rise and fall times in electro-magnetically controlled injection nozzles. The effect can be compensated by adding a voltage dependant time correction $\Delta t(U_b)$. The compensated time is

$$t_{inj} + \Delta t(U_b) \quad . \tag{3.35}$$

Instead of direct measurement, the mass air flow $\dot{m}_a$ can be estimated from intake manifold pressure p_m or the throttle angle α_t at throttled SI engines. The air flow into the cylinders also depends on the dynamic pressure changes in the intake manifold. It is a function of

$$\dot{m}_a = f_0(p_m, \dot{p}_m, n) \quad , \tag{3.36}$$

where f_0 must be measured for all possible $\dot{m}_a$ at stationary engine operation and corrected for dynamic pressure changes (Section 3.2.6).

Figure 3.15 shows a map for the required injection time t_{inj} of a high-pressure piezoelectric injector over the desired injection fuel mass m_f and the injection pressure difference Δp.

3.2.5 Air Mass per Combustion Cycle

The relative air supply λ_a at low engine speeds can be increased by acoustic resonances in the inlet pipes to each cylinder. These resonances are exited by the periodic opening and closing of the inlet valves. The geometry of the inlet pipes is designed for resonances at lower engine speeds. It is intended that a pressure maximum from the resonance occurs at the inlet valve precisely when it is opened. Hence, more air flows into the combustion chamber and increases the relative air supply λ_a and the effective work w_e. Typical resonant frequencies are between 2000 and 3000 rpm. For even lower resonant frequencies the geometric dimensions of the inlet pipes become too large. The frequency of air pulsation in the inlet pipe is

$$f_p = \frac{n \cdot CYL}{2} \quad .$$

(3.37)

The factor 2 is due to the fact that air is aspirated only every second cycle in a four stroke process. For example, the pulsation frequency for a six cylinder engine ($CYL = 6$) at an engine speed of $n = 6000\,rpm$ is $f_p = 300\,Hz$. The air mass per cylinder can be calculated by integrating the mass air flow $\dot{m}_a$ over one pulsation period.

$$m_a = \int_{t_a}^{t_b} \dot{m}_a \, dt$$

(3.38)

The limits (begin t_a and end t_b) of integration are given by

$$t_b - t_a = \frac{1}{f_p} = \frac{2}{n \cdot CYL} \quad ,$$

(3.39)

and therefore, the aspirated air for one cylinder per cycle is

$$m_a = \int_0^{\frac{1}{f_p}} \dot{m}_a \, dt \quad .$$

(3.40)

The air supply m_a can be calculated by integration of the mass air flow signal. The sampling rate must be high enough to avoid aliasing, and therefore it is about $5 - 10$ times higher as the highest pulsation frequency. Eventual non-linear characteristics of the air flow meter must be compensated for before the integration. A linear characteristic can be obtained by e.g. multiplying the sensor characteristic with it's inverse. Thus an eventual bias introduced by the integration can be avoided [42].

The proper timing for integration (t_a, t_b) can be derived from the crankshaft angle α_{cs} signal. For example, if the crankshaft sensor has 60 teeth, the duration of $t_b - t_a = \frac{1}{f_p}$ is equivalent to $\Delta\alpha_{CS} = 120°$ in a six cylinder engine. This is given by the turn of 20 teeth of the crankshaft sensor. Unfortunately, mass air flow is synchronised to time and not to the crankshaft angle α_{CS}. Since mass air flow $\dot{m}_a$ is not sampled at start and stop times t_a and t_b, it must be interpolated:

$$\dot{m}_a(t_a) = \dot{m}_a(t_0)\frac{t_1 - t_a}{T_s} + \dot{m}_a(t_1)\left(1 - \frac{t_1 - t_a}{T_s}\right)$$

$$\dot{m}_a(t_b) = \dot{m}_a(t_n)\frac{t_{n+1} - t_b}{T_s} + \dot{m}_a(t_{n+1})\left(1 - \frac{t_{n+1} - t_b}{T_s}\right)$$

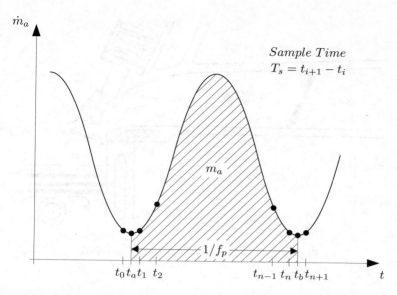

Figure 3.16 Air mass m_a obtained by integration of the air flow $\dot{m}_a$ over period $t_b - t_a$.

The integration is approximated e.g. by the trapazoidal rule:

$$m_a \approx \frac{T_s}{CYL}\left[(\dot{m}_a(t_a) + \dot{m}_a(t_1))\frac{t_1 - t_a}{T_s} + \dot{m}_a(t_1) + 2\dot{m}_a(t_2) + \cdots \right.$$
$$\left. \cdots + 2\dot{m}_a(t_{n-1}) + \dot{m}_a(t_n) + (\dot{m}_a(t_n) + \dot{m}_a(t_b))\left(1 - \frac{t_{n+1} - t_b}{T_s}\right)\right]$$

which is simplified to:

$$m_a \approx \frac{T_s}{CYL}\left[\dot{m}_a(t_0)\frac{(t_1 - t_a)^2}{T_s^2} - \dot{m}_a(t_1)\left(1 - \frac{(t_1 - t_a)^2}{T_s^2}\right) + 2\sum_{i=1}^{n}\dot{m}_a(t_i) - \right.$$
$$\left. -\dot{m}_a(t_n)\frac{(t_{n+1} - t_b)^2}{T_s^2} + \dot{m}_a(t_{n+1})\left(1 - \frac{(t_{n+1} - t_b)^2}{T_s^2}\right)\right]$$

3.2.6 Intake Manifold Dynamics

Figure 3.17 shows a cross-section of the intake manifold. The throttle angle controls the mass air flow $\dot{m}_{a,in}$ into the manifold. Diesel engines are either unthrottled or very moderately throttled in some operating points in order to ensure a sufficient exhaust gas recirculation.

The mass air flow out from the manifold into the cylinders $\dot{m}_{a,out}$ depends on the pressure level in the intake manifold p_m (and the pressure in the cylinder p_c). To control the air-fuel ratio λ correctly also in transients, the injected amount of fuel must be adapted to the mass air flow into the cylinder $\dot{m}_{a,out}$ rather than to the mass air flow into the intake manifold $m_{a,in}$.

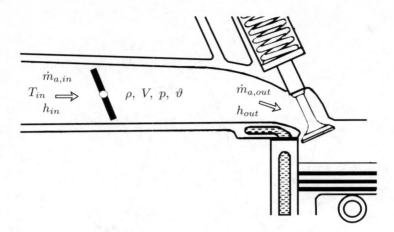

Figure 3.17 Cross-section of intake manifold

The pressure oscillations shown in Figure 3.16 shall be neglected in the following deduction (averaged model). A change in mass air flow $\dot{m}_a$ results in a delayed change in manifold pressure p_m. The according differential equation is derived from an energy equilibrium: The change of the internal energy of the air mass in the intake manifold is equal to the sum of in- and outgoing energy flows plus the balance of energy changes of the gas due to the displacement work pV. By introducing the specific internal energy $u = U/m$ and the specific enthalpy $h = H/m$ the differential equation becomes:

$$\frac{d}{dt}(m_{a,in}u_{in}) = \dot{m}_{a,in}u_{in} - \dot{m}_{a,out}u_{out} + p_a\dot{V}_{in} - p_m\dot{V}_{out} \qquad (3.41)$$

In this model, resonances within the manifold are neglected by assuming identical pressure p_m at the throttle and cylinders [1]. Additionally, the heat radiation from the engine is supposed to match the thermal heat required for the evaporation of the fuel. Therefore, no additional terms are added to Equation 3.41. The enthalpies at the inlet and outlet are equivalent to:

$$\dot{m}_{a,in}h_{in} = \dot{m}_{a,in}u_{in} + p_a\dot{V}_{in} \qquad (3.42)$$
$$\dot{m}_{a,out}h_{out} = \dot{m}_{a,out}u_{out} + p_m\dot{V}_{out} \qquad (3.43)$$

which can be inserted in Equation 3.41:

$$m_{a,in}\dot{u}_{in} + \dot{m}_{a,in}u_{in} = \dot{m}_{a,in}h_{in} - \dot{m}_{a,out}h_{out} \qquad (3.44)$$

Using the specific heat coefficients $c_v = \partial u/\partial\vartheta$ and $c_p = \partial h/\partial\vartheta$ as well as the air density $\rho = m/V$ we get

$$\rho_m V_m c_v\dot{\vartheta}_m + c_v\vartheta_m\dot{\rho}_m V_m = \dot{m}_{a,in}c_p\vartheta_a - \dot{m}_{a,out}c_p\vartheta_m \qquad (3.45)$$

---

[1]This relates to an averaged pressure model, which has proved to be sufficiently accurate for mass air flow transients.

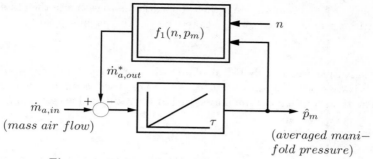

Figure 3.18 Dynamic model of intake manifold

and after division by $c_v V_m$

$$\rho_m \dot{\vartheta}_m + \dot{\rho}_m \vartheta_m = \frac{c_p}{c_v} \frac{\vartheta_a}{V_m} \left(\dot{m}_{a,in} - \frac{\vartheta_m}{\vartheta_a} \dot{m}_{a,out} \right) \quad . \tag{3.46}$$

Inserting the adiabatic exponent $\kappa = c_p/c_v$ and the ideal gas equation $pV = m R \vartheta$, this yields the following equation for the pressure change:

$$\dot{p}_m = \frac{\kappa R \vartheta_a}{V_m} \left(\dot{m}_{a,in} - \frac{\vartheta_m}{\vartheta_a} \dot{m}_{a,out} \right) \tag{3.47}$$

It is difficult to measure the mass air flow from the manifold into the cylinder $\dot{m}_{a,out}$. Because the dynamic response of $\dot{m}_{a,out}$ is much faster than that of the manifold pressure p_m, only the static behaviour of $\dot{m}_{a,out}$ shall be considered by a look-up table $f_1(n, p_m)$. The mass air flow $\dot{m}_{a,out}$ depends on the engine speed n and the manifold pressure p_m at stationary operation, where the derivatives are $\dot{n} = 0$ and $\dot{p}_m = 0$:

$$\dot{m}_{a,out}^* = \dot{m}_{a,out} \frac{\vartheta_m}{\vartheta_a} = f_1(n, p_m) \tag{3.48}$$

The pressure change in the intake manifold is given by:

$$\dot{p}_m = \frac{1}{\tau}(\dot{m}_{a,in} - f_1(n, p_m)) \tag{3.49}$$

with the integration constant τ:

$$\tau = \frac{V_m}{\kappa R \vartheta_a} \tag{3.50}$$

The look-up table can be measured on an engine test bed at stationary operating points, where the derivative of the averaged manifold pressure $\dot{p}_m = 0$. Under these conditions the incoming mass air flow $\dot{m}_{a,in}$ is equal to the values in the look-up table for $\dot{m}_{a,out}^*$. Figure 3.18 shows the block diagram of the pressure model of the intake manifold. By integration of Equation 3.49 the average manifold pressure can be estimated in realtime. This can be utilized at engine idle speed control (Section 4.2). Another application is to estimate the mass air flow $\dot{m}_{a,in}$ from the measured manifold pressure p_m and engine speed n:

$$\dot{m}_{a,in} = \tau \cdot \dot{p}_m + f_1(n, p_m) \quad . \tag{3.51}$$

The derivative $\dot{p}_m$ can only be calculated with some delay. In some applications, the derivative of the throttle angle $\dot{\alpha}_t$ is therefore used as an additional variable.

The time constant can be normalised at operating points $p_{m,0}$ and $\dot{m}_{a,0}$:

$$\tau_n = \frac{p_{m,0}}{\dot{m}_{a,0}} \tau \tag{3.52}$$

This normalised parameter τ_n is the integration time constant in seconds. The pressure change $\dot{p}_m$ is then:

$$\tau_n \frac{d}{dt} \left(\frac{p_m}{p_{m,0}} \right) = \frac{\dot{m}_{a,in}}{\dot{m}_{a,0}} - \frac{f_1(n, p_m)}{\dot{m}_{a,0}} \tag{3.53}$$

The time constant τ_n depends mainly on the air flow $\dot{m}_{a,0}$ which can be seen in the following example: Assuming a manifold volume of $V_m = 4,25\,l$ at an ambient temperature of $\vartheta_a = 300\,^{\circ}K$ and an adiabatic coefficient $\kappa = 1.4$, the time constant τ_n at minimum and maximum power can be calculated:

- at maximum power, the manifold pressure is $p_{m,0} = 1\,bar$ and the mass air flow shall be $\dot{m}_{a,0} = 600\,kg/h$. This leads to a time constant of:

$$\tau_{n,1} = 21\,ms \tag{3.54}$$

- at minimum power (e.g. idling), the pressure is $p_{m,0} = 0.35\,bar$ and the mass air flow shall be $\dot{m}_{a,0} = 6\,kg/h$ which leads to:

$$\tau_{n,2} = 740\,ms \tag{3.55}$$

It can be seen that the dynamic behaviour of the intake manifold has an impact on engine dynamics especially at low power such as idling.

3.2.7 Compensation of Wall Wetting

This chapter relates to manifold injection systems, where fuel is injected into the inlet pipes in front of the input valves.

Short deviations of the air-fuel ratio must be compensated because the state variables in the inlet pipe vary during dynamic transitions. For example an air pressure variation or a change in the wall fuel mass m_W deposited on the wall of the inlet pipe (wall wetting) leads to a mismatch of the air-fuel ratio λ in the cylinders [2]. Short-time deviations caused by wall wetting can be compensated by a dynamic modelling of the system.

Figure 3.19 shows the main effects of wall wetting. The variation of the wall fuel mass m_W over time results from the depositing fuel flow $\dot{m}_D$ and fuel flow from evaporation $\dot{m}_E$:

$$\frac{dm_W}{dt} = \dot{m}_D - \dot{m}_E \tag{3.56}$$

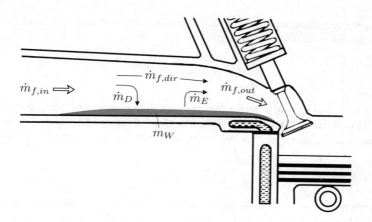

Figure 3.19 Compensation of wall wetting

The fuel flow injected into the inlet pipe $m_{f,in}$ is split up into a fuel flow directly into the cylinder $\dot{m}_{f,dir} = (1 - c)\dot{m}_{f,in}$ and a depositing fuel flow $\dot{m}_D = c \cdot \dot{m}_{f,in}$:

$$\dot{m}_{f,in} = \dot{m}_D + \dot{m}_{f,dir} = c \cdot \dot{m}_{f,in} + (1 - c) \cdot \dot{m}_{f,in} \qquad (3.57)$$

The factor c in that is called deposition rate. The fuel flow from evaporation $\dot{m}_E$ is supposed to be proportional to the wall fuel mass m_W:

$$\dot{m}_E = \frac{1}{T} \cdot m_W \qquad (3.58)$$

Inserting Equation 3.57 and 3.58 into Equation 3.56 leads to

$$\dot{m}_W = c \cdot \dot{m}_{f,in} - \frac{1}{T} \cdot m_W \quad . \qquad (3.59)$$

The resulting fuel flow into the cylinder $\dot{m}_{f,out}$ is composed of the fuel flow directly into the cylinder $\dot{m}_{f,dir}$ and the fuel flow from evaporation $\dot{m}_E$. This yields

$$\dot{m}_{f,out} = (1 - c)\dot{m}_{f,in} + \frac{1}{T} \cdot m_W \qquad (3.60)$$

Equation 3.59 and 3.60 can be Laplace transformed into

$$M_W = \frac{c \cdot T}{1 + Ts} \cdot \dot{M}_{f,in} \qquad (3.61)$$

and

$$\dot{M}_{f,out} = (1 - c) \cdot \dot{M}_{f,in} + \frac{1}{T} \cdot M_W \quad . \qquad (3.62)$$

Inserting Equation 3.61 in 3.62 yields

$$\dot{M}_{f,out} = \left[(1 - c) + \frac{c}{1 + Ts}\right]\dot{M}_{f,in} \quad . \qquad (3.63)$$

The transfer function between fuel flow injected into the inlet pipe and fuel flow sucked into the cylinder results to

$$\frac{\dot{M}_{f,out}}{\dot{M}_{f,in}} = \frac{1 + (1-c)Ts}{1 + Ts} \qquad . \qquad (3.64)$$

The step response of this transfer function consists of a proportional part $(1-c)$ and a delayed part with a gain c and a time constant T. For wall wetting compensation the inverted transfer function is put on the allocated fuel mass:

$$\frac{1 + Ts}{1 + (1-c)Ts} \qquad (3.65)$$

The compensator is a PDT_1-element with a gain of $\frac{1}{1-c}$ and a time constant $(1-c)T$. The parameters c and T are dependent on the operation point of the engine. They are determined on a test bench at dynamic transients by varying these parameters until the lambda deviations are minimized. Fig 3.20 shows test results of such a process. The λ-deviations are reduced effectively leading to less noxious emissions after the catalytic converter.

This model shows an unproportional reinforcement of possible disruptions because of the differential effect of the compensator. However, the consequences on λ can be limited. At cold engine operation this wall wetting model is completed by a second model with simular structure but bigger time constant.

3.3 Ignition Control in SI Engines

This chapter relates to SI engines only. Diesel engines do not require a spark ignition, since combustion is triggered by self inflammation due to compressional heat. In diesel engines, the injection start angle replaces the ignition angle.

3.3.1 Ignition Angle Control

Correct ignition timing over the entire engine operating range is very important as it has a major impact on fuel consumption as well as on emission rates. Combustion within the cylinder can be divided into two phases:

1. **Inflammation delay (Time Proportional)**
   In-cylinder pressure and temperature do not rise considerably within this time period. The inflammation delay time τ_d depends on the temperature, pressure and air-fuel ratio. The lag can be convoluted into an equivalent crankshaft angle which increases with engine speed.

2. **Combustion (Angle Proportional)**
   The equivalent crankshaft angle for the second phase is almost constant over the entire engine operating range. Induced by the piston movement, turbulances accelerate with engine speed, as well as the combustion process.

If combustion starts too late because of retarded ignition angles, the emission of hydrocarbons HC will increase. High pressure amplitudes at advanced ignition

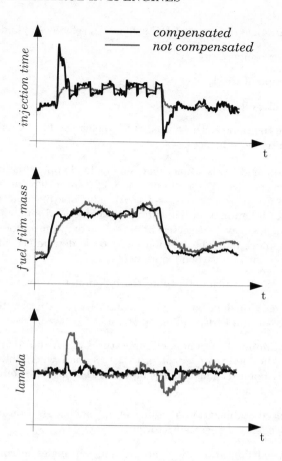

Figure 3.20 Compensation of fuel film dynamics at a test engine

angles increase the emission of NO_x. NO_x can be reduced by delaying the ignition at the expense of a higher fuel consumption [2]. The following parameters are used to control the ignition angle:

- Intake manifold pressure p_m

- Mass air flow $\dot{m}_a$

- Engine speed n

- Throttle angle α_t

- Air-fuel ratio λ

---

[2]Over all, the determination of the right ignition angle is a compromise between different objectives.

- Crankshaft angle α_{CS} and TDC signal of a reference cylinder

- Ambient air temperature ϑ_a

- Engine temperature ϑ_e

- Battery voltage U_b

These values are the same as those needed for fuel control. The ignition angle α_i is dependent on many influences:

- The ignition angle α_i is a function of engine load approximated by injection time $t_{inj} \sim \dot{m}_a/(n \cdot \lambda)$ (see Equation 3.32), and of engine speed n. This can be described by a map $\alpha_i = f(t_i, n)$. The look-up table also covers the variation of inflammation depending on engine load and speed. Retarded ignition angles may be selected in order to compromise for reduced emissions and knocking. The ignition angle α_i is determined for each engine operating point by test bed experiments.

- Air-fuel ratio λ, which determines the inflammation delay τ_d.

- Retarded ignition angle at high ambient air temperature ϑ_a to avoid knocking. A look-up table depending on t_{inj} and ϑ_a may be used.

- Engine warm-up at low engine temperatures ϑ_e. A retarded ignition angle α_i retards the energy conversion process to a phase where the exhaust valves are already opened. The exhaust pipe and the catalytic converter are then heated very fast.

- Engine speed stabilization at idling by advancing ignition angles at lower engine speeds, thus increasing torque.

- Engine speed limitation by retarding ignition angles in conjunction with fuel cut off.

- Retarded ignition angles during acceleration in order to avoid knocking.

- Closed-loop knock control

- The battery voltage U_b has an impact on the ignition energy.

Figure 3.21 shows an ignition angle map depending on engine speed and load. Angles α_i before Top Dead Center (TDC) are positive.

3.3.2   Optimisation of Engine Maps

The fuel amount and ignition angle are the two most important parameters that influence the fuel consumption as well as the emission of pollutants. This has already been shown in Sections 3.1.2 and 3.1.6. There is a conflict between minimising either fuel consumption or emissions. This is shown in Figure 3.22.

If the ignition angle is chosen to minimise fuel consumption, the engine raw emission rates for NO_x and HC will be fairly high. On the other hand, if the

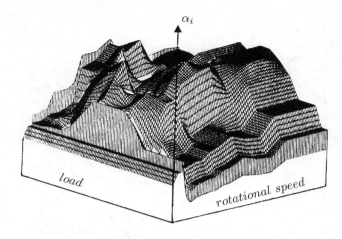

Figure 3.21 Ignition angle map

ignition angle is selected to minimise emissions, the fuel consumption will be higher. A compromise must consider fuel consumption **and** emission levels at all engine operating points. Emission levels can be very high at some particular operating points. There, the optimisation must focus on the emissions. Other operating points show acceptable emission rates. At these points the optimisation must focus on fuel consumption.

Fuel consumption and emission levels are measured in special road driving cycles like the ECE-test or FTP-test. These tests specify the vehicle velocity over time. Translating vehicle to engine speeds, a test cycle is equivalent to a sequence of different engine operating points over time. Every operating point is defined by several control parameters including engine speed and load.

The fuel consumption can be described by the volume $\dot{V}$ of combusted fuel over time. The minimisation criterium is the integral over the test cycle.

$$V = \int_0^T \dot{V}(t) \, dt \to min \qquad (3.66)$$

The total fuel consumption V for a test cycle time T can also be obtained by a discrete summation over the engine operating points.

$$V = \sum_{i=1}^N \dot{V}_i(\alpha_i, \lambda_i) \, t_i \to min \qquad (3.67)$$

An analysis of the test cycle shows that most operating points are visited several times. The individual time periods where the engine stays in the same operating point i can be summarised into a total time period t_i. The fuel consumption over time $\dot{V}_i$ can then be minimised independently for each operating point. The resulting values of α_i and λ_i are stored into look-up tables $\alpha_i(t_{inj}, n)$ and $\lambda_i(t_{inj}, n)$ for every operating point.

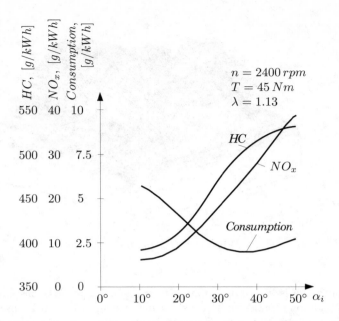

Figure 3.22 Fuel consumption and emission levels over ignition angle α_i.

When optimising fuel consumption, the maximum allowable emission levels are treated as optimisation constraints. The maximum emission rates are fixed by laws which specify the maximum integral masses of the different pollutants generated during a test cycle.

$$HC \;\; = \;\; \sum_{i=1}^{N} \dot{H}C(\alpha_i, \lambda_i)\; t_i \;\; \leq \hat{H}C \qquad\qquad (3.68)$$

$$CO \;\; = \;\; \sum_{i=1}^{N} \dot{C}O(\alpha_i, \lambda_i)\; t_i \;\; \leq \hat{C}O \qquad\qquad (3.69)$$

$$NO_x \;\; = \;\; \sum_{i=1}^{N} \dot{N}O_x(\alpha_i, \lambda_i)\; t_i \;\; \leq \hat{N}O_x \qquad\qquad (3.70)$$

The emission levels per time $\dot{H}C, \dot{C}O, \dot{N}O$ can be influenced by the values of α_i and λ_i at each operating point i. The emission limits are only given for the integral mass over the whole test cycle. It is therefore not obvious which α_i and λ_i values must be adopted at each operating point i. Such an optimisation problem with constraints can be solved by using the Lagrange multiplication method [4]. The differences between actually achieved and acceptable emission levels are weighted by Lagrange factors L. Equation 3.67 and equations 3.68 to

3.70 are combined into a single criterium.

$$W = V + L_{HC}(HC - \hat{HC}) + L_{CO}(CO - \hat{CO}) + L_{NO_x}(NO_x - \hat{NO}_x) \to \min$$
(3.71)

Now the cost function W must be minimised. For example, if all emission rates were at the acceptable limits ($HC = \hat{HC}$, etc.), all terms except V for fuel consumption would disappear. This would minimise V as before. The value W can be divided into two parts: a constant part W_o which is independent of the operating points i and a variable part influenced by α_i and λ_i.

$$W = \sum_{i=1}^{N} \dot{V}_i(\alpha_i, \lambda_i)t_i +$$

$$\sum_{i=1}^{N} [L_{HC}\dot{HC}(\alpha_i, \lambda_i)t_i + L_{CO}\dot{CO}(\alpha_i, \lambda_i)t_i + L_{NO_x}\dot{NO}_x(\alpha_i, \lambda_i)t_i]$$

$$-L_{HC}\hat{HC} - L_{CO}\hat{CO} - L_{NO_x}\hat{NO}_x$$

$$W = \sum_{i=1}^{N} Z(\alpha_i, \lambda_i)t_i - W_0$$

where:

$$W_0 = L_{HC}\hat{HC} + L_{CO}\hat{CO} + L_{NO_x}\hat{NO}_x = const$$
(3.72)

and:

$$Z(\alpha_i, \lambda_i) = \dot{V}(\alpha_i, \lambda_i)$$
$$+L_{HC}\dot{HC}(\alpha_i, \lambda_i)$$
$$+L_{CO}\dot{CO}(\alpha_i, \lambda_i)$$
$$+L_{NO_x}\dot{NO}_x(\alpha_i, \lambda_i)$$

The value of W can be minimised by minimising the function $Z(\alpha_i, \lambda_i)$ at each operating point:

$$Z_i(\alpha_i, \lambda_i) \to min$$
(3.73)

Figure 3.23 shows $\dot{V}(\alpha_i, \lambda_i)$ and $\dot{NO}_x(\alpha_i, \lambda_i)$ for one operating point i depending on ignition angle α_i and air-fuel ratio λ_i. The values were measured in an engine test bed run. The pair α_i, λ_i for minimum $Z(\alpha_i, \lambda_i)$ is marked by a rectangle.

It can be seen that fuel consumption $\dot{V}(\alpha_i, \lambda_i)$ at minimum $Z(\alpha_i, \lambda_i)$ is slightly higher than the absolute minimum in order to compromise with emissions $NO_x(\alpha_i, \lambda_i)$. The value W is a minimum for the entire test cycle if correct values for the Lagrange factors L_{HC}, L_{CO} and L_{NO_x} were selected. In practice, several iterations with modified Lagrange factors must be passed to obtain a minimum W which also meets the legal emission constraints. For example, in a first iteration, low fuel consumption V is attained. However, emissions (HC, CO, NO_x) are still

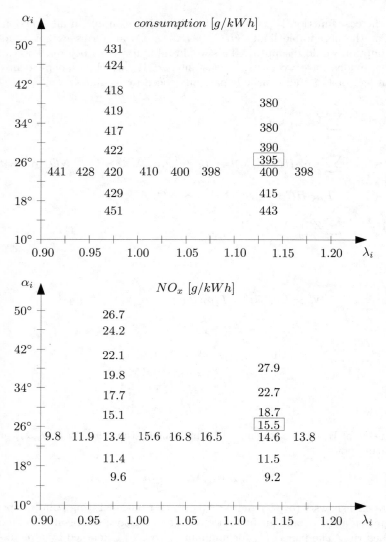

Figure 3.23 Fuel consumption and NO_x emissions over ignition angle α_i and air-fuel ratio λ at an operating point i with $L_{NO_x} = 3$.

relatively close to or above the legal limits. The Lagrange weighting factors L are then increased for the next iteration. Practical experience shows that only a few iterations are needed to minimise the function Z at a small number of representative operating points i. Values for other operating points can be obtained by interpolation. Figure 3.24 shows resulting look-up tables for the ignition angle α and the air-fuel ratio λ. In engines at stochiometric $\lambda = 1$ operation, only the ignition angle α_i is calculated.

3.3.3   Ignition Power Amplifier

A power transistor switches the current through the ignition coil. The timing is controlled by the micro computer of the engine control unit.

Power Amplifier

Figure 3.25 shows the circuit of the ignition power amplifier. The current through the ignition coil is flowing when the transistor is turned on:

$$i_1(t) = \frac{U_b - U_{CE}}{R_1}(1 - e^{-t/\tau}) \tag{3.74}$$

where $\tau = L_1/R_1$ is the time constant. The current increases almost linearly at the beginning of the loading period. The energy stored in the coil after loading is controlled to:

$$E_L = \frac{1}{2}L_1 \hat{i}_1^2 \tag{3.75}$$

In this equation, $\hat{i}_1$ shall be the current at the time when the transistor is switched off. The switch-on time period must be limited in order to protect the power transistor from too high currents i_1.

The switch-off of the transistor induces a high voltage at the collector of the transistor and at the coil L_1 because the current is interrupted. This voltage is amplified in the coupled coil L_2 and transferred to the spark plug.

The capacitors C_1 and C_2 caused by parasitic effects have an impact on the maximum induced voltage $\hat{U}$ at the spark plug. Both capacitors can be summarised by C':

$$C' = C_1 + \left(\frac{w_2}{w_1}\right)C_2 \tag{3.76}$$

where w_2/w_1 is the winding ratio between coil L_2 and coil L_1. The energy stored in capacitor C' is:

$$E_C = \frac{1}{2}C' \hat{U}_1^2 \tag{3.77}$$

Assuming an ideal energy conversion $E_L = E_C$, the maximum voltage $\hat{U}_1$ on the primary side is given by:

$$\hat{U}_1 = \hat{i}_1\sqrt{\frac{L_1}{C'}} \tag{3.78}$$

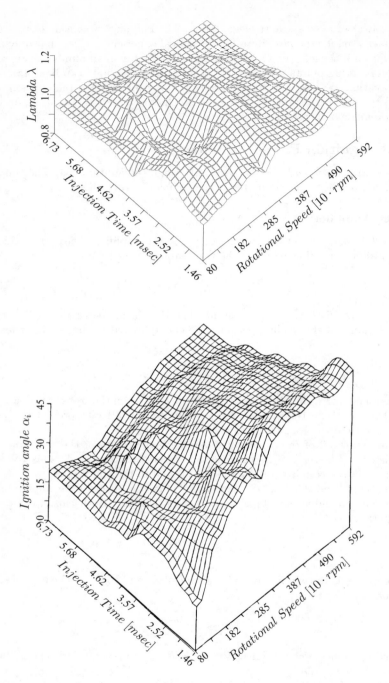

Figure 3.24 Look-up tables of optimum air-fuel ratio λ and ignition angle α for an FTP test cycle.

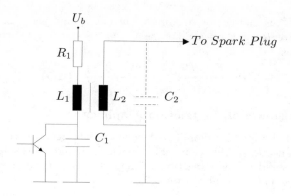

Figure 3.25 Ignition power amplifier

The resonant frequency f_r of the circuit is

$$f_r = \frac{1}{2\pi\sqrt{L_1 C'}} \quad , \tag{3.79}$$

which has typical values in the range of $1 - 3\,kHz$. Due to a non-ideal coupling factor $K \approx 0.85 < 1$ between the coils, the resonances are not exactly sinusoidal.

A numerical example is given below: The voltage on the secondary side without load is specified to be above $25\,kV$:

$$\hat{U}_2 \geq 25\,kV$$

The voltage with parasitic load must be above a lower level, considering bad conditions like dirty or damp spark plugs.

$$\hat{U}_2^* \geq 12\,kV$$

The worst-case parasitic resistances parallel to the plug are about:

$$R_p \approx 300\,k\Omega$$

Assuming a winding ratio of $w_2/w_1 = 100$ and a coupling factor of $K = 0.85$, the maximum voltage $\hat{U}_1$ on the primary side is

$$\hat{U}_1 = \frac{w_1}{w_2}\frac{\hat{U}_2}{K} = 300\,V \quad ,$$

which the power transistor must be selected to withstand. The maximum current is

$$\hat{i}_1 = \frac{w_2}{w_1}\frac{\hat{U}_2^*}{K R_p} = 5\,A \quad .$$

The voltage $\hat{U}_2^*$ is chosen for maximum current $\hat{i}_1$ and the case of a parallel parasitic resistor R_p on the secondary side. The resistor on the primary side can be estimated as:

$$R_1 \leq \frac{U_b - U_{CE}}{\hat{i}_1} = \frac{14\,V - 1.5\,V}{5\,A} = 2.5\,\Omega$$

Internal Resistance of the Ignition Amplifier

The quality of the ignition amplifier depends on the ignition circuit's effective internal resistance R_i on the secondary side which should be as small as possible. It can be measured by inserting two different resistors R_{p1} and R_{p2} parallel to the spark plug. The internal resistance is:

$$R_i = \frac{\Delta U_2}{\Delta i_2} \tag{3.80}$$

The voltage ΔU_2 is equivalent to:

$$\Delta U_2 = U_{21} - U_{22} \tag{3.81}$$

where U_{21} is the voltage at R_{p1} and U_{22} is the voltage at R_{p2}. The current Δi_2 can be calculated by assuming $R_{p1} > R_{p2}$:

$$\Delta i_2 = \frac{U_{22}}{R_{p2}} - \frac{U_{21}}{R_{p1}} \tag{3.82}$$

which yields:

$$R_i = \frac{(U_{21} - U_{22})R_{p1}R_{p2}}{U_{22}R_{p1} - U_{21}R_{p2}} \tag{3.83}$$

As an example, parallel resistor values of $R_{p1} = 1\,M\Omega$ and $R_{p2} = 100\,k\Omega$ were used. The resulting two secondary voltages

$$U_{21} = 24\,kV \quad , \qquad U_{22} = 10\,kV$$

are measured to calculate the internal resistance:

$$R_i = 185\,k\Omega$$

Protection for the Power Transistor

Switch-on Limitations: To reduce the energy dissipated in the transistor, the transistor is shut off completely at low engine speed, e.g. below $0.5\,s^{-1} = 30\,rpm$.

Over Voltage Protection: Peak voltages at the collector of the power transistor can exceed allowable values at switch off. If, for example, the connection to the spark plug is interrupted, the secondary circuit will not be discharged. The peak voltage during the next cycle will then be higher because of the already loaded capacitor C_2. This can be avoided by using the protection circuit shown in Figure 3.26. The voltage at the diode is proportional to the ratio of $R_2/(R_1 + R_2)$ and the voltage at the collector.

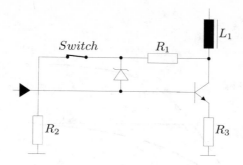

Figure 3.26 Overvoltage protection.

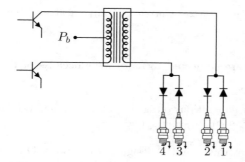

Figure 3.27 Circuit of the ignition power amplifier.

Ignition cutoff: When the engine is turned off, the ignition circuit is also switched off. A resulting voltage peak might cause undesired combustion of the remaining fuel mixture. Ignition can be prevented by opening the switch indicated in Figure 3.26. In this case, the maximum collector voltage is reduced to the voltage of the diode. This is not enough to generate a spark on the secondary side.

Electronic Distribution

In four cylinder engines, the ignition can be distributed without mechanical switches according to Figure 3.27.

The two transistors on the left side work intermittently and use the same induction coil. Each spark plug is connected to a high voltage diode. Plugs 2 and 3 are connected in series as are plugs 1 and 4. Therefore, two plugs receive the high secondary voltage simultaneously. However, because the two cylinders are in opposite phases (one in compression, the other in exhaust) only one of the two cylinders will fire. The other two plugs are blocked because of the diodes. The problems of such an approach are:

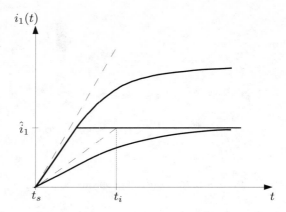

Figure 3.28 Current in ignition coil over time.

- Spark plugs are subjected to more wear because of the doubled ignition rate.

- Slightly reduced ignition voltage because of a small voltage loss at the spark plug of the non-combusting cylinder.

- Conflicting restraints on the design of the diodes: On one hand, good electrical conduction is required which leads to poor heat conduction. On the other hand, a high threshold voltage in the conducting state generates a lot of heat which can be better dissipated with little insulation.

Advantages of electronic distribution:

- The ignition angle may be selected independently of the position of mechanical distribution.

- Good suppression of interference due to the diodes.

Alternatively to using a double ignition coil for four cylinders as shown or for each pair of plugs, one coil for each plug can be used. If the amplifiers are integrated together with the ignition coils at the spark plugs, the high voltage parts can be shielded.

3.3.4 Dwell Angle Control

The dwell time of the power transistor can be reduced by a lower resistor R_1 on the primary side of the ignition coil without changing the time constant L_1/R_1 (see Equation 3.74). The current of the power transistor is limited when reaching its maximum level $\hat{i}_1$ according to the device in Figure 3.29. The current over time is shown in Figure 3.28.

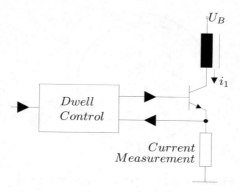

Figure 3.29 Measurement of the current through the ignition coil.

If the dwell time is too long, the energy E_t dissipated in the transistor can destroy the device. The thermal energy is equivalent to:

$$E_t = \int\limits_0^{t_d} P(t)\, dt \approx \hat{i} \int\limits_0^{t_d} U_{CE}(t)\, dt \tag{3.84}$$

The dwell time t_d depends on the time interval between the start of the current flow at t_s and the ignition at t_i:

$$t_d = t_i - t_s \tag{3.85}$$

The starting time t_s is controlled to maintain a constant dwell time t_d to protect the transistor. The respective crankshaft angle α_{CS} is proportional to the engine speed n according to:

$$\alpha_{CS} = 360°\, n\, t_d \tag{3.86}$$

Example:
A dwell time of $t_d = 3\,ms$ at $n_1 = 600\,rpm$ corresponds to a dwell angle of:

$$\alpha_{cs1} = 10.8°$$

At maximum engine speed $n_2 = 6000\,rpm$ the dwell angle is now

$$\alpha_{cs2} = 108°$$

3.3.5   Ignition Angle Errors in Transients

In many engine control systems engine speed is measured at the crankshaft by means of a pick-up wheel with 60 teeth. Getting an edge every 6°, there are only small errors in transients. A different pick-up configuration is a wheel with 60° segments on it. In a four cylinder engine, the crankshaft wheel has two segments

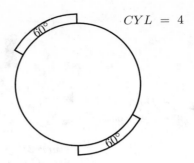

Figure 3.30 Segmental engine speed sensor.

as two cycles are passed per revolution (Figure 3.30).The engine speed can be derived from the segment signal $t_{60°}$:

$$n = \frac{1}{6 \cdot t_{60°}} \tag{3.87}$$

The actual engine speed value is calculated after measuring $t_{60°}$. This engine speed value is then used for ignition timing at the next cylinder, which is half a crankshaft revolution later. In engine speed transients, significant ignition angle errors occur.

The following counter configuration could be implemented in the I/O portion of a micro-controller. Figure 3.31 explains the different signals. There should be two counters: The first one counts the segment time $t_{60°}$ which is indicated in (2). The second counter subdivides the time between subsequent negative edges of segments (3). The dwell time t_d and the ignition time t_i are determined from the threshold values calculated by the micro-controller.

For a given speed n, the ignition time t_i depends on the ignition angle α_i:

$$t_i = \frac{\alpha_i}{n \, 360°} \tag{3.88}$$

The ignition release time t_r triggers the next ignition:

$$t_r = \frac{2}{CYL} t_{360°} - t_i = \frac{1}{n} \left(\frac{1}{2} - \frac{\alpha_i}{360°} \right) \tag{3.89}$$

where $CYL = 4$ is the number of cylinders in this example. This calculation is correct for a constant engine speed only. We shall now estimate the errors introduced by a given acceleration. We assume an engine speed profile according to (5) in Figure 3.31, which relates to a constant acceleration from n_0 to n_1. The ignition release time error is approximated by a Taylor expansion:

$$
\begin{aligned}
\Delta t_r &= \left. \frac{\partial t_r}{\partial n} \right|_{n_0} \Delta n + \left. \frac{\partial t_r}{\partial \alpha_i} \right|_{\alpha_0} \Delta \alpha_i (\Delta n) \tag{3.90} \\
&= -\frac{1}{n_0{}^2} \left(\frac{2}{CYL} - \frac{\alpha_i(n_0)}{360°} \right) \Delta n - \frac{1}{n_0 \, 360°} \Delta \alpha_i (\Delta n) \tag{3.91}
\end{aligned}
$$

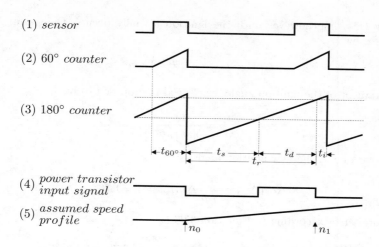

Figure 3.31 Segment based ignition control.

where the engine speed difference is:

$$\Delta n = n_1 - n_0 \tag{3.92}$$

and the ignition angle difference is:

$$\Delta \alpha_i(\Delta n) = \alpha_i(n_1) - \alpha_i(n_0) \tag{3.93}$$

The error of the ignition release time results in an ignition angle error:

$$\alpha_i \;=\; 360° \left(\frac{2}{CYL} - n_1 t_r \right) \tag{3.94}$$

$$\Delta \alpha_i \;=\; -360° \, n_1 \, \Delta t_r \tag{3.95}$$

$$\;=\; \left[\frac{n_1^2}{n_0^2} \left(\frac{2}{CYL} 360° - \alpha_i(n_0) \right) \frac{\Delta n}{n_1} \right] + \frac{n_1}{n_0} \left[\alpha_i(n_1) - \alpha_i(n_0) \right] \tag{3.96}$$

The error consists of two portions. The first part is the release error caused by the engine speed change and the second part is due to a new ignition angle value at the new speed.

Example:
A four cylinder engine $CYL = 4$ at $n_0 = 600\,rpm = 10/s$ has an ignition angle of $\alpha_i(n_0) = 20°$. The engine speed acceleration is supposed to be $1000\,rpm$ per second:

$$a = 1000 \frac{1}{min\ s} = 16.6\,s^{-2}$$

The ignition release time t_r is calculated based upon the engine speed n_0.

$$t_r(n_0) = 44.4\,ms \qquad = \frac{1}{10}\left(\frac{1}{2} - \frac{20}{360} \right)$$

During this time however until the ignition actually occurs, the engine speed increases by

$$\Delta n(t = t_r) = a\,t_r = 44\,rpm\quad.$$

The gradient of the ignition angle over speed is supposed to be

$$\frac{\partial\alpha_i}{\partial n} = \frac{20°}{500\;rpm}\quad.$$

The error due to the new ignition angle is:

$$\Delta\alpha_i(\Delta n) = \frac{\partial\alpha_i}{\partial n}\Delta n(t = t_r) = 1.76°$$

The total error according to Equation 3.96 is:

$$\Delta\alpha_i = \left(\frac{644\,rpm}{600\,rpm}\right)^2 (180° - 20°)\frac{44\,rpm}{644\,rpm} + \frac{644\,rpm}{600\,rpm}1.76° = 12.59° + 1.89°$$

The release error can be very high when using a segmental speed sensor. It can be avoided by using an incremental sensor with a 60 tooth wheel. Then only the error of 1.89° remains during the dynamic transient in the above example. Therefore, in most applications a segmental sensor is only additionally used at the camshaft to distinguish between the first and the second crankshaft rotation of a cycle (720°). In case of crankshaft sensor failure, the second camshaft sensor serves as a back-up device. In speed transients, ignition angle errors may be then tolerated.

4 Engine Control Systems

4.1 Lambda Control

In stoichiometric engine operation, emission levels heavily depend on how accurate the air-fuel ratio can be kept at $\lambda = 1$. Due to measurement and computational tolerances, sufficiently accurate stoichiometric operation requires a closed loop control.

4.1.1 Stochiometric Operation of SI Engines

In SI engines, the air-fuel ratio λ is either very lean at part load or stochiometric at medium and high load. A stoichiometric ratio of $\lambda = 1$ should lead to an ideal combustion. Figure 4.1 shows the emissions at different air-fuel ratios. For $\lambda = 1$, the emissions of HC, CO and NO_x are relatively low. Due to turbulence and local inhomogeneity of the gas mixture, real combustion actually produces HC, CO and NO_x at the same time. By means of a catalytic converter, these raw emissions can be effectively reduced.

It can be seen in Figure 4.2 that the emission rates after the catalytic converter vary highly with the air-fuel ratio λ: A change of the average $\Delta\lambda = 0.1\,\%$ would already double the emission rates. Therefore, it is important to have an accurate closed loop lambda control to guarantee an average air-fuel ratio within a window smaller than $0.1\,\%$ around $\lambda = 1$. When engine speed and torque change, lambda deviations of $2 - 3\,\%$ over a short period of time are allowed. If the average accuracy can be held, such deviations go into both directions. Within the volume of the catalytic converter excursions of the air-fuel ratio in one direction are compensated by those in the opposite direction. At the exhaust pipe tail, short time lambda deviations of a few percent do not deteriorate the emissions after the catalytic converter.

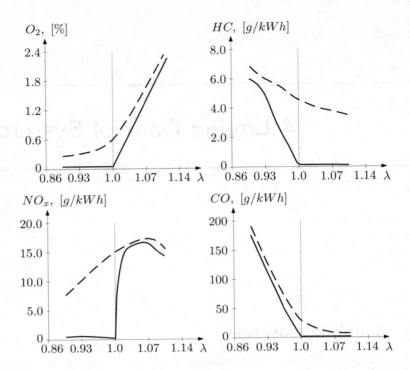

Figure 4.1 Measurement of exhaust gases: oxygen O_2, hydrocarbon HC, nitrogen oxide NO_x and carbon monoxide CO. The concentration before the catalytic converter are indicated by dotted and the concentrations after the catalytic converter by straight lines.

The block diagram of the lambda controlled SI engine is shown in Figure 4.3. The amount of injected fuel is controlled by the engine control unit which gets its feedback from the lambda sensor in the exhaust pipe as well as the mass air flow signal in the inlet pipe. Additional variables like engine speed and engine temperature are also used in the control scheme.

Catalytic Converter

The catalytic aftertreatment reduces the emissions considerably (supposing a correct lambda control at $\lambda = 1$). Due to turbulences and flame propagation, the air-fuel mixture is still uncompletely burned. Noxious gases like HC, CO and NO_x are converted to CO_2, H_2O and N_2 by the catalytic converter. The converter is integrated into the exhaust pipe. It consists of a ceramic or metal carrier substrate covered by a wash coat with an extremely large surface which is again covered with a thin layer of platinum and rhodium as shown in Figure 4.4.

The ratio of platinum to rhodium is approximately 2 to 1. Depending on the engine size about $1 - 3\,g$ of the precious metals are used. They both support

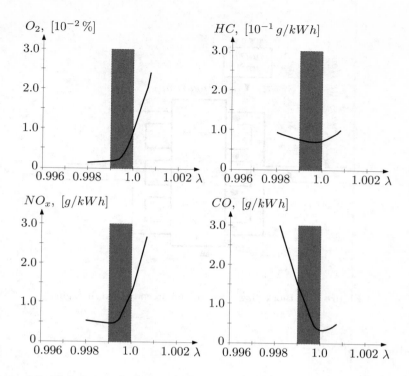

Figure 4.2 Emission rates of an engine after the catalytic converter at a static operating point (engine speed $1800\,rpm$ and torque $T = 65\,Nm$). Average lambda should be within the indicated window.

the chemical reactions: Platin supports more the oxidation of CO and HC and rhodium supports more the reduction of the nitrogen oxides NO_x.

Reduction and oxidation processes are simultaneously running in the catalytic converter. The conversion ratio is defined as the relative change of the gas concentration before and after the catalytic process.

$$c_r = \frac{c_{in} - c_{out}}{c_{in}} \tag{4.1}$$

The conversion ratio has typical values of $c_r > 90\,\%$. The most important chemical reactions are listed below:

Oxidation of HC and CO:

$$H_nC_m + \left(m + \frac{n}{4}\right)O_2 \quad \rightarrow \quad m\,CO_2 + \frac{n}{2}H_2O \tag{4.2}$$

$$H_nC + 2H_2O \quad \rightarrow \quad CO_2 + \left(2 + \frac{n}{2}\right)H_2 \tag{4.3}$$

$$CO + \frac{1}{2}O_2 \quad \rightarrow \quad CO_2 \tag{4.4}$$

$$CO + H_2O \quad \rightarrow \quad CO_2 + H_2 \tag{4.5}$$

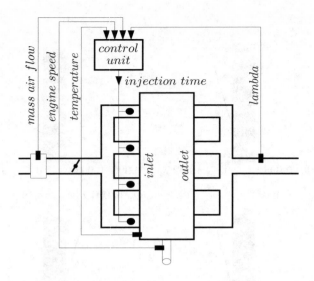

Figure 4.3 Block diagram of a lambda controlled SI engine.

Reduction of NO_x:

$$CO + NO \; \rightarrow \; \frac{1}{2}N_2 + CO_2 \tag{4.6}$$

$$H_nC_m + 2\left(m + \frac{n}{4}\right)NO \; \rightarrow \; \left(m + \frac{n}{4}\right)N_2 + \frac{n}{2}H_2O + m\,CO_2 \tag{4.7}$$

$$H_2 + NO \; \rightarrow \; \frac{1}{2}N_2 + H_2O \tag{4.8}$$

Other catalytic reactions:

$$SO_2 + \frac{1}{2}O_2 \; \rightarrow \; SO_3 \tag{4.9}$$

$$SO_2 + 3H_2 \; \rightarrow \; H_2S + 2H_2O \tag{4.10}$$

$$\frac{5}{2}H_2 + NO \; \rightarrow \; NH_3 + H_2O \tag{4.11}$$

$$2NH_3 + \frac{5}{2}O_2 \; \rightarrow \; 2NO + 3H_2O \tag{4.12}$$

$$NH_3 + CH_4 \; \rightarrow \; HCN + 3H_2 \tag{4.13}$$

$$H_2 + \frac{1}{2}O_2 \; \rightarrow \; H_2O \tag{4.14}$$

The conversion ratio is influenced by the air-fuel ratio and the converter volume. Deviations of $\Delta\lambda < 3\,\%$ can be compensated for a short period of time. At stationary engine operation, the conversion ratio is high, even if the converter would be already partly damaged. During transients, excursions in the air-fuel

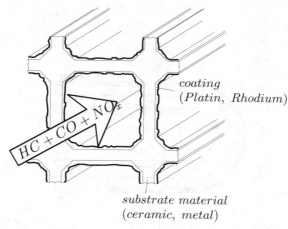

coating
(*Platin*, *Rhodium*)

$HC + CO + NO_x$

substrate material
(*ceramic*, *metal*)

Figure 4.4 Exploded view of a catalytic converter.

ratio occur, leading to higher emissions. During the warm-up phase of the engine and the exhaust pipe, temperatures are too low for chemical reactions and the conversion ratio is poor. The catalytic converter has to reach temperatures beyond $300\,°C$ to be effective. There are several possibilities to accelerate engine warm-up.

- A fast heating of the exhaust pipe can be obtained by an ignition angle retard of e.g. $10° < \Delta\alpha_i < 20°$. The combustion is shifted to a phase of the thermodynamic cycle, where the exhaust valves are already opened.

- An additional start-up catalytic converter is mounted very close to the engine where the exhaust gases get hotter soon. After the warm-up period, this converter is bypassed.

- Fresh air is added to the exhaust gases by a secondary air pump. The engine runs with a rich mixture ($\lambda < 1$). The additional combustion process in the exhaust pipe heats up the catalytic converter.

- The catalytic converter is electrically heated. In order to reduce the required heating power, the heater is concentrated in the region of the converter where the exothermic reaction first starts.

4.1.2 Oxygen Sensor

A lambda sensor is used to measure the concentration of oxygen O_2 in the exhaust pipe. The sensor is mounted in the collective exhaust pipe where the individual exhaust pipes from the cylinders end in. In engines with 6 or more cylinders two lambda sensors are used. In Figure 4.6 it can be seen, that the output voltage increases sharply at $\lambda = 1$. Thus the stochiometric point can be determined.

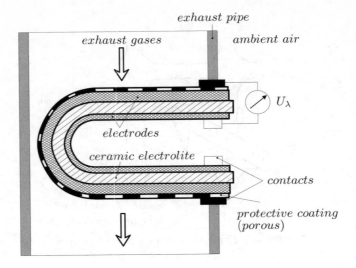

Figure 4.5 Zirconium dioxyde sensor

Zirconium Dioxyde Sensor

The sensor consists of a solid ceramic electrolyte (zirconium dioxyde), which conducts oxygen ions at temperatures above $250\,^\circ C$. The outer electrode is covered with platinum. The oxygen partial pressure on the surface of the ceramic material is thus identical with the one inside the catalytic converter. The inner electrode has a direct contact with the ambient air. The exhaust gases flow around the outer electrodes. Figure 4.5 shows the construction of a Zirconium Dioxyde Sensor.

Because of a difference in the partial oxygen pressure $p(O_2)$ inside and outside of the exhaust pipe, there is an electrolytic voltage between the electrodes:

$$U_\lambda = k\; T_{Sensor}\; ln\frac{p(O_2)_{ambient}}{p(O_2)_{exhaust}} \qquad (4.15)$$

The internal resistance ranges from $10^7\,\Omega$ at $200\,^\circ C$ to $5\cdot 10^3\,\Omega$ at $800\,^\circ C$. Figure 4.6 shows a characteristic step in the sensor voltage curve close to $\lambda = 1$. This step is caused by the increase of the oxygen partial pressure over several orders of magnitude inside the exhaust pipe around $\lambda = 1$. Typical values for the open circuit voltages are:

$$U_\lambda(rich) \quad = \quad 800 - 1000\,mV$$
$$U_\lambda(lean) \quad = \quad 50 - 200\,mV$$

The response time ranges from 15 to $30\,ms$.

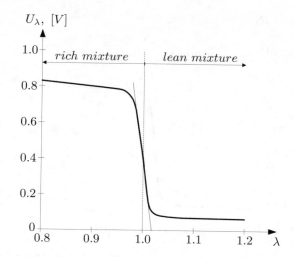

Figure 4.6 Output voltage of zirconium dioxyde sensor

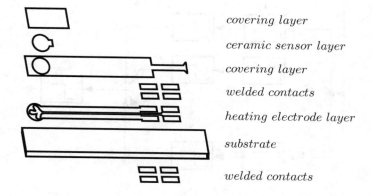

Figure 4.7 Planar structure of the strontium titanate sensor

Strontium Titanate Sensor

Strontium Titanate is a ceramic semiconductor material. Its conductivity depends on the material temperature and oxygen partial pressure. Conductivity in strontium titanate is less influenced by surface effects at high temperatures than in other materials. The dependance of the probe resistance from the temperature decreases at higher temperatures leaving the dependance on lambda only. As can be seen in Figure 4.7, the strontium titanate sensor has a planar structure.

The resistance characteristic of the sensor is shown in Figure 4.8.

An advantage of the planar device is its short response time of a few milliseconds after lambda deviations. The protection pipe around the sensing device adds

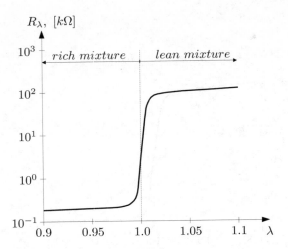

Figure 4.8 Resistance characteristic of the strontium titanate sensor

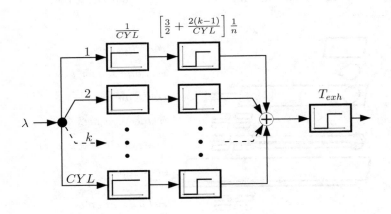

Figure 4.9 Engine model for lambda control

however further delays. Because of its operation at temperatures around $800\,°C$ it can be fitted closer to the engine. In the engine model (see Chapter 4.1.3) this leads to shorter time delays T_{exh} between exhaust valve and lambda sensor.

4.1.3 Engine Model for Lambda Control

Figure 4.9 shows a suitable model of the engine for lambda control,

CYL	is the number of cylinders
k	is the respective cylinder $1, \ldots, CYL$
$\frac{1}{n}$	is the time needed for one crankshaft revolution
T_{exh}	is the time delay between exhaust valve and lambda sensor

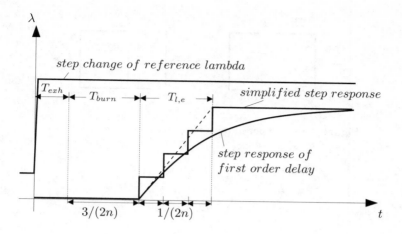

Figure 4.10 Step response and its approximation by a first-order delay (CYL=4)

Its simplified step response can be seen in Figure 4.10.

Fuel is injected into the intake manifold and sucked into the cylinders at phase-shifted time periods. This leads to the stair-step characteristic in the simplified step response. For controller design the steps are approximated by a first-order delay element with the following structure (see also Figure 4.10):

$$\frac{K_{l,e}}{1 + T_{l,e}\, s} \tag{4.16}$$

The combustion can be modeled as dead time T_{burn} continuing until the opening of the exhaust valve. Another dead time T_{exh} results from the time the exhaust gas needs to get to the lambda sensor.

T_{exh} : varies in dependence of the mass air flow between 20 and 500 ms
T_{burn} : time between opening of inlet and exhaust valves
$T_{l,e}$: the approximation delivers $\frac{2(CYL-1)}{n \cdot CYL}$

The dead times can be summed up to:

$$T_{d,e} = T_{exh} + T_{burn}$$

Figure 4.11 shows the simplified engine model containing only one delay time $T_{l,e}$ and only one dead time $T_{d,e}$.

Typical values of the parameters are:

$T_{d,e}$: 100 ms ... 1.0 s
$T_{l,e}$: 50 ms ... 0.5 s

Since the model parameters vary significantly with the operating condition of the engine, the parameters of the lambda control are adapted in dependance of

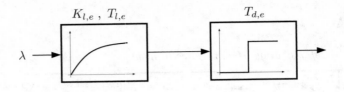

Figure 4.11 Simplified dynamic portion of the engine model

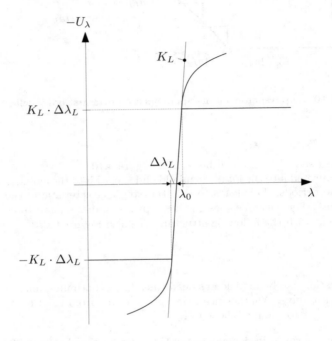

Figure 4.12 Inverted λ-characteristic with limiting range $\pm\Delta\lambda_L$

the engine operating point (feed forward adaption). Each control parameter is stored in a map over the engine's operating points.

4.1.4   Lambda Control Circuit

The characteristic between the output voltage U_λ and the air-fuel ratio λ is non-linear. After operation for many years this characteristic slightly ages. Therefore the most stable measuring range of the characteristic is taken for the control. Figure 4.12 shows, that it is located in the steep linear range of the characteristic. The sensitivity factor in this range is K_L.

Outside the measurement range the characteristic is cut off. The center of the

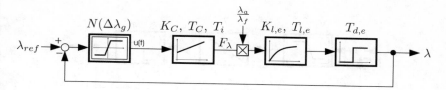

Figure 4.13 Closed loop-control circuit of the lambda-control

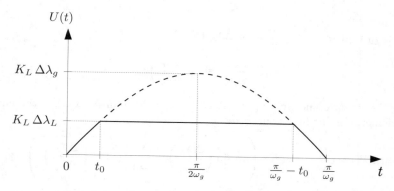

Figure 4.14 Limiting of the output sine function $U(t)$

measurement range λ_0 is not at the desired reference value λ_{ref} but is determined exclusively by the stability of the characteristic. The lambda reference value λ_{ref} must however lie within the range $[\lambda_0 - \Delta\lambda_L, \lambda_0 + \Delta\lambda_L]$. The offset of λ_0 against the reference value λ_{ref} can be compensated e.g. by a direction-dependant integral time constant of the PI controller.

To get the classical structure of a control loop, the sign of the characteristic voltage $U_\lambda(\lambda)$ is inverted. At the input of the controller a non-linear function is doing the range cut-off.

The closed loop-control circuit comprises a non-linear element and a dead time. Therefore it performs a limit cycle. For an analytic calculation the method of the harmonic balance [22] is used where the input of the non-linear element receives a sine function with the limit cycle $\Delta\lambda_g$:

$$\lambda(t) = \Delta\lambda_g \cdot \sin(\omega_g t) \tag{4.17}$$

From the output signal $U(t)$ only the first term $U_1(t)$ of a Fourier expansion is taken. The amplitude of $U_1(t)$ equals the Fourier coefficient U_1 (see Figure 4.14).

$$U_1 = \frac{4\omega_g}{\pi} K_L \left(\int_0^{t_0} \Delta\lambda_g \sin^2(\omega_g t)\, dt + \int_{t_0}^{\frac{\pi}{2\omega_g}} \Delta\lambda_L \sin(\omega_g t)\, dt \right)$$

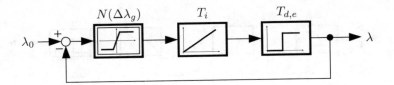

Figure 4.15 Control loop after delay compensation

The time t_0 is given by the ratio of $\Delta\lambda_L$ to $\Delta\lambda_g$:

$$t_0 = \frac{1}{\omega_g} \arcsin\left(\frac{\Delta\lambda_L}{\Delta\lambda_g}\right)$$

Solving the integral and dividing by $\Delta\lambda_g$ leads to the gain $N(\Delta\lambda_g)$ of the non-linear element for the first Fourier term:

$$N(\Delta\lambda_g) = \frac{U_1}{\Delta\lambda_g} = \frac{2}{\pi} K_L \left(\arcsin\left(\frac{\Delta\lambda_L}{\Delta\lambda_g}\right) + \frac{\Delta\lambda_L}{\Delta\lambda_g} \sqrt{1 - \left(\frac{\Delta\lambda_L}{\Delta\lambda_g}\right)^2} \right)$$

If the output range is strongly limited, meaning $\Delta\lambda_L \ll \Delta\lambda_g$, the gain can be approximated by:

$$N(\Delta\lambda_g) \approx \frac{4}{\pi} \left(\frac{\Delta\lambda_L}{\Delta\lambda_g}\right) K_L \tag{4.18}$$

We assume the controller to be a PI-element with the following structure:

$$\frac{1 + T_C s}{T_i s} \cdot \frac{1}{K_C} \tag{4.19}$$

The factor $\frac{1}{K_C}$ represents the steady-state relationship between controller variable and air-fuel ratio λ. First the time parameter T_C is chosen to compensate the time delay $T_{l,e}$ of the engine:

$$T_C \approx T_{l,e} \tag{4.20}$$

Because $T_{l,e}$ depends strongly on the operation point of the engine, T_C needs to be adapted. Figure 4.15 shows the resulting structure of the control loop after compensation. The open-loop transfer function results to

$$G(s) = N(\Delta\lambda_g) \frac{1}{s\, T_i} \frac{1}{K_C} \cdot e^{-T_{d,e} s} \quad , \tag{4.21}$$

and the open-loop frequency response to

$$G(j\omega) = N(\Delta\lambda_g) \frac{1}{j\omega T_i} \frac{1}{K_C} \cdot \left[\cos\left(\omega T_{d,e}\right) - j \sin\left(\omega T_{d,e}\right)\right] \quad . \tag{4.22}$$

The stability limit of the closed-loop system is at

$$G(j\omega) = -1 \quad . \tag{4.23}$$

The frequency of the limit cycle ω_g results from the imaginary part of $G(j\omega)$:

$$Im\{G(j\omega_g)\} = 0 \quad \Rightarrow \quad \cos(\omega_g T_{d,e}) = 0 \tag{4.24}$$

$$\Rightarrow \quad \omega_g = \frac{\pi}{2 \cdot T_{d,e}} \tag{4.25}$$

With $\omega_g = \frac{\pi}{2 \cdot T_{d,e}}$ the real part yields:

$$Re\{G(j\omega_g)\} = -N(\Delta\lambda_g)\frac{2}{\pi}\frac{1}{K_C}\frac{T_{d,e}}{T_i} \tag{4.26}$$

The stability criterion of the control loop is given by (Figure 4.16):

$$|Re\{G(j\omega_g)\}| \leq 1 \tag{4.27}$$

Inserting Equation 4.26 into Equation 4.27 leads to

$$T_i > N(\Delta\lambda_g)\frac{2}{\pi}\frac{1}{K_C}T_{d,e} \tag{4.28}$$

or with Equation 4.18

$$T_i > \frac{8}{\pi^2} \cdot \frac{\Delta\lambda_L}{\Delta\lambda_g} \cdot \frac{K_L}{K_C} \cdot T_{d,e} \quad . \tag{4.29}$$

The dependence of the parameter $T_{d,e}$ on the operating point of the engine leads to a controlled adaption of the parameter T_i. The maximum amplitude of the limit cycle has been constrained by the lambda-window to:

$$\frac{\Delta\lambda_g}{\lambda} \leq 3\% \tag{4.30}$$

This equation determines the minimum value of the integration parameter T_i. Consequently the control loop reacts relatively slow to dynamic transitions between operating points (see also Figure 4.20). During long transient times noxious emissions can no longer be reduced by the catalytic converter.

4.1.5 Measurement Results

If we assume the volume of the catalytic converter to be around $V_C \approx 0.016\,m^3$, then it contains about $m_a = 0.02\,kg$ of air (and noxious exhaust gases). At full engine load and speed, a mass air flow of $\dot{m}_a = 600\,kg/h$ shall run through the exhaust pipe. It will stay $t_C = m_a/\dot{m}_a \approx 120\,ms$ in the catalytic converter. At engine idling, mass air flow might be at $6\,kg/s$. This would stay $t_C \approx 12\,s$ in the converter. The frequency of the lambda control limit cycle must therefore be above

- $0.1\,Hz$ at idling,

- $10\,Hz$ at full load and speed.

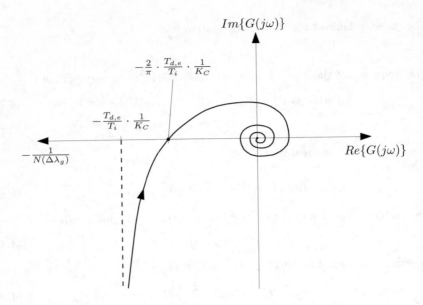

Figure 4.16 Root locus diagram of lambda-control

Figure 4.17 shows measurement results of the lambda control F_λ at an approximately stationary operating point of the engine. Noxious emissions and λ before and after catalytic treatment are shown in one diagramm. At stationary engine operation the catalytic converter has a high conversion ratio.

Figure 4.18 and 4.19 show measurement results of the lambda control during dynamic engine transients of a driving test cycle. Rotational speed and load vary a lot during acceleration and deceleration. At dynamic engine transients we observe fast rotational speed variations e.g. caused by gear changes. Since the integration time constant is limited by the lambda control limit cycle amplitude, mismatches occur where the lambda window is left and high peaks of noxious emissions are generated.

4.1.6 Adaptive Lambda Control

The dynamic performance of the lambda control is strongly restricted by the following parameters:

- given dead time of the engine $T_{d,e}$ (see Chapter 4.1.3)

- amplitude of limit cycle $\Delta\lambda_g$ limited at short-time deviations $< 3\%$ (see Equation 4.30)

The integration time constant T_i of the controller is constrained to the lower limit given in Equation 4.29. At engine transients to another operating point, the lambda control needs up to several seconds for arriving back to the stochiometric mixture (see Figure 4.20).

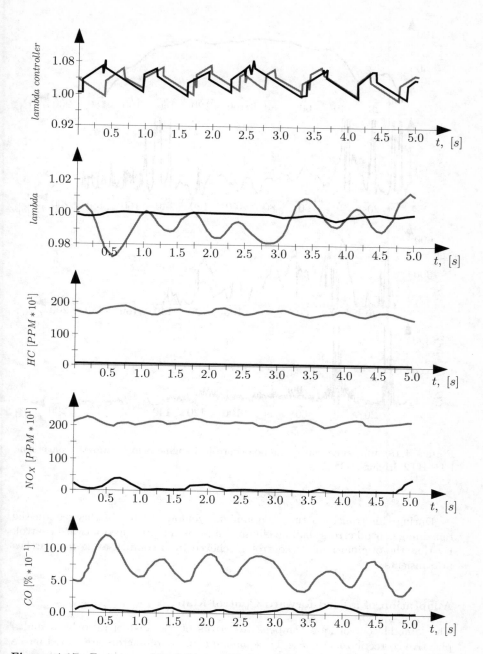

Figure 4.17 Emissions of lambda-controlled engine at stationary engine operation with $n = 1800/min$, $T = 65\,Nm$, before and after catalytic converter

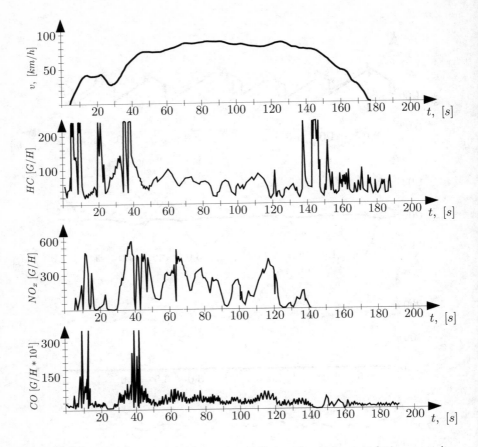

Figure 4.18 Raw emissions of lambda-controlled engine before catalytic conversion, FTP-HT2 driving-cycle

During this transition time the lambda window is left. In this section the remaining control errors shall be eliminated by an adaptive feed-forward control. By that the original lambda control is relieved from compensating mismatches in transients.

Adaptation of a Feed-forward Control Map

The lambda control loop compensates errors of the air-fuel ratio by a multiplicative correction factor F_λ. These lambda correction factors are stored into a feed-forward control map in all engine operating points. Instead of performing the error compensation by the original lambda control loop, it can now be performed by the right F_λ from the feed-forward control map without time delay. The lambda mismatches during transients are thus overcome.

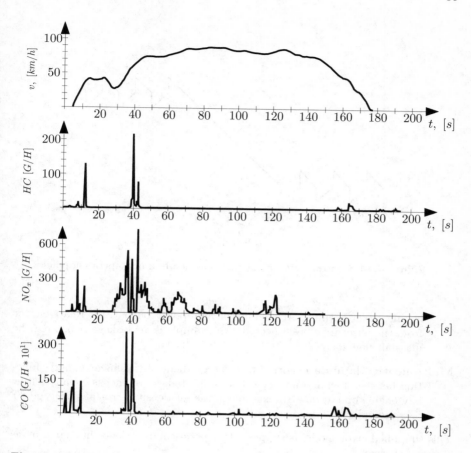

Figure 4.19 Emissions of lambda-controlled engine after catalytic conversion, FTP-HT2 driving-cycle

The problem is how to adapt the correction factors F_λ in the feed-forward control map, when some engine operating points are only very rarely visited, due to special habits of individual drivers. Eventually an adaptation is even impossible. High noxious exhaust emissions would thus remain during transients into these rarely visited operation points. Therefore a globally valid lambda compensation approach is used rather than a local adaptation of correction factors in all engine operating points.

Globally Valid Lambda Compensation

The air-fuel ratio errors are assumed to consist of two components (4.21):

Additive lambda offset error: since the absolute value of this offset is identical over the entire engine operating range, its impact is mostly felt at low

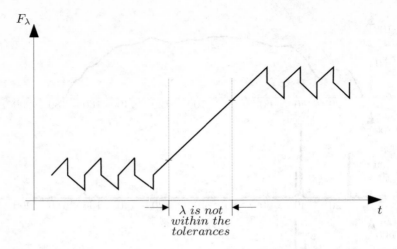

Figure 4.20 Control action F_λ at the transition to a new operating point

engine power outputs. At medium or high power output, the relative error from the offset may be neglected. An example is air leakage bypassing the mass air flow meter.

Multiplicative lambda errors: since the gradient of the linear lambda function between fuel and air mass flow is affected, its impact is equally felt at any engine operation. An example is the air density error at flap type air flow meters.

This simplified error model is supported by practical experience in engine management systems.

The additive and multiplicative errors shall now be compensated. The correct air mass flow would have been

$$\dot{m}_{a,o} = \lambda_0 L_{St} \dot{m}_f \quad . \tag{4.31}$$

The corrupted characteristic is then

$$\begin{aligned}
\dot{m}_a &= \lambda L_{St} \dot{m}_f + \Delta \dot{m}_a \\
&= \frac{\lambda}{\lambda_0} \dot{m}_{a,0} + \Delta \dot{m}_a \quad .
\end{aligned} \tag{4.32}$$

The compensation scheme comprises two steps.

a.) At **medium** and **high** engine power outputs, the additive error can be neglected.

$$\frac{\dot{m}_a}{\dot{m}_{a,0}} = \frac{\lambda}{\lambda_0} + \underbrace{\frac{\Delta \dot{m}_a}{\dot{m}_{a,0}}}_{\approx 0} \approx \frac{\lambda}{\lambda_0} \tag{4.33}$$

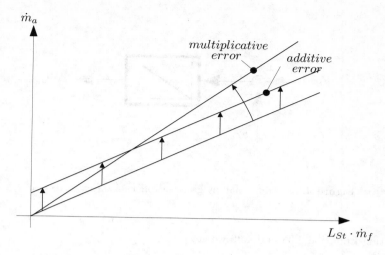

Figure 4.21 Simplified error model for the lambda characteristic

The remaining multiplicative lambda error can then be compensated by the regular lambda control loop which generates a control output factor F_λ inversely proportional to $\frac{\lambda}{\lambda_0}$. It is averaged to suppress the limit cycle.

$$\overline{F}_\lambda = \frac{\lambda_0}{\lambda} \tag{4.34}$$

In the absence of errors, $F_{\lambda 0}$ would have been equal to 1 (stochiometric). The product

$$\overline{F}_\lambda \cdot \frac{\dot{m}_a}{\dot{m}_{a,0}} \approx 1 \tag{4.35}$$

recovers the uncorrupted air-fuel ratio. The control output is low-pass filtered into $\overline{F}_\lambda$ and is stored in a non-volatile memory at medium and high engine power outputs.

$$F_{Hi} = \overline{F}_\lambda \tag{4.36}$$

Taking advantage of the compensation factor F_{Hi}, the corrected mass air flow $\dot{m}_{a,0}$ can be calculated from the measured one $\dot{m}_a$.

$$F_{Hi} \cdot \dot{m}_a \approx \dot{m}_{a,0} \tag{4.37}$$

By application of F_{Hi}, the gradient of the lambda characteristic is turned back to λ_0.

b.) This is now employed at **low** engine power outputs. The additive offset error $\Delta \dot{m}_a$ can no longer be neglected.

$$\dot{m}_a = \frac{\lambda}{\lambda_0} \dot{m}_{a,0} + \Delta \dot{m}_a \tag{4.38}$$

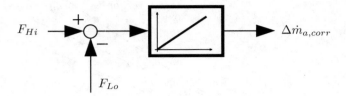

Figure 4.22 Additional integral controller for offset correction

Inserting Equation 4.34 and 4.36 we get

$$\dot{m}_{a,0} = F_{Hi} \cdot \dot{m}_a - F_{Hi} \cdot \Delta\dot{m}_a \quad . \tag{4.39}$$

The lambda control loop generates a multiplicative correction factor F_λ also at low engine power output. It is averaged to suppress the limit cycle.

$$F_{Lo} = \overline{F}_\lambda \tag{4.40}$$

The correct mass air flow can be calculated as

$$\dot{m}_{a,0} = F_{Lo} \cdot \dot{m}_a \quad . \tag{4.41}$$

Merging Equation 4.39 and 4.41 yields

$$\frac{\Delta\dot{m}_a}{\dot{m}_a} = \frac{F_{Lo} - F_{Hi}}{F_{Hi}} \quad . \tag{4.42}$$

If the offset error $\Delta\dot{m}_a$ could be eliminated, then the two correction factors

$$F_{Lo} = F_{Hi} \quad , \quad \text{for} \quad \Delta\dot{m}_a = 0 \tag{4.43}$$

would be identical.

   This is achieved by an additional integral control loop, which gets the difference $F_{Hi} - F_{Lo}$ at it's input, and which generates the unknown offset $\Delta\dot{m}_{a,corr}$ at it's output.

   The lambda characteristic can now be corrected by subtracting $\Delta\dot{m}_{a,corr}$. The corrected lambda characteristic is

$$F_{Hi} \cdot \dot{m}_a = \underbrace{F_{Hi} \cdot \frac{\lambda}{\lambda_0}}_{\approx 1} \cdot \dot{m}_{a,0} + F_{Hi} \underbrace{\left(\Delta\dot{m}_a - \Delta\dot{m}_{a,corr} \right)}_{\approx 0} \approx \dot{m}_{a,0} \quad . \tag{4.44}$$

Since the original lambda control loop is unloaded from the correction task, there are no more mismatches during engine transients.

   Both F_{Hi} and $\Delta\dot{m}_{a,corr}$ are stored in a non-volatile memory, so that they are correcting the lambda characteristic even at open-loop operation.

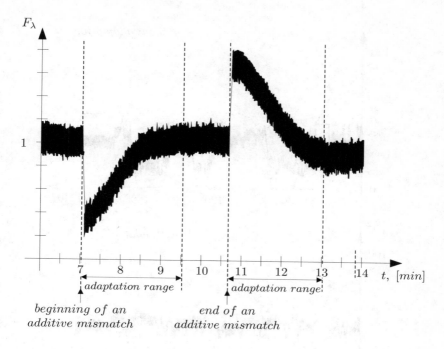

Figure 4.23 Control output factor F_λ with a bypass leakage in the intake system

Results of the Globally Valid Compensation

In Figure 4.23, a bypass leakage of $0.1\,mm^2$ was introduced into the intake system. At stationary engine operation, the control output factor F_λ first corrects the resulting air-fuel ratio. This correction is then slowly shifted from the closed loop control to the adaptive compensation scheme. The control output factor F_λ slowly returns to a limit cycle around an average value of 1.

The real gain of global compensation comes when driving through engine transients such as shown in Figure 4.24. The vehicle is following the speed profile of an emission test. The control output factor F_λ is limited in its adaptation speed by the minimum value of the integration time constant. When the major portion of all lambda mismatches is globally compensated, the closed loop control is mostly relieved from the correction task. The limited transient speed of F_λ is no longer leading to noxious exhaust emission spikes.

4.2   Idle Speed Control

As a rule of thumb, fuel consumption of internal combustion engines increases proportional to engine speed at idling. Therefore, the idle speed should be made as low as possible. The reduced engine idle speed can be held up with less engine power output. Contrary to that, load torque variations such as the switch-on of

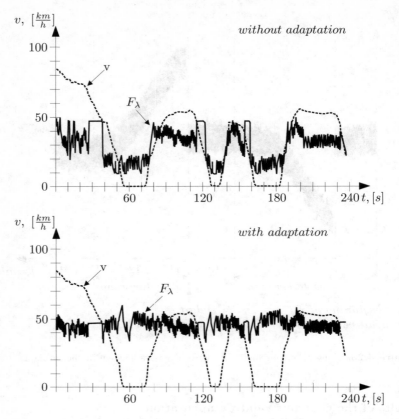

Figure 4.24 Results of globally valid lambda compensation when driving through test cycle

the air condition compressor motor stay constant. Engine torque output steps compensating such loads thus increase relative to the basic torque required to keep the engine running. This is a challenge for the idle speed control. The actuation variable at SI engines is the mass air flow into the engine, at Diesel engines the injected fuel amount.

A problem are gas pedal movements of the driver at idling. They modulate the actuation variable in competition to the control actuator, which also varies the same variable. When the driver e.g. slowly increases the mass air flow in SI engines, the controller will reduce its actuator signal in order to regulate the speed to the reference level. If in a next step the driver would release the gas pedal, the control actuation takes some time to adapt to this. With an improper design, the engine might stall in such situations.

The control scheme of SI engines presented in this section measures the engine speed and estimates the intake manifold pressure. The dynamic behaviour of the control loop is determined by the intake manifold (see Section 3.2.6), the energy conversion process and the torque balance at the crankshaft, which are modeled in the following section. At Diesel engines, the intake manifold model and the feedback of the intake manifold pressure are dropped.

4.2.1 Energy Conversion Model and Torque Balance

The energy conversion process is extremely complex and highly nonlinear. In a simplified approach, the stationary dependence of the combustion torque T_{comb} from intake manifold pressure and engine speed shall be represented by a nonlinear map $f_2(n, p_m)$, which can be measured at all engine operating points. The dynamic behaviour is separately considered by a combination of first order lag time $T_{l,e}$ and a dead time $T_{d,e}$. The lag time approximates the phase-shifted operation of the engine cylinders, as seen in lambda control (see Section 4.1.3).

$$T_{l,e} \approx \frac{2(CYL - 1)}{CYL} \cdot \frac{1}{n} \quad . \tag{4.45}$$

The dead time $T_{d,e}$ covers the delay between the average open position of the intake valves of a cylinder and the average position of the energy conversion process. It shall be approximated by

$$T_{d,e} \approx 3/(4n) \quad , \tag{4.46}$$

which is only half the value compared to that at lambda control. Both time constants vary inversely proportional to engine speed.

The torque balance at the crankshaft is

$$2\pi J \frac{dn}{dt} = T_{comb} - T_{load} \quad . \tag{4.47}$$

An engine with open clutch, i.e. without the driveline, has a moment of inertia in the range of

$$J = 0.15 \ldots 0.30 \, kg \, m^2 \quad .$$

By introducing normalised variables, we get

$$\underbrace{2\pi \cdot \frac{J \cdot n_0}{T_0}}_{T_J} \cdot \frac{d(n/n_0)}{dt} = \frac{T_{comb}}{T_0} - \frac{T_{load}}{T_0} \tag{4.48}$$

with a time constant

$$T_J = 2\pi \frac{J \cdot n_0}{T_0} \quad . \tag{4.49}$$

At maximum torque output and engine speed

$$\begin{aligned} J &= 0.3 \, kg \, m^2, \\ n_0 &= 6000 \, min^{-1}, \\ T_0 &= 300 \, Nm, \end{aligned}$$

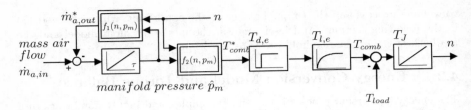

Figure 4.25 Plant model for idle speed control of SI engines

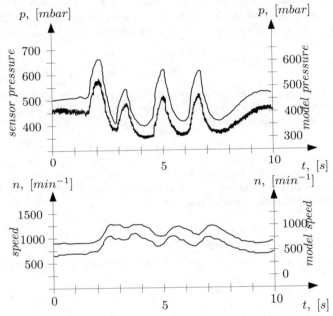

Figure 4.26 Comparison of measured and calculated manifold pressure

the time constant is $T_J = 0.63\,s$. When accelerating from low engine speed with maximum torque, the moment of inertia J is an order of magnitude smaller. Contrary, T_J is an order of magnitude larger at high engine speed and minimum torque output, e.g. when coasting. The load torque comprises friction, auxiliary drives and disturbances. The complete plant model for idle speed control is shown in Fig 4.25.

The mass air flow $\dot{m}_a$ into the engine is measured, whereas the intake manifold pressure $\hat{p}_m$ is calculated by integrating model Equation 3.49. A comparison of measured and calculated manifold pressure is shown in Figure 4.26.

Taking into account the shifted scale for the model variables, there is an excellent tracking of the model to the real engine.

4.2.2 State Space Control

In many vehicles, the idle speed is actually controlled with a PID controller. The differentiating D portion is sometimes shifting the ignition angle, due to the smaller delays between angle advance/retard and torque response. For SI engines, a state space controller shall be used, which feeds back the model pressure $\hat{p}_m$ and the measured engine speed n. Any unwanted driver actuation of the mass air flow generates a much faster response of the manifold pressure compared to that of the engine speed. The engine dead time $T_{d,e}$ cannot be compensated by the differentiating D portion of the PID control. For this reason, state space control is superior to PID control of the idle speed at SI engines.

In a first step, the two maps $f_1(n, p_m)$ and $f_2(n, p_m)$ are linearised at the idle speed operation point $\dot{m}_{a,0}, n_0, p_{m0}$. Introducing first order differentials

$$
FN_1 = \left.\frac{\partial f_1}{\partial n}\right|_{n=n_0}
$$

$$
FP_1 = \left.\frac{\partial f_1}{\partial p_m}\right|_{p_m=p_{m0}}
$$

$$
FN_2 = \left.\frac{\partial f_2}{\partial n}\right|_{n=n_0}
$$

$$
FP_2 = \left.\frac{\partial f_2}{\partial p_m}\right|_{p_m=p_{m0}} \tag{4.50}
$$

and difference variables, we get

$$
\frac{\Delta \dot{m}_{a,out}^*}{\dot{m}_{a,0}} = FN_1 \frac{n_0}{\dot{m}_{a,0}} \frac{\Delta n}{n_0} + FP_1 \frac{p_{m,0}}{\dot{m}_{a,0}} \frac{\Delta p_m}{p_{m,0}} \quad , \tag{4.51}
$$

$$
\frac{\Delta T_{comb}^*}{T_0} = FN_2 \frac{n_0}{T_0} \frac{\Delta n}{n_0} + FP_2 \frac{p_{m,0}}{T_0} \frac{\Delta p_m}{p_{m,0}} \quad . \tag{4.52}
$$

The differential equation from the manifold model (Eq. 3.53) is Laplace-transformed, and becomes together with Eq. 4.51

$$
s \cdot \tau_n \cdot \frac{\Delta P_m}{p_{m,0}} = -FN_1 \frac{n_0}{\dot{m}_{a,0}} \frac{\Delta N}{n_0} - FP_1 \frac{p_{m,0}}{\dot{m}_{a,0}} \frac{\Delta P_m}{p_{m,0}} + \frac{\Delta \dot{M}_{a,in}}{\dot{m}_{a,0}} \quad . \tag{4.53}
$$

The incoming air flow $\Delta \dot{M}_{a,in}$ serves as a control input ΔU. Eq. 4.52 is also Laplace-transformed and extended by the engine lag and delay times.

$$
\frac{\Delta T_{comb}}{T_0} = FN_2 \frac{n_0}{T_0} \frac{e^{-s\,T_{d,e}}}{1+sT_{l,e}} \frac{\Delta N}{n_0} + FP_2 \frac{p_{m,0}}{T_0} \frac{e^{-s\,T_{d,e}}}{1+sT_{l,e}} \frac{\Delta P_m}{p_{m,0}} \quad . \tag{4.54}
$$

This is now inserted into the torque balance (Eq. 4.48). Neglecting the disturbance load torque T_{load} for control purposes, we get

$$
s\,T_J \cdot \frac{\Delta N}{n_0} = \frac{e^{-s\,T_{d,e}}}{1+sT_{l,e}} \left(FN_2 \frac{n_0}{T_0} \frac{\Delta N}{n_0} + FP_2 \frac{p_{m,0}}{T_0} \frac{\Delta P_m}{p_{m,0}} \right) \quad . \tag{4.55}
$$

The stability analysis of the plant model and the controller design shall now be done by neglecting time constants $T_{d,e}$ and $T_{l,e}$. The subsequent approach simplifies to a second order linear state space model

$$
s \cdot \begin{bmatrix} \frac{\Delta P_m}{p_{m,0}} \\ \frac{\Delta N}{n_0} \end{bmatrix} = \underbrace{\begin{bmatrix} -\frac{FP_1}{\tau_n}\frac{p_{m,0}}{\dot{m}_{a,0}} & -\frac{FN_1}{\tau_n}\frac{n_0}{\dot{m}_{a,0}} \\ \frac{FP_2}{T_J}\frac{p_{m,0}}{T_0} & \frac{FN_2}{T_J}\frac{n_0}{T_0} \end{bmatrix}}_{\mathbf{A}} \cdot \begin{bmatrix} \frac{\Delta P_m}{p_{m,0}} \\ \frac{\Delta N}{n_0} \end{bmatrix} + \underbrace{\begin{bmatrix} \frac{1}{\tau_n} \\ 0 \end{bmatrix}}_{\mathbf{b}} \cdot \frac{\Delta U}{\dot{m}_{a,0}} \quad .
$$

$$(4.56)$$

The poles of the open-loop system are obtained from the characteristic equation

$$det(s\underline{\mathbf{I}} - \underline{\mathbf{A}}) = 0 \qquad (4.57)$$

or

$$
s^2 + \left(\frac{FP_1}{\tau_n}\frac{p_{m,0}}{\dot{m}_{a,0}} - \frac{FN_2}{T_J}\frac{n_0}{T_0} \right) s + \left(\frac{FN_1 \cdot FP_2 - FP_1 \cdot FN_2}{\tau_n \cdot T_J} \right) \frac{p_{m,0}}{\dot{m}_{a,0}} \cdot \frac{n_0}{T_0} = 0 \quad .
$$

$$(4.58)$$

Inserting Eq. 4.49 for T_J and Eq. 3.52 for τ_n, this becomes

$$
s^2 + \left(\frac{FP_1}{\tau} - \frac{FN_2}{2\pi J} \right) s + \left(\frac{FN_1 \cdot FP_2 - FP_1 \cdot FN_2}{\tau \cdot 2\pi J} \right) = 0 \quad . \qquad (4.59)
$$

The characteristic equation is independent of a specific normalisation of the variables. The two poles are

$$
s_{1,2} = -\frac{1}{2}\left(\frac{FP_1}{\tau} - \frac{FN_2}{2\pi J} \right) \pm
$$

$$
\pm \sqrt{\frac{1}{4}\left(\frac{FP_1}{\tau} - \frac{FN_2}{2\pi J} \right)^2 - \left(\frac{FN_1 \cdot FP_2 - FP_1 \cdot FN_2}{\tau \cdot 2\pi J} \right)} \quad . (4.60)
$$

The poles are real for

$$
\frac{FP_1}{\tau} - \frac{FN_2}{2\pi J} \geq 2\sqrt{\frac{FN_1 \cdot FP_2 - FP_1 \cdot FN_2}{\tau \cdot 2\pi J}} \quad . \qquad (4.61)
$$

For

$$
\frac{FN_2}{2\pi J} > \frac{FP_1}{\tau} \quad , \qquad (4.62)
$$

the open-loop idle speed plant becomes unstable.

The controller shall be implemented by a proportional feedback of the manifold pressure and the engine speed.

$$
\frac{\Delta U}{\dot{m}_{a,0}} = \begin{bmatrix} -K_P, & -K_N \end{bmatrix} \cdot \begin{bmatrix} \frac{\Delta P_m}{p_{m,0}} \\ \frac{\Delta N}{n_0} \end{bmatrix} \qquad (4.63)
$$

The second order model of the closed-loop system is then

$$s \cdot \begin{bmatrix} \frac{\Delta P_m}{p_{m,0}} \\ \frac{\Delta N}{n_0} \end{bmatrix} = \underbrace{\begin{bmatrix} -\left(\frac{FP_1}{\tau_n}\frac{p_{m,0}}{\dot{m}_{a,0}} + \frac{K_P}{\tau_n}\right) & -\left(\frac{FN_1}{\tau_n}\frac{n_0}{\dot{m}_{a,0}} + \frac{K_N}{\tau_n}\right) \\ \frac{FP_2}{T_J}\frac{p_{m,0}}{T_0} & \frac{FN_2}{T_J}\frac{n_0}{T_0} \end{bmatrix}}_{\mathbf{A}^*} \cdot \begin{bmatrix} \frac{\Delta P}{p_{m,0}} \\ \frac{\Delta N}{n_0} \end{bmatrix} \quad .$$

(4.64)

The control dynamics shall be determined by pole placement. The characteristic equation of the closed-loop system is

$$det(s\mathbf{I} - \mathbf{A}^*) = 0 \quad ,$$

$$s^2 + \left(\frac{FP_1}{\tau_n}\frac{p_{m,0}}{\dot{m}_{a,0}} + \frac{K_p}{\tau_n} - \frac{FN_2}{T_J}\frac{n_0}{T_0}\right)s -$$
$$- \left[\left(\frac{FP_1}{\tau_n}\frac{p_{m,0}}{\dot{m}_{a,0}} + \frac{K_p}{\tau_n}\right)\frac{FN_2}{T_J}\frac{n_0}{T_0} - \left(\frac{FN_1}{\tau_n}\frac{n_0}{\dot{m}_{a,0}} + \frac{K_N}{\tau_n}\right)\frac{FP_2}{T_J}\frac{p_{m,0}}{T_0}\right] = 0 \quad .$$

(4.65)

The characteristic equation of a second order system with desired poles s_1 and s_2 is

$$s^2 - (s_1 + s_2) \cdot s - s_1 \cdot s_2 = 0 \quad .$$ (4.66)

A comparison yields the control parameters

$$K_P = -\tau_n(s_1 + s_2) - FP_1 \cdot \frac{p_{m,0}}{\dot{m}_{a,0}} + \frac{\tau_n}{T_J} \cdot FN_2 \cdot \frac{n_0}{T_0}$$ (4.67)

and

$$K_N = \frac{T_J \cdot \tau_n}{FP_2 \cdot \frac{p_{m,0}}{T_0}}(s_1 \cdot s_2) - FN_1 \cdot \frac{n_0}{\dot{m}_{a,0}} -$$
$$- \frac{FN_2 \cdot \frac{n_0}{T_0}}{FP_2 \cdot \frac{p_{m,0}}{T_0}} \cdot \tau_n \cdot (s_1 + s_2) + \frac{\tau_n}{T_J} \cdot \frac{FN_2^2 \cdot \frac{n_0^2}{T_0^2}}{FP_2 \cdot \frac{p_{m,0}}{T_0}} \quad .$$ (4.68)

In the practical calibration process of the idle speed control to an actual engine, these parameters can be tuned to make up for the neglected lag time $T_{l,e}$ and dead time $T_{d,e}$. The complete block diagram of idle speed control is shown in Figure 4.27.

The multiplication factor K_R for the reference speed n_{ref} is selected, so that the closed-loop system has no offset, i.e. $\Delta n = 0$ and $\Delta p_m = 0$. This is applying for the absence of disturbance load torques. A proportional control does however show still a stationary control offset in the case of noise inputs or parameter variations. This is why an additional integral controller is introduced, which reduces stationary offset to zero. The problem with integral control is, that a disturbance input from the driver could result in control actions integrating to its range boundaries. If the driver relinquishes his input, the engine might stall.

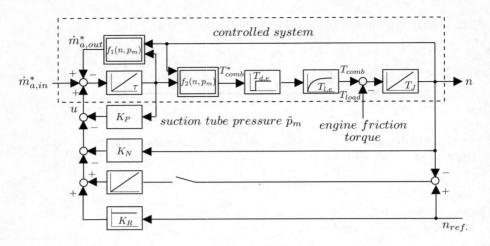

Figure 4.27 Block diagram of idle speed control

There are however a number of ways to overcome such a so-called wind-up effect. A heuristic approach could be used to interrupt integration, when a disturbance input from the driver is detected.

If SI engines would be throttled by a modulation of their intake valves instead of the throttle body butterfly, the intake manifold model could be deleted, simplifying the controller design. The same applies for Diesel engines.

4.2.3   Measurement Results

The idle speed controller was applied to a two-liter four cylinder SI-engine with power steering, automatic transmission and air condition. The idle speed n_0 in the absence of load disturbance torques was $720\,min^{-1}$. Figure 4.28 shows an aperiodic decay of the speed response after an acceleration impulse from the driver. No additional integral control was applied in this test.

There is no undershoot when the speed levels off into its stationary value. In Figure 4.29 various disturbance loads are applied to the state space control without integral control. The stationary speed level is going down with increasing load torque. The stationary offset can be eliminated by means of additional integral control and feed-forward control of disturbance torques. This is demonstrated in Figure 4.30.

A very critical case has been tried out in Figure 4.31. When the engine speed sharply drops after a disturbance input from the driver, the position stick of the automatic transmission is shifted to Drive. The resultant speed response shows only a small undershoot even in this case.

The idle speed control of Diesel engines can be done in a similar way. There are two major differences of the plant in comparison to SI-engines:

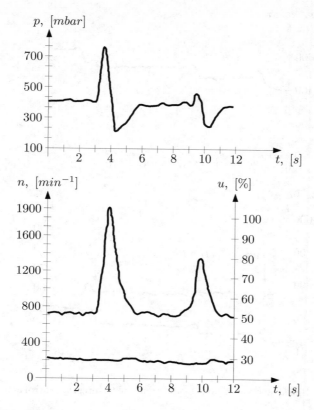

Figure 4.28 Speed response after driver impulse input, without integral control

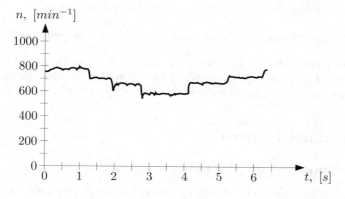

Figure 4.29 Speed levels at various load torques, without integral control

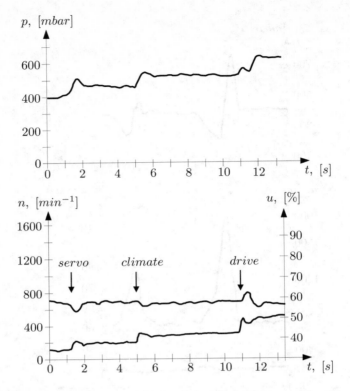

Figure 4.30 Speed levels at various load torques, with integral control and feed-forward control

1. The intake manifold is unthrottled, so that the engine is getting the maximum possible mass air flow $\dot{m}_a$ in each operation point.

2. With direct fuel injection, the delay time $T_{l,e}$ may be significantly reduced.

These two points simplify the control design. A complication would be turbo charging, which introduces a significant time constant for the response of the mass air flow $\dot{m}_a$ to gas pedal transients.

4.3   Knock Control

4.3.1   Knocking at SI Engines

During a combustion cycle, the compressed however not yet inflamed portion of the air-fuel mixture may self-inflame, before it is reached by the flame front coming from the spark plug. The condition for this to happen is, that the self-inflammation time is shorter than the propagation time of the flame front. The

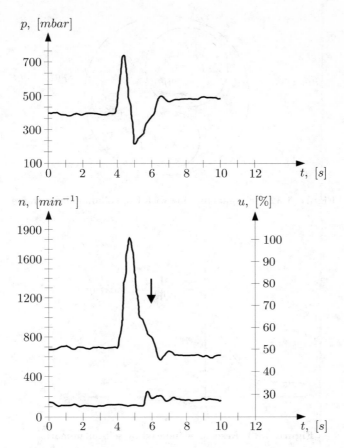

Figure 4.31 Disturbance input from driver and simultaneous gear shift to Drive position

self-inflammation delay τ_d is approximated by Woschni [80] as

$$\tau_d = 0.44\,ms \cdot \exp(4650\,°K/\vartheta) \cdot (p/p_0)^{-1.19}   . \tag{4.69}$$

Self-inflammation preferably happens at locations within the combustion chamber, which are distant from the spark plug, and which show high temperature levels. In the case of mixture self-inflammation in a remote spot, two flame fronts with opposite directions are generated (Figure 4.32). When colliding, the resulting pressure peak excites acoustical eigen-oscillations, which depend of the geometry of the combustion chamber. These resonances are superimposed to the normal pressure curve (Figure 4.33). Due to very high pressure gradients knock oscillations can lead to significant engine damages. In extreme cases, the entire engine may be destroyed in a fraction of a minute.

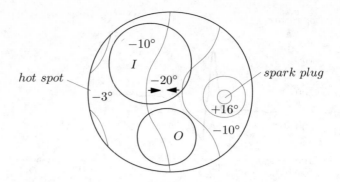

Figure 4.32 Self-inflammation with two colliding flame fronts

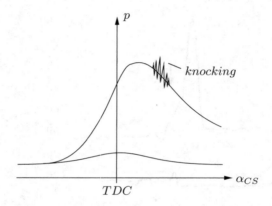

Figure 4.33 Resonance induced by self-inflammation

The sensitivity of SI engines to fuel self-inflammation depends upon several parameters.

- Increased ambient temperature, which leads to higher peak temperatures within the combustion process.

- Increased load pressure, which also increases peak temperatures. This can be caused by higher bariometric pressures, by higher engine load conditions or by turbo charging.

- Bad fuel quality, e.g. low octane number.

The knocking sensitivity of engines can be reduced by a proper design.

- Compact combustion chamber geometry in order to avoid hot spots.

- Central position of the spark plug in order to minimize flame propagation.

- Increased turbulence for faster flame propagation.

• Limitation or regulation of boost pressure at turbo-charged engines.

By retarding the ignition angle, the entire energy conversion process is shifted backwards. Since the combustion pressure is then superimposed to a lower pressure due to adiabatic compression, resulting peak pressures are reduced.

After a short response time gas oscillations lead to resonance waves in the combustion chamber. When the piston is at top dead center (TDC), the radial resonaces with frequency modes

$$f_{mn} = c_0 \sqrt{\vartheta/273\,°K} \cdot \beta_{mn}/d \qquad (4.70)$$

dominate. The parameters are

$$c_0 \quad \text{sound propagation velocity at } 273\,°K$$
$$\vartheta \quad \text{Temperature within combustion chamber}$$
$$d \quad \text{cylinder diameter}$$
$$\beta_{mn} \quad \text{Bessel function, e.g.}$$
$$\beta_{10} = 0.5861$$
$$\beta_{20} = 0.9722$$
$$\beta_{30} = 1.2197$$

The variable geometry of the combustion chamber due to the piston movement is neglected.

Example: Knock resonance frequencies
From the parameters

$$c_0 = 330\,m/s \quad ,$$
$$\vartheta = 2500\,°K \quad ,$$
$$d = 0.089\,m \quad ,$$

we can calculate

$$f_{10} = 6.6\,kHz \quad ,$$
$$f_{20} = 10.9\,kHz \quad ,$$
$$f_{30} = 13.7\,kHz \quad .$$

At the real engine, a resonance frequency of $f_{10} = 6.8\,kHz$ was measured.

4.3.2 Knock Sensors

There are several approaches to measure knock oscillations.

a.) Combustion pressure sensor
The direct approach is to measure the combustion pressure. The knock oscillations superimposed to the pressure curve may be filtered out e.g. by a band pass.

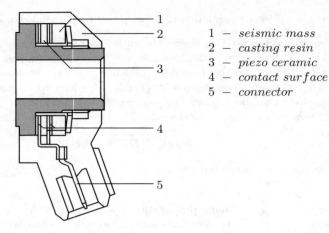

1 — *seismic mass*
2 — *casting resin*
3 — *piezo ceramic*
4 — *contact surface*
5 — *connector*

Figure 4.34 Mechanical knock sensor

Advantage :   • Integral acquisition of all oscillations
                    in the combustion chamber

Disadvantages :   • High costs to harden pressure sensors for the
                    operation in the combustion chamber.
                  • Engine head design may leave no room for
                    a pressure sensor.

b.) Mechanical Vibration Sensors at engine block
The engine block is transmitting knock oscillations from the different cylinders,
which can be sensed by mechanical resonators. An example is shown in Figure 4.34. With a sensor eigen frequency around $25\,kHz$, several knock resonances
can be measured. Four cylinder engines need one or two sensors, six and more
cylinder engines at least two sensors.

Advantage :   • Low Costs
                  • Straight forward mounting

Disadvantages :   • Strong disturbance noise from closing valves or
                    piston tilting

c.) Ion Current Measurement
As sensors, the standard spark plugs may be used. During the combustion process of hydro-carbons, electrically charged ions and electrons are generated. The
intensity of the chemical reaction and thus the intensity of the ionisation depend
on the flame temperature, on the air fuel ratio and on the fuel quality. The un-
moved mass of a positive ion H_3O^+ is approximately 30,000 time larger than that
of a negative electron. The voltage polarity at the spark plug gap is therefore
selected such that the small area electrode is positive and the large area electrode is negative. The light electrons are accelerated much more than the heavy
ions, crossing through a large distance per time. Therefore, the same number of

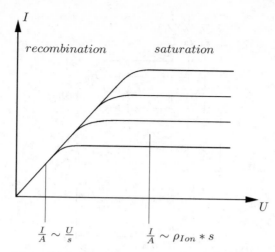

Figure 4.35 Ion current versus supply voltage

negative electrons can reach the small area electrode as positive ions can reach the large area electrode of the spark plug.

When a low electrical field U/s is applied to the spark plug gap (width s), the ion current density i/A is proportional to the electrical field (A electrode area). The ohm law is applying in this type of operation. Ions and electrons generated in the combustion process and not attracted to one of the spark plug gaps are recombining. Ion currents must therefore be measured under high electrical fields at the spark plug gap, so that all ions and electrons arrive at their electrode. This type of operation is called saturation mode. The ion current density then depends only on the ion density ρ_{Ion} within the combustion process and the gap distances (Figure 4.35). The resistance of the measurement loop must be kept below approximately $0.5\,M\Omega$.

The ion current measurement circuit must be protected from high ignition voltages. The two requirements for

- a low resistance at sensing

- a high resistance for protection

can be considered by high voltage diodes (Figure 4.36).

The capacitor C at the primary side of the ignition coil is loaded to e.g. $300 - 400\,V$ during dwell time. After the ignition, the secondary ignition voltage (from Pin 4) decays. After top dead center, the voltage stored in C drives the ionisation measurement circuit, in which the current through R_m indicates the ion density and thus the combustion intensity.

A problem with ion current measurement is that it represents only the combustion intensity in a very small volume around the spark plug, not in the entire combustion chamber. Knock detection therefore heavily depends on the position of the spark plug. A central position is advantageous for knock detection, since

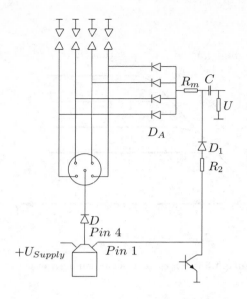

Figure 4.36 Ion current measurement via high voltage diodes

the first resonance wave has a pressure minimum and a velocity maximum there. The second resonance wave has a pressure maximum and a velocity minimum at the center of the combustion chamber. It is not suitable for knock detection by ion current, but rather for an indirect combustion pressure measurement.

Advantages :   • In-cylinder measurement
                    • No mechanical disturbances

Disadvantages :   • Dependence on spark plug position
                    • Measurement in a small portion of the
                      combustion chamber

d.) Light Intensity of Combustion Process
Knock oscillations modulate the intensity of the combustion process. With that comes a modulation of light intensity and colour in the combustion chamber. Light measurement is therefore another approach to measure knocking. A cone-formed portion of the combustion chamber is monitored.

A fiber-glass cable is fed through the central electrode of the spark plug, from where the light is forwarded to a remote photo transistor. A severe problem with light measurement in the combustion chamber is that the quartz glas window at the cable end is coated by soot in varying thickness. The measurement sensitivity is thus changing over several orders of magnitude.

Advantages :   • In-cylinder measurement
                    • No mechanical disturbances

Disadvantages :   • Extreme sensitivity variations

automatic gain
control

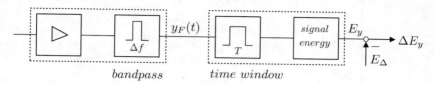

bandpass   time window

Figure 4.37 Signal processing of knock signal

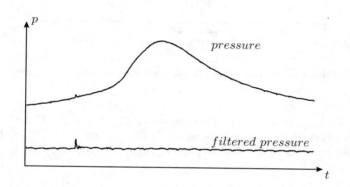

Figure 4.38 Bandpass output signal for non-knocking combustion

4.3.3 Signal Processing

If we disregard sensor-specific adaptation circuitry, a uniform methodology for signal processing can be applied (Figure 4.37).

At first the sensor signal amplitude is regulated to a constant level by automatic gain control. The amplifier output signal $y(t)$ is shown in Figure 4.38 for non-knocking and in Figure 4.39 for knocking combustion.

The next step is a bandpass filter $r_{\Delta f}(f)$ which suppresses all spectral information outside the selected knock resonance frequency window $[f_r - \Delta f/2, f_r + \Delta f/2]$. The adiabatic pressure curve is suppressed as well (Figs 4.38 and 4.39). The bandpass-filtered signal in the time domain is the convolution

$$y_F(t) = y(t) * r_{\Delta f}(t) \tag{4.71}$$

with the inverse Fourier transform of the rectangular frequency window

$$r_{\Delta f}(t) = \Delta f \frac{\sin(\pi \Delta f t)}{(\pi \Delta f t)} \exp\left(j 2\pi f_r t\right) \quad . \tag{4.72}$$

Knocking can only occur in a limited time interval during combustion. The signal $y_F(t)$ is therefore multiplied by a time window function. In the first place

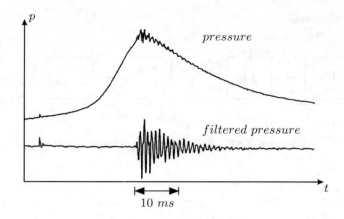

Figure 4.39 Bandpass output signal for knocking combustion

this is a rectangular window $r_T(t)$ with width T. If leakage shall be reduced, more sophisticated windows can be applied. Due to windowing, the subsequent integration stretches over a limited time interval. The resulting signal energy is

$$E_y(t) = \int_{t-T/2}^{t+T/2} y_F^2(t)dt = y_F^2(t) * r_T(t) = \Big(y(t) * r_{\Delta f}(t)\Big)^2 * r_T(t) \quad . \qquad (4.73)$$

At each discrete combustion cycle n, the signal energy $E_y(n)$ is derived. After substraction of an operation-point depending threshold E_0, we get the so-called knock signal

$$\Delta E_y(n) = \begin{cases} E_y(n) - E_0 &, E_y \geq E_0 \\ 0 &, \text{otherwise} \end{cases} \qquad (4.74)$$

$\Delta E_y(n)$ may be classified into a few steps in order to simplify knock control.

4.3.4   Knock Control

In a classical control circuit, a reference value is given, which must be approached as close as possible by the actual control variable. At knock control, no such reference is available. Because of the high damage potential of only a very few subsequent high-energy knockings in a cylinder, a reaction must be taken immediately after a single knock already.

The usual actuation is a retardation of the ignition angle, shifting the energy conversion process backwards and thus reducing peak pressures and temperatures. An alternative input may be to lower the boost pressure of a turbo charger. The knock control ignition angle is calculated at discrete combustion cycles n as

$$\alpha_k(n) = \alpha_k(n-1) + \Delta \alpha_k - \beta \cdot \Delta E_y(n) \quad , \qquad (4.75)$$

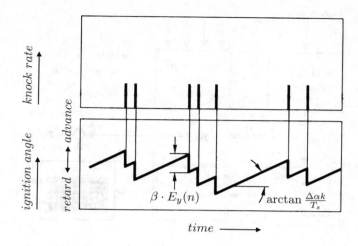

Figure 4.40 Control of knock occurance rate by ignition angle shifting

where $\Delta\alpha_k$ is a permanent ignition angle advance, and $\beta \cdot \Delta E_y(n)$ the ignition angle retard at knocking. A typical control cycle is shown in Figure 4.40. The knock control ignition angle $\alpha_k(n)$ is added to the ignition angle obtained from the ignition map (Section 3.3.2).

The two parameters $\Delta\alpha_k$ and β determine the average knock occurance rate. For safety reasons, the knock control advance is limited at

$$\alpha_k(n) \leq 0 \quad . \tag{4.76}$$

In case of errors, the ignition angle map determines the most advanced ignition angle. Knock control compensates the influence of parameter variations such as

- ambient temperatures

- bariometric pressures at different altitudes

- octane values at different fuel qualities

- engine manufacturing tolerances and ageing.

The compression ratio of knock controlled engines may be increased by at least 1. Fuel consumption is reduced by around 7 %. At turbo-charged engines, fuel savings are even higher.

4.3.5 Adaptive Knock Control

At dynamic engine transients, mismatches of the ignition angle occur resulting in increased knock occurance rates. The response time of knock control can be reduced by a feed-forward control angle $\alpha_l(n)$ stored in an adaptive ignition angle

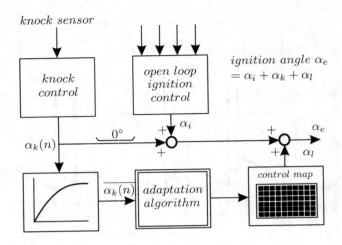

Figure 4.41 Knock control with feed-forward adaptive ignition angle map

map. Contrary to lambda control, a successful global error model has not yet been found. The values of the ignition angle map must therefore be adapted in every individual engine operating point for all cylinders (Figure 4.41).

The ignition angle at one cylinder is the sum

$$\alpha_e(n) = \alpha_i(n) + \alpha_k(n) + \alpha_l(n) \quad , \tag{4.77}$$

with

α_e : effective ignition angle
α_i : open loop ignition angle from fixed map
α_k : knock control ignition angle
α_l : learned ignition angle from adaptive map

The average knock control ignition angle $\bar{\alpha}_k(n)$ is the basis to teach the adaptive ignition angle map $\alpha_l(n)$ into the direction of retarding. A fixed advance angle α_a is superimposed to the teaching process providing a forgetting function of the thought angles. The learned ignition angle is

$$\alpha_l(n) = (1 - k_l)\alpha_l(n - 1) + k_l(\bar{\alpha}_k(n - 1) + \alpha_a(n - 1)) \quad . \tag{4.78}$$

The factor k_l determines how fast the learning process is. Z-Transformation of this equation yields

$$\alpha_l(z) = (1 - k_l)z^{-1} \cdot \alpha_l(z) + k_l z^{-1} (\bar{\alpha}_k(z) + \alpha_a(z)) \tag{4.79}$$

$$\alpha_l(z) = \frac{k_l z^{-1}}{1 - (1 - k_l)z^{-1}} (\bar{\alpha}_k(z) + \alpha_a(z)) \tag{4.80}$$

For an evaluation of the learning dynamics, the response of $\alpha_l(n)$ to an input step function

$$\bar{\alpha}_k(z) + \alpha_a(z) = \frac{\alpha_0}{1 - z^{-1}} \tag{4.81}$$

is considered.

$$\alpha_l(z) = \frac{k_l \cdot \alpha_0 \, z^{-1}}{(1 - z^{-1}) \, (1 - (1 - k_l)z^{-1})}$$

$$= \alpha_0 \left(\frac{1}{1 - z^{-1}} - \frac{1}{1 - (1 - k_l)z^{-1}} \right) \tag{4.82}$$

The discrete response function is then

$$\alpha_l(n) = \alpha_0 \left(1 - (1 - k_l)^n \right) \quad . \tag{4.83}$$

Reconstructing the continous-time function with $t = nT_s$, we get

$$\alpha_l(t) \approx \alpha_0 \left(1 - \exp\left(-k_l t/T_s \right) \right) \quad . \tag{4.84}$$

The learning time constant is the sample time T_s devided by the factor k_l.

$$T_l \approx T_s/k_l \tag{4.85}$$

Since the sampling is done at each combustion cycle, the sampling time T_s is inversely proportional to engine speed. A compensation may be achieved by letting the factor k_l become also inversely proportional to engine speed.

In Figure 4.42 the effect of the adaptive feed-forward control on knock control is shown. The knock control angle is oscillating around an average $\bar{\alpha}_k$. In order to prevent the engine from knocking to often, the angle $\bar{\alpha}_k$ is negative, corresponding to a retard from the fixed ignition angle map. Transferring the average knock control angle $\bar{\alpha}_k$ into the adaptive feed-forward control map α_l, the knock control angle can return to its maximum advance $\alpha_k = 0$. In Figure 4.42 this transfer has been simplified to happen in one step. In reality the transfer response happens with time constant T_l. After the adaptation, the knock control α_k will retard in the event of knocking, however advance only against the maximum limit $\alpha_k = 0$ with steps $\Delta \alpha_k$. Since the advance can not go beyond the limit, ignition angle oscillations are reduced, resulting in a reduced knock occurance rate in comparison to non-adaptive approaches.

When the engine enters a new operating area (Figure 4.43), the average knock control angle $\bar{\alpha}_k$ follows a transient into a stationary angle. The transient shall be terminated after n_{max} combustion cycles, and the adaptation could start from there on. Since the engine may however stay in the operating area for a shorter time than n_{max} cycles, the adaptation is allowed to start already after n_{min} combustion cycles. In this case, the average knock control angle $\bar{\alpha}_k$ is still somewhat deviating from the stationary value. Therefore, the adaptation factor k_l must be reduced.

$$k_l = \begin{cases} 0, & n_{Comb} < n_{min} \\ \frac{n_{Comb}}{n_{max}} k_{l0} \quad , & n_{min} \leq n_{Comb} \leq n_{max} \\ k_{l0} \quad , & n_{Comb} > n_{max} \end{cases} \tag{4.86}$$

Typical values are

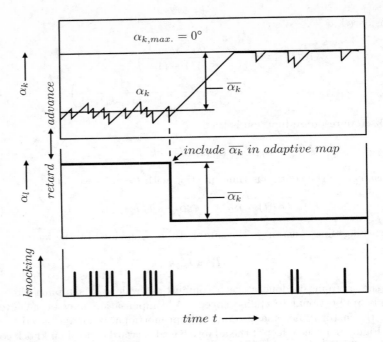

Figure 4.42 Reduction of knock occurance rate by transfer from α_k to learned angle α_l

$$n_{min} = 2\ldots10$$
$$n_{max} \leq 500 \quad.$$

In the medium range, the adaptation time constant T_l is increased to compensate for the uncertainty of the average knock control angle $\bar{\alpha}_k$ at $n_{Comb} \leq n_{max}$. The approach allows to adapt the adaptive ignition angle map also in engine operating areas, which are very shortly visited.

Figs 4.44 and 4.45 show the performance of the adaptive knock control. The resulting ignition angle retard $(-\alpha_l)$ is plotted over manifold pressure p_m and engine speed n. In Figure 4.44, the engine is operated with a 50 : 50 mixture of 91 octane and 98 octane fuel. The adaptive map must learn a retard in some of the operating points. After returning to an engine operation with 100 % of 98 octane fuel, the retard angles are forgotten by integration of the α_a-steps.

4.4 Combustion Torque Estimation

4.4.1 Crankshaft Moment of Inertia

For diagnostic purposes, the correct combustion must be monitored during engine operation. In case of misfires, unburnt gases would be generated. The engine would then no longer meet legal limits for noxious emissions. Therefore, the

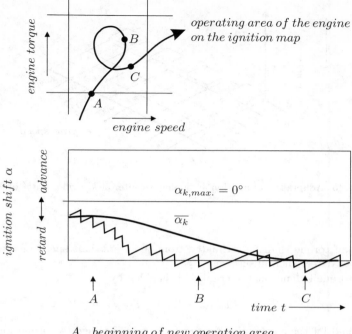

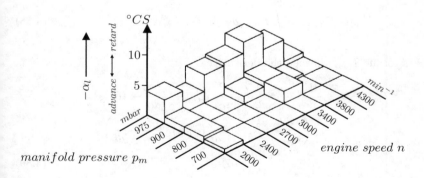

A   beginning of new operation area
B   minimum number n_{min} of ignitions reached
C   maximum number n_{max} of ignitions reached

Figure 4.43 Operation time in one operating area

Figure 4.44 Adaptation of ignition angle map α_l after $50\,km$ ride, $50:50$ mixture of 91 and 98 octane fuel.

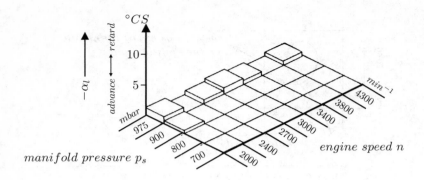

Figure 4.45 Adaptation of ignition angle map α_l after $50\,km$ ride, $100\,\%$ of 98 octane fuel.

combustion torque shall be estimated from the crankshaft speed of the engine, in order to detect such misfires.

The torque balance at the crankshaft is given by

$$T_{comb} - T_{mass} - T_{load} - T_{fric} = 0 \quad . \tag{4.87}$$

In Section 3.1.1 the combustion torque T_{comb} was obtained (see Equation 3.7) as

$$T_{comb} = \sum_{j=1}^{CYL} (p_j(\alpha_{CS}) - p_0)A_p \cdot \frac{ds_j(\alpha_{CS})}{d\alpha_{CS}} \quad .$$

The mass torque shall be derived from the kinetic energy E_{mass} of the engine masses in motion.

$$E_{mass} = \int_0^{2\pi} T_{mass} d\alpha_{CS} = \frac{1}{2} J \dot\alpha_{CS}^2 \quad . \tag{4.88}$$

The mass torque T_{mass} is then the derivative

$$
\begin{aligned}
T_{mass} &= \frac{dE_{mass}}{d\alpha_{CS}} = \frac{1}{2}\left(\frac{dJ}{d\alpha_{CS}}\dot\alpha_{CS}^2 + J\frac{d}{d\alpha_{CS}}\left(\dot\alpha_{CS}^2\right)\right) \\
&= \frac{1}{2}\left(\frac{dJ}{d\alpha_{CS}}\dot\alpha_{CS}^2 + J\frac{d}{dt}\left(\dot\alpha_{CS}^2\right)\cdot\frac{1}{d\alpha_{CS}/dt}\right) \\
&= J\ddot\alpha_{CS} + \frac{1}{2}\frac{dJ}{d\alpha_{CS}}\dot\alpha_{CS}^2
\end{aligned}
\tag{4.89}
$$

The first term represents the rotational masses, the second term the oscillating ones.

In [20] a two-mass approach is presented as a model of the connecting rod. The overall rod mass m_{rod} is separated into

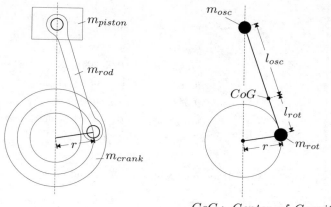

CoG : Center of Gravity

Figure 4.46 Two-mass model for oscillating and rotating masses.

- an oscillating portion

$$m_{rod,osc} = m_{rod} \cdot \frac{l_{osc}}{l} \quad , \tag{4.90}$$

- and a rotational portion

$$m_{rod,rot} = m_{rod} \cdot \frac{l_{rot}}{l} \quad . \tag{4.91}$$

The two lengths l_{osc} and l_{rot} with

$$l_{osc} + l_{rot} = l$$

are defined by the location of the center of gravity of the connecting rod. Thus the oscillating mass at each cylinder is

$$m_{osc} = m_{piston} + m_{rod} \cdot \frac{l_{osc}}{l} \quad , \tag{4.92}$$

and the rotational mass of the crankshaft portion at one cylinder

$$\frac{m_{rot}}{CYL} = \frac{m_{crank}}{CYL} + m_{rod} \cdot \frac{l_{rot}}{l} \quad . \tag{4.93}$$

The crankshaft mass is deducted from the moment of inertia

$$m_{crank} = \frac{J_{crank}}{r^2} \quad . \tag{4.94}$$

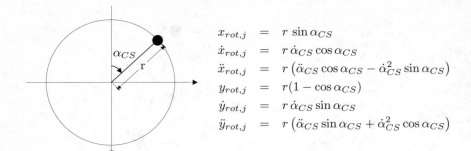

$$\begin{aligned}
x_{rot,j} &= r\sin\alpha_{CS}\\
\dot{x}_{rot,j} &= r\,\dot{\alpha}_{CS}\cos\alpha_{CS}\\
\ddot{x}_{rot,j} &= r\left(\ddot{\alpha}_{CS}\cos\alpha_{CS}-\dot{\alpha}_{CS}^2\sin\alpha_{CS}\right)\\
y_{rot,j} &= r(1-\cos\alpha_{CS})\\
\dot{y}_{rot,j} &= r\,\dot{\alpha}_{CS}\sin\alpha_{CS}\\
\ddot{y}_{rot,j} &= r\left(\ddot{\alpha}_{CS}\sin\alpha_{CS}+\dot{\alpha}_{CS}^2\cos\alpha_{CS}\right)
\end{aligned}$$

Figure 4.47 Rotational Motion at the Crankshaft

The kinetic energy of the engine masses in motion shall now be calculated.

$$E_{mass} = \frac{1}{2}\frac{m_{rot}}{CYL}\sum_{j=1}^{CYL}v_{rot,j}^2 + \frac{1}{2}m_{osc}\sum_{j=1}^{CYL}v_{osc,j}^2 \tag{4.95}$$

The speed of the oscillating mass $v_{osc,j}$ is the time derivative of the respective piston stroke s_j (see Equation 3.8).

$$v_{osc,j} = \dot{s}_j(\alpha_{CS}) = \dot{s}\left(\alpha_{CS}-(j-1)\frac{4\pi}{CYL}\right) \quad , \quad j=1,...,CYL \tag{4.96}$$

The rotational speed must be composed from the two components

$$\underline{v}_{rot,j} = [\dot{x}_{rot,j},\dot{y}_{rot,j}]^T \quad , \quad |\underline{v}_{rot,j}|^2 = \dot{x}_{rot,j}^2 + \dot{y}_{rot,j}^2 \quad . \tag{4.97}$$

The time derivative of the kinetic energy E_{mass} is

$$\begin{aligned}
\frac{dE_{mass}}{dt} &= \frac{dE_{mass}}{d\alpha_{CS}}\cdot\frac{d\alpha_{CS}}{dt} = T_{mass}\cdot\dot{\alpha}_{CS}\\
&= \frac{m_{rot}}{CYL}\sum_{j=1}^{CYL}\left(\dot{x}_{rot,j}\cdot\ddot{x}_{rot,j}+\dot{y}_{rot,j}\cdot\ddot{y}_{rot,j}\right) + m_{osc}\sum_{j=1}^{CYL}\dot{s}_j\ddot{s}_j\\
&= \frac{m_{rot}}{CYL}\sum_{j=1}^{CYL}\left(r^2\cos^2(\alpha_{CS})\dot{\alpha}_{CS}\,\ddot{\alpha}_{CS}+r^2\sin^2(\alpha_{CS})\dot{\alpha}_{CS}\,\ddot{\alpha}_{CS}\right)+\\
&\quad +m_{osc}\sum_{j=1}^{CYL}\frac{ds_j}{d\alpha_{CS}}\cdot\dot{\alpha}_{CS}\left(\frac{d^2s_j}{d\alpha_{CS}^2}\cdot\dot{\alpha}_{CS}^2+\frac{ds_j}{d\alpha_{CS}}\cdot\ddot{\alpha}_{CS}\right)
\end{aligned}$$

$$\frac{dE_{mass}}{dt} =$$

$$\underbrace{\left[\underbrace{\left(m_{rot} \cdot r^2 + m_{osc} \sum_{j=1}^{CYL} \left(\frac{ds_j}{d\alpha_{CS}}\right)^2\right)}_{J} \ddot{\alpha}_{CS} + \frac{1}{2} \underbrace{\left(2m_{osc} \sum_{j=1}^{CYL} \frac{ds_j}{d\alpha_{CS}} \cdot \frac{d^2 s_j}{d\alpha_{CS}^2}\right)}_{\frac{dJ}{d\alpha_{CS}}} \dot{\alpha}_{CS}^2 \right] \dot{\alpha}_{CS}}_{T_{mass}}$$

$$(4.99)$$

In this, the equations in Figure 4.47 and Eq. 3.5 in Section 3.1.1 are used. The moment of inertia is

$$J(\alpha_{CS}) = m_{rot} \cdot r^2 + m_{osc} \sum_{j=1}^{CYL} \left(\frac{ds_j}{d\alpha_{CS}}\right)^2 \quad . \tag{4.100}$$

4.4.2 Crankshaft Torque Balance

The friction torque T_{fric} is given by the Coulomb law as

$$\begin{aligned}
T_{fric} &= \sum_{j=1}^{CYL} \underbrace{F_{fric,j}}_{c_f \cdot \dot{s}_j} \cdot \frac{ds_j}{d\alpha_{CS}} \\
&= \sum_{j=1}^{CYL} c_f \frac{ds_j}{d\alpha_{CS}} \cdot \frac{d\alpha_{CS}}{dt} \cdot \frac{ds_j}{d\alpha_{CS}} \\
&= c_f \sum_{j=1}^{CYL} \left(\frac{ds_j}{d\alpha_{CS}}\right)^2 \cdot \dot{\alpha}_{CS}
\end{aligned} \tag{4.101}$$

The torque balance (see Eq. 4.87) is then

$$\sum_{j=1}^{CYL} (p_j(\alpha_{CS}) - p_0) A_p \frac{ds_j(\alpha_{CS})}{d\alpha_{CS}} - \left[m_{rot} r^2 + m_{osc} \sum_{j=1}^{CYL} \left(\frac{ds_j(\alpha_{CS})}{d\alpha_{CS}}\right)^2\right] \ddot{\alpha}_{CS} -$$

$$-\frac{1}{2}\left[2m_{osc} \sum_{j=1}^{CYL} \frac{ds_j(\alpha_{CS})}{d\alpha_{CS}} \cdot \frac{d^2 s_j(\alpha_{CS})}{d\alpha_{CS}^2}\right] \dot{\alpha}_{CS}^2 -$$

$$(4.103)$$

$$-c_f \sum_{j=1}^{CYL} \left(\frac{ds_j(\alpha_{CS})}{d\alpha_{CS}}\right)^2 \dot{\alpha}_{CS} - T_{load}(\alpha_{CS}) = 0$$

4.4.3 Transformation into Linear System Representation

For further calculations, the torque balance is regrouped into an angle-dependent differential equation with time-derivatives.

$$J(\alpha_{CS})\ddot{\alpha}_{CS} = T_{comb}(\alpha_{CS}) - f(\alpha_{CS}) \cdot \dot{\alpha}_{CS}^2 - T_{load}^*(\alpha_{CS}) \tag{4.104}$$

The angle-dependent function is

$$f(\alpha_{CS}) = \sum_{j=1}^{CYL} \left(m_{osc} \frac{ds_j(\alpha_{CS})}{d\alpha_{CS}} \cdot \frac{d^2 s_j(\alpha_{CS})}{d\alpha_{CS}^2} \right) \quad . \tag{4.105}$$

The extended load torque

$$T_{load}^*(\alpha_{CS}) = T_{load}(\alpha_{CS}) + \underbrace{c_f \sum_{j=1}^{CYL} \left(\frac{ds_j(\alpha_{CS})}{d\alpha_{CS}} \right)^2 \dot{\alpha}_{CS}}_{T_{fric}}$$

is an approximation and shall comprise also the friction torque T_{fric}. The combustion torque is

$$T_{comb}(\alpha_{CS}) = \sum_{j=1}^{CYL} (p_j(\alpha_{CS}) - p_0) A_p \cdot \frac{ds_j(\alpha_{CS})}{d\alpha_{CS}} \quad .$$

The second derivative of the crankshaft angle may be reformulated by substituting

$$\ddot{\alpha}_{CS} = \frac{d^2 \alpha_{CS}}{dt^2} = \frac{d}{dt}(\dot{\alpha}_{CS}) = \frac{d\dot{\alpha}_{CS}}{d\alpha_{CS}} \cdot \frac{d\alpha_{CS}}{dt} = \frac{d\dot{\alpha}_{CS}}{d\alpha_{CS}} \cdot \dot{\alpha}_{CS}$$

into Equation 4.104.

$$\dot{\alpha}_{CS} \cdot d\dot{\alpha}_{CS} = \frac{1}{J(\alpha_{CS})} \Big(T_{comb}(\alpha_{CS}) - f(\alpha_{CS}) \cdot \dot{\alpha}_{CS}^2 - T_{load}^*(\alpha_{CS}) \Big) d\alpha_{CS} \tag{4.106}$$

Integration results into an equation which depends only on the square of the crankshaft angle speed $\dot{\alpha}_{CS}$ instead on both crankshaft angle and time.

$$\dot{\alpha}_{CS}^2(n+1) - \dot{\alpha}_{CS}^2(n) =$$

$$\frac{2}{J(\alpha_{CS})} \int_{\alpha_{CS}(n)}^{\alpha_{CS}(n+1)} \Big(T_{comb}(\alpha_{CS}) - f(\alpha_{CS}) \cdot \dot{\alpha}_{CS}^2 - T_{load}^*(\alpha_{CS}) \Big) d\alpha_{CS} \tag{4.107}$$

Over the discrete angular step $\Delta\alpha_{CS} = \alpha_{CS}(n+1) - \alpha_{CS}(n)$, the integration may be approximated as

$$\dot{\alpha}_{CS}^2(n+1) - \dot{\alpha}_{CS}^2(n) \approx \frac{2\Delta\alpha_{CS}}{J(n)} \Big(T_{comb}(n) - f(n)\dot{\alpha}_{CS}^2(n) - T_{load}^*(n) \Big) \quad . \tag{4.108}$$

With a 60 teeth crankshaft sensor wheel, the angular step $\Delta\alpha_{CS}$ is $6°$. Instead of multiples of the sample time $n \cdot T_s$, we are now calculating with multiples of the angular step $n \cdot \Delta\alpha_{CS}$. By regarding the square of the crankshaft rotational speed $\dot\alpha^2(n)$ as a state variable x_1, we can linearise the calculation. By this we obtain a linear discrete space model of the crankshaft motion.

$$x_1(n+1) = \left(1 - \frac{2\Delta\alpha_{CS}}{J(n)} \cdot f(n)\right) x_1(n) + \frac{2\Delta\alpha_{CS}}{J(n)} x_2(n) \qquad (4.109)$$

with the state variables

$$\begin{aligned}
x_1(n) &= \dot\alpha_{CS}^2(n) \quad, \\
x_2(n) &= T_{comb}(n) - T_{load}^*(n) \quad, \\
x_3(n) &= x_2(n+1) \quad.
\end{aligned} \qquad (4.110)$$

4.4.4 Kalman Filter Design

The combustion torque is the physical cause which generates the crankshaft motion. Kalman filters employ a Markovian system model, i.e. a first order time-discrete linear system which is excited by white noise. Oscillations of the combustion pressure torque and load torque decrease at higher engine order. This behaviour is not reflected by a white noise excitation. Therefore the torque state variable $x_2(n)$ is modelled to be the output of a second order low pass system $H(z)$ which is excited by white noise $U(z)$ [29].

$$X_2(z) = H(z) \cdot U(z) \qquad (4.111)$$

The filter output $x_2(n)$ is a so-called coloured noise, the power density spectrum of which decreases indeed over increasing engine order. $H(z)$ has a double pole on the real axis.

$$H(z) = \frac{(1 - exp(-\delta \cdot \Delta\alpha_{CS}))^2}{(z - exp(-\delta \cdot \Delta\alpha_{CS}))^2} \qquad (4.112)$$

In the discrete angle domain, the state variable $x_2(n)$ is modelled as

$$x_2(n+2) - 2x_2(n+1) \cdot exp(-\delta \cdot \Delta\alpha_{CS}) + x_2(n) \cdot exp(-2\delta \cdot \Delta\alpha_{CS})$$
$$= \big(1 - exp(-\delta \cdot \Delta\alpha_{CS})\big)^2 \cdot u(n) \quad. \qquad (4.113)$$

Introducing another state variable $x_3(n) = x_2(n+1)$, this can be expressed in first order state space form as a basis for Kalman filtering.

$$\underline{\mathbf{x}}(\mathbf{n}) = \left(\dot\alpha_{CS}^2(n) \quad T_{comb}(n) - T_{load}^*(n) \quad T_{comb}(n+1) - T_{load}^*(n+1) \right)^T \qquad (4.114)$$

$$\underline{\mathbf{y}}(n) = \dot\alpha_{CS}^2(n) \qquad (4.115)$$

$$\underline{\mathbf{A}}(\mathbf{n}) = \begin{pmatrix} 1 - \frac{2 \cdot f(n) \cdot \Delta\alpha_{CS}}{J(n)} & \frac{2 \cdot \Delta\alpha_{CS}}{J(n)} & 0 \\ 0 & 0 & 1 \\ 0 & -exp(-2\delta \cdot \Delta\alpha_{CS}) & 2 \cdot exp(-\delta \cdot \Delta\alpha_{CS}) \end{pmatrix} \qquad (4.116)$$

$$\underline{\mathbf{B}}(\mathbf{n}) = \left(0 \quad 0 \quad \big(1 - exp(-\delta \cdot \Delta\alpha_{CS})\big)^2 \right)^T \qquad (4.117)$$

$$\underline{\mathbf{C}}^{\mathbf{T}}(\mathbf{n}) = \left(1 \quad 0 \quad 0 \right) \qquad (4.118)$$

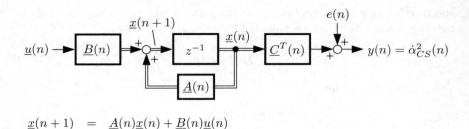

$$x(n+1) = \underline{A}(n)\underline{x}(n) + \underline{B}(n)\underline{u}(n)$$
$$y(n) = \underline{C}(n)\underline{x}(n) + \underline{e}(n)$$

Figure 4.48 Linear model for Kalman estimation of squared crankshaft speed.

Based upon this linearised model, a Kalman estimation can be performed [7]. Appropriate values for δ, $R_{uu}(n) = \sigma_u^2$ and $R_{ee}(n) = \sigma_e^2$ are chosen. By measuring the square of the rotational crankshaft speed $y(n) = \dot{\alpha}_{CS}^2(n)$, the torque difference $\hat{x}_2(n) = T_{comb}(n) - T_{load}^*(n)$ can be estimated.

$$\underline{\hat{x}}(n+1) = \underline{H}(n)\,\underline{\hat{x}}(n) + \underline{K}(n)\,\underline{y}(n) \tag{4.119}$$

$$\underline{\hat{x}}(n+1) = \underline{A}(n)\,\underline{\hat{x}}(n) + \underline{K}(n)\left(\underline{y}(n) - \underline{\hat{y}}(n)\right) \tag{4.120}$$

For various applications such as engine misfire detection, the absolute combustion torque must be obtained. At top and bottom dead centers (TDC and BDC) of a four-cylinder engine, the combustion torque is zero, because the piston stroke derivative $ds_j(\alpha_{CS})/d\alpha_{CS}$ is zero in those points. Thus, the load torque can be separately calculated in the TDC and BDC points.

$$\hat{x}_2(n_{TDC,BDC}) \approx -T_{load}^*(n) \tag{4.121}$$

When the estimated torque difference $\hat{x}_2(n)$ is corrected by an interpolated load torque $\hat{x}_2(n_{TDC,BDC})$ between TDC/BDC-Points, the combustion torque $T_{comb}(n)$ can be also calculated separately.

4.4.5   Results

In the case of a misfire, driveline oscillations are excited. The estimation process is required to distinguish between crankshaft speed and rotational driveline oscillations. Figure 4.49 shows the measured crankshaft speed signal of a test engine at 1500 *rpm*. At the end of the first cycle a misfire occurs. Figure 4.50 shows the combustion torque estimated by the Kalman filter, and the load torque interpolated between the TDCs. Figure 4.51 contains the corrected combustion torque. The torque fluctuations induced by the driveline are now effectively suppressed.

At higher engine speeds the oscillating mass torques increase. The signal-to-noise ratio decreases rapidly, and the performance of the Kalman filter decreases. The current estimation limit of this approach is between 3000 and 4000 *rpm*.

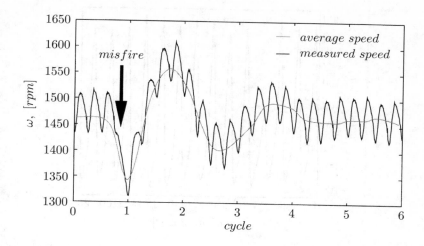

Figure 4.49 Measured angular speed signal with single misfire

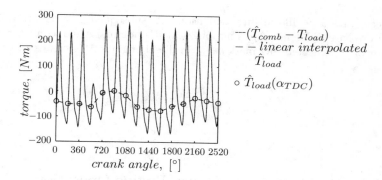

Figure 4.50 Estimated combustion torque by Kalman filter

4.5 Cylinder Balancing

In this section an approach to compensate errors of the injected fuel mass

$$\Delta m_{f,i} = m_{f,i} - m_{f,ref} \qquad (4.122)$$

at individual cylinders i is presented. The reference fuel mass $m_{f,ref}$ has been calculated by the engine management system and been transformed into an injection time t_{inj} (see section 3.2.4). The injection time t_{inj} is decomposed into several very short time portions. Errors due to varying injector rise and fall times thus introduce a relatively large fuel mass error. Another source of errors is the injection pressure difference Δp in equation 3.31. At the first time portion of the injection procedure, the pressure in the fuel rail is decreased at the location of the

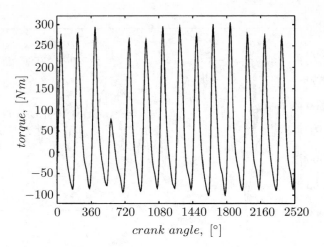

Figure 4.51 Estimated combustion torque T_{comb} by Kalman filter with load torque correction

injector, resulting in pressure oscillations. At subsequent injection time portions, the pressure difference Δp is no longer at it's nominal value, contributing to an error of the injected fuel mass $m_{f,i}$. In diesel engines, this error can be as large as

$$\frac{\Delta m_{f,i}}{m_{f,ref}} \leq 25\% \quad . \tag{4.123}$$

4.5.1   Residues at Stationary Engine Operation

The non-disturbed fuel mass m_f determines the effective work generated by the combustion in one cylinder (equ. 3.11).

$$\omega_{e,ref} \cdot \frac{V_d}{CYL} = \eta_e \cdot m_{f,ref} \cdot H_f \tag{4.124}$$

The individual fuel mass error $\Delta m_{f,i}$ shall now be indirectly determined by the error of the effective work $\Delta \omega_{e,i}$ contributed by cylinder i. Integration of the torque balance at the crankshaft (equ. 4.106) over one cylinder-related segment of crankshaft angle yields

$$J \int_{\alpha_i - \frac{2\pi}{CYL}}^{\alpha_i + \frac{2\pi}{CYL}} \dot{\alpha}_{CS} \frac{d\dot{\alpha}_{CS}}{d\alpha_{CS}} \, d\alpha_{CS} = \int_{\alpha_i - \frac{2\pi}{CYL}}^{\alpha_i + \frac{2\pi}{CYL}} (T_{comb} - T_{osc} - T^*_{load}) \, d\alpha_{CS} \quad . \tag{4.125}$$

The crankshaft angle α_i represents the center of the combustion process at cylinder i.

$$\frac{J}{2}\left(\dot{\alpha}_{CS}^2(\alpha_i + \frac{2\pi}{CYL}) - \dot{\alpha}_{CS}^2(\alpha_i - \frac{2\pi}{CYL})\right) = \frac{V_d}{CYL}(\omega_{e,i} - \omega_{osc,i} - \omega_{load,i}^*) \quad .$$

$$(4.126)$$

The effective work is partitioned into the reference work $\omega_{e,ref}$, which is identical for all cylinders in one stationary operating point of the engine, and into the error of the effective work $\Delta\omega_{e,i}$ at cylinder i.

$$\omega_{e,i} = \omega_{e,ref} + \Delta\omega_{e,i} \qquad (4.127)$$

Since the work balance at stationary engine operation

$$\omega_{e,ref} - \omega_{osc,i} - \omega_{load,i}^* = 0 \qquad (4.128)$$

is zero (the load work does not change as fast), we get the absolute effective work error

$$\Delta\omega_{e,i} \cdot \frac{V_d}{CYL} = \frac{J}{2}\left(\dot{\alpha}_{CS}^2(\alpha_i + \frac{2\pi}{CYL}) - \dot{\alpha}_{CS}^2(\alpha_i - \frac{2\pi}{CYL})\right) \qquad (4.129)$$

and the relative error (residue)

$$R_i = \frac{2\,\eta_e\,m_{f,ref}\,H_f}{J} \cdot \frac{\Delta\omega_{e,i}}{\omega_{e,ref}} = \dot{\alpha}_{CS}^2(\alpha_i + \frac{2\pi}{CYL}) - \dot{\alpha}_{CS}^2(\alpha_i - \frac{2\pi}{CYL}) \quad . \quad (4.130)$$

At stationary engine operation, there is a typical residue R_i for each cylinder i (Figure 4.52). The sum of all residues is zero.

$$\sum_{i=1}^{CYL} R_i = 0 \qquad (4.131)$$

This is the basis for the compensation of the fuel mass errors $\Delta m_{f,i}$.

4.5.2   Residues at Engine Transients

At engine transients, the work balance in equation 4.128 is unequal zero. This is due to the fact, that a portion of the effective work $\omega_{e,ref}$ is now dedicated to the increase of the engine speed, i. e. of the rotational energy E_{kin}. Disregarding this would lead to a bias in the residue calculation, violating equation 4.131. Figure 4.53 shows the uncompensated residues R_i (equ. 4.130) at nonstationary engine operation.

The increase of the rotational kinetic energy due to speed increase over one cylinder-related segment of crankshaft angle is

$$\Delta E_{kin,i} = \frac{J}{2}\left(\bar{\dot{\alpha}}_{CS}^2(\alpha_i + \frac{2\pi}{CYL}) - \bar{\dot{\alpha}}_{CS}^2(\alpha_i - \frac{2\pi}{CYL})\right) \quad . \qquad (4.132)$$

This can be easily verified since the average engine speed does not change at stationary operation. Under such conditions, the kinetic energy would remain constant, i. e. $\Delta E_{kin,i} = 0$.

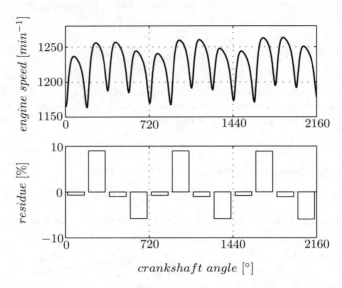

Figure 4.52 Engine speed and residues at 4-cylinder engine (stationary operation)

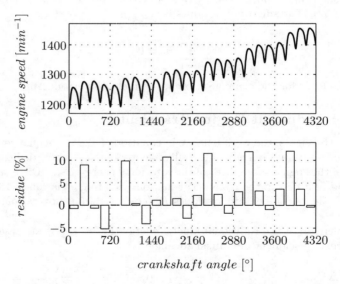

Figure 4.53 Uncompensated residues at 4-cylinder engine during transient

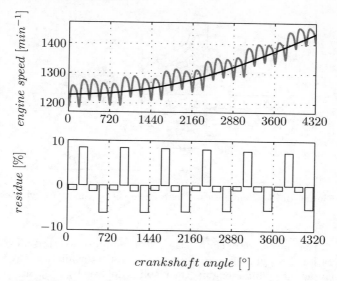

Figure 4.54 Compensated residues at 4-cylinder engine during transient

At engine transients, the work balance becomes

$$\omega_{e,ref} - \Delta E_{kin,i} - \omega_{osc,i} - \omega_{load,i}^* = 0 \quad . \tag{4.133}$$

A compensated residue can therefore be formulated as

$$R_{comp,i} = \left(\dot{\alpha}_{CS}^2(\alpha_i + \frac{2\pi}{CYL}) - \dot{\alpha}_{CS}^2(\alpha_i - \frac{2\pi}{CYL}) \right) - \\ - \left(\bar{\dot{\alpha}}_{CS}^2(\alpha_i + \frac{2\pi}{CYL}) - \bar{\dot{\alpha}}_{CS}^2(\alpha_i - \frac{2\pi}{CYL}) \right) \quad . \tag{4.134}$$

Figure 4.54 shows that equation 4.131 is valid again for such compensated residues.

$$\sum_{i=1}^{CYL} R_{comp,i} = 0 \tag{4.135}$$

The average crankshaft speed $\bar{\dot{\alpha}}$ in equation 4.132 is calculated by means of an acausal FIR filter. For an even number of cylinders it is

$$\bar{\dot{\alpha}}(\beta_i) = \frac{1}{CYL} \left[\frac{1}{2} \dot{\alpha}(\beta_{i-\frac{CYL}{2}}) + \sum_{j=i-\frac{CYL}{2}+1}^{i+\frac{CYL}{2}-1} \dot{\alpha}(\beta_j) + \frac{1}{2} \dot{\alpha}(\beta_{i+\frac{CYL}{2}}) \right] \quad . \tag{4.136}$$

The angle β_i stands for the two angles

$$\beta_i = \alpha_i \pm \frac{2\pi}{CYL} \tag{4.137}$$

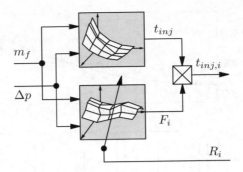

Figure 4.55 Compensation map for injection timing at cylinder i

before and after the center of combustion. The computational result of an acausal·
filter operation for cylinder i in equation 4.136 is available only at cylinder
$i+\frac{CYL}{2}$. For a four-cylinder engine, the result is delayed by two cylinder segments.
Fortunately, this delay does not create any problems, since the residue R_i is
required only two crankshaft revolutions later, when the injection for cylinder i
is calculated again (see Equation 4.138).

4.5.3   Adaptation of Injection Map

The injector map Figure 3.15 in section 3.2.4 shall now be adapted such that
the injection time t_{inj} is compensated by the residues derived in the previous
section. Since the original map $t_{inj}(m_f, \Delta p)$ is identical for all cylinders, the
compensation is introduced by an additional learning map $F_i(m_f, \Delta p)$ for each
cylinder i (Figure 4.55).

The compensation factor for cylinder i is

$$F_i(n) = (1 - k_l)\, F_i(n-1) - k_l \left[R_{comp,i}(n-1) - \right.$$

$$\left. -\frac{1}{(CYL - 1)} \sum_{j=1;\, j \neq i}^{CYL} R_{comp,j}(n-1) \right] \quad , \qquad (4.138)$$

with n being the discrete iteration time and $k_l < 1$ the weighting factor determining the learning time constant (see section 4.3.5). After having compensated
the injection time at all cylinders, the overall amount of fuel measured to the
engine must remain unchanged. Therefore, the weighted residues $R_{comp,j}$ of all
other cylinders $j \neq i$ are subtracted from residue $R_{comp,i}$. For a positive term
in the bracket of equation 4.138, the compensation factor F_i is decreased, since
too much fuel has been injected into cylinder i. Figure 4.56 shows how the
compensation factors F_i are settling at one operation point of the engine. The
above adaptation procedure has been verified with an engine running through
various operation points where different compensation factors F_i are required for
cylinder i. Figure 4.57 shows how F_i is settling rapidly after approaching new
engine operation points for the first time every 2 seconds.

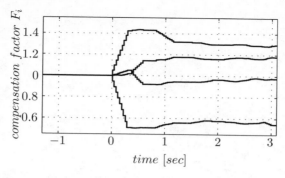

Figure 4.56 Transient behaviour of compensation factors F_i at one operation point

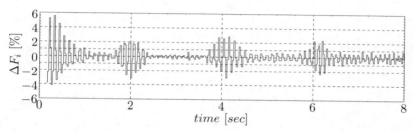

Figure 4.57 Settling of compensation factor change ΔF_i after approaching new operation points for the first time

When already compensated operation points are revisited, the compensation factors F_i remain at their respective prior values with a tolerance of under 1% (Figure 4.58). This behaviour verifies the effectiveness of injector map adaptation for transient engine operation.

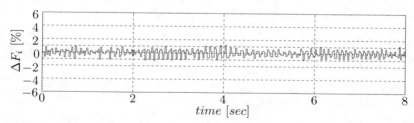

Figure 4.58 Compensation factor change ΔF_i at repeated visits of already compensated operation points

5 Driveline Control

5.1 Driveline Modeling

The main parts of a vehicular driveline are engine, clutch, transmission, shafts and wheels. The driveline is a fundamental part of a vehicle and its dynamics has been modeled in different ways depending on the purpose. The frequency range important for control is the regime including the lowest resonance modes of the driveline [55, 61]. Vibrations and noise contribute to a higher frequency range [73, 25] which is not treated here.

Section 5.1.1 covers the derivation of basic equations describing a driveline. An illustrative example is presented in Section 5.1.2. Experiments are performed with a Scania heavy truck. The aim of the modeling is to find the most important physical effects explaining the oscillations in the measured engine speed, transmission speed, and wheel speed. The models are combinations of rotating inertias connected by damped shaft flexibilities. The generalized Newton's second law is used to derive the models. The main part of the experiments used for modeling considers low gears. The reason for this is that the lower the gear is, the higher the torque transferred in the drive shaft is. This means that the shaft torsion is higher for lower gears, and hereby also the problems with oscillations. Furthermore, the amplitudes of the resonances in the wheel speed are higher for lower gears, since the load and vehicle mass appear reduced by the high conversion ratio. Section 5.2 treats the modeling when the driveline is separated in two parts, which is the case when in neutral gear or when the clutch is disengaged.

5.1.1 Basic Driveline Equations

Figure 5.1 depicts a driveline of a rear-driven vehicle. It consists of engine, clutch, transmission, propeller shaft, final drive, drive shafts, and wheels. Fundamental

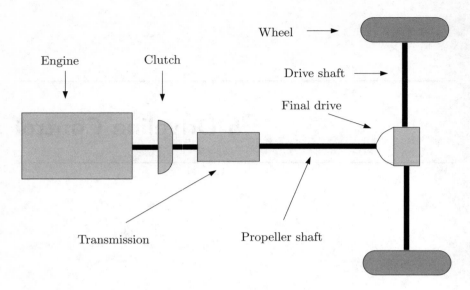

Figure 5.1 A rear-driven vehicular driveline.

equations for the driveline will be derived by using the generalized Newton's second law of motion [50]. Some basic equations regarding the forces acting on the wheel are obtained, influenced by the complete dynamics of the vehicle. This means that effects from, for instance, vehicle mass and trailer will be included in the equations describing the wheels. Figure 5.2 shows the labels, the inputs, and the outputs of each subsystem of the driveline type considered in this work. Relations between inputs and outputs will in the following be described for each part.

Engine: The output torque of the engine is characterized by the driving torque (T_e) resulting from the combustion, the internal friction from the engine ($T_{fric,e}$), and the external load from the clutch (T_c). Newton's second law of motion gives the following model

$$J_m \ddot{\alpha}_{cs} = T_e - T_{fric,e} - T_c \qquad (5.1)$$

where J_m is the mass moment of inertia of the engine and α_{cs} is the angle of the flywheel.

Clutch: A friction clutch found in vehicles equipped with a manual transmission consists of a clutch disk connecting the flywheel of the engine and the transmission's input shaft. When the clutch is engaged, and no internal friction is assumed, $T_c = T_t$ is obtained. The transmitted torque is a function of the angular difference ($\alpha_{cs} - \alpha_c$) and the angular velocity difference ($\dot{\alpha}_{cs} - \dot{\alpha}_c$) over the clutch

$$T_c = T_t = f_c(\alpha_{cs} - \alpha_c, \ \dot{\alpha}_{cs} - \dot{\alpha}_c) \qquad (5.2)$$

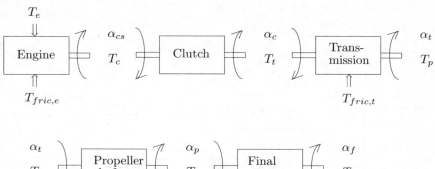

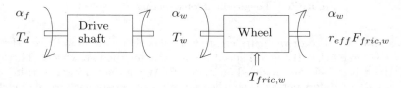

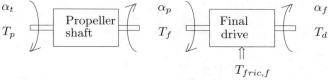

Figure 5.2 Subsystems of a vehicular driveline with their respective angle and torque labels.

Transmission: A transmission has a set of gears, each with a conversion ratio i_t. This gives the following relation between the input and output torque of the transmission

$$T_p = f_t(T_t,\ T_{fric,t},\ \alpha_c - \alpha_t i_t,\ \dot{\alpha}_c - \dot{\alpha}_t i_t,\ i_t) \qquad (5.3)$$

where the internal friction torque of the transmission is labeled $T_{fric,t}$. The reason for considering the angle difference $\alpha_c - \alpha_t i_t$ in (5.3) is the possibility of having torsional effects in the transmission.

Propeller shaft: The propeller shaft connects the transmission's output shaft with the final drive. No friction is assumed ($\Rightarrow T_p = T_f$), giving the following model of the torque input to the final drive

$$T_p = T_f = f_p(\alpha_t - \alpha_p,\ \dot{\alpha}_t - \dot{\alpha}_p) \qquad (5.4)$$

Final drive: The final drive is characterized by a conversion ratio i_f in the same way as for the transmission. The following relation for the input and output torque holds

$$T_d = f_f(T_f,\ T_{fric,f},\ \alpha_p - \alpha_f i_f,\ \dot{\alpha}_p - \dot{\alpha}_f i_f, i_f) \qquad (5.5)$$

where the internal friction torque of the final drive is labeled $T_{fric,f}$.

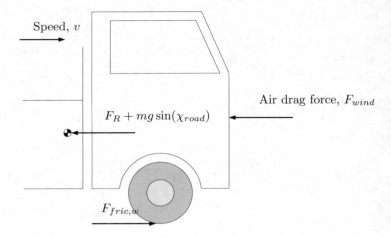

Figure 5.3 Longitudinal forces acting on a vehicle.

Drive shafts: The drive shafts connect the wheels to the final drive. Here it is assumed that the wheel speed is the same for the two wheels. Therfore, the drive shafts are modeled as one shaft. When the vehicle is turning and the speed differs between the wheels, both drive shafts have to be modeled. No friction ($\Rightarrow T_w = T_d$) gives the model equation

$$T_w = T_d = f_d(\alpha_f - \alpha_w, \ \dot{\alpha}_f - \dot{\alpha}_w) \tag{5.6}$$

Wheel: Figure 5.3 shows the forces acting on a vehicle with mass m_{CoG} and speed v_{CoG}. Newton's second law in the longitudinal direction gives

$$F_{fric,w} = m_{CoG}\dot{v}_{CoG} + F_{wind} + F_R + m_{CoG}g\sin(\chi_{road}) \tag{5.7}$$

The friction force ($F_{fric,w}$) is described by the sum of the following quantities [25].

- F_{wind}, the air drag, is approximated by

$$F_{wind} = \frac{1}{2}c_{air}A_L\rho_a v_{CoG}^2 \tag{5.8}$$

  where c_{air} is the drag coefficient, A_L the maximum vehicle cross section area, and ρ_a the air density. However, effects from, for instance, open or closed windows will make the force difficult to model.

- F_R, the rolling resistance, is approximated by

$$F_R = m_{CoG}(c_{r1} + c_{r2}v_{CoG}) \tag{5.9}$$

  where c_{r1} and c_{r2} depend on, for instance, tires and tire pressure.

- $m_{CoG}g\sin(\chi_{road})$, the gravitational force, where χ_{road} is the slope of the road.

The resulting torque due to $F_{fric,w}$ is equal to $F_{fric,w}r_{eff}$, where r_{eff} is the wheel radius. Newton's second law gives

$$J_W \ddot{\alpha}_w = T_w - F_{fric,w}r_{eff} - T_{fric,w} \qquad (5.10)$$

where J_W is the mass moment of inertia of the wheel, T_w is given by (5.6), and $T_{fric,w}$ is the friction torque. Including (5.7) to (5.9) in (5.10) together with $v = r_{eff}\dot{\alpha}_w$ gives

$$(J_W + m_{CoG}r_{eff}^2)\ddot{\alpha}_w = T_w - T_{fric,w} - \frac{1}{2}c_{air}A_L\rho_a r_{eff}^3 \dot{\alpha}_w^2 \qquad (5.11)$$
$$-r_{eff}m_{CoG}(c_{r1} + c_{r2}r_{eff}\dot{\alpha}_w) - r_{eff}m_{CoG}g\sin(\chi_{road})$$

The dynamical influence from the tire has been neglected in the equation describing the wheel.

A complete model of the driveline with the clutch engaged is described by Equations (5.1) to (5.11). So far the functions f_c, f_t, f_p, f_f, f_d, and the friction torques $T_{fric,t}$, $T_{fric,f}$, and $T_{fric,w}$ are unknown. In the following section assumptions will be made about these, resulting in a series of driveline models, with different complexities.

5.1.2 An Illustrative Modeling Example

A Scania heavy truck is used for experiments. Figure 5.4 shows a Scania 144L 6x2 truck that has the configuration as follows.

- 14 liter V8 turbo-charged diesel engine with maximum power of 530 Hp and maximum torque of 2300 Nm. The fuel metering is governed by an in-line injection pump system [6].

- The engine is connected to a manual range-splitter transmission GRS900R (Figure 5.6) via a clutch. The transmission has 14 gears and a hydraulic retarder. It is also equipped with the automatic gear shifting system Opti-Cruise [58].

- The weight of the truck is $m = 24\,000$ kg.

Engine

The V8 engine in the 144L truck uses an in-line pump system with one fuel pump supplying all eight cylinders with fuel. Driveline modeling will be influenced by a number of subsystems of the engine that are common for both engine types. These are

Maximum torque delimiter The injected fuel amount is restricted by the physical character of the engine (i.e., engine size, number of cylinders, etc.), together with restrictions that the engine control system uses, for utilizing the engine in the best possible way. The maximum torque decreases below 1100 rpm and above 1500 rpm.

Figure 5.4 Scania 144L truck.

Figure 5.5 Scania 14 liter V8 DSC14 engine.

Figure 5.6 Scania GRS900R range-splitter transmission with retarder and OptiCruise automatic gear-shifting system.

Diesel smoke delimiter If the turbo pressure is low and a high engine torque is demanded, diesel smoke emissions will increase to an unacceptable level. This is prevented by restricting the fuel amount to a level with acceptable emissions at low turbo pressures.

Transfer function from fuel amount to engine torque The engine torque is the torque resulting from the explosions in the cylinders. A static function relating the engine torque to injected fuel can be obtained in a dynamometer test. For a diesel engine this function is fairly static, and no dynamical models are used in this work.

Engine friction The engine output torque transferred to the clutch is equal to the engine torque (the torque resulting from the explosions) subtracted by the engine internal friction. Friction modeling is thus fundamental for driveline modeling and control.

Sensor System

The velocity of a rotating shaft is measured by using an inductive sensor [57], which detects the time when cogs from a rotating cogwheel are passing. This time sequence is then inverted to get the angle velocity. Hence, the bandwidth of the measured signal depends on the speed and the number of cogs the cogwheel is equipped with.

Three speed sensors are used to measure the speed of the flywheel of the engine ($\dot{\alpha}_{cs}$), the speed of the output shaft of the transmission ($\dot{\alpha}_t$), and the speed of the driving wheel ($\dot{\alpha}_w$). The transmission speed sensor has fewer cogs than the other two sensors, indicating that the bandwidth of this signal is lower.

Measured Variables			
Variable	*Node*	*Resolution*	*Rate*
Engine speed, $\dot{\alpha}_{cs}$	Engine	0.013 rad/s	20 ms
Engine torque, T_e	Engine	1% of max torque	20 ms
Engine temp, ϑ_e	Engine	1° C	1 s
Wheel speed, $\dot{\alpha}_w$	ABS	0.033 rad/s	50 ms
Transmission speed, $\dot{\alpha}_t$	Transmission	0.013 rad/s	50 ms

Table 5.1 Measured variables transmitted on the CAN-bus.

By measuring the amount of fuel, m_f, that is fed to the engine, a measure of the driving torque, $T_e(m_f)$, is obtained from dynamometer tests, as mentioned before. The output torque of the engine is the driving torque subtracted by the engine friction, $T_{fric,e}$. This signal, $u = T_e(m_f) - T_{fric,e}$, is the torque acting on the driveline, which is a pulsating signal with torque pulses from each cylinder explosion. However, the control signal $u = T_e(m_f) - T_{fric,e}$ is treated as a continuous signal, which is reasonable for the frequency range considered for control design. A motivation for this is that an eight-cylinder engine makes 80 strokes/s at an engine speed of 1200 rev/min. This means that a mean-value engine model is assumed (neglects variations during the engine cycle).

The truck is equipped with a set of control units, each connected with a CAN-bus [62]. These CAN nodes are the engine control node, the transmission node, and the ABS brake system node. Each node measures a number of variables and transmits them via the bus.

Experiments for Driveline Modeling

A number of test roads at Scania were used for testing. They have different known slopes. The variables in Table 5.1 are logged during tests that excite driveline resonances. Figure 5.7 shows a test with the 144L truck where step inputs in accelerator position excite driveline oscillations. In Figure 5.7 it is seen that the main flexibility of the driveline is located between the output shaft of the transmission and the wheel, since the largest difference in speed is between the measured transmission speed and wheel speed.

Engine Friction Modeling

The engine friction $T_{fric,e}$ is modeled as a function of the engine speed and the engine temperature

$$T_{fric,e} = T_{fric,e}(\dot{\alpha}_{cs}, \vartheta_e) \tag{5.12}$$

The influence from the load is neglected. With neutral gear engaged, the engine speed is controlled to 20 levels between 600 and 2300 RPM, while measuring the engine torque and temperature. The resulting friction map for the 144L truck is shown in Figure 5.8.

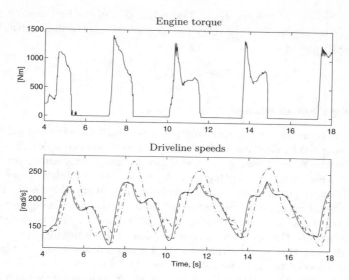

Figure 5.7 Logged data on the CAN-bus during step inputs in accelerator position with the 144L truck. The transmission speed (dashed) and the wheel speed (dash-dotted) are scaled to engine speed in solid. The main flexibility of the driveline is located between the output shaft of the transmission and the wheel, since the largest difference in speed is between the measured transmission speed and wheel speed.

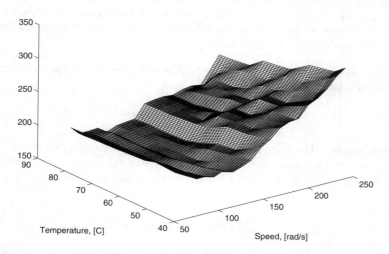

Figure 5.8 Engine friction for the 144L truck, modeled as a function of engine speed and engine temperature.

The logged engine torque, $T_e(m_f)$, as a function of the fuel amount, is recalculated to control signal to the driveline by subtracting the engine friction from the engine torque as

$$u = T_e(m_f) - T_{fric,e}(\dot\alpha_{cs}, \vartheta_e) \tag{5.13}$$

Obtaining a Set of Models

The measured engine speed, transmission speed, and wheel speed for the 144L truck is explained by deriving a set of models of increasing complexity. Figure 5.7 shows that the main difference in speed is between the measured transmission speed and wheel speed, indicating that the important flexibility of the driveline is located between the output shaft of the transmission and the wheel. This leads to a first model with a lumped engine and transmission inertia connected to the wheel inertia by a drive-shaft flexibility. The reason for this is that the drive shaft is subject to the relatively largest torsion. This is mainly due to the high torque difference that results from the amplification of the engine torque by the conversion ratio of the transmission (i_t) and the final drive (i_f). This number ($i_t i_f$) can be as high as 60 for the lowest gear. A total of three models will be derived for the 144L truck, all based on the basic driveline equations derived in Section 5.1.1.

Model with Drive-Shaft Flexibility

The simplest model with a drive-shaft flexibility is developed first. Assumptions about the fundamental equations in Section 5.1.1 are made in order to obtain a model with a lumped engine and transmission inertia and a drive-shaft flexibility. Labels are according to Figure 5.2. The clutch and the propeller shafts are assumed to be stiff, and the drive shaft is described as a damped torsional flexibility. The transmission and the final drive are assumed to multiply the torque by the conversion ratio, without losses.

Clutch: The clutch is assumed to be stiff, which gives the following equations for the torque and the angle

$$T_c = T_t, \quad \alpha_{cs} = \alpha_c \tag{5.14}$$

Transmission: The transmission is described by one rotating inertia J_t. The friction torque is assumed to be described by a viscous damping coefficient d_t. The model of the transmission, corresponding to (5.3), is

$$\alpha_c = \alpha_t i_t \tag{5.15}$$
$$J_t \ddot\alpha_t = T_t i_t - d_t \dot\alpha_t - T_p \tag{5.16}$$

By using (5.14) and (5.15), the model can be rewritten as

$$J_t \ddot\alpha_{cs} = T_c i_t^2 - d_t \dot\alpha_{cs} - T_p i_t \tag{5.17}$$

Propeller shaft: The propeller shaft is also assumed to be stiff, which gives the following equations for the torque and the angle

$$T_p = T_f, \quad \alpha_t = \alpha_p \tag{5.18}$$

Final drive: In the same way as for the transmission, the final drive is modeled by one rotating inertia J_f. The friction torque is assumed to be described by a viscous damping coefficient d_f. The model of the final drive, corresponding to (5.5), is

$$\alpha_p = \alpha_f i_f \tag{5.19}$$
$$J_f \ddot{\alpha}_f = T_f i_f - d_f \dot{\alpha}_f - T_d \tag{5.20}$$

Equation (5.20) can be rewritten with (5.18) and (5.19) which gives

$$J_f \ddot{\alpha}_t = T_p i_f^2 - d_f \dot{\alpha}_t - T_d i_f \tag{5.21}$$

Converting (5.21) to a function of engine speed is done by using (5.14) and (5.15) resulting in

$$J_f \ddot{\alpha}_{cs} = T_p i_f^2 i_t - d_f \dot{\alpha}_{cs} - T_d i_f i_t \tag{5.22}$$

By replacing T_p in (5.22) with T_p in (5.17), a model for the lumped transmission, propeller shaft, and final drive is obtained

$$(J_t i_f^2 + J_f)\ddot{\alpha}_{cs} = T_c i_t^2 i_f^2 - d_t \dot{\alpha}_{cs} i_f^2 - d_f \dot{\alpha}_{cs} - T_d i_f i_t \tag{5.23}$$

Drive shaft: The drive shaft is modeled as a damped torsional flexibility, having stiffness k, and internal damping c. Hence, (5.6) becomes

$$
\begin{aligned}
T_w = T_d &= k(\alpha_f - \alpha_w) + d(\dot{\alpha}_f - \dot{\alpha}_w) = k(\alpha_{cs}/i_t i_f - \alpha_w) \\
&+ d(\dot{\alpha}_{cs}/i_t i_f - \dot{\alpha}_w)
\end{aligned} \tag{5.24}
$$

where (5.14), (5.15), (5.18), and (5.19) are used. By replacing T_d in (5.23) with (5.24) the equation describing the transmission, the propeller shaft, the final drive, and the drive shaft, becomes

$$
\begin{aligned}
(J_t i_f^2 + J_f)\ddot{\alpha}_{cs} &= T_c i_t^2 i_f^2 - d_t \dot{\alpha}_{cs} i_f^2 - d_f \dot{\alpha}_{cs} \\
&- k(\alpha_{cs} - \alpha_w i_t i_f) - d(\dot{\alpha}_{cs} - \dot{\alpha}_w i_t i_f)
\end{aligned} \tag{5.25}
$$

Wheel: If (5.11) is combined with (5.24), the following equation for the wheel is obtained:

$$
\begin{aligned}
(J_W + m r_{eff}^2)\ddot{\alpha}_w &= k(\alpha_{cs}/i_t i_f - \alpha_w) + d(\dot{\alpha}_{cs}/i_t i_f - \dot{\alpha}_w) - d_w \dot{\alpha}_w \\
&- \frac{1}{2}c_{air} A_L \rho a r_{eff}^3 \dot{\alpha}_w^2 - m c_{r2} r_{eff}^2 \dot{\alpha}_w - r_{eff} m (c_{r1} + g \sin(\chi_{road}))
\end{aligned} \tag{5.26}
$$

where the friction torque is described as viscous damping, with label d_w.

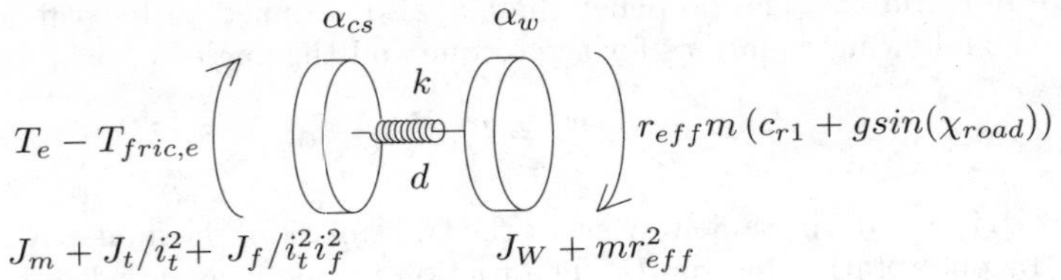

Figure 5.9 The Drive-shaft model consists of a lumped engine and transmission inertia connected to the wheel inertia by a damped torsional flexibility.

The complete model, named the **Drive-shaft model**, is obtained by inserting T_c from (5.25) into (5.1), together with (5.26), which gives the following equations. An illustration of the model can be seen in Figure 5.9.

Model 5.1 The Drive-Shaft Model

$$(J_m + J_t/i_t^2 + J_f/i_t^2 i_f^2)\ddot{\alpha}_{cs} = T_e - T_{fric,e} - (d_t/i_t^2 + d_f/i_t^2 i_f^2)\dot{\alpha}_{cs} \quad (5.27)$$
$$-k(\alpha_{cs}/i_t i_f - \alpha_w)/i_t i_f$$
$$-d(\dot{\alpha}_{cs}/i_t i_f - \dot{\alpha}_w)/i_t i_f$$
$$(J_W + mr_{eff}^2)\ddot{\alpha}_w = k(\alpha_{cs}/i_t i_f - \alpha_w) + d(\dot{\alpha}_{cs}/i_t i_f - \dot{\alpha}_w) \quad (5.28)$$
$$-(d_w + mc_{r2}r_{eff}^2)\dot{\alpha}_w - \frac{1}{2}c_{air}A_L\rho_a r_{eff}^3\dot{\alpha}_w^2$$
$$-r_{eff}m(c_{r1} + gsin(\chi_{road}))$$

The Drive-shaft model is the simplest model of three considered. The drive-shaft torsion, the engine speed, and the wheel speed are used as states according to

$$x_1 = \alpha_{cs}/i_t i_f - \alpha_w, \quad x_2 = \dot{\alpha}_{cs}, \quad x_3 = \dot{\alpha}_w \quad (5.29)$$

More details of state-space descriptions are given in Chapter 5.3.4. For low gears, the influence from the air drag is low and by neglecting $\frac{1}{2}c_{air}A_L\rho_a r_{eff}^3\dot{\alpha}_w^2$ in (5.28), the model is linear in the states, but nonlinear in the parameters.

Parameter estimation of the **Drive-shaft model**

A data set containing engine torque, engine speed, and wheel speed measurements are used to estimate the parameters and the initial conditions of the **Drive-shaft** model. The estimated parameters are

$$i = i_t i_f, \quad l = r_{eff}m(c_{r1} + gsin(\chi_{road}))$$
$$J_1 = J_m + J_t/i_t^2 + J_f/i_t^2 i_f^2, \quad J_2 = J_W + mr_{eff}^2 \quad (5.30)$$
$$d_1 = d_t/i_t^2 + d_f/i_t^2 i_f^2, \quad d_2 = d_w + mc_{r2}r_{eff}^2$$

together with the stiffness, k, and the internal damping, d, of the drive shaft. The estimated initial conditions of the states are labeled x_{10}, x_{20}, and x_{30}, according to (5.29).

Figure 5.10 shows an example of how the model fits the measured data. The measured driveline speed are shown together with the model output, x_1, x_2, and x_3. According to the model, the clutch is stiff, and therefore, the transmission speed is equal to the engine speed scaled with the conversion ratio of the transmission (i_t). In the figure, this signal is shown together with the measured transmission speed. The plots are typical examples that show that a major part of the driveline dynamics is captured with a linear mass-spring model with the drive shafts as the main flexibility.

Results of parameter estimation

- The main contribution to driveline dynamics from driving torque to engine speed and wheel speed is the drive shaft, explaining the first main resonance of the driveline.

- The true drive-shaft torsion (x_1) is unknown, but the value estimated by the model has physically reasonable values. These values will be further validated in Chapter 5.5.6.

- The model output transmission speed (x_2/i_t) fits the measured transmission speed data reasonably well, but there is still a systematic dynamics lag between model outputs and measurements.

Influence from Propeller-Shaft Flexibility

The Drive-shaft model assumes stiff driveline from the engine to the final drive. The propeller shaft and the drive shaft are separated by the final drive, which has a small inertia compared to other inertias, e.g., the engine inertia. This section covers an investigation of how the model parameters of the Drive-shaft model are influenced by a flexible propeller shaft.

A model is derived with a stiff driveline from the engine to the output shaft of the transmission. The propeller shaft and the drive shafts are modeled as damped torsional flexibilities. As in the derivation of the Drive-shaft model, the transmission and the final drive are assumed to multiply the torque with the conversion ratio, without losses.

The derivation of the Drive-shaft model is repeated here with the difference that the model for the propeller shaft (5.18) is replaced by a model of a flexibility with stiffness k_p and internal damping d_p

$$T_p = T_f = k_p(\alpha_t - \alpha_p) + d_p(\dot{\alpha}_t - \dot{\alpha}_p) = k_p(\alpha_{cs}/i_t - \alpha_p) + d_p(\dot{\alpha}_{cs}/i_t - \dot{\alpha}_p) \tag{5.31}$$

where (5.14) and (5.15) are used in the last equality. This formulation means that there are two torsional flexibilities, the propeller shaft and the drive shaft. Inserting (5.31) into (5.17) gives

$$J_t\ddot{\alpha}_{cs} = T_c i_t^2 - d_t\dot{\alpha}_{cs} - (k_p(\alpha_{cs}/i_t - \alpha_p) + d_p(\dot{\alpha}_{cs}/i_t - \dot{\alpha}_p)) i_t \tag{5.32}$$

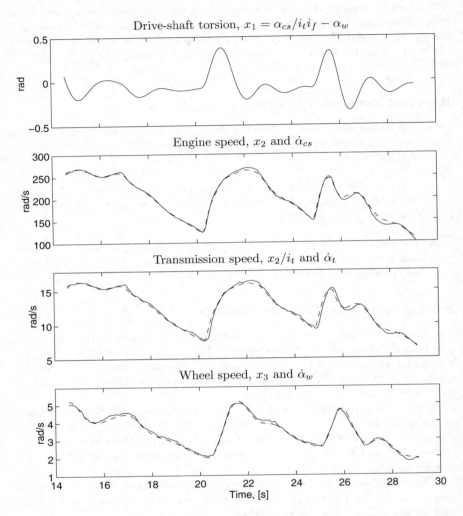

Figure 5.10 The parameters of the Drive-shaft model estimated on data with step inputs in accelerator position using gear 1. The top figure shows the estimated drive-shaft torsion, and the bottom figures show the model outputs (x_2, x_3) in dashed lines, together with the measured driveline speeds in solid. The plots are typical examples of that a major part of the dynamics is captured by a linear model with a drive-shaft flexibility.

By combining this with (5.1) the following differential equation describing the lumped engine and transmission results

$$(J_m + J_t/i_t^2)\ddot{\alpha}_{cs} = T_e - T_{fric,e} - d_t/i_t^2\dot{\alpha}_{cs} \qquad (5.33)$$
$$-\frac{1}{i_t}(k_p(\alpha_{cs}/i_t - \alpha_p) + d_p(\dot{\alpha}_{cs}/i_t - \dot{\alpha}_p))$$

The final drive is described by inserting (5.31) in (5.20) and using (5.19)

$$\alpha_p = \alpha_f i_f \qquad (5.34)$$
$$J_f\ddot{\alpha}_f = i_f(k_p(\alpha_{cs}/i_t - \alpha_p) + d_p(\dot{\alpha}_{cs}/i_t - \dot{\alpha}_p)) - d_f\dot{\alpha}_f - T_d \qquad (5.35)$$

Including (5.34) in (5.35) gives

$$J_f\ddot{\alpha}_p = i_f^2(k_p(\alpha_{cs}/i_t - \alpha_p) + d_p(\dot{\alpha}_{cs}/i_t - \dot{\alpha}_p)) - d_f\dot{\alpha}_p - i_f T_d \qquad (5.36)$$

The equation for the drive shaft (5.24) is repeated with new labels

$$T_w = T_d = k_d(\alpha_f - \alpha_w) + d_d(\dot{\alpha}_f - \dot{\alpha}_w) = k_d(\alpha_p/i_f - \alpha_w) + d_d(\dot{\alpha}_p/i_f - \dot{\alpha}_w) \qquad (5.37)$$

where (5.34) is used in the last equality.

The equation for the final drive (5.36) now becomes

$$J_f\ddot{\alpha}_p = i_f^2(k_p(\alpha_{cs}/i_t - \alpha_p) + d_p(\dot{\alpha}_{cs}/i_t - \dot{\alpha}_p)) - d_f\dot{\alpha}_p \qquad (5.38)$$
$$-i_f(k_d(\alpha_p/i_f - \alpha_w) + d_d(\dot{\alpha}_p/i_f - \dot{\alpha}_w))$$

The equation for the wheel is derived by combining (5.11) with (5.37). The equation describing the wheel becomes

$$(J_W + mr_{eff}^2)\ddot{\alpha}_w = k_d(\alpha_p/i_f - \alpha_w) + d_d(\dot{\alpha}_p/i_f - \dot{\alpha}_w) \qquad (5.39)$$
$$-d_w\dot{\alpha}_w - \frac{1}{2}c_{air}A_L\rho_a r_{eff}^3\dot{\alpha}_w^2 - mc_{r2}r_{eff}^2\dot{\alpha}_w - r_{eff}m(c_{r1} + g\sin(\chi_{road}))$$

where again the friction torque is assumed to be described by a viscous damping coefficient d_w. The complete model with drive shaft and propeller shaft flexibilities is the following, which can be seen in Figure 5.11.

$$(J_m + J_t/i_t^2)\ddot{\alpha}_{cs} = T_e - T_{fric,e} - d_t/i_t^2\dot{\alpha}_{cs} \qquad (5.40)$$
$$-\frac{1}{i_t}(k_p(\alpha_{cs}/i_t - \alpha_p) + d_p(\dot{\alpha}_{cs}/i_t - \dot{\alpha}_p))$$
$$J_f\ddot{\alpha}_p = i_f^2(k_p(\alpha_{cs}/i_t - \alpha_p) + d_p(\dot{\alpha}_{cs}/i_t - \dot{\alpha}_p)) - d_f\dot{\alpha}_p \qquad (5.41)$$
$$-i_f(k_d(\alpha_p/i_f - \alpha_w) + d_d(\dot{\alpha}_p/i_f - \dot{\alpha}_w))$$
$$(J_W + mr_{eff}^2)\ddot{\alpha}_w = k_d(\alpha_p/i_f - \alpha_w) + d_d(\dot{\alpha}_p/i_f - \dot{\alpha}_w) \qquad (5.42)$$
$$-(d_w + mc_{r2}r_{eff}^2)\dot{\alpha}_w - \frac{1}{2}c_{air}A_L\rho_a r_{eff}^3\dot{\alpha}_w^2 \qquad (5.43)$$
$$-r_{eff}m(c_{r1} + g\sin(\chi_{road}))$$

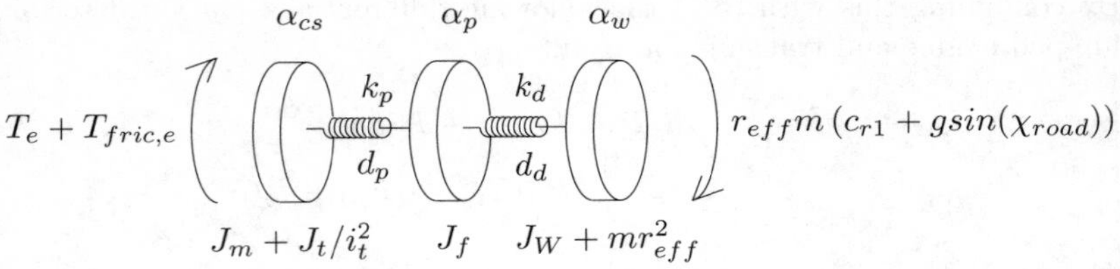

Figure 5.11 Model with flexible propeller shaft and drive shaft.

The model equations (5.40) to (5.42) describe the Drive-shaft model extended with the propeller shaft with stiffness k_p and damping d_p. The three inertias in the model are

$$
\begin{aligned}
J_1 &= J_m + J_t/i_t^2 \\
J_2 &= J_f \\
J_3 &= J_W + mr_{eff}^2
\end{aligned}
\tag{5.44}
$$

If the magnitude of the three inertias are compared, the inertia of the final drive (J_f) is considerably less than J_1 and J_2 in (5.44). Therefore, the model will act as if there are two damped springs in series. The total stiffness of two undamped springs in series is

$$
k = \frac{k_p i_f^2 k_d}{k_p i_f^2 + k_d}
\tag{5.45}
$$

whereas the total damping of two dampers in series is

$$
d = \frac{d_p i_f^2 d_d}{d_p i_f^2 + d_d}
$$

The damping and the stiffness of the drive shaft in the previous section will thus typically be underestimated due to the flexibility of the propeller shaft. This effect will increase with lower conversion ratio in the final drive, i_f. The individual stiffness values obtained from parameter estimation are somewhat lower than the values obtained from material data.

Deviations between Engine Speed and Transmission Speed

As mentioned above, there is good agreement between model output and experimental data for $u = T_e - T_{fric,e}$, $\dot{\alpha}_{cs}$, and $\dot{\alpha}_w$, but there is a slight deviation between measured and estimated transmission speed. With the Drive-shaft model, stiff dynamics between the engine and the transmission is assumed, and hence the only difference between the model outputs engine speed and transmission speed is the gain i_t (conversion ratio of the transmission). However, a comparison between the measured engine speed and transmission speed shows that there is not only a gain difference according to Figure 5.12. This deviation has a character of a phase shift and some smoothing (signal levels and shapes agree). This indicates

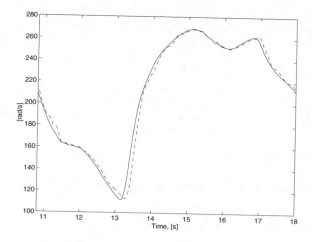

Figure 5.12 Measured engine speed (solid) and transmission speed (dashed). The transmission speed is multiplied with the conversion ratio of the transmission, i_t.

that there is some additional dynamics between engine speed, $\dot{\alpha}_{cs}$, and transmission speed, $\dot{\alpha}_t$. Two natural candidates are additional mass-spring dynamics in the driveline, or sensor dynamics. The explanation is that there is a combined effect, with the major difference explained by the sensor dynamics. The motivation for this is that the high stiffness of the clutch flexibility (given from material data) cannot result in a phase shift form of the magnitude shown in Figure 5.12. Neither can backlash in the transmission explain the difference, because then the engine and transmission speeds would be equal when the backlash is at its endpoints.

As mentioned before, the bandwidth of the measured transmission speed is lower than the measured engine and wheel speeds, due to fewer cogs in the sensor. It is assumed that the engine speed and the wheel speed sensor dynamics are not influencing the data for the frequencies considered. The speed dependence of the transmission sensor dynamics is neglected. The following sensor dynamics are assumed, after some comparison between sensor filters of different order,

$$
\begin{aligned}
f_m &= 1 \\
f_t &= \frac{1}{1 + \gamma s} \\
f_w &= 1
\end{aligned}
\tag{5.46}
$$

where a first order filter with an unknown parameter γ models the transmission sensor. Figure 5.13 shows the configuration with the **Drive-shaft model** and sensor filter f_m, f_t, and f_w. The outputs of the filters are y_m, y_t, and y_w.

Now the parameters, the initial condition, and the unknown filter constant γ can be estimated such that the model outputs (y_m, y_t, y_w) fit the measured data. The result of this is seen in Figure 5.14 for gear 1. The conclusion is that the main part of the deviation between engine speed and transmission speed is due to sensor dynamics. Figure 5.15 shows an enlarged plot of the transmission

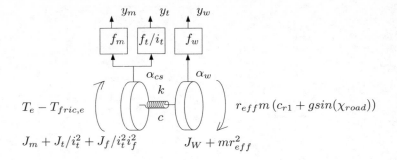

Figure 5.13 The Drive-shaft model with sensor dynamics.

speed, with the model output from the Drive-shaft model with and without sensor filtering.

Results of parameter estimation

- If the Drive-shaft model is extended with a first order sensor filter for the transmission speed, all three velocities ($\dot{\alpha}_{cs}$, $\dot{\alpha}_t$, $\dot{\alpha}_w$) are estimated by the model. The model outputs fit the data except for some time intervals where there are deviations between model and measured data (see Figure 5.15). However, these deviations will in the following be related to nonlinearities at low clutch torques.

Model with Flexible Clutch and Drive Shaft

The clutch has so far been assumed stiff and the main contribution to low-frequency oscillations is the drive-shaft flexibility. However, measured data suggests that there is some additional dynamics between the engine and the transmission. The candidate which is most flexible is the clutch. Hence, the model will include two torsional flexibilities, the drive shaft, and the clutch. With this model structure, the first and second resonance modes of the driveline are explained. The reason to this ordering in frequency is the relatively higher stiffness in the clutch, because the relative stiffness of the drive shaft is reduced by the conversion ratio.

A model with a linear clutch flexibility and one torsional flexibility (the drive shaft) is derived by repeating the procedure for the Drive-shaft model with the difference that the model for the clutch is a flexibility with stiffness k_c and internal damping d_c

$$T_c = T_t = k_c(\alpha_{cs} - \alpha_c) + d_c(\dot{\alpha}_{cs} - \dot{\alpha}_c) = k_c(\alpha_{cs} - \alpha_t i_t) + d_c(\dot{\alpha}_{cs} - \dot{\alpha}_t i_t) \quad (5.47)$$

where (5.15) is used in the last equality. By inserting this into (5.1) the equation describing the engine inertia is given by

$$J_m \ddot{\alpha}_{cs} = T_e - T_{fric,e} - (k_c(\alpha_{cs} - \alpha_t i_t) + d_c(\dot{\alpha}_{cs} - \dot{\alpha}_t i_t)) \quad (5.48)$$

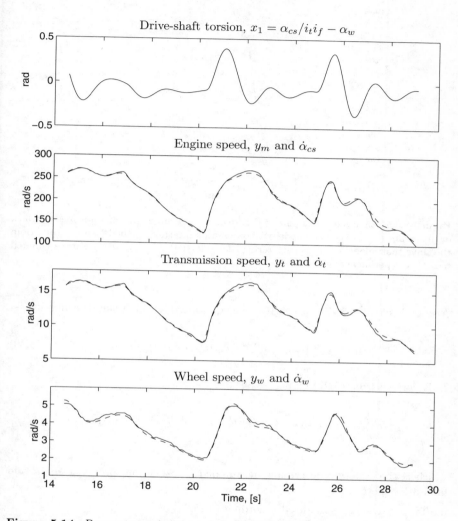

Figure 5.14 Parameter estimation of the **Drive-shaft model** as in Figure 5.10, but with sensor dynamics included. The top figure shows the estimated drive-shaft torsion, and the bottom figures show the model outputs (y_m, y_t, y_w) in dashed, together with the measured data in solid. The main part of the deviation between engine speed and transmission speed is due to sensor dynamics. See also Figure 5.15.

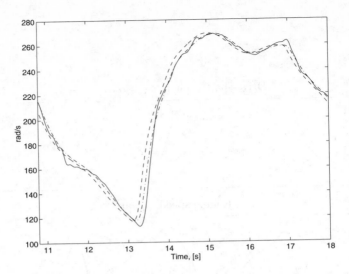

Figure 5.15 Enlargement of part of Figure 5.14. Measured transmission speed (solid), output from the Drive-shaft model without sensor filtering (dashed), and output from the Drive-shaft model with sensor filtering (dash-dotted). The parameters are estimated based on experiments with gear 1.

Also by inserting (5.47) into (5.16), the equation describing the transmission is

$$J_t \ddot{\alpha}_t = i_t \left(k_c (\alpha_{cs} - \alpha_t i_t) + d_c (\dot{\alpha}_{cs} - \dot{\alpha}_t i_t) \right) - d_t \dot{\alpha}_t - T_p \qquad (5.49)$$

T_p is derived from (5.21) giving

$$(J_t + J_f/i_f^2) \ddot{\alpha}_t = i_t \left(k_c (\alpha_{cs} - \alpha_t i_t) + d_c (\dot{\alpha}_{cs} - \dot{\alpha}_t i_t) \right) - (d_t + d_f/i_f^2) \dot{\alpha}_t - T_d/i_f \qquad (5.50)$$

which is the equation describing the lumped transmission, propeller shaft, and final drive inertia.

The drive shaft is modeled according to (5.24) as

$$T_w = T_d = k_d (\alpha_f - \alpha_w) + d_d (\dot{\alpha}_f - \dot{\alpha}_w) = k_d (\alpha_t/i_f - \alpha_w) + d_d (\dot{\alpha}_t/i_f - \dot{\alpha}_w) \qquad (5.51)$$

where (5.18) and (5.19) are used in the last equality.

The complete model, named the Clutch and drive-shaft model, is obtained by inserting (5.51) into (5.50) and (5.11). An illustration of the model can be seen in Figure 5.16.

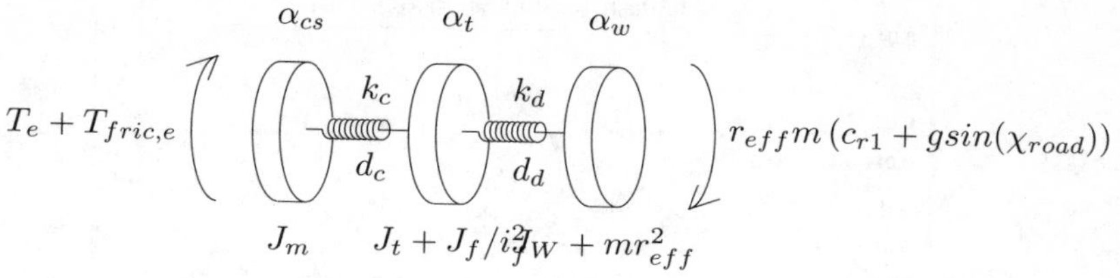

$$T_e + T_{fric,e} \left(\overbrace{\begin{array}{ccc} \alpha_{cs} & \alpha_t & \alpha_w \\[4pt] \bigcirc \!\! \stackrel{k_c}{\underset{d_c}{\sim}} \!\! \bigcirc \!\! \stackrel{k_d}{\underset{d_d}{\sim}} \!\! \bigcirc \end{array}} \right) r_{eff} m \left(c_{r1} + g sin(\chi_{road}) \right)$$

$$J_m \qquad J_t + J_f/i_f^2 \qquad J_W + mr_{eff}^2$$

Figure 5.16 The Clutch and drive-shaft model: Linear clutch and drive-shaft torsional flexibility.

Model 5.2 The Clutch and Drive-Shaft Model

$$J_m \ddot{\alpha}_{cs} = T_e - T_{fric,e} - (k_c(\alpha_{cs} - \alpha_t i_t) + d_c(\dot{\alpha}_{cs} - \dot{\alpha}_t i_t)) \tag{5.52}$$

$$(J_t + J_f/i_f^2)\ddot{\alpha}_t = i_t \left(k_c(\alpha_{cs} - \alpha_t i_t) + d_c(\dot{\alpha}_{cs} - \dot{\alpha}_t i_t) \right) \tag{5.53}$$

$$-(d_t + d_f/i_f^2)\dot{\alpha}_t - \frac{1}{i_f}(k_d(\alpha_t/i_f - \alpha_w) + d_d(\dot{\alpha}_t/i_f - \dot{\alpha}_w))$$

$$(J_W + mr_{eff}^2)\ddot{\alpha}_w = k_d(\alpha_t/i_f - \alpha_w) + d_d(\dot{\alpha}_t/i_f - \dot{\alpha}_w) \tag{5.54}$$

$$-(d_w + c_{r2}r_{eff})\dot{\alpha}_w - \frac{1}{2}c_{air}A_L\rho_a r_{eff}^3\dot{\alpha}_w^2 \tag{5.55}$$

$$-r_{eff}m\left(c_{r1} + g sin(\chi_{road})\right)$$

The clutch torsion, the drive-shaft torsion, and the driveline speeds are used as states according to

$$x_1 = \alpha_{cs} - \alpha_t i_t, \quad x_2 = \alpha_t/i_f - \alpha_w, \quad x_3 = \dot{\alpha}_{cs}, \quad x_4 = \dot{\alpha}_t, \quad x_5 = \dot{\alpha}_w \tag{5.56}$$

More details about state-space representations and parameters are covered in Chapter 5.3.4. For low gears, the influence from the air drag is low and by neglecting $\frac{1}{2}c_{air}A_L\rho_a r_{eff}^3\dot{\alpha}_w^2$ in (5.54), the model is linear in the states, but non-linear in the parameters. The model equipped with the sensor filter in (5.46) gives the true sensor outputs (y_m, y_t, y_w).

Parameter estimation of the Clutch and drive-shaft model

The parameters and the initial conditions of the Clutch and drive-shaft model are estimated with the sensor dynamics described above, in the same way as the Drive-shaft model in this section. A problem when estimating the parameters of the Clutch and drive-shaft model is that the bandwidth of the measured signals is not enough to estimate the stiffness k_c in the clutch. Therefore, the value of the stiffness given from material data is used and fixed, and the rest of the parameters are estimated.

The resulting clutch torsion (x_1) and the drive-shaft torsion (x_2) are shown in Figure 5.17. The true values of these torsions are not known, but the figure shows that the amplitude of the drive-shaft torsion has realistic values that agree

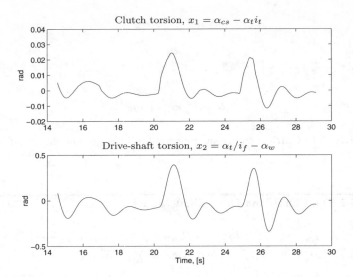

Figure 5.17 Clutch torsion (top figure) and drive-shaft torsion (bottom figure) result-ing from parameter estimation of the Clutch and drive-shaft model with sensor filtering, on data with gear 1. The true values of these torsions are not known, but the plots show that the drive-shaft torsion has realistic values.

with material data. However, the clutch torsion does not have realistic values (explained later), which can be seen when comparing with the static nonlinearity in Figure 5.18.

The model output velocities ($\dot{\alpha}_{cs}$, $\dot{\alpha}_t$, $\dot{\alpha}_w$) show no improvement compared to those generated by the Drive-shaft model with sensor dynamics, displayed in Figure 5.14.

Results of parameter estimation

- The model including a linear clutch does not improve the data fit. The interpretation of this is that the clutch model does not add information for frequencies in the measured data.

Nonlinear Clutch and Drive-Shaft Flexibility

When studying a clutch in more detail it is seen that the torsional flexibility is a result of an arrangement with smaller springs in series with springs with much higher stiffness. The reason for this arrangement is vibration insulation. When the angle difference over the clutch starts from zero and increases, the smaller springs, with stiffness k_{c1}, are being compressed. This ends when they are fully compressed at α_{c1} radians. If the angle is increased further, the stiffer springs, with stiffness k_{c2}, are beginning to be compressed. When α_{c2} is reached, the clutch hits a mechanical stop. This clutch characteristics can be modeled as in Figure 5.18. The resulting stiffness $k_c(\alpha_{cs} - \alpha_c)$ of the clutch is given by

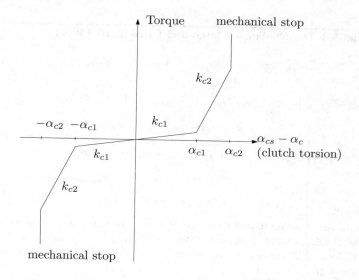

Figure 5.18 Nonlinear clutch characteristics.

$$k_c(x) = \begin{cases} k_{c1} & \text{if } |x| \leq \alpha_{c1} \\ k_{c2} & \text{if } \alpha_{c1} < |x| \leq \alpha_{c2} \\ \infty & \text{otherwise} \end{cases} \qquad (5.57)$$

The torque $M_{kc}(\alpha_{cs} - \alpha_c)$ from the clutch nonlinearity is

$$M_{kc}(x) = \begin{cases} k_{c1}x & \text{if } |x| \leq \alpha_{c1} \\ k_{c1}\alpha_{c1} + k_{c2}(x - \alpha_{c1}) & \text{if } \alpha_{c1} < x \leq \alpha_{c2} \\ -k_{c1}\alpha_{c1} + k_{c2}(x + \alpha_{c1}) & \text{if } -\alpha_{c2} < x \leq -\alpha_{c1} \\ \infty & \text{otherwise} \end{cases} \qquad (5.58)$$

If the linear clutch in the Clutch and drive-shaft model is replaced by the clutch nonlinearity according to Figure 5.18, the following model, called the Nonlinear clutch and drive-shaft model, is derived.

Model 5.3 The Nonlinear Clutch and Drive-Shaft Model

$$J_m \ddot{\alpha}_{cs} = T_e - T_{fric,e} - M_{kc}(\alpha_{cs} - \alpha_t i_t) \tag{5.59}$$
$$-d_c(\dot{\alpha}_{cs} - \dot{\alpha}_t i_t)$$
$$(J_t + J_f/i_f^2)\ddot{\alpha}_t = i_t \left(M_{kc}(\alpha_{cs} - \alpha_t i_t) + d_c(\dot{\alpha}_{cs} - \dot{\alpha}_t i_t)\right) \tag{5.60}$$
$$-(d_t + d_f/i_f^2)\dot{\alpha}_t - \frac{1}{i_f}\left(k_d(\alpha_t/i_f - \alpha_w) + d_d(\dot{\alpha}_t/i_f - \dot{\alpha}_w)\right)$$
$$(J_W + mr_{eff}^2)\ddot{\alpha}_w = k_d(\alpha_t/i_f - \alpha_w) + d_d(\dot{\alpha}_t/i_f - \dot{\alpha}_w) \tag{5.61}$$
$$-(d_w + mc_{r2}r_{eff})\dot{\alpha}_w - \frac{1}{2}c_{air}A_L\rho_a r_{eff}^3\dot{\alpha}_w^2 \tag{5.62}$$
$$-r_{eff}m\left(c_{r1} + gsin(\chi_{road})\right)$$

Nonlinear driveline model with five states. (The same state-space representation as for the Clutch and drive-shaft model can be used.) The function $M_{kc}(\cdot)$ is given by (5.58). The model equipped with the sensor filter in (5.46) gives the true sensor outputs (y_m, y_t, y_w).

Parameter estimation of the Nonlinear clutch and drive-shaft model

When estimating the parameters and the initial conditions of the Nonlinear clutch and drive-shaft model, the clutch static nonlinearity is fixed with known physical values and the rest of the parameters are estimated, except for the sensor filter which is the same as in the previous model estimations.

The resulting clutch torsion ($x_1 = \alpha_{cs} - \alpha_t i_t$) and drive-shaft torsion ($x_2 = \alpha_t/i_f - \alpha_w$) are shown in Figure 5.19. The true values of these torsions are not known as mentioned before. However, the figure shows that both angles have realistic values that agree with other experience. The model output velocities ($\dot{\alpha}_{cs}$, $\dot{\alpha}_t$, $\dot{\alpha}_w$) show no improvement compared to those generated by the Drive-shaft model with sensor dynamics, displayed in Figure 5.14.

In Figure 5.15 it was seen that the model with the sensor filtering fitted the signal except for a number of time intervals with deviations. The question is if this is a result of some nonlinearity. Figure 5.20 shows the transmission speed plotted together with the model output and the clutch torsion. It is clear from this figure that the deviation between model and experiments occurs when the clutch angle passes the area with the low stiffness in the static nonlinearity (see Figure 5.18).

Results of parameter estimation

- The model including the nonlinear clutch does not improve the overall data fit for frequencies in the measured data.

- The model is able to estimate a clutch torsion with realistic values.

- The estimated clutch torsion shows that when the clutch passes the area with low stiffness in the nonlinearity, the model deviates from the data. The reason is unmodeled dynamics at low clutch torques [3].

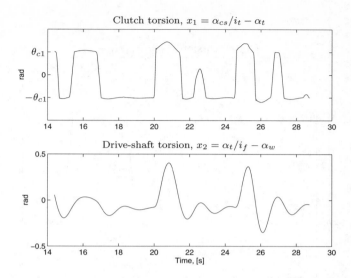

Figure 5.19 Clutch torsion (top figure) and drive-shaft torsion (bottom figure) resulting from parameter estimation of the **Nonlinear clutch and drive-shaft model** with sensor filtering, on data with gear 1. The true values of these torsions are not known, but the plots show that they have realistic values.

Model Validity

In the parameter estimation, the unknown load, l, which vary between the trials, is estimated. The load can be recalculated to estimate road slope, and the calculated values agree well with the known values of the road slopes at Scania. Furthermore, the estimation of the states describing the torsion of the clutch and the drive shaft shows realistic values. This gives further support to model structure and parameters.

The assumption about sensor dynamics in the transmission speed influencing the experiments, agrees well with the fact that the engine speed sensor and the wheel speed sensor have considerably higher bandwidth (more cogs) than the transmission speed sensor.

When estimating the parameters of the **Drive-shaft model**, there is a problem when identifying the viscous friction components d_1 and d_2. The sensitivity in the model to variations in the friction parameters is low, and the same model fit can be obtained for a range of friction parameters. However the sum $d_1 i^2 + d_2$ is constant during these tests. The problem with estimating viscous parameters will be further discussed later.

Summary of Modeling Example

Parameter estimation shows that a model with one torsional flexibility and two inertias is able to fit the measured engine speed and wheel speed in a frequency regime including the first main resonance of the driveline. By considering the difference between measured transmission speed and wheel speed it is reasonable to deduce that the main flexibility is the drive shafts.

Clutch torsion, $x_1 = \alpha_{cs}/i_t - \alpha_t$

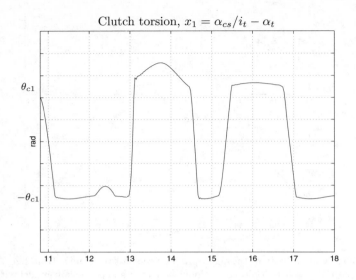

Transmission speed, $y_t = x_4/(1 + \gamma s)$ and $\dot{\alpha}_t$

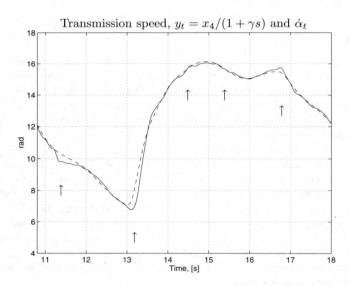

Figure 5.20 Clutch torsion (top figure) and measured and estimated transmission speeds (bottom figure) from the Nonlinear clutch and drive-shaft model with sensor dynamics with gear 1. The result is that the main differences between model (dashed) and experiments (solid) occur when the clutch torsion passes the area with the low stiffness ($|\theta| < \theta_{c1}$) in the static clutch nonlinearity.

In order for the model to also fit the measured transmission speed, a first order sensor filter is added to the model, in accordance with properties of the sensor system. It is shown that all three velocities are fitted accurately enough. Parameter estimation of a model with a nonlinear clutch explains that the difference between the measured data and the model outputs occurs when the clutch transfers zero torque.

Further supporting facts of the validity of the models are that they give values to the non-measured variables, drive shaft and clutch torsion, that agree with experience from other sources. Furthermore, the known road slopes are well estimated.

The result is a series of models that describe the driveline in increasing detail by, in each extension, adding the effect that seems to be the major cause for the deviation still left.

The result, from a user perspective, is that, within the frequency regime interesting for control design, the Drive-shaft model with some sensor dynamics gives good agreement with experiments. It is thus suitable for control design. The major deviations left are captured by the nonlinear effects in the Nonlinear clutch and drive-shaft model, which makes this model suitable for verifying simulation studies in control design.

5.2 Modeling of Neutral Gear

An important basis for design of driveline management is to understand the dynamic behavior of the driveline before and after going from a gear to neutral. This requires additional modeling of the driveline since it is separated in two parts when in neutral. Such a decoupled model is the topic of this section, together with its use for analysis of possible oscillation patterns of the decoupled driveline.

A decoupled model has several applications. It is the basis for a diagnosis system of gear-shift quality. The analysis cast light on the sometimes, at first sight, surprising oscillations that occur in an uncontrolled driveline. It is also an indication for the value of feedback control.

5.2.1 Stationary Gear-Shift Experiments

First, a series of gear-shifts with a stationary driveline are performed without using driveline torque control. This means that a speed controller controls the engine speed to a desired level, and when the driveline speeds have reached stationary levels, engagement of neutral gear is commanded. Figure 5.21 shows two of these trials where the engine speed is 1400 RPM and 2100 RPM respectively, on a flat road with gear 1. The behavior of the engine speed, the transmission speed, and the wheel speed is shown in the figure. At $t = 14$ s, a shift to neutral is commanded. A gear shift is performed by using a gear lever actuator driven by air pressure. A delay-time from commanded gear shift to activated gear-lever movement is seen in the experiments. This is a combined effect from a delay in the actuator, and a delay in building up the air pressure needed to overcome friction. This delay is longer the higher the speed is.

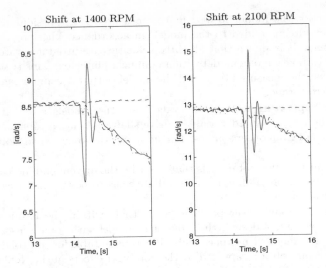

Figure 5.21 Engagement of neutral gear commanded at 14 s, with stationary driveline at 1400 RPM and 2100 RPM on a flat road with gear 1. Engine speed (dashed) and wheel speed (dash-dotted) are scaled to transmission speed which is seen in solid lines. After a delay time, neutral gear is engaged, causing the driveline speeds to oscillate. The amplitude of the oscillating transmission speed is higher the higher the speed is.

After the shift, the driveline is decoupled into two parts. The movement of the engine speed is independent of the movement of the transmission speed and the wheel speed, which are connected by the propeller shaft and the drive shaft, according to Figure 5.1. The speed controller maintains the desired engine speed also after the gear shift. The transmission speed and the wheel speed, on the other hand, are only affected by the load (rolling resistance, air drag, and road inclination), which explains the decreasing speeds in the figure.

The transient behavior of the transmission speed and the wheel speed differ however, and the energy built up in the shafts is seen to affect the transmission speed more than the wheel speed, giving an oscillating transmission speed. The higher the speed is, the higher amplitude of the oscillations is obtained. The amplitude value of the oscillations for 1400 RPM is 2.5 rad/s, and 5 rad/s for 2100 RPM.

5.2.2   Dynamical Gear-Shift Experiments

In the previous trials there was no relative speed difference, since the driveline was in a stationary mode. If a relative speed difference is present prior to the gear-shift, there will be a different type of oscillation. Figures 5.22 and 5.23 describe two trials where neutral gear is engaged with an oscillating driveline without torque control. The oscillations are a result of an engine torque pulse at 11.7 s.

There is only a small difference between the measured engine speed and transmission speed prior to the gear shift. This difference was in Chapter 5.1 explained

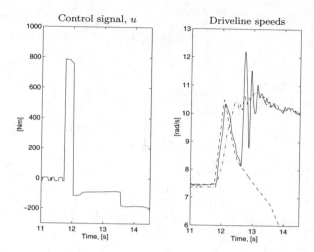

Figure 5.22 Engaged neutral gear without torque control at 12.5 s in a trial with oscillating driveline as a result of a provoking engine torque pulse at 11.7 s in the left figure. Engine speed (dashed) and wheel speed (dash-dotted) are scaled to transmission speed (solid) in the right figure. After the gear shift the transmission speed oscillates.

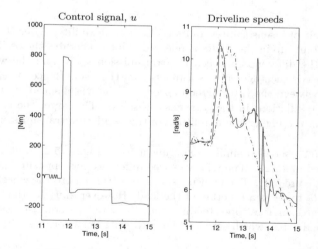

Figure 5.23 Same field trial as in Figure 5.22, but with engaged neutral gear at 13.2 s. Engine speed (dashed) and wheel speed (dash-dotted) are scaled to transmission speed (solid) in the right figure. After the gear shift the transmission speed oscillates.

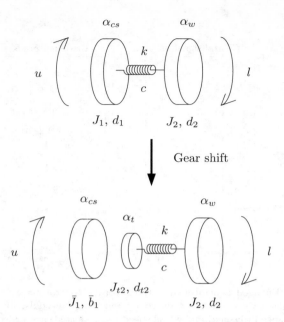

Figure 5.24 Description of how the driveline model changes after engagement of neutral gear. The first model is the Drive-shaft model, which is then separated into two sub-models when neutral gear is engaged. The left part consists of the engine and one part of the transmission. The right part of the model consists of the rest of the transmission and the drive shaft out to the wheels, called the Decoupled model.

to be a result of a sensor filter and a stiff clutch flexibility. After the gear shift, the energy built up in the shafts is released, which generates the oscillations and minimizes the difference between the transmission speed and the wheel speed. The two speeds then decrease as a function of the load. Hence, a relative speed difference between the transmission speed and the wheel speed at the shift moment gives oscillations in the transmission speed. The larger the relative speed difference is, the higher the amplitude of the oscillating transmission speed will be.

Figure 5.23 shows a similar experiment as in Figure 5.22, but with neutral gear engaged at 13.2 s. The relative speed difference has opposite sign compared to that in Figure 5.22. The transmission speed transfers to the wheel speed, and these two decrease as a function of the load. However, initially the transmission speed deviates in the opposite direction compared to how the relative speed difference indicates, which seems like a surprising behavior.

5.2.3   A Decoupled Model

A decoupled model is needed to analyze and explain the three different types of oscillations described by Figures 5.21, 5.22, and 5.23. Engaging neutral gear can be described as in Figure 5.24. Before the gear shift, the driveline dynamics is described by the Drive-shaft model. This model assumes a lumped engine and transmission inertia, as described previously. When neutral gear is engaged, the driveline is separated into two parts as indicated in the figure. The two parts move independent of each other, as mentioned before. The engine side of the model consists of the engine, the clutch, and part of the transmission (characterized by the parameters J_{t1} and d_{t1} according to Section 5.1.2). The parameters describing the lumped engine, clutch, and part of transmission are $\bar{J}_1$ and $\bar{b}_1$ according to the figure. The wheel side of the model consists of the rest of the transmission (characterized by the parameters J_{t2} and d_{t2}) and the drive-shaft flexibility out to the wheels, which is named the Decoupled model. The model is described by the following equations.

Model 5.4 The Decoupled Model

$$J_{t2}\ddot{\alpha}_t = -d_{t2}\dot{\alpha}_t - k(\alpha_t/i_f - \alpha_w)/i_f - d(\dot{\alpha}_t/i_f - \dot{\alpha}_w)/i_f \tag{5.63}$$

$$J_2\ddot{\alpha}_w = k(\alpha_t/i_f - \alpha_w) + d(\dot{\alpha}_t/i_f - \dot{\alpha}_w) - d_2\dot{\alpha}_w - l \tag{5.64}$$

The model equipped with the sensor filter in (5.46) gives the true sensor outputs (y_t, y_w).

All these parameters were estimated in Section 5.1.2, except the unknown parameters J_{t2} and d_{t2}. The model is written in state-space form by using the states x_1 = drive-shaft torsion, x_2 = transmission speed, and x_3 = wheel speed.

Note that the Decoupled model after the gear shift has the same model structure as the Drive-shaft model, but with the difference that the first inertia is considerable less in the Decoupled model, since the engine and part of the transmission are decoupled from the model.

Quality of the Decoupled Model

The unknown parameters J_{t2} and d_{t2} can be estimated if the dynamics described by the Decoupled model is excited. This is the case when engaging neutral gear at a transmission torque level different from zero, giving oscillations. One such case is seen in Figure 5.25, where the oscillating transmission speed is seen together with the Decoupled model with estimated parameters J_{t2} and d_{t2}, and initial drive-shaft torsion, x_{10}. The rest of the parameters are the same as in the Drive-shaft model, which were estimated in Section 5.1.2. The rest of the initial condition of the states (transmission speed and wheel speed) are the measured values at the time for the gear shift. The model output (y_t and y_w with sensor filter) are fitted to the measured transmission speed and wheel speed. The conclusion is that the Decoupled model is able to capture the main resonance in the oscillating transmission speed.

If the initial states (drive-shaft torsion, transmission speed, and wheel speed) of the Decoupled model are known at the time for engaging neutral gear, the behavior of the speeds after the shift can be predicted.

The different characteristic oscillations seen in the experiments after engaged neutral gear are explained by the value of the drive-shaft torsion and the relative speed difference at the time of engagement. The Decoupled model can be used to

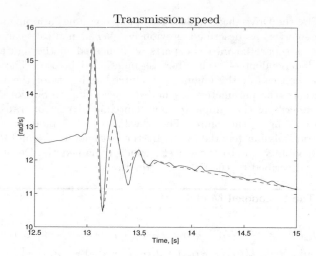

Figure 5.25 Measured oscillations after a gear shift at 13.0 s in solid line. The outputs of the Decoupled model are fitted to data, shown in dashed line. The Decoupled model is able to capture the main resonance in the oscillating transmission speed after the gear shift.

predict the behavior of the driveline speeds if these initial variables are known. The demonstration of problems with an uncontrolled driveline motivates the need for feedback control in order to minimize the oscillations after a gear shift.

5.3   Driveline Control

There are two types of variables that are of special interest in driveline control:

- (rotational) velocities

- torques

Since the parts of a vehicular driveline (engine, clutch, transmission, shafts, and wheels) are elastic, velocities and torques differ along the driveline. It also means that mechanical resonances may occur. The handling of such resonances is basic for functionality and driveability, but is also important for reducing mechanical stress and noise. New driveline-management applications and high-powered engines increase the need for strategies for how to apply engine torque in an optimal way.

Two important applications for driveline control are

- driveline speed control

- driveline control for gear shifting

These two applications will be treated in the following chapters. The first application is important to handle wheel-speed oscillations following from a change in accelerator pedal position or from impulses from towed trailers and road roughness, known as vehicle shuffle.

The second application, driveline control for gear shifting, is used to implement automatic gear shifting. In todays traffic it is desired to have an automatic gear shifting system on heavy trucks. One approach at the leading edge of technology is gear shifting by engine control [58]. With this approach, disengaging the clutch is replaced by controlling the engine to a state where the transmission transfers zero torque, and by that realizing a virtual clutch. After neutral gear is engaged, the engine speed is controlled to a speed such that the new gear can be engaged. The gear shifting system uses a manual transmission with automated gear lever, and a normal friction clutch that is engaged only at start and stop.

The total time needed for a gear shift is an important quality measure. One reason for this is that the vehicle is free-rolling, since there is no driving torque, which may be serious with heavy loads and large road slopes. The difference in engine torque before a gear shift and at the state where the transmission transfers zero torque is often large. Normally, this torque difference is driven to zero by sliding the clutch. With gear shifting by engine control, the aim is to decrease the time needed for this phase by using engine control. However, a fast step in engine torque may lead to excited driveline resonances. If these resonances are not damped, the time to engage neutral gear increases, since one has to wait for satisfactory gear-shift conditions. Furthermore, engaging neutral gear at a non-zero transmission torque results in oscillations in the transmission speed, which is disturbing for the driver, and increases the time needed to engage the new gear. These problems motivate the need for using feedback control in order to reach zero transmission torque. Two major problems must be addressed to obtain this. First, the transmission torque must be estimated and validated. Then a strategy must be derived that drives this torque to zero with damped driveline resonances.

5.3.1 Background

Fuel-Injection Strategy for Speed Control

As described in the previous chapter, fuel-injection strategy can be of torque control type or speed control type. For diesel engines, speed control is often referred to as RQV control, and torque control referred to as RQ control [5]. With RQ control, the driver's accelerator pedal position is interpreted as a desired engine torque, and with RQV control the accelerator position is interpreted as a desired engine speed. RQV control is essentially a proportional controller calculating the fuel amount as function of the difference between the desired speed set by the driver and the actual measured engine speed. The reason for this controller structure is the traditionally used mechanical centrifugal governor for diesel pump control [5]. This means that the controller will maintain the speed demanded by the driver, but with a stationary error (velocity lag), which is a function of the controller gain and the load (rolling resistance, air drag, and road inclination). With a cruise controller, the stationary error is compensated for, which means that the vehicle will maintain the same speed independent of load changes. This requires an integral part of the controller which is not used in the RQV control concept.

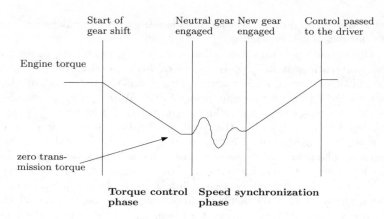

Figure 5.26 Engine torque during the different phases in automatic gear shifting by engine control. The engine torque is controlled to a state where the transmission transfers zero torque, whereafter neutral gear is engaged without using the clutch. After the speed synchronization phase, the new gear is engaged, and control is transferred back to the driver.

Automatic Gear Shifting in Heavy Trucks

Traditionally a gear shift is performed by disengaging the clutch, engaging neutral gear, shifting to a new gear, and engaging the clutch again. In todays traffic it is desired to have an automatic gear shifting system on heavy trucks. The following three approaches are used:

Automatic transmission This approach is seldom used for the heaviest trucks, due to expensive transmissions and problems with short life time. Another drawback is the efficiency loss compared to manual transmissions.

Manual transmission and automatic clutch A quite common approach, which needs an automatic clutch system [56]. This system has to be made robust against clutch wear.

Manual transmission with gear shifting by engine control With this approach the automatic clutch is replaced by engine control, realizing a virtual clutch. The only addition needed to a standard manual transmission is an actuator to move the gear lever. Lower cost and higher efficiency characterize this solution.

With this last approach a gear shift includes the phases described in Figure 5.26, where the engine torque during the shift event is shown.

5.3.2 Field Trials for Problem Demonstration

A number of field trials are performed in order to describe how driveline resonances influence driveline management.

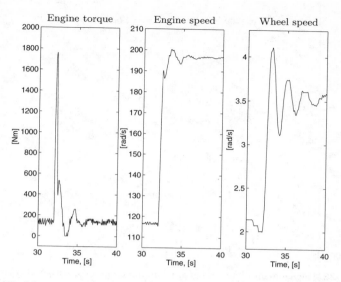

Figure 5.27 Measured speed response of a step in accelerator position at t=32 s. An RQV speed controller controls the engine speed to 2000 RPM. The engine speed is well damped, but the resonances in the driveline is seen to give oscillating wheel speed, resulting in vehicle shuffle.

Driveline speed control

A specific example of how the RQV speed controller performs is seen in Figure 5.27. The figure shows how the measured engine speed and wheel speed respond to a step input in accelerator position. It is seen how the engine speed is well behaved with no oscillations. With a stiff driveline this would be equivalent with also having well damped wheel speed. The more flexible the driveline is, the less sufficient a well damped engine speed is, since the flexibility of the driveline will lead to oscillations in the wheel speed. This will be further discussed and demonstrated in later chapters.

If it is desired to decrease the response time of the RQV controller (i.e., increase the bandwidth), the controller gain must be increased. Then the amplitude of the oscillations in the wheel speed will be higher.

Driveline torque control

When using gear shifting by engine control, the phases in Figure 5.26 are accomplished. First, control is transferred from the driver to the control unit, entering the *torque control phase*. The engine is controlled to a torque level corresponding to zero transferred torque in the transmission. After neutral gear is engaged, the *speed synchronization phase* is entered. Then the engine speed is controlled to track the transmission speed (scaled with the conversion ratio of the new gear), whereafter the new gear is engaged. Finally, the torque level is transferred back to the level that the driver demands.

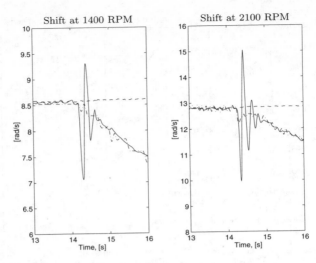

Figure 5.28 Engagement of neutral gear commanded at 14 s, with stationary driveline at 1400 RPM and 2100 RPM on a flat road with gear 1. The engine speed (dashed) and wheel speed (dash-dotted) are scaled to transmission speed (solid) with the conversion ratio of the driveline. After a short delay time, neutral gear is engaged, causing the driveline speeds to oscillate. The amplitude of the oscillating transmission speed is higher the higher the stationary speed is.

The total time needed for a gear shift is important to minimize, since the vehicle is free-rolling with zero transmission torque. In Figure 5.28, neutral gear is engaged, without a torque control phase, at a constant speed. This means that there is a driving torque transferred in the transmission, which clearly causes the transmission speed to oscillate. The amplitude of the oscillations is increasing the higher the stationary speed is. This indicates that there must be an engine torque step in order to reach zero transmission torque and no oscillations in the transmission speed.

Figure 5.29 shows the transmission speed when the engine torque is decreased to 46 Nm at 12.0 s. Prior to that, the stationary speed 2200 RPM was maintained, which requested an engine torque of about 225 Nm. Four trials are performed with this torque profile with engaged neutral gear at different time delays after the torque step. After 12.4 s there is a small oscillation in the transmission speed, after 13.3 s and 14.8 s there are oscillations with high amplitude, and at 13.8 s there are no oscillations in the transmissions speed. This indicates how driveline resonances influence the transmission torque, which is clearly close to zero for the gear shift at 12.4 s and 13.8 s, but different from zero at 13.3 s and 14.8 s. The amplitude of the oscillating transmission torque will be higher if the stationary speed is increased or if the vehicle is accelerating.

One way this can be handled is to use a ramp in engine torque according to the scheme in Figure 5.26. However, this approach is no good for optimizing shift time, since the ramp must be conservative in order to wait until the transmission torque fluctuations are damped out.

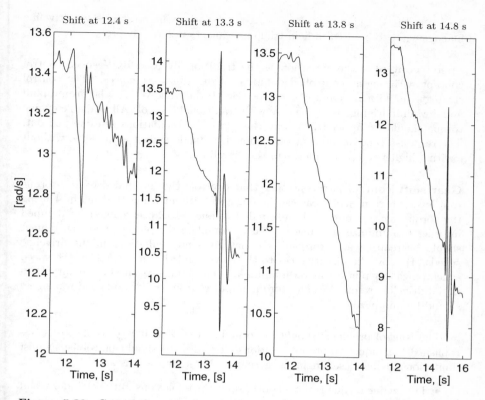

Figure 5.29 Gear shifts with the engine at the stationary speed 2200 RPM with gear 1. At 12.0 s there is a decrease in engine torque to 46 Nm in order to reach zero transmission torque. The transmission speed is plotted when neutral gear is engaged at 12.4 s, 13.3 s, 13.8 s, and 14.8 s (with the same torque profile). The different amplitudes in the oscillations show how the torque transmitted in the transmission is oscillating after the torque step. Note that the range of the vertical axes differ between the plots.

The gear shift at 13.3 s in Figure 5.29 shows the effect of a gear shift at a transmission torque different from zero. This leads to the following problems:

- Disturbing to the driver, both in terms of noise and speed impulse.

- Increased wear on transmission.

- Increased time for the speed synchronization phase, since the transmission speed, which is the control goal, is oscillating. The oscillations are difficult to track for the engine and therefore one has to wait until they are sufficiently damped.

5.3.3 Goals of Driveline Control

Based on the field-trial demonstration of problems with driveline handling, the goals for reducing the influence from oscillations in performance and driveability are outlined. These will be the basis when deriving strategies for driveline management, to be used in field-trial experiments in later chapters.

Speed control is the extension of the traditionally used RQV speed control concept with engine controlled damping of driveline resonances. The control strategy should maintain a desired speed with the same velocity lag from uphill and downhill driving, as in the case with traditional control. All available engine torque should be applied in a way that driveline oscillations are damped out. The response time of the controller should be made as fast as possible without exciting higher resonance modes of the driveline.

Gear-shift control is a controller that controls the internal driveline torque to a level where neutral gear can be engaged without using the clutch. During the torque control phase, the excited driveline resonances should be damped in order to minimize the time needed to complete the phase. The engagement should be realized at a torque level that gives no oscillations in the driveline speeds. Hereby, the disturbances to the driver and the time spent in the speed synchronization phase can be minimized. The influence on shift quality from initial driveline resonances and torque impulses from trailer and road roughness should be minimized.

The control problems should be formulated so that it is possible to use established techniques to obtain solutions. The designs should be robust against limitations in the diesel engine as actuator. These limitations are:

- The engine torque is not smooth, since the explosions in the cylinder result in a pulsating engine torque.

- The output torque of the engine is not exactly known. The only measure of it is a static torque map from dynamometer tests.

- The dynamical behavior of the engine is also characterized by the engine friction, which must be estimated. Many variables influence engine friction and it is necessary to find a simple yet sufficiently detailed model of the friction.

- The engine output torque is limited in different modes of operation. The maximum engine torque is restricted as a function of the engine speed, and the torque level is also restricted at low turbo pressures.

The resulting strategies should be possible to implement on both in-line pump and unit pump injection engines, with standard automotive driveline sensors.

5.3.4   Comment on Architectures for Driveline Control

There is one architectural issue in driveline control that should be noted. There are different possible choices in driveline control between using different sensor locations, since the driveline normally is equipped with at least two sensors for rotational speed, but sometimes more. If the driveline was rigid, the choice of sensor would not matter, since the sensor outputs would differ only by a scaling factor. However, it will be demonstrated that the presence of torsional flexibilities implies that sensor choice gives different control problems. The difference can be formulated in control theoretic terms e.g., by saying that the poles are the same, but the zeros differ both in number and values. A principle study should not be understood as a study on where to put a single sensor. Instead, it aims at an understanding of where to invest in increased sensor performance in future driveline management systems. This issue will also be investigated in later design chapters.

5.3.5 State-Space Formulation

The input to the open-loop driveline system is $u = T_e - T_{fric,e}$, i.e., the difference between the driving torque and the friction torque. Possible physical state variables in the models of Chapter 5.1 are torques, angle differences, and angle velocity of any inertia. The angle difference of each torsional flexibility and the angle velocity of each inertia are used as state variables. The state space representation is

$$\dot{\underline{x}} = \underline{A}\underline{x} + \underline{B}u + \underline{H}l \tag{5.65}$$

where $\underline{A}$, $\underline{B}$, $\underline{H}$, $\underline{x}$, and l are defined next for the Drive-shaft model and for the Clutch and drive-shaft model defined in Chapter 5.1.

State-space formulation of the linear Drive-shaft model:

$$
\begin{aligned}
x_1 &= \alpha_{cs}/i_t i_f - \alpha_w \\
x_2 &= \dot{\alpha}_{cs} \\
x_3 &= \dot{\alpha}_w \\
l &= r_{eff} m \left(c_{r1} + g \sin(\chi_{road}) \right)
\end{aligned} \tag{5.66}
$$

giving

$$
\underline{A} = \begin{pmatrix}
0 & 1/i & -1 \\
-k/iJ_1 & -(d_1 + d/i^2)/J_1 & d/iJ_1 \\
k/J_2 & d/iJ_2 & -(d + d_2)/J_2
\end{pmatrix}, \tag{5.67}
$$

$$
\underline{B} = \begin{pmatrix} 0 \\ 1/J_1 \\ 0 \end{pmatrix}, \quad
\underline{H} = \begin{pmatrix} 0 \\ 0 \\ -1/J_2 \end{pmatrix} \tag{5.68}
$$

where

$$
\begin{aligned}
i &= i_t i_f \\
J_1 &= J_m + J_t/i_t^2 + J_f/i_t^2 i_f^2 \\
J_2 &= J_W + m r_{eff}^2 \\
d_1 &= d_t/i_t^2 + d_f/i_t^2 i_f^2 \\
d_2 &= d_w + m c_{r2} r_{eff}^2
\end{aligned} \tag{5.69}
$$

State-space formulation of the linear Clutch and drive-shaft model:

$$
\begin{aligned}
x_1 &= \alpha_{cs} - \alpha_t i_t \\
x_2 &= \alpha_t/i_f - \alpha_w \\
x_3 &= \dot{\alpha}_{cs} \\
x_4 &= \dot{\alpha}_t \\
x_5 &= \dot{\alpha}_w
\end{aligned}
\tag{5.70}
$$

$\underline{A}$ is given by the matrix

$$
\begin{pmatrix}
0 & 0 & 1 & -i_t & 0 \\
0 & 0 & 0 & 1/i_f & -1 \\
-k_c/J_1 & 0 & -d_c/J_1 & d_c i_t/J_1 & 0 \\
k_c i_t/J_2 & -k_d/i_f J_2 & d_c i_t/J_2 & -(d_c i_t^2 + d_2 + d_d/i_f^2)/J_2 & d_d/i_f J_2 \\
0 & k_d/J_3 & 0 & d_d/i_f J_3 & -(d_3 + d_d)/J_3
\end{pmatrix}
$$

and

$$
\underline{B} = \begin{pmatrix} 0 \\ 0 \\ 1/J_1 \\ 0 \\ 0 \end{pmatrix}, \quad
\underline{H} = \begin{pmatrix} 0 \\ 0 \\ 0 \\ 0 \\ -1/J_2 \end{pmatrix}
\tag{5.71}
$$

where

$$
\begin{aligned}
J_1 &= J_m \\
J_2 &= J_t + J_f/i_f^2 \\
J_2 &= J_W + m r_{eff}^2 \\
d_2 &= d_t + d_f/i_f^2 \\
d_3 &= d_w + c_{r2} r_{eff}
\end{aligned}
\tag{5.72}
$$

The model equipped with the sensor filter derived in (5.46) gives the true sensor outputs (y_m, y_t, y_w), according to Chapter 5.1.

Disturbance Description

The influence from the road is assumed to be described by the slow-varying load l and an additive disturbance v. A second disturbance n is a disturbance acting on the input of the system. This disturbance is considered because the firing pulses in the driving torque can be seen as an additive disturbance acting on the input. The state-space description then becomes

$$
\underline{\dot{x}} = \underline{A}\,\underline{x} + \underline{B}\,u + \underline{B}\,n + \underline{H}\,l + \underline{H}\,v
\tag{5.73}
$$

with $\underline{x}, \underline{A}, \underline{B}, \underline{H}$, and l defined in (5.66) to (5.69) or in (5.70) to (5.72), depending on model choice.

Measurement Description

For controller synthesis it is of fundamental interest which physical variables of the process that can be measured. In the case of a vehicular driveline the normal sensor alternative is an inductive sensor mounted on a cogwheel measuring the angle, as mentioned before. Sensors that measure torque are expensive, and are seldom used in production vehicular applications.

The output of the process is defined as a combination of the states given by the matrix $\underline{\mathbf{C}}$ in

$$y = \underline{\mathbf{C}} x + e \tag{5.74}$$

where e is a measurement disturbance.

In this work, only angle velocity sensors are considered, and therefore, the output of the process is one/some of the state variables defining an angle velocity. Especially, the following C-matrices are defined (corresponding to a sensor on $\dot{\alpha}_{cs}$ and $\dot{\alpha}_w$ for the Drive-shaft model).

$$\underline{\mathbf{C}}_m = (0\ 1\ 0) \tag{5.75}$$
$$\underline{\mathbf{C}}_w = (0\ 0\ 1) \tag{5.76}$$

5.3.6 Controller Formulation

The performance output z is the combination of states that has requirements to behave in a certain way. This combination is described by the matrices M and D in the following way

$$z = \underline{\mathbf{M}} x + Du \tag{5.77}$$

The resulting control problem can be seen in Figure 5.30. The unknown controllers F_r and F_y are to be designed so that the performance output (5.77) meets its requirements (defined later).

If state-feedback controllers are used, the control signal u is a linear function of the states (if they are all measured) or else the state estimates, $\hat{x}$, which are obtained from a Kalman filter. The control signal is described by

$$u = l_0 r - \underline{\mathbf{K}}_c \hat{x} \tag{5.78}$$

where r represents the commanded signal with the gain l_0, and K_c is the state-feedback matrix. The equations describing the Kalman filter is

$$\dot{\hat{\mathbf{x}}} = \underline{\mathbf{A}}\,\hat{\mathbf{x}} + \underline{\mathbf{B}}\,u + \underline{\mathbf{K}}_f(y - \underline{\mathbf{C}}\,\hat{\mathbf{x}}) \tag{5.79}$$

where $\underline{\mathbf{K}}_f$ is the Kalman gain.

Identifying the matrices $F_r(s)$ and $F_y(s)$ in Figure 5.30 gives

$$F_y(s) = \underline{\mathbf{K}}_c(s\underline{\mathbf{I}} - \underline{\mathbf{A}} + \underline{\mathbf{B}}\,\underline{\mathbf{K}}_c + \underline{\mathbf{K}}_f\underline{\mathbf{C}})^{-1}\underline{\mathbf{K}}_f \tag{5.80}$$
$$F_r(s) = l_0\left(1 - \underline{\mathbf{K}}_c(s\underline{\mathbf{I}} - \underline{\mathbf{A}} + \underline{\mathbf{B}}\,\underline{\mathbf{K}}_c + \underline{\mathbf{K}}_f\underline{\mathbf{C}})^{-1}\underline{\mathbf{B}}\right)$$

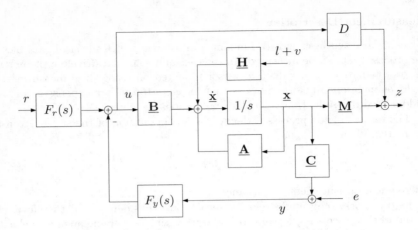

Figure 5.30 Plant and controllers F_r and F_y.

The closed-loop transfer functions from r, v, and e to the control signal u are given by

$$G_{ru} = \left(\mathbf{I} - \mathbf{K}_c(s\mathbf{I} - \mathbf{A} + \mathbf{B}\,\mathbf{K}_c)^{-1}\mathbf{B}\right) l_0 \qquad (5.81)$$

$$G_{vu} = \mathbf{K}_c(s\mathbf{I} - \mathbf{A} + \mathbf{K}_f\mathbf{C})^{-1}N - \mathbf{K}_c(s\mathbf{I} - \mathbf{A} + \mathbf{B}\,\mathbf{K}_c)^{-1}N \qquad (5.82)$$
$$\quad -\mathbf{K}_c(s\mathbf{I} - \mathbf{A} + \mathbf{B}\,\mathbf{K}_c)^{-1}\mathbf{B}\,\mathbf{K}_c(s\mathbf{I} - \mathbf{A} + \mathbf{K}_f\mathbf{C})^{-1}N$$

$$G_{eu} = \mathbf{K}_c\left((s\mathbf{I} - \mathbf{A} + \mathbf{B}\,\mathbf{K}_c)^{-1}\mathbf{B}\,\mathbf{K}_c - I\right)(s\mathbf{I} - \mathbf{A} + \mathbf{K}_f\mathbf{C})^{-1}\mathbf{K}_f \quad (5.83)$$

The transfer functions to the performance output z are given by

$$G_{rz} = (\mathbf{M}(s\mathbf{I} - \mathbf{A})^{-1}\mathbf{B} + D)G_{ru} \qquad (5.84)$$

$$G_{vz} = \mathbf{M}(s\mathbf{I} - \mathbf{A} + \mathbf{B}\,\mathbf{K}_c)^{-1}\mathbf{B}\,\mathbf{K}_c(s\mathbf{I} - \mathbf{A} + \mathbf{K}_f\mathbf{C})^{-1}N \qquad (5.85)$$
$$\quad +\mathbf{M}(s\mathbf{I} - \mathbf{A} + \mathbf{B}\,\mathbf{K}_c)^{-1}N + DG_{vu}$$

$$G_{ez} = (\mathbf{M}(s\mathbf{I} - \mathbf{A})^{-1}\mathbf{B} + D)G_{vu} \qquad (5.86)$$

Two return ratios (loop gains) result, which characterize the closed-loop behavior at the plant output and input respectively

$$GF_y = \mathbf{C}(s\mathbf{I} - \mathbf{A})^{-1}\mathbf{B}\,F_y \qquad (5.87)$$

$$F_yG = F_y\mathbf{C}(s\mathbf{I} - \mathbf{A})^{-1}\mathbf{B} \qquad (5.88)$$

When only one sensor is used, these return ratios are scalar and thus equal.

5.3.7 Some Feedback Properties

The performance output when controlling the driveline to a certain speed is the velocity of the wheel, defined as

$$z = \dot{\alpha}_w = \mathbf{C}_w x \qquad (5.89)$$

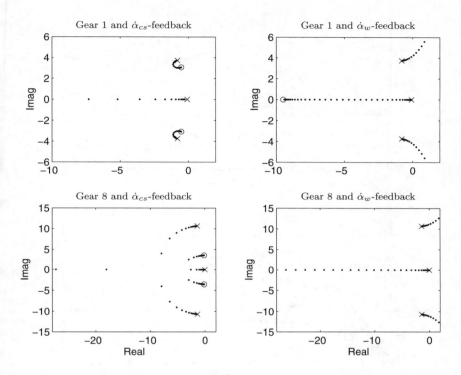

Figure 5.31 Root locus with respect to a P-controller gain, for gear 1 (top figures) and gear 8 (bottom figures), with sensor on $\dot{\alpha}_{cs}$ (left figures), or $\dot{\alpha}_w$ (right figures). The cross represent the open-loop poles, while the rings represent the open-loop zeros. The system goes unstable when the $\dot{\alpha}_w$-gain is increased, but is stable for all $\dot{\alpha}_{cs}$-gains.

When studying the closed-loop control problem with a sensor on $\dot{\alpha}_{cs}$ or $\dot{\alpha}_w$, two different control problems result. Figure 5.31 shows a root locus with respect to a P-controller gain for two gears using velocity sensor $\dot{\alpha}_{cs}$ and $\dot{\alpha}_w$ respectively. The open-loop transfer functions from control signal to engine speed G_{um} has three poles and two zeros, as can be seen in Figure 5.31. G_{uw} on the other hand has one zero and the same poles. Hence, the relative degree [34] of G_{um} is one and G_{uw} has a relative degree of two. This means that when $\dot{\alpha}_w$-feedback is used, and the gain is increased, two poles must go to infinity which makes the system unstable. When the velocity sensor $\dot{\alpha}_{cs}$ is used, the relative degree is one, and the closed-loop system is stable for all gains. (Remember that $\dot{\alpha}_w$ is the performance output and thus desirable to use.)

The same effect can be seen in step response tests when the P-controller is used. Figure 5.32 demonstrates the problem with resonances that occur with increasing gain for the two cases of feedback. When the engine-speed sensor is used, the engine speed is well damped when the gain is increased, but the resonance in the drive shaft makes the wheel speed oscillate. When using $\dot{\alpha}_w$-

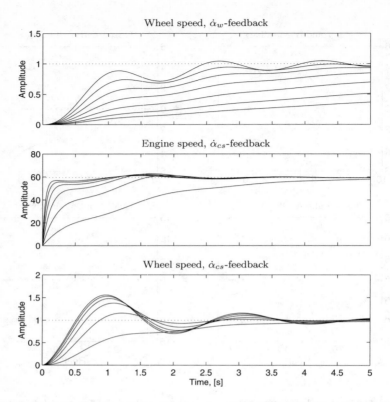

Figure 5.32 Step responses when using a P-controller with different gains on the Drive-shaft model with gear 1. With $\dot{\alpha}_w$-feedback (top figure), increased gain results in instability. With $\dot{\alpha}_{cs}$-feedback (bottom figures), increased gain results in a well damped engine speed, but an oscillating wheel speed.

feedback it is difficult to increase the bandwidth, since the poles moves closer to the imaginary axis, and give a resonant system.

The characteristic results in Figures 5.31 and 5.32 only depend on the relative degree, and are thus parameter independent. However, this observation may depend on feedback structure, and therefore a more detailed analysis is performed in the following section.

5.3.8   Driveline Control with LQG/LTR

Different sensor locations result in different control problems with different inherent characteristics, as illustrated in the previous section. The topic of this section is to show how this influences control design when using Linear Quadratic design with Loop Transfer Recovery (LQG/LTR) with design of the return ratio at the output of the plant [48].

Important comment: LQG/LTR is *one* method to obtain the parameters in a controller structure with state feedback using an observer. Even if the method is unknown to the reader, the presentation should be easy to follow if the reader has a basic course in control and accepts that LQG/LTR is a method to compute l_0, $\mathbf{K}_c$, and $\mathbf{K}_f$ in Eq. 5.78 and Eq. 5.79.

The reason for using LQG/LTR, in this principle study, is that it offers a control design method resulting in a controller and observer of the same order as the plant model, and it is also an easy method for obtaining robust controllers.

Transfer Functions

When comparing the control problem of using $\dot{\alpha}_{cs}$ or $\dot{\alpha}_w$ as sensor, the open-loop transfer functions G_{um} and G_{uw} results. These have the same number of poles but different number of zeros, as mentioned before. Two different closed-loop systems are obtained depending on which sensor that is being used.

Feedback from $\dot{\alpha}_w$

A natural feedback configuration is to use the performance output, $\dot{\alpha}_w$. Then among others the following transfer functions result

$$G_{rz} = \frac{G_{uw} F_y F_r}{1 + G_{uw} F_y} = T_w F_r \tag{5.90}$$

$$G_{nu} = \frac{1}{1 + G_{uw} F_y} = S_w \tag{5.91}$$

where (5.81) to (5.86) are used together with the matrix inversion lemma [34], and n is the input disturbance. The transfer functions S_w and T_w are the *sensitivity* function and the *complementary sensitivity* function [48]. The relation between these transfer function is, as usual,

$$S_w + T_w = 1 \tag{5.92}$$

Feedback from $\dot{\alpha}_{cs}$

The following transfer functions result if the $\dot{\alpha}_{cs}$-sensor is used.

$$G_{rz} = \frac{G_{uw} F_y F_r}{1 + G_{um} F_y} \tag{5.93}$$

$$G_{nu} = \frac{1}{1 + G_{um} F_y} \tag{5.94}$$

The difference between the two feedback configurations is that the return difference is $1 + G_{uw} F_y$ or $1 + G_{um} F_y$.

It is desirable to have sensitivity functions that corresponds to $y = \dot{\alpha}_{cs}$ and $z = \dot{\alpha}_w$. The following transfer functions are defined

$$S_m = \frac{1}{1 + G_{um} F_y}, \quad T_m = \frac{G_{um} F_y}{1 + G_{um} F_y} \tag{5.95}$$

These transfer functions correspond to a configuration where $\dot{\alpha}_{cs}$ is the output (i.e. $y = z = \dot{\alpha}_{cs}$). Using (5.93) it is natural to define $\overline{T}_m$ by

$$\overline{T}_m = \frac{G_{uw}F_y}{1 + G_{um}F_y} = T_m \frac{G_{uw}}{G_{um}} \qquad (5.96)$$

The functions S_m and $\overline{T}_m$ describe the design problem when feedback from α_{cs} is used.

When combining (5.95) and (5.96), the corresponding relation to (5.92) is

$$S_m + \overline{T}_m \frac{G_{um}}{G_{uw}} = 1 \qquad (5.97)$$

If S_m is made zero for some frequencies in (5.97), then $\overline{T}_m$ will not be equal to one, as in (5.92). Instead, $\overline{T}_m = G_{uw}/G_{um}$ for these frequency domains.

Limitations on Performance

The relations (5.92) and (5.97) will be the fundamental relations for discussing design considerations. The impact of the ratio G_{uw}/G_{um} will be analyzed in the following sections.

Definition 5.1 $\overline{T}_m$ in (5.96) is the modified complementary sensitivity function. $G_{w/m} = G_{uw}/G_{um}$ is the dynamic output ratio.

Design Example with a Simple Mass-Spring Model

Linear Quadratic Design with Loop-Transfer Recovery will be treated in four cases, being combinations of two sensor locations, $\dot{\alpha}_{cs}$ or $\dot{\alpha}_w$, and two models with the same structure, but with different parameters. Design without pre-filter ($F_r = 1$) is considered.

The section covers a general plant with n inertias connected by $k - 1$ torsional flexibilities, without damping and load, and with unit conversion ratio. There are $(2n - 1)$ poles, and the location of the poles is the same for the different sensor locations. The number of zeros depends on which sensor that is used, and when using $\dot{\alpha}_w$ there are no zeros. When using feedback from $\dot{\alpha}_{cs}$ there are $(2n - 2)$ zeros. Thus, the transfer functions G_{um} and G_{uw}, have the same denominators, and a relative degree of 1 and $(2n - 1)$ respectively.

Structural Properties of Sensor Location

The controller (5.80) has a relative degree of one. The relative degree of $G_{um}F_y$ is thus 2, and the relative degree of $G_{uw}F_y$ is $2n$. When considering design, a good alternative is to have relative degree one in GF_y, implying infinite gain margin and high phase margin.

When using $G_{um}F_y$, one pole has to be moved to infinity, and when using $G_{uw}F_y$, $2n-1$ poles have to be moved to infinity, in order for the ratio to resemble a first order system at high frequencies.

When the return ratio behaves like a first order system, also the closed-loop transfer function behaves like a first order system. This conflicts with the design goal of having a steep roll-off rate for the closed-loop system in order to attenuate measurement noise. Hence, there is a trade-off when using $\dot{\alpha}_w$-feedback.

When using $\dot{\alpha}_{cs}$-feedback, there is no trade-off, since the relative degree of G_{um} is one.

Structure of $G_{w/m}$

We have in the previous simple examples seen that the relative degree and the zeros are important. The dynamic output ratio contains exactly this information and nothing else.

For low frequencies the dynamic output ratio has gain equal to one,

$$\left| G_{w/m}(0) \right| = 1$$

(if the conversion ratio is equal to one). Furthermore, $G_{w/m}$ has a relative degree of $2n - 2$ and thus, a high frequency gain roll-off rate of $20(2n - 2)$ dB/decade. Hence, the dynamic output ratio gives the closed-loop transfer function $\overline{T}_m$ a high frequency gain roll-off rate of $q_m + 20(2n - 2)$ dB/decade, where q_m is the roll-off rate of $G_{um}F_y$. When using $\dot{\alpha}_w$-feedback, T_w will have the same roll-off rate as $G_{uw}F_y$.

Parametric properties of $G_{w/m}$

Typical parametric properties of $G_{w/m}$ can be seen in the following example.

Example 5.1 *Two different plants of the form (5.66) to (5.69) are considered with the following values:*
a) $J_1 = 0.0974$, $J_2 = 0.0280$, $k = 2.80$, $c = 0$, $d_1 = 0.0244$, $d_2 = 0.566$, $l = 0$.
b) $J_1 = 0.0974$, $J_2 = 0.220$, $k = 5.50$, $c = 0$, $d_1 = 1.70$, $d_2 = 0.660$, $l = 0$.
with labels according to the state-space formulation in Section 5.3.5. The shape of $G_{w/m}$ can be seen in Figure 5.33. The rest of the chapter will focus on control design of these two plant models.

LQG Designs

Integral action is included by augmenting the state to attenuate step disturbances in v [48]. The state-space realization $\mathbf{A}_a$, $\mathbf{B}_a$, $\mathbf{M}_a$, $\mathbf{C}_{wa}$, and $\mathbf{C}_{ma}$ results. The Kalman-filter gain, $\mathbf{K}_f$, is derived by solving the Riccati equation [48]

$$\underline{\mathbf{P}}_f\mathbf{A}^T + \underline{\mathbf{A}}\underline{\mathbf{P}}_f - \underline{\mathbf{P}}_f\underline{\mathbf{C}}^T\underline{\mathbf{V}}^{-1}\underline{\mathbf{C}}\underline{\mathbf{P}}_f + \underline{\mathbf{B}}W\underline{\mathbf{B}}^T = 0 \qquad (5.98)$$

The covariances W and $\underline{\mathbf{V}}$, for disturbances v and e respectively, are adjusted until the return ratio

$$\underline{\mathbf{C}}(s\underline{\mathbf{I}} - \underline{\mathbf{A}})^{-1}\underline{\mathbf{K}}_f, \qquad \underline{\mathbf{K}}_f = \underline{\mathbf{P}}_f\underline{\mathbf{C}}^T\underline{\mathbf{V}}^{-1} \qquad (5.99)$$

and the closed-loop transfer functions S and T show satisfactory performance. The Nyquist locus remains outside the unit circle centered at -1. This means that there is infinite gain margin, and a phase margin of at least $60°$. Furthermore, the relative degree is one, and $|S| \leq 1$.

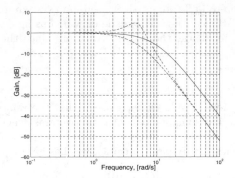

Figure 5.33 Dynamic output ratio $G_{w/m}$ for Example 5.1a (solid line) and Example 5.1b (dashed line).

Design for $\dot{\alpha}_w$-feedback. W is adjusted (and thus $F_y(s)$) such that S_w and T_w show satisfactory performance, and that the desired bandwidth is obtained. The design of the driveline models in Example 5.1 is shown in Figure 5.34. Note that the roll-off rate of T_w is 20 dB/decade.

Design for $\dot{\alpha}_{cs}$-feedback. W is adjusted (and thus $F_y(s)$) so that S_m and T_m (and thus $\dot{\alpha}_{cs}$) show satisfactory performance. Depending on the shape of $G_{w/m}$ for middle high frequencies, corrections in W must be taken so that $\overline{T}_m$ achieves the desired bandwidth. If there is a resonance peak in $G_{w/m}$, the bandwidth in $\overline{T}_m$ is chosen such that the peak is suppressed. Figure 5.34 shows such an example (the plant in Example 5.1b with $\dot{\alpha}_{cs}$-feedback), where the bandwidth is lower in order to suppress the peak in $G_{w/m}$. Note also the difference between S_w and S_m.

The parameters of the dynamic output ratio are thus important in the LQG step of the design.

Loop-Transfer Recovery, LTR

The next step in the design process is to include $\underline{\mathbf{K}}_c$, and recover the satisfactory return ratio obtained previously. When using the combined state feedback and Kalman filter, the return ratio is $GF_y = \underline{\mathbf{C}}(s\mathbf{I} - \underline{\mathbf{A}})^{-1}\underline{\mathbf{B}}\underline{\mathbf{K}}_c(s\mathbf{I} - \underline{\mathbf{A}} + \underline{\mathbf{B}}\underline{\mathbf{K}}_c + \underline{\mathbf{K}}_f\underline{\mathbf{C}})^{-1}\underline{\mathbf{K}}_f$. A simplistic LTR can be obtained by using $\underline{\mathbf{K}}_c = \rho C$ and increasing ρ. As ρ is increased, $2n - 1$ poles move towards the open system zeros. The remaining poles move towards infinity (compare to Section 5.3.5). If the Riccati equation

$$\underline{\mathbf{A}}^T\underline{\mathbf{P}}_c + \underline{\mathbf{P}}_c\underline{\mathbf{A}} - \underline{\mathbf{P}}_c\underline{\mathbf{B}}R^{-1}\underline{\mathbf{B}}^T\underline{\mathbf{P}}_c + \underline{\mathbf{C}}^TQ\underline{\mathbf{C}} = 0 \qquad (5.100)$$

is solved with $Q = \rho$, and $R = 1$, $\underline{\mathbf{K}}_c = \sqrt{\rho}C$ is obtained in the limit, and to guarantee stability, this $\underline{\mathbf{K}}_c$ is used for recovery.

Figure 5.35 shows the recovered closed-loop transfer functions for Example 5.1. Nyquist locus and control signal transfer function, $G_{ru} = F_y/(1 + G_{uw}F_y)$, are shown in Figure 5.36.

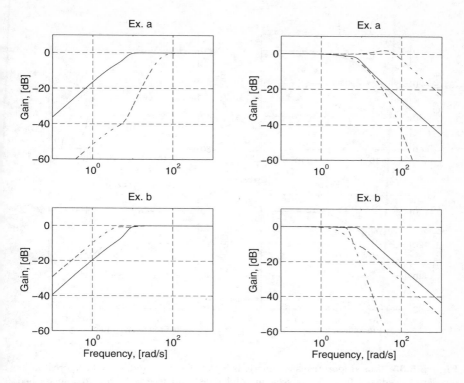

Figure 5.34 Closed-loop transfer functions S (left figures), and T (right figures). Feedback from $\dot{\alpha}_w$ is seen in solid lines, and feedback from $\dot{\alpha}_{cs}$ in dashed lines. $\overline{T}_m$ is seen in the right figures in dash-dotted lines. For the $\dot{\alpha}_{cs}$-design, $W = 5 \cdot 10^4$ (Ex. 5.1a) and $W = 50$ (Ex. 5.1b) are used, and for the $\dot{\alpha}_w$-design, $W = 15$ (Ex. 5.1a) and $W = 5 \cdot 10^2$ (Ex. 5.1b) are used.

Recovery for $\dot{\alpha}_w$-feedback. There is a trade-off when choosing an appropriate ρ. A low ρ gives good attenuation of measurement noise and a low control signal, but in order to have good stability margins, a high ρ must be chosen. This gives an increased control signal, and a 20 dB/decade roll-off rate in T_w for a wider frequency range.

Recovery for $\dot{\alpha}_{cs}$-feedback. There is no trade-off when choosing ρ. It is possible to achieve good recovery with reasonable stability margins and control signal, together with a steep roll-off rate.

The structural properties, i.e. the relative degrees are thus dominant in determining the LTR step of the design.

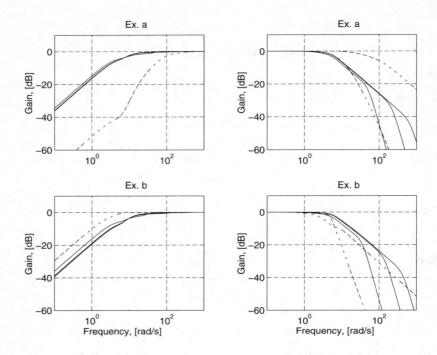

Figure 5.35 Closed-loop transfer functions S (left figures), and T (right figures) after recovery. Feedback from $\dot{\alpha}_w$ is seen in solid lines, and feedback from $\dot{\alpha}_{cs}$ in dashed lines. $\overline{T}_m$ is seen in the right figures in dash-dotted lines. For the $\dot{\alpha}_{cs}$-design, $\rho = 10^6$ (Ex. 5.1a) and $\rho = 10^5$ (Ex. 5.1b) are used, and for the $\dot{\alpha}_w$-design, $\rho = 10^4$, 10^8, and 10^{11} are used in both Ex. 5.1a and b.

5.4   Driveline Speed Control

The background and problems with traditional diesel engine speed control (RQV) were covered in Chapter 5.3. Driveline speed control is here defined as the extension of RQV control with engine controlled active damping of driveline resonances. Active damping is obtained by using a feedback law that calculates the fuel amount so that the engine inertia works in the opposite direction of the oscillations, at the same time as the desired speed is obtained. The calculated fuel amount is a function of the engine speed, the wheel speed, and the drive-shaft torsion, which are states of the **Drive-shaft model**, derived in Chapter 5.1. These variables are estimated by a Kalman filter with either the engine speed or the wheel speed as input. The feedback law is designed by deriving a criterion in which the control problem is given a mathematical formulation.

The RQV control scheme gives a specific character to the driving feeling e.g., when going uphill and downhill. This driving character is possible to maintain when extending RQV control with active damping. Traditional RQV control is further explained in Section 5.4.1. Thereafter, the speed control problem keeping

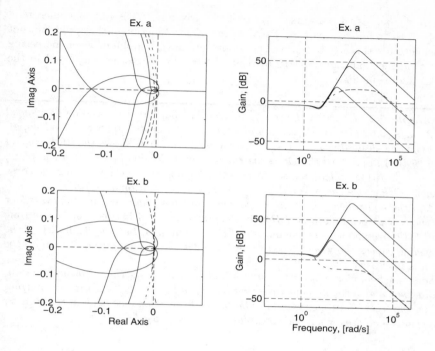

Figure 5.36 Nyquist plot of return ratio (left figures) and control signal transfer function $F_y/(1 + G_{uw}F_y)$ (right figures). Feedback from $\dot{\alpha}_w$ is seen in solid lines, and feedback from $\dot{\alpha}_{cs}$ in dashed lines. For the $\dot{\alpha}_{cs}$-design, $\rho = 10^6$ (Ex. 5.1a) and $\rho = 10^5$ (Ex. 5.1b) are used, and for the $\dot{\alpha}_w$-design, $\rho = 10^4$, 10^8, and 10^{11} are used in both Ex. 5.1a and b. A dash-dotted circle with radius one, centered at -1, is also shown in the Nyquist plots.

RQV characteristics is formulated in Section 5.4.2. The problem formulation is then studied in the following sections. The design based on the **Drive-shaft model** is simulated together with the more complicated **Nonlinear clutch and drive-shaft model** as vehicle model. Some important disturbances are simulated that are difficult to generate in systematic ways in real experiments. Finally, some field experiments are shown.

5.4.1 RQV Control

RQV control is the traditional diesel engine control scheme covered in Chapter 5.3. The controller is essentially a proportional controller with the accelerator as reference value and a sensor measuring the engine speed. The RQV controller has no information about the load, and a nonzero load, e.g., when going uphill or downhill, gives a stationary error. The RQV controller is described by

$$u = u_0 + K_p(ri - \dot{\alpha}_{cs}) \tag{5.101}$$

where $i = i_t i_f$ is the conversion ratio of the driveline, K_p is the controller gain, and r is the reference velocity. The constant u_0 is a function of the speed, but not the load since this is not known. The problem with vehicle shuffle when increasing the controller gain, in order to increase the bandwidth, is demonstrated in the following example.

Example 5.2 *Consider the truck modeled in Chapters 5.1 traveling at a speed of 2 rad/s (3.6 km/h) with gear 1 and a total load of 3000 Nm ($\approx$ 2 % road slope). Let the new desired velocity be $r = 2.3$ rad/s. Figure 5.37 shows the RQV control law (5.101) applied to the Drive-shaft model with three gains, K_p. In the plots, u_0 from (5.101) is calculated so that the stationary level is the same for the three gains. (Otherwise there would be a gain dependent stationary error.)*

When the controller gain is increased, the rise time decreases and the overshoot in the wheel speed increases. Hence, there is a trade-off between short rise time and little overshoot. The engine speed is well damped, but the flexibility of the driveline causes the wheel speed to oscillate with higher amplitude the more the gain is increased.

The same behavior is seen in Figure 5.38, which shows the transfer functions from load and measurement disturbances, v and e, to the performance output, when the RQV controller is used. The value of the resonance peak in the transfer functions increases when the controller gain is increased.

5.4.2 Problem Formulation

The goals of the speed control concept were outlined in Chapter 5.3. These are here given a mathematical formulation, which is solved for a controller using established techniques and software.

The performance output for the speed controller is the wheel speed, $z = \dot{\alpha}_w$, as defined in Chapter 5.3.4, since the wheel speed rather than the engine speed determines vehicle behavior. Figure 5.39 shows the transfer functions from control signal (u) and load (l) to the wheel speed (z) for both the Drive-shaft model and the Clutch and drive-shaft model. The Clutch and drive-shaft model adds a second resonance peak originating from the clutch. Furthermore, the high frequency roll-off rate is steeper for the Clutch and drive-shaft model than for the Drive-shaft model. Note that the transfer function from the load to the performance output is the same for the two models. This chapter deals with the development of a controller based on the Drive-shaft model, neglecting the influence from the clutch for higher frequencies.

A first possible attempt for speed control is a scheme of applying the engine torque to the driveline such that the following cost function is minimized

$$\lim_{T \to \infty} \int_0^T (z - r)^2 \tag{5.102}$$

where r is the reference velocity given by the driver. The cost function (5.102) can be made arbitrarily small if there are no restrictions on the control signal u, since the plant model is linear. However, a diesel engine can only produce torque

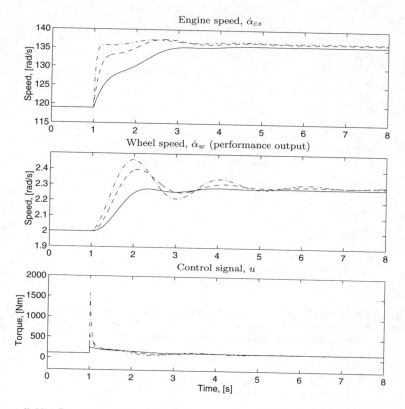

Figure 5.37 Response of step in accelerator position at t=1 s, with RQV control (5.101) controlling the **Drive-shaft model**. Controller gains $K_p=8$, $K_p=25$, and $K_p=85$ are shown in solid, dashed, and dash-dotted lines respectively. Increased gain results in a well damped engine speed and an oscillating wheel speed.

in a certain range, and therefore, (5.102) is extended such that a large control signal is penalized in the cost function.

The stationary point $z = r$ is reached if a stationary control signal, u_0, is used. This torque is a function of the reference value, r, and the load, l. For a given wheel speed, $\dot{\alpha}_w$, and load, the driveline has the following stationary point

$$x_0(\dot{\alpha}_w, l) = \begin{pmatrix} d_2/k & 1/k \\ i & 0 \\ 1 & 0 \end{pmatrix} \begin{pmatrix} \dot{\alpha}_w \\ l \end{pmatrix} = \delta_x \dot{\alpha}_w + \delta_l l \qquad (5.103)$$

$$u_0(\dot{\alpha}_w, l) = \begin{pmatrix} (d_1 i^2 + d_2)/i & 1/i \end{pmatrix} \begin{pmatrix} \dot{\alpha}_w \\ l \end{pmatrix} = \lambda_x \dot{\alpha}_w + \lambda_l l \qquad (5.104)$$

The stationary point is obtained by solving

$$\underline{\mathbf{A}}\,\underline{\mathbf{x}} + \underline{\mathbf{B}}\,u + \underline{\mathbf{H}}\,l = 0 \qquad (5.105)$$

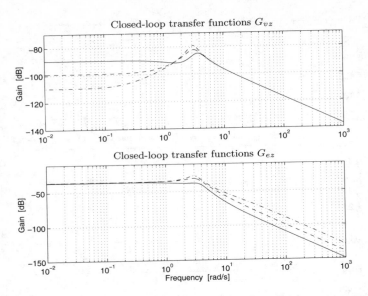

Figure 5.38 Closed-loop transfer functions G_{vz} and G_{ez} when using the RQV control law (5.101) for the controller gains K_p=8 (solid), K_p=25 (dashed), and K_p=85 (dash-dotted). The resonance peaks increase with increasing gain.

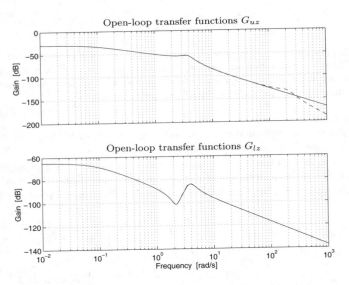

Figure 5.39 Transfer functions from control signal, u, and load, l, to performance output, z. The **Drive-shaft model** is shown in solid and the **Clutch and drive-shaft model** is shown in dashed. The modeled clutch gives a second resonance peak and a steeper roll-off rate.

for $\underline{x}$ and u, where $\underline{\mathbf{A}}$, $\underline{\mathbf{B}}$, and $\underline{\mathbf{H}}$ are given by (5.66) to (5.69).

The cost function is modified by using (5.103) and (5.104), such that a control signal that deviates from the stationary value $u_0(r, l)$ adds to the cost function. The extended cost function is given by

$$\lim_{T \to \infty} \int_0^T (z - r)^2 + \eta(u - u_0(r, l))^2 \qquad (5.106)$$

where η is used to control the trade-off between short rise time and control signal amplitude.

The controller that minimizes (5.106), called the speed controller, has no stationary error, since the load, l, is included and thus compensated for. However, it is desirable that the stationary error characteristic for the RQV controller is maintained in the speed controller, as mentioned before. A stationary error comparable with that of the RQV controller can be achieved by using only a part of the load in the criterion (5.106), as will be demonstrated in Section 5.4.3.

5.4.3 Speed Control with Active Damping and RQV Behavior

Before continuing, the following is repeated:

Important comment: LQG/LTR is *one* method to obtain the parameters in a controller structure with state feedback using an observer. Even if the method is unknown to the reader, the presentation should be easy to follow if the reader has a basic course in control and accepts that LQG/LTR is a method to compute l_0, $\underline{\mathbf{K}}_c$, and $\underline{\mathbf{K}}_f$ in Eq. 5.78 and Eq. 5.79.

The problem formulation (5.106) will be treated in two steps. First without RQV behavior i.e., using the complete load in the criterion, and then extending to RQV behavior. The problem formulation (5.106) is in this section solved with LQG technique. This is done by linearizing the driveline model and rewriting (5.106) in terms of the linearized variables. A state-feedback matrix is derived that minimizes (5.106) by solving a Riccati equation. The derived feedback law is a function of η which is chosen such that high bandwidth together with a feasible control signal is obtained.

The model (5.65)

$$\underline{\dot{x}} = \underline{\mathbf{A}}\underline{x} + \underline{\mathbf{B}}u + \underline{\mathbf{H}}l \qquad (5.107)$$

is affine since it includes a constant term, l. The model is linearized in the neighborhood of the stationary point (x_0, u_0). The linear model is described by

$$\Delta\underline{\dot{x}} = \underline{\mathbf{A}}\,\Delta\underline{x} + \underline{\mathbf{B}}\,\Delta u \qquad (5.108)$$

where

$$
\begin{aligned}
\Delta\underline{x} &= \underline{x} - \underline{x}_0 \\
\Delta u &= u - u_0 \\
\underline{x}_0 &= \underline{x}_0(x_{30}, l) \\
u_0 &= u_0(x_{30}, l)
\end{aligned}
\qquad (5.109)
$$

where the stationary point (x_0, u_0) is given by (5.103) and (5.104) (x_{30} is the initial value of x_3). Note that the linear model is the same for all stationary points.

The problem is to devise a feedback control law that minimizes the cost function (5.106). The cost function is expressed in terms of Δx and Δu by using (5.109)

$$\lim_{T \to \infty} \int_0^T (\mathbf{M}\,(\underline{\mathbf{x}}_0 + \Delta \underline{\mathbf{x}}) - r)^2 + \eta(u_0 + \Delta u - u_0(r, l))^2 \quad (5.110)$$

$$= \lim_{T \to \infty} \int_0^T (\mathbf{M}\,\Delta \underline{\mathbf{x}} + r_1)^2 + \eta(\Delta u + r_2)^2 \quad (5.111)$$

with

$$\begin{aligned} r_1 &= \mathbf{M}\,\underline{\mathbf{x}}_0 - r \\ r_2 &= u_0 - u_0(r, l) \end{aligned} \quad (5.112)$$

In order to minimize (5.110) a Riccati equation is used. Then the constants r_1 and r_2 must be expressed in terms of state variables. This can be done by augmenting the plant model (A, B) with models of the constants r_1 and r_2. Since these models will not be controllable, they must be stable in order to solve the Riccati equation [48]. Therefore the model $\dot r_1 = \dot r_2 = 0$ is not used because the poles are located on the imaginary axis. Instead the following models are used

$$\begin{aligned} \dot r_1 &= -\sigma r_1 \\ \dot r_2 &= -\sigma r_2 \end{aligned} \quad \begin{aligned} (5.113) \\ (5.114) \end{aligned}$$

which with a low σ indicates that r is a slow-varying constant.

The augmented model is given by

$$\mathbf{A}_r = \begin{pmatrix} & & & 0 & 0 \\ & \underline{\mathbf{A}} & & 0 & 0 \\ & & & 0 & 0 \\ 0 & 0 & 0 & -\sigma & 0 \\ 0 & 0 & 0 & 0 & -\sigma \end{pmatrix}, \quad (5.115)$$

$$\mathbf{B}_r = \begin{pmatrix} \underline{\mathbf{B}} \\ 0 \\ 0 \end{pmatrix}, \quad \underline{\mathbf{x}}_r = (\Delta \underline{\mathbf{x}}^T \ r_1 \ r_2)^T \quad (5.116)$$

By using these equations, the cost function (5.110) can be written in the form

$$\lim_{T \to \infty} \int_0^T x_r^T \mathbf{Q}\, x_r + R\Delta u^2 + 2x_r^T \mathbf{N}\, \Delta u \quad (5.117)$$

with

$$\begin{aligned} \mathbf{Q} &= (\mathbf{M}\ 1\ 0)^T (\mathbf{M}\ 1\ 0) + \eta(0\ 0\ 0\ 0\ 1)^T(0\ 0\ 0\ 0\ 1) \\ \mathbf{N} &= \eta(0\ 0\ 0\ 0\ 1)^T \\ R &= \eta \end{aligned} \quad (5.118)$$

The cost function (5.110) is minimized by using

$$\Delta u = -\underline{\mathbf{K}}_c \underline{\mathbf{x}}_r \qquad (5.119)$$

with

$$\underline{\mathbf{K}}_c = \underline{\mathbf{Q}}^{-1}(\mathbf{B}_r^T \underline{\mathbf{P}}_c + \underline{\mathbf{N}}^T) \qquad (5.120)$$

where $\underline{\mathbf{P}}_c$ is the stabilizing solution to the Riccati equation

$$\underline{\mathbf{A}}_r^T \underline{\mathbf{P}}_c + \underline{\mathbf{P}}_c \underline{\mathbf{A}}_r + R - (\underline{\mathbf{P}}_c \underline{\mathbf{B}}_r + \underline{\mathbf{N}})\underline{\mathbf{Q}}^{-1}(\underline{\mathbf{P}}_c \underline{\mathbf{B}}_r + \underline{\mathbf{N}})^T = 0 \qquad (5.121)$$

The control law (5.119) becomes

$$\Delta u = -\underline{\mathbf{K}}_c \underline{\mathbf{x}}_r = - \begin{pmatrix} K_{c1} & K_{c2} & K_{c3} \end{pmatrix} \Delta \underline{\mathbf{x}} - K_{c4} r_1 - K_{c5} r_2 \qquad (5.122)$$

By using (5.109) and (5.112) the control law for the speed controller is written as

$$u = K_0 x_{30} + K_l l + K_r r - \begin{pmatrix} K_{c1} & K_{c2} & K_{c3} \end{pmatrix} \underline{\mathbf{x}} \qquad (5.123)$$

with

$$\begin{aligned} K_0 &= \begin{pmatrix} K_{c1} \ K_{c2} \ K_{c3} \end{pmatrix} \delta_x - K_{c4} M \delta_x + \lambda_x - K_{c5}\lambda_x \\ K_r &= K_{c4} + K_{c5}\lambda_x \\ K_l &= \begin{pmatrix} K_{c1} \ K_{c2} \ K_{c3} \end{pmatrix} \delta_l - K_{c4} M \delta_l + \lambda_l \end{aligned} \qquad (5.124)$$

where δ_x, δ_l, λ_x, and λ_l are described in (5.103) and (5.104).

When this control law is applied to Example 5.2 the controller gain becomes

$$u = 0.230 x_{30} + 4470 r + 0.125 l - \begin{pmatrix} 7620 & 0.0347 & 2.36 \end{pmatrix} \underline{\mathbf{x}} \qquad (5.125)$$

where $\eta = 5 \cdot 10^{-8}$ and $\sigma = 0.0001$ are used. With this controller the phase margin is guaranteed to be at least 60° with infinite amplitude margin [48]. A step-response simulation with the speed controller (5.125) is shown in Figure 5.40.

The rise time of the speed controller is shorter than for the RQV controller. Also the overshoot is less when using speed control. The driving torque is controlled such that the oscillations in the wheel speed are actively damped. This means that the controller applies the engine torque in a way that the engine inertia works in the opposite direction of the oscillation. Then the engine speed oscillates, but the important wheel speed is well behaved as seen in Figure 5.40.

Extending with RQV Behavior

The RQV controller has no information about the load, l, and therefore a stationary error will be present when the load is different from zero. The speed controller (5.123) is a function of the load, and the stationary error is zero if the load is estimated and compensated for. There is however a demand from the driver that the load should give a stationary error, and only when using a cruise controller the stationary error should be zero.

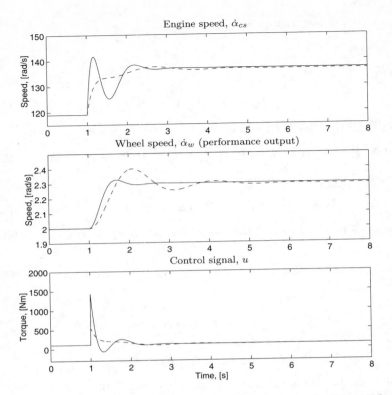

Figure 5.40 Response of step in accelerator position at t=1 s. The Drive-shaft model is controlled with the speed control law (5.125) in solid lines. RQV control (5.101) with K_p=25 is seen in dashed lines. With active damping, the engine speed oscillates, resulting in a well damped wheel speed.

The speed controller can be modified such that a load different from zero gives a stationary error. This is done by using βl instead of the complete load l in (5.123). The constant β ranges from $\beta = 0$ which means no compensation for the load, to $\beta = 1$ which means fully compensation of the load and no stationary error. The compensated speed control law becomes

$$u = K_0 x_{30} + K_l \beta l + K_r r - \begin{pmatrix} K_{c1} & K_{c2} & K_{c3} \end{pmatrix} \underline{\mathbf{x}} \qquad (5.126)$$

In Figure 5.41, the RQV controller with its stationary error (remember the reference value $r = 2.3$ rad/s) is compared to the compensated speed controller (5.126) applied to Example 5.2 for three values of β. By adjusting β, the speed controller with active damping is extended with a stationary error comparable with that of the RQV controller.

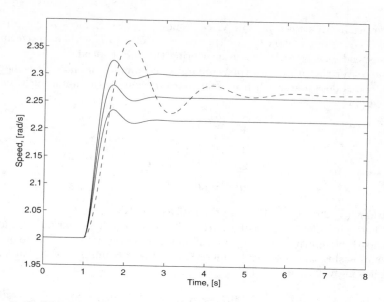

Figure 5.41 Wheel-speed response of step in accelerator position at t=1 s. The Drive-shaft model is controlled with the RQV controller (5.101) in dashed line, and the speed controller with stationary error (5.126) with $\beta = 0$, 0.5, 1 in solid lines. The speed controller achieves the same stationary level as the RQV controller by tuning β.

5.4.4 Influence from Sensor Location

The speed controller investigated in the previous section uses feedback from all states ($x_1 = \alpha_{cs}/i_t i_f - \alpha_w$, $x_2 = \dot{\alpha}_{cs}$, and $x_3 = \dot{\alpha}_w$). A sensor measuring shaft torsion (e.g., x_1) is normally not used, and therefore an observer is needed to estimate the unknown states. In this work, either the engine speed or the wheel speed is used as input to the observer. This results in different control problems depending on sensor location. Especially the difference in disturbance rejection is investigated.

The observer gain is calculated using Loop-Transfer Recovery (LTR) [48]. The speed control law (5.123) then becomes

$$u = K_0 x_{30} + K_r r + K_l l - \begin{pmatrix} K_{c1} & K_{c2} & K_{c3} \end{pmatrix} \underline{\hat{x}} \tag{5.127}$$

with K_0, K_r, and K_l given by (5.124). The estimated states $\underline{\hat{x}}$ are given by the Kalman filter

$$\Delta \underline{\dot{\hat{x}}} = \underline{A} \, \Delta \underline{\hat{x}} + \underline{B} \, \Delta u + \underline{K}_f (\Delta y - \underline{C} \, \Delta \underline{\hat{x}}) \tag{5.128}$$

$$\underline{K}_f = \underline{P}_f \underline{C}^T \underline{V}^{-1} \tag{5.129}$$

where $\underline{P}_f$ is derived by solving the Riccati equation

$$\underline{P}_f \underline{A}^T + \underline{A} \underline{P}_f - \underline{P}_f \underline{C}^T \underline{V}^{-1} \underline{C} \underline{P}_f + W = 0 \tag{5.130}$$

The covariance matrices W and $\underline{V}$ correspond to disturbances v and e respectively. The output matrix $\underline{C}$ is either equal to $\underline{C}_m$ (5.75) when measuring the engine speed, or $\underline{C}_w$ (5.76) when measuring the wheel speed.

To recover the properties (phase margin and amplitude margin) achieved in the previous design step when all states are measured, the following values are selected [48]

$$
\begin{aligned}
V &= 1 \\
W &= \rho BB^T \\
\underline{C} &= \underline{C}_m \ \text{or} \ \underline{C}_w \\
\rho &= \rho_m \ \text{or} \ \rho_w
\end{aligned}
\tag{5.131}
$$

Equations (5.129) and (5.130) are then solved for $\underline{K}_f$.

When using LQG with feedback from all states, the phase margin, φ, is at least $60°$ and the amplitude margin, a, is infinity as stated before. This is obtained also when using the observer by increasing ρ towards infinity. For Example 5.2 the following values are used

$$
\begin{aligned}
\rho_m &= 5 \cdot 10^5 \ \Rightarrow \ \varphi_m = 60.5°, \ a_m = \infty \\
\rho_w &= 10^{14} \ \Rightarrow \ \varphi_w = 59.9°, \ a_w = 35.0
\end{aligned}
\tag{5.132}
$$

where the aim has been to have at least $60°$ phase margin. The large difference between ρ_m and ρ_w in (5.132) is due to the structural difference between the two sensor locations, according to Chapter 5.3.4.

The observer dynamics is cancelled in the transfer functions from reference value to performance output ($z = \dot{\alpha}_w$) and to control signal (u). Hence, these transfer functions are not affected by sensor location. However, the observer dynamics will be included in the transfer functions from disturbances v and e to both z and u.

Influence from Load Disturbances

Figure 5.42 shows how the performance output and the control signal are affected by the load disturbance v. There is a resonance peak in G_{vz} when using feedback from the engine-speed sensor, which is not present when feedback from the wheel-speed sensor is used. The reason for this can be seen when studying the transfer function G_{vz} in (5.85). By using the matrix inversion lemma [34] (5.85) is rewritten as

$$
(G_{vz})_{cl} = \frac{G_{vz} + F_y(G_{uy}G_{vz} - G_{uz}G_{vy})}{1 + G_{uy}F_y}
\tag{5.133}
$$

where G_{ab} denotes the transfer function from signal a to b, and cl stands for closed loop. The subscript y in (5.133) represents the output of the system, i.e., either $\dot{\alpha}_w$ or $\dot{\alpha}_{cs}$. The controller F_y is given by (5.80) as

$$
F_y(s) = \underline{K}_c(s\underline{I} - \underline{A} + \underline{B}\,\underline{K}_c + \underline{K}_f\underline{C})^{-1}\underline{K}_f
\tag{5.134}
$$

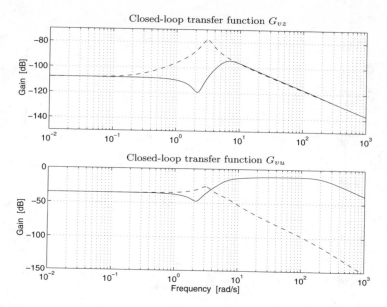

Figure 5.42 Closed-loop transfer functions from load disturbance, v, to performance output, z, and to control signal, u. Feedback from $\dot{\alpha}_w$ is shown in solid and feedback from $\dot{\alpha}_{cs}$ is shown in dashed lines. With $\dot{\alpha}_{cs}$-feedback the transfer functions have a resonance peak, resulting from the open-loop zeros.

with C either being C_m for engine-speed feedback, or C_w for wheel-speed feedback. For the speed controller ($z = \dot{\alpha}_w$), Equation (5.133) becomes

$$(G_{vz})_{cl} = \frac{G_{vw}}{1 + G_{uw}F_y} \qquad (5.135)$$

when the sensor measures the wheel speed. Equation (5.135) is obtained by replacing the subscript y in (5.133) by the subscript w. Then the parenthesis in (5.133) equals zero. In the same way, the resulting equation for the $\dot{\alpha}_{cs}$-feedback case is

$$(G_{vz})_{cl} = \frac{G_{vw} + F_y(G_{um}G_{vw} - G_{uw}G_{vm})}{1 + G_{um}F_y} \qquad (5.136)$$

Hence, when using the wheel-speed sensor, the controller is cancelled in the numerator, and when the engine-speed sensor is used, the controller is not cancelled.

The optimal return ratio in the LQG step is

$$\underline{\mathbf{K}}_c(s\underline{\mathbf{I}} - \underline{\mathbf{A}})^{-1}\underline{\mathbf{B}} \qquad (5.137)$$

Hence, the poles from $\underline{\mathbf{A}}$ is kept, but there are new zeros that are placed such that the relative degree of (5.137) is one, assuring a phase margin of at least $60°$ ($\varphi > 60°$), and an infinite gain margin. In the LTR step the return ratio is

$$F_yG_{uy} = \underline{\mathbf{K}}_c(s\underline{\mathbf{I}} - \underline{\mathbf{A}} - \underline{\mathbf{B}}\underline{\mathbf{K}}_c - \underline{\mathbf{K}}_f\underline{\mathbf{C}})^{-1}\underline{\mathbf{K}}_f\underline{\mathbf{C}}(s\underline{\mathbf{I}} - \underline{\mathbf{A}})^{-1}\underline{\mathbf{B}} \qquad (5.138)$$

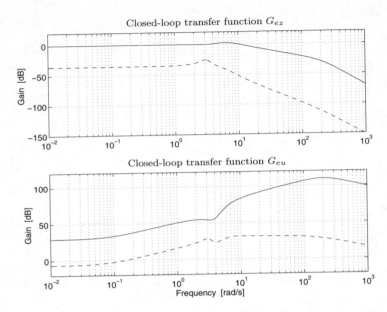

Figure 5.43 Closed-loop transfer functions from measurement noise, e, to performance output, z, and to control signal, u. Feedback from $\dot\alpha_w$ is shown in solid and feedback from $\dot\alpha_{cs}$ is shown in dashed lines. The difference between the two feedback principles is described by the dynamic output ratio. The effect increases with lower gears.

When ρ in (5.131) is increased towards infinity, (5.137) equals (5.138). This means that the zeros in the open-loop system $\underline{\mathbf{C}}\,(s\underline{\mathbf{I}}-\underline{\mathbf{A}}\,)^{-1}\underline{\mathbf{B}}$ are cancelled by the controller. Hence, the open-loop zeros will become poles in the controller F_y. This means that the closed-loop system will have the open-loop zeros as poles when using the engine-speed sensor. The closed-loop poles become $-0.5187 \pm 3.0753j$, which causes the resonance peak in Figure 5.42.

Influence from Measurement Disturbances

The influence from measurement disturbances e is shown in Figure 5.43. The transfer functions from measurement noise to output, (5.86), can be rewritten via the matrix inversion lemma as

$$(G_{ez})_{cl} = -\frac{G_{uz}F_y}{1 + G_{uy}F_y} \qquad (5.139)$$

The complementary sensitivity function is defined for the two sensor alternatives as

$$T_w = \frac{G_{uw}F_y}{1 + G_{uw}F_y}, \quad T_m = \frac{G_{um}F_y}{1 + G_{um}F_y} \qquad (5.140)$$

Then by replacing the subscript y in (5.139) with m or w (for $\dot\alpha_{cs}$-feedback or

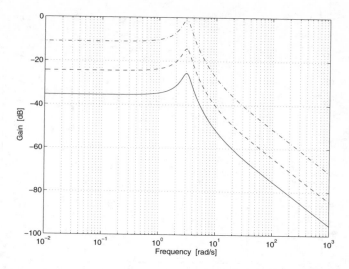

Figure 5.44 The dynamic output ratio $G_{w/m}$ for gear 1 (solid), gear 7 (dashed), and gear 14 (dash-dotted).

$\dot{\alpha}_w$-feedback), and comparing with (5.140), the following relations hold

$$(G_{ez})_{cl} = -T_w \text{ with } \dot{\alpha}_w-\text{feedback} \tag{5.141}$$

$$(G_{ez})_{cl} = -T_m \frac{G_{uw}}{G_{um}} = T_m G_{w/m} \text{ with } \dot{\alpha}_{cs}-\text{feedback} \tag{5.142}$$

where the dynamic output ratio $G_{w/m}$ was defined in Definition 5.1. For the Drive-shaft model the dynamic output ratio is

$$G_{w/m} = \frac{ds + k}{i(J_2 s^2 + (d + d_2)s + k)} \tag{5.143}$$

where the state-space description in Chapter 5.3.4 is used. Especially for low frequencies, $G_{w/m}(0) = 1/i = 1/i_t i_f$. The dynamic output ratio can be seen in Figure 5.44 for three different gears.

When ρ in (5.131) is increased towards infinity, (5.137) equals (5.138), which means that $T_m = T_w$. Then (5.141) and (5.142) gives

$$(G_{ez})_{cl,m} = (G_{ez})_{cl,w} G_{w/m} \tag{5.144}$$

where cl, m and cl, w means closed loop with feedback from $\dot{\alpha}_{cs}$ and $\dot{\alpha}_w$ respectively.

The frequency range in which $T_m = T_w$ is valid depends on how large ρ in (5.131) is made. Figure 5.45 shows the sensitivity functions

$$S_w = \frac{1}{1 + G_{uw}F_y}, \quad S_m = \frac{1}{1 + G_{um}F_y} \tag{5.145}$$

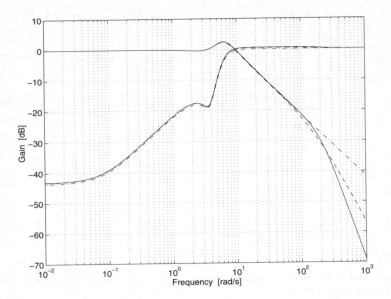

Figure 5.45 Sensitivity function S and complementary sensitivity function T. The dash-dotted lines correspond to the case with all states known. When only one velocity is measured, the solid lines correspond to $\dot{\alpha}_w$-feedback, and the dashed lines correspond to $\dot{\alpha}_{cs}$-feedback.

and the complementary sensitivity functions T_w and T_m (5.140) for the two cases of feedback. It is seen that $T_m = T_w$ is valid up to about 100 rad/s (≈ 16 Hz). The roll-off rate at higher frequencies differ between the two feedback principles. This is due to that the open-loop transfer functions G_{uw} and G_{um} have different relative degrees. G_{uw} has a relative degree of two, and G_{um} has a relative degree of one. Therefore, T_w has a steeper roll-off rate than T_m.

Hence, the difference in G_{ez} depending on sensor location is described by the dynamic output ratio $G_{w/m}$. The difference in low-frequency level is equal to the conversion ratio of the driveline. Therefore, this effect increases with lower gears.

Load Estimation

The feedback law with unknown load is

$$u = K_0 x_{30} + K_r r + K_l \hat{l} - \left(\begin{array}{ccc} K_{c1} & K_{c2} & K_{c3} \end{array} \right) \hat{\underline{x}} \qquad (5.146)$$

where $\hat{l}$ is the estimated load. In order to estimate the load, the model used in the Kalman filter is augmented with a model of the load. The load is hard to model correctly since it is a function of road slope. However it can be treated as a slow-varying constant. A reasonable augmented model is

$$x_4 = \hat{l}, \quad \text{with} \quad \dot{x}_4 = 0 \qquad (5.147)$$

This gives

$$\dot{\hat{\underline{\mathbf{x}}}} = \underline{\mathbf{A}}_l\hat{\underline{\mathbf{x}}}_l + \underline{\mathbf{B}}_l u + \underline{\mathbf{K}}_f(y - \underline{\mathbf{C}}_l\hat{\underline{\mathbf{x}}}_l) \tag{5.148}$$

with

$$\hat{\underline{\mathbf{x}}}_l = \begin{pmatrix} \hat{\underline{\mathbf{x}}} & \hat{l} \end{pmatrix}^T, \tag{5.149}$$

$$\underline{\mathbf{A}}_l = \begin{pmatrix} & \underline{\mathbf{A}} & & 0 \\ & & & 0 \\ & & & -1/J_2 \\ 0 & 0 & 0 & 0 \end{pmatrix}, \tag{5.150}$$

$$\underline{\mathbf{B}}_l = \begin{pmatrix} \underline{\mathbf{B}} \\ 0 \end{pmatrix}, \quad \underline{\mathbf{C}}_l = \begin{pmatrix} \underline{\mathbf{C}} & 0 \end{pmatrix} \tag{5.151}$$

The feedback law is

$$u = K_0 x_{30} + K_r r - \begin{pmatrix} K_{c1} & K_{c2} & K_{c3} & -K_l \end{pmatrix}\hat{\underline{\mathbf{x}}}_l \tag{5.152}$$

5.4.5 Simulations

An important step in demonstrating feasibility for real implementation is that a controller behaves well when simulated on a more complicated vehicle model than it was designed for. Even more important in a principle study is that such disturbances can be introduced that hardly can be generated in systematic ways in real experiments. One such example is impulse disturbances from a towed trailer.

The control law based on the reduced driveline model is simulated with a more complete nonlinear model, derived in Chapter 5.1. The purpose is also to study effects from different sensor locations as discussed in Section 5.4.4. The simulation situation is seen in Figure 5.46. The Nonlinear clutch and drive-shaft model, given by (5.59) to (5.61), is used as vehicle model. The steady-state level for the Nonlinear clutch and drive-shaft model is calculated by solving the model equations for the equilibrium point when the load and speed are known.

The controller used is based on the Drive-shaft model , as was derived in the previous sections. The wheel speed or the engine speed is the input to the observer (5.128), and the control law (5.127) with $\beta = 0$ generates the control signal.

The simulation case presented here is the same as in Example 5.2, i.e., a velocity step response, but a load disturbance is also included. The stationary point is given by

$$\dot{\alpha}_w = 2, \; l = 3000 \;\Rightarrow\; x_0 = \begin{pmatrix} 0.0482 & 119 & 2.00 \end{pmatrix}^T, \quad u_0 = 109 \tag{5.153}$$

where (5.103) and (5.104) are used, and the desired new speed is $\dot{\alpha}_w = 2.3$ rad/s. At steady state, the clutch transfers the torque $u_0 = 109$ Nm. This means that the clutch angle is in the area with higher stiffness ($\alpha_{c1} < \alpha_c \leq \alpha_{c2}$) in the clutch nonlinearity, seen in Figure 5.18. This is a typical driving situation when speed control is used. However, at low clutch torques ($\alpha_c < \alpha_{c1}$) the clutch nonlinearity

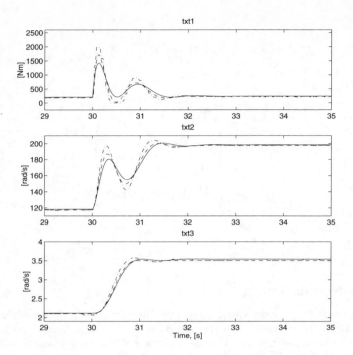

Figure 5.46 Simulation configuration. As a step for demonstrating feasibility for real implementation, the Nonlinear clutch and drive-shaft model is simulated with the controller based on the Drive-shaft model.

can produce limit cycle oscillations [3]. This situation occurs when the truck is traveling downhill with a load of the same size as the friction in the driveline, resulting in a low clutch torque. This is however not treated here. At $t = 6$ s, a load impulse disturbance is simulated. The disturbance is generated as a square pulse with 0.1 s width and 1200 Nm height, added to the load according to (5.73).

In order to simulate the nonlinear model, the differential equations (5.59) to (5.61) are scaled such that the five differential equations (one for each state) have about the same magnitude. The model is simulated using the Runge Kutta (45) method [72] with a low step size to catch the effect of the nonlinearity.

Figures 5.47 to 5.49 show the result of the simulation. These figures should be compared to Figure 5.40, where the same control law is applied to the Drive-shaft model. From these plots it is demonstrated that the performance does not critically depend on the simplified model structure. The design still works if the extra dynamics is added. Further evidence supporting this is seen in Figure 5.49. The area with low stiffness in the clutch nonlinearity ($\alpha_c < \alpha_{c1}$) is never entered. The load impulse disturbance is better attenuated with feedback from the wheel-speed sensor, which is a verification of the behavior that was discussed in Section 5.4.4.

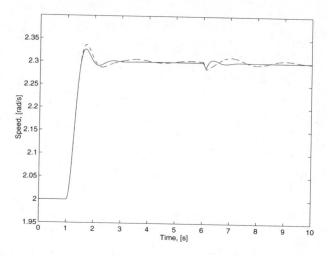

Figure 5.47 Wheel-speed response of step in accelerator position at t=1 s with the speed controller (5.127) derived from the **Drive-shaft model**, controlling the **Nonlinear clutch and drive-shaft model**. The solid line corresponds to $\dot{\alpha}_w$-feedback and feedback from $\dot{\alpha}_{cs}$ is seen in dashed line. At t=6 s, an impulse disturbance v acts on the load. The design still works when simulated with extra clutch dynamics.

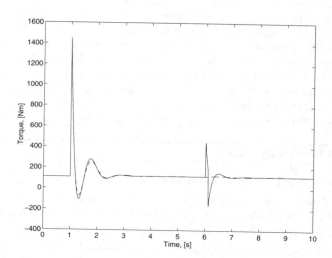

Figure 5.48 Control signal corresponding to Figure 5.47. There is only little difference between the two sensor alternatives in the step response at t=1 s. However, the load impulse (at t=6 s) generates a control signal that damps the impulse disturbance when feedback from the wheel-speed sensor is used, but not with engine-speed feedback.

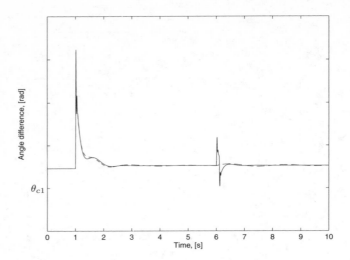

Figure 5.49 Clutch-angle difference corresponding to Figure 5.47. The influence from the clutch nonlinearity can be neglected, because the area with low stiffness ($\alpha_c < \alpha_{c1}$) is never entered.

5.4.6 Speed Controller Experiments

Experiments are used to demonstrate that the method is applicable for real implementations in a heavy truck. The goal is further to demonstrate that the simplified treatment of the diesel engine (smooth torque, dynamical behavior, etc, according to Chapter 5.3) holds in field trials.

The speed control strategy is implemented by discretizing the feedback law and the observer. The controller parameters are tuned for the practical constraints given by the measured signals. Step response tests in engine speed are performed with the strategy and the results are compared to the traditionally used RQV controller for speed control.

The algorithm computed every iteration is as follows.

Model 5.5 Control algorithm

---

1. *Read engine speed $(\dot{\alpha}_{cs})$ and engine temperature (ϑ_e).*

2. *Calculate engine friction torque, $T_{fric,e}(\dot{\alpha}_{cs}, \vartheta_e)$, as function of the engine speed and the engine temperature. The friction values are obtained from a map, described in Section 5.1.2, by an interpolation routine.*

3. *Read the engine torque (T_e) and the variable used as input to the observer (engine speed, $\dot{\alpha}_{cs}$, or wheel speed, $\dot{\alpha}_w$).*

4. *Calculate the control signal $u_k = (T_e - T_{fric,e}(\dot{\alpha}_{cs}, \vartheta_e))$, and update the observer equations.*

5. *Read the reference value (r_k), and use the feedback law to calculate the new control signal, u_{k+1}.*

6. *The new control signal is transferred to requested engine torque by adding the engine friction torque to the control signal $(u_{k+1} + T_{fric,e}(\dot{\alpha}_{cs}, \vartheta_e))$. The requested engine torque is then sent to the engine control unit.*

The repetition-rate of the algorithm is chosen the same as the sampling rate of the input variable to the observer. This means that the sampling-rate is 50 Hz using feedback from the engine-speed sensor. More information about the measured variables are found in Table 5.1. The parameters of the implemented algorithm are in the following sections tuned for the practical constraints given by the sensor characteristics.

An almost flat test road has been used for field trials with a minimum of changes from test to test. The focus of the tests is low gears, with low speeds and thus little impact from air drag. Reference values are generated by the computer to generate the same test situation from time to time. Only one direction of the test road is used so that there will be no difference in road inclination. The test presented here is a velocity step response from 2.1 rad/s to 3.6 rad/s (about 1200 RPM to 2000 RPM) with gear 1. In Figure 5.50, the speed controller is compared to traditional RQV control. The engine torque, the engine speed, and the wheel speed are shown. The speed controller uses feedback from the engine speed, and the RQV controller has the gain $K_p = 50$. With this gain the rise-time and the peak torque output is about the same for the two controllers.

With RQV control, the engine speed reaches the desired speed but the wheel speed oscillates, as in the simulations made earlier. Speed control with active damping significantly reduces the oscillations in the wheel speed. This means that the controller applies the engine torque in a way that the engine inertia works in the opposite direction of the oscillation. This gives an oscillating engine speed, according to Figure 5.50. Hence, it is demonstrated that the assumption about the simplified model structure (Drive-shaft model) is sufficient for control design. It is further demonstrated that the design is robust against nonlinear speed dependent torque limitations (maximum torque limitations), and the assumption about static transfer function between engine torque and fuel amount is sufficient.

5.4.7 Summary

RQV control is the traditional way speed control is performed in diesel engines, which gives a certain driving character with a load dependent stationary error when going uphill or downhill. With RQV, there is no active damping of wheel-speed oscillations, resulting in vehicle shuffle. An increased controller gain results in increased wheel-speed oscillations while the engine speed is well damped.

Speed control is the extension of the traditionally used diesel engine speed-control scheme with engine controlled damping of wheel-speed oscillations. The simplified linear model with drive-shaft flexibility is used to derive a controller which shows significant reduction in wheel-speed oscillations in field trials with a heavy truck.

The response time of the diesel engine, with unit-pump injection system, is demonstrated to be fast enough for controlling the first resonance mode of the

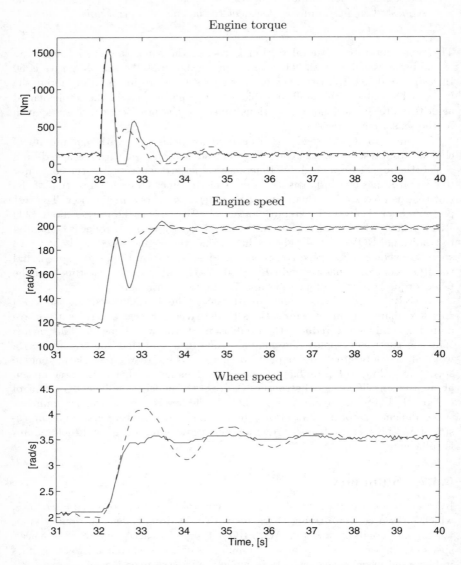

Figure 5.50 Speed step at t=32 s with active damping and engine-speed feedback (solid) compared to traditional RQV control with K_p=50 (dashed). Experiments are performed on a flat road. After 32.5 s, the control signals differ depending on control scheme. With speed control, the engine inertia works in the opposite direction of the oscillations, which are significantly reduced.

driveline. This means that the static torque map used for relating injected fuel amount to engine torque, together with a friction model as function of the engine speed and temperature, is sufficient for control.

An investigation using LQG/LTR was done. The open-loop zeros are cancelled by the controller. With engine-speed feedback this is critical, because the open-loop transfer function has a resonant zero couple. It is shown that this zero couple becomes poles of the transfer functions from load disturbances to wheel speed. This results in undamped load disturbances when engine-speed feedback is used. When feedback from the wheel-speed sensor is used, no resonant open-loop poles are cancelled. Load disturbances are thus better attenuated with this feedback configuration. Measurement disturbances are better attenuated when the engine-speed sensor is used, than when using the wheel-speed sensor. This effect increases with lower gears.

To summarize, the controller improves performance and driveability since driving response is increased while still reducing vehicle shuffle.

5.5 Driveline Control for Gear-Shifting

Gear shifting by engine control realizes fast gear shifts by controlling the engine instead of sliding the clutch to a torque-free state in the transmission, as described in Section 5.3. This is done by controlling the internal torque of the driveline. The topic of this chapter is to derive a control strategy based on a model of the transmitted torque in the transmission. There are other alternatives of internal torques that can be used as control objectives, e.g. drive-shaft torque, but this is not used here except in the final subsection. Thus, there is a detailed study of the dynamical behavior of the transmission torque, which should be zero in order to engage neutral gear. A transmission-torque controller is derived that controls the estimated transmission torque to zero while having engine controlled damping of driveline resonances. With this approach, the specific transmission-torque behavior for each gear is described and compensated for.

A model of the transmission is developed in Section 5.5.1, where the torque transmitted in the transmission is modeled as a function of the states and the control signal of the **Drive-shaft model**. The controller goal was stated in Chapter 5.3, and is formulated in mathematical terms as a gear-shift control criterion in Section 5.5.2. The control law in Section 5.5.3 minimizes the criterion. Influence from sensor location, simulations, and experiments are presented in the sections following.

5.5.1 Internal Driveline Torque

There are many possible definitions of internal driveline torque. Since the goal is to engage neutral gear without using the clutch, it is natural to use the minimization of the torque transferred in the transmission as a control goal. The following sections cover the derivation of an expression for this torque, called the *transmission torque*, as function of the state variables and the control signal.

Transmission

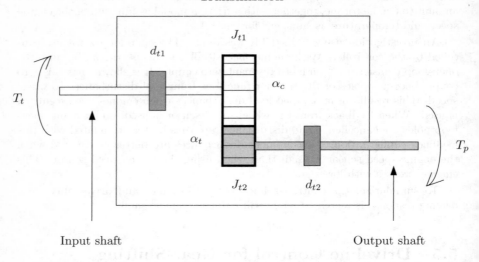

Figure 5.51 Simplified model of the transmission with two cogwheels with conversion ratio i_t. The cogwheels are connected to the input and output shafts respectively. The torque transmitted between the cogwheels is the transmission torque, z.

Transmission Torque

The performance output, z, for the gear-shift controller is the transmission torque transferred between the cogwheels in the transmission. A simplified model of the transmission is depicted in Figure 5.51. The input shaft is connected to bearings with a viscous friction component d_{t1}. A cogwheel is mounted at the end of the input shaft which is connected to a cogwheel mounted on the output shaft. The conversion ratio between these are i_t, as mentioned in Chapter 5.1. The output shaft is also connected to bearings with the viscous friction component d_{t2}.

By using Newton's second law, the transmission can be modeled by the following two equations

$$J_{t1}\ddot{\alpha}_c = T_t - d_{t1}\dot{\alpha}_c - z \tag{5.154}$$
$$J_{t2}\ddot{\alpha}_t = i_t z - d_{t2}\dot{\alpha}_t - T_p \tag{5.155}$$

In the following subsections, the expression for the transmission torque is derived for the three models developed in Chapter 5.1. Furthermore, assumptions are made about the unknown variables characterizing the different parts of the transmission.

Transmission Torque for the Drive-Shaft Model

The Drive-shaft model is defined by Equations (5.27) and (5.28). The model is here extended with the model of the transmission depicted in Figure 5.51, and the expression for the transmission torque is derived. By using the equation describing the engine inertia (5.1)

$$J_m \ddot{\alpha}_{cs} = T_e - T_{fric,e} - T_c \tag{5.156}$$

together with (5.14)

$$T_c = T_t, \quad \alpha_{cs} = \alpha_c \tag{5.157}$$

equation (5.154) is expressed in terms of engine speed

$$(J_m + J_{t1})\ddot{\alpha}_{cs} = T_e - T_{fric,e} - d_{t1}\dot{\alpha}_{cs} - z \tag{5.158}$$

To describe the performance output in terms of state variables, $\ddot{\alpha}_{cs}$ (which is not a state variable) is replaced by (5.27), which is one of the differential equations describing the **Drive-shaft model**

$$
\begin{aligned}
(J_m + J_t/i_t^2 + J_f/i_t^2 i_f^2)\ddot{\alpha}_{cs} =\ & T_e - T_{fric,e} - (d_t/i_t^2 + d_f/i_t^2 i_f^2)\dot{\alpha}_{cs} \\
& -k(\alpha_{cs}/i_t i_f - \alpha_w)/i_t i_f \\
& -d(\dot{\alpha}_{cs}/i_t i_f - \dot{\alpha}_w)/i_t i_f
\end{aligned} \tag{5.159}
$$

which together with $u = T_e - T_{fric,e}$ gives

$$
\begin{aligned}
u - d_{t1}\dot{\alpha}_{cs} - z =\ & \frac{J_m + J_{t1}}{J_m + J_t/i_t^2 + J_f/i_t^2 i_f^2} \Big(u - (d_t/i_t^2 + d_f/i_t^2 i_f^2)\dot{\alpha}_{cs} \\
& -k(\alpha_{cs}/i_t i_f - \alpha_w)/i_t i_f - d(\dot{\alpha}_{cs}/i_t i_f - \dot{\alpha}_w)/i_t i_f \Big)
\end{aligned} \tag{5.160}
$$

From this equation it is possible to express the performance output, z, as a function of the control signal, u, and the state variables, $\mathbf{x}$, according to the state-space description (5.66) to (5.69).

Model 5.6 Transmission Torque for the Drive-Shaft Model

$$z = \mathbf{M}\mathbf{x} + Du \quad \text{with}$$

$$
\mathbf{M}^T = \begin{pmatrix} \frac{(J_m + J_{t1})k}{J_1 i} \\ \frac{J_m + J_{t1}}{J_1}(d_1 + d/i^2) - d_{t1} \\ -\frac{(J_m + J_{t1})d}{J_1 i} \end{pmatrix} \tag{5.161}
$$

$$D = 1 - \frac{J_m + J_{t1}}{J_1}$$

The transmission torque, z, is modeled as a function of the states and the control signal for the *Drive-shaft model*, where the labels from (5.69) are used.

The unknown parameters in (5.161) are $J_m + J_{t1}$ and d_{t1}. The other parameters were estimated in Chapter 5.1. One way of estimating these unknowns would be to decouple the **Drive-shaft model** into two models, corresponding to neutral gear. Then a model including the engine, the clutch, and the input shaft of the transmission results, in which the performance output is equal to zero ($z = 0$).

Trials with neutral gear would then give a possibility to estimate the unknowns. This will be further investigated in Chapter 5.2.

In the derivation of the **Drive-shaft model** in Chapter 5.1 the performance output, z, is eliminated. If z is eliminated in (5.154) and (5.155) and (5.157) is used, the equation for the transmission is

$$(J_{t1}i_t^2 + J_{t2})\ddot{\alpha}_{cs} = i_t^2 T_c - i_t T_p - (d_{t1}i_t^2 + d_{t2})\dot{\alpha}_{cs} \qquad (5.162)$$

By comparing this with the equation describing the transmission in Chapter 5.1, (5.17)

$$J_t\ddot{\alpha}_{cs} = i_t^2 T_c - d_t\dot{\alpha}_{cs} - i_t T_p \qquad (5.163)$$

the following equations relating the parameters are obtained

$$J_t = i_t^2 J_{t1} + J_{t2} \qquad (5.164)$$
$$d_t = i_t^2 d_{t1} + d_{t2} \qquad (5.165)$$

In order to further investigate control and estimation of the transmission torque, the unknowns are given values. It is arbitrarily assumed that the gear shift divides the transmission into two equal inertias and viscous friction components, giving

$$J_{t1} = J_{t2} \qquad (5.166)$$
$$d_{t1} = d_{t2}$$

A more detailed discussion of these parameters will be performed in Chapter 5.5.6. Equations (5.164) and (5.165) then reduce to

$$J_{t1} = \frac{J_t}{1 + i_t^2} \qquad (5.167)$$

$$d_{t1} = \frac{d_t}{1 + i_t^2} \qquad (5.168)$$

The following combinations of parameters from the **Drive-shaft model** were estimated in Chapter 5.1

$$J_1 = J_m + J_t/i_t^2 + J_f/i_t^2 i_f^2 \qquad (5.169)$$
$$d_1 = d_t/i_t^2 + d_f/i_t^2 i_f^2 \qquad (5.170)$$

according to the labels from the state-space formulation in (5.69). From (5.167) and (5.169) $J_m + J_{t1}$ can be derived as

$$
\begin{aligned}
J_m + J_{t1} &= J_m + \frac{J_t}{1 + i_t^2} = J_m + \frac{i_t^2}{1 + i_t^2}(J_1 - J_m - J_f/i_t^2 i_f^2) \\
&= J_m \frac{1}{1 + i_t^2} + J_1 \frac{i_t^2}{1 + i_t^2} - J_f \frac{1}{i_f^2(1 + i_t^2)} \qquad (5.171)
\end{aligned}
$$

A combination of (5.168) and (5.170) gives d_{t1}

$$d_{t1} = \frac{d_t}{1 + i_t^2} = \frac{i_t^2}{1 + i_t^2}(d_1 - d_f/i_t^2 i_f^2) \qquad (5.172)$$

For low gears i_t has a large value. This together with the fact that J_f and d_f are considerably less than J_1 and d_1 gives the following approximation about the unknown parameters

$$J_m + J_{t1} \approx J_1 \frac{i_t^2}{1 + i_t^2} \tag{5.173}$$

$$d_{t1} \approx d_1 \frac{i_t^2}{1 + i_t^2} \tag{5.174}$$

Transmission Torque for the Clutch and Drive-Shaft Model

The performance output expressed for the Clutch and drive-shaft model is given by replacing T_t in (5.154) by equation (5.47)

$$T_c = T_t = k_c(\alpha_{cs} - \alpha_t i_t) + d_c(\dot{\alpha}_{cs} - \dot{\alpha}_t i_t) \tag{5.175}$$

Then the performance output is

$$z = k_c(\alpha_{cs} - \alpha_t i_t) + d_c(\dot{\alpha}_{cs} - \dot{\alpha}_t i_t) - d_{t1} i_t \dot{\alpha}_t - J_{t1} i_t \ddot{\alpha}_t \tag{5.176}$$

This is expressed in terms of state variables by using (5.53)

$$(J_t + J_f/i_f^2)\ddot{\alpha}_t = i_t \left(k_c(\alpha_{cs} - \alpha_t i_t) + d_c(\dot{\alpha}_{cs} - \dot{\alpha}_t i_t) \right) \tag{5.177}$$

$$-(d_t + d_f/i_f^2)\dot{\alpha}_t - \frac{1}{i_f} \left(k_d(\alpha_t/i_f - \alpha_w) + d_d(\dot{\alpha}_t/i_f - \dot{\alpha}_w) \right)$$

leading to the following model.

Model 5.7 Transmission Torque for the Clutch and Drive-Shaft Model

---

$$z = \mathbf{M}\mathbf{x} \text{ with} \tag{5.178}$$

$$\mathbf{M}^T = \begin{pmatrix} k_c(1 - \frac{J_{t1} i_t^2}{J_2}) \\ \frac{J_{t1} i_t k_d}{J_2 i_f} \\ d_c(1 - \frac{J_{t1} i_t^2}{J_2}) \\ \frac{J_{t1} i_t^2}{J_2}(i_t^2 d_c + d_2 + d_d/i_f^2) - d_c i_t - d_{t1} i_t \\ -\frac{J_{t1} i_t d_d}{J_2 i_f} \end{pmatrix}$$

with states and labels according to to the state-space description (5.70) to (5.72).

The following combinations of parameters from the Clutch and drive-shaft model were estimated in Chapter 5.1

$$J_2 = J_t + J_f/i_f^2 \tag{5.179}$$

$$d_2 = d_t + d_f/i_f^2 \tag{5.180}$$

according to (5.72). From (5.167), (5.168), (5.179), and (5.180), J_{t1} and d_{t1} can be written as

$$J_{t1} = \frac{i_t^2}{1 + i_t^2}(J_2 - J_f/i_f^2) \tag{5.181}$$

$$d_{t1} = \frac{i_t^2}{1 + i_t^2}(d_2 - d_f/i_f^2) \tag{5.182}$$

which are approximated to

$$J_{t1} \approx \frac{i_t^2}{1 + i_t^2}J_2 \tag{5.183}$$

$$d_{t1} \approx \frac{i_t^2}{1 + i_t^2}d_2 \tag{5.184}$$

since J_f and d_f are considerably less than J_1 and d_1.

Transmission Torque for the Nonlinear Clutch and Drive-Shaft Model

The performance output for the Nonlinear clutch and drive-shaft model is derived in the same way as for the Clutch and drive-shaft model, with the difference that (5.175) is replaced by

$$T_c = T_t = M_{kc}(\alpha_{cs} - \alpha_t i_t) + d_c(\dot{\alpha}_{cs} - \dot{\alpha}_t i_t) \tag{5.185}$$

where M_{kc} is the torque transmitted by the clutch nonlinearity, given by (5.58). Then the performance output is defined as

---

Model 5.8 Transmission Torque for the Nonlinear Clutch and Drive-Shaft Model

$$z = (M_{kc} \;\; \dot{\alpha}_t/i_f - \dot{\alpha}_w \;\; \alpha_{cs} \;\; \dot{\alpha}_t \;\; \dot{\alpha}_w) \begin{pmatrix} 1 - \frac{J_{t1}i_t^2}{J_2} \\ \frac{J_{t1}i_t k_d}{J_2 i_f} \\ d_c(1 - \frac{J_{t1}i_t^2}{J_2}) \\ \frac{J_{t1}i_t^2}{J_2}(i_t^2 d_c + d_2 + d_d/i_f^2) - d_c i_t - d_{t1}i_t \\ -\frac{J_{t1}i_t d_d}{J_2 i_f} \end{pmatrix}$$

The parameters not estimated in the definition above are approximated in the same way as for the performance output for the Clutch and drive-shaft model.

Model Comparison

Figure 5.52 shows the transmission torque during a test with step inputs in accelerator position with the 144L truck using gear 1. The transmission torque is calculated with (5.161) for the Drive-shaft model, and with (5.178) for the Clutch and drive-shaft model. Figure 5.53 shows the performance output in the frequency domain. The low-frequency level differs between the two models, and the main

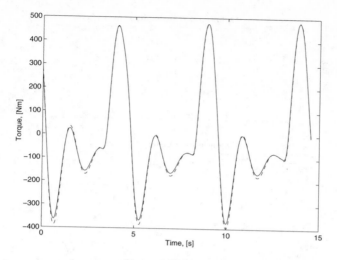

Figure 5.52 Estimated transmission torque, z, in (5.161) and (5.178) for a test with step inputs in accelerator position with the 144L truck. The solid line corresponds to the Drive-shaft model and the dashed line corresponds to the Clutch and drive-shaft model.

reason for this is the difficulties to estimate the viscous damping coefficients described in Chapter 5.1. The difference at higher frequencies is due to the clutch, which gives a second resonance peak for the Clutch and drive-shaft model. Furthermore, the roll-off rate of the Clutch and drive-shaft model is steeper than for the Drive-shaft model.

5.5.2 Transmission-Torque Control Criterion

Problem Formulation

The transmission-torque controller is the controller that drives the transmission torque to zero with engine controlled damping of driveline resonances. Then the time spent in the torque control phase (see Chapter 5.3) is minimized. The engagement of neutral gear should be at a torque level that gives no oscillations in the driveline speeds. Hereby, the disturbances to the driver and the time spent in the speed synchronization phase can be minimized. The influence on shift quality from initial driveline resonances, and torque impulses from trailer and road roughness should be minimized.

Control Criterion

The transmission-torque controller is realized as a state-feedback controller, based on the Drive-shaft model. The controller is obtained by deriving a control criterion that describes the control problem of minimizing the transmission torque. The criterion is then minimized by standard software for a controller solving the control problem.

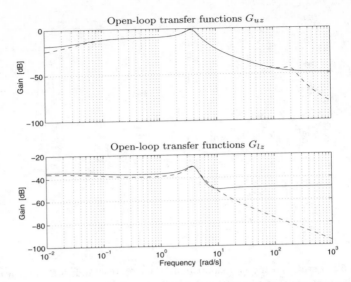

Figure 5.53 Transfer functions from control signal, u, and load, l, to transmission torque, z. The Drive-shaft model is shown in solid and the Clutch and drive-shaft model is shown in dashed lines. The modeled clutch adds a second resonance peak and a steeper roll-off rate.

The gear-shift problem can be described as minimizing the transmission torque, z, but with a control signal, u, possible to realize by the diesel engine. Therefore, the criterion consists of two terms. The first term is z^2 which describes the deviation from zero transmission torque. The second term describes the deviation in control signal from the level needed to obtain $z = 0$. Let this level be u_{shift}, which will be speed-dependent as described later. Then the criterion is described by

$$\lim_{T \to \infty} \int_0^T z^2 + \eta(u - u_{shift})^2 \tag{5.186}$$

The controller that minimizes this cost function will utilize engine controlled damping of driveline resonances (since z^2 is minimized) in order to obtain $z = 0$. At the same time, the control signal is prevented from having large deviations from the level u_{shift}. The trade-off is controlled by tuning the parameter η.

In the following subsections, the influence from each term in the criterion (5.186) will be investigated, and then how these can be balanced together for a feasible solution by tuning the parameter η.

Unconstrained Active Damping

The influence from the first term in the criterion (5.186) is investigated by minimizing z^2. The performance output, $z = \mathbf{M}\mathbf{x} + Du$, is derived in (5.161) for the Drive-shaft model as a function of the states and the control signal. The term z^2 can be minimized for a control law, since z includes the control signal and D is

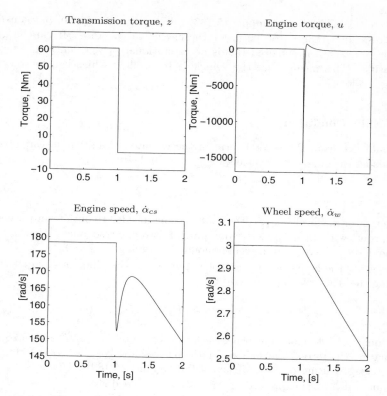

Figure 5.54 Unconstrained active damping of the Drive-shaft model. At t=1 s, a gear shift is commanded and the control law (5.187) calculates the engine torque such that the transmission torque is driven to zero instantaneously. The oscillations in the transmission torque are damped with an unrealizable large control signal. The wheel speed decreases linearly.

scalar. If u is chosen as

$$u = -D^{-1}\mathbf{M}\mathbf{x} \tag{5.187}$$

$z = 0$ is guaranteed. This control law is called *unconstrained active damping* and the reason for this is illustrated in the following example.

Example 5.3 *Consider the 144L truck modeled in Chapter 5.1 traveling at a speed of 3 rad/s (5.4 km/h) with gear 1 and a total load of 3000 Nm ($\approx$ 2 % road slope).*

Figure 5.54 shows the resulting transmission torque, the control signal, the engine speed, and the wheel speed, when a gear shift is commanded at t=1 s, with the control signal chosen according to (5.187). Unconstrained active damping is achieved which obtains $z = 0$ instantaneously. The wheel speed decreases linearly, while the engine speed is oscillating.

Unconstrained active damping (5.187) fulfills the control goal, but generates a control signal that is too large for the engine to generate. It can be noted that despite $z = 0$ is achieved this is not a stationary point, since the speed is decreasing. This means that the vehicle is free-rolling which can be critical if lasting too long.

Gear-Shift Condition

The influence from the second term in the criterion (5.186) is investigated by minimizing $(u - u_{shift})^2$, resulting in the control law

$$u = u_{shift} \qquad (5.188)$$

where the torque level u_{shift} is the control signal needed to obtain zero transmission torque, without using active damping of driveline resonances. Hence, u_{shift} can be derived from a stiff driveline model, by solving for $z = 0$.

By using the labels according to Chapter 5.3.4, the differential equation describing the stiff driveline is

$$(J_1 i + J_2/i)\ddot{\alpha}_w = u - (d_1 i + d_2/i)\dot{\alpha}_w - l/i \qquad (5.189)$$

This equation is developed by using the **Drive-shaft model** in (5.27) and (5.28), and eliminating the torque transmitted by the drive shaft, $k(\alpha_{cs}/i - \alpha_w) + c(\dot{\alpha}_{cs}/i - \dot{\alpha}_w)$. Then, by using $\dot{\alpha}_{cs} = \dot{\alpha}_w i$ (i.e., stiff driveline), (5.189) results.

Equation (5.158) expressed in terms of wheel speed is

$$z = u - d_{t1} i \dot{\alpha}_w - (J_m + J_{t1}) i \ddot{\alpha}_w \qquad (5.190)$$

Combining (5.189) and (5.190) gives the performance output for the stiff driveline.

$$z = (1 - \frac{(J_m + J_{t1})i^2}{J_1 i^2 + J_2})u - (d_{t1} i - \frac{(J_m + J_{t1})i}{J_1 i^2 + J_2}(d_1 i^2 + d_2))\dot{\alpha}_w + \frac{(J_m + J_{t1})i}{J_1 i^2 + J_2}l \qquad (5.191)$$

The control signal to force $z = 0$ is given by solving (5.191) for u while $z = 0$. Then the torque level u_{shift} becomes

$$
\begin{aligned}
u_{shift}(\dot{\alpha}_w, l) &= \mu_x \dot{\alpha}_w + \mu_l l \quad \text{with} \\
\mu_x &= (d_{t1} i - \frac{(J_m + J_{t1})i}{J_1 i^2 + J_2}(d_1 i^2 + d_2))(1 - \frac{(J_m + J_{t1})i^2}{J_1 i^2 + J_2})^{-1} \\
\mu_l &= -\frac{(J_m + J_{t1})i}{J_1 i^2 + J_2}(1 - \frac{(J_m + J_{t1})i^2}{J_1 i^2 + J_2})^{-1}
\end{aligned}
\qquad (5.192)
$$

This control law is called the *gear-shift condition*, since it implies zero transmission torque. The following example illustrates the control performance when using (5.192).

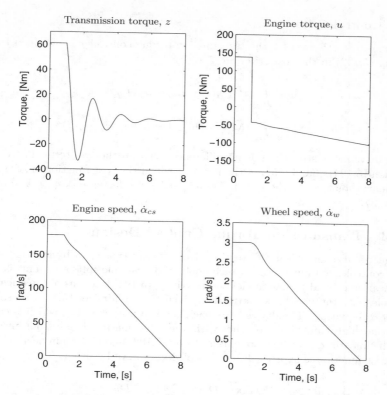

Figure 5.55 The Drive-shaft model controlled with the gear-shift condition (5.192). At t=1 s, a gear shift is commanded. The speed dependent realizable control signal drives the transmission torque to zero. Undamped oscillations in the transmission torque increase the time needed to fulfill the goal of controlling the transmission torque to zero.

Example 5.4 *Consider the 144L truck in the same driving situation as in Example 5.3. The stationary point is obtained by using (5.103) and (5.104).*

$$x_{30} = 3, \quad l = 3000 \quad \Rightarrow \quad x_0 = \begin{pmatrix} 0.0511 & 178 & 3.00 \end{pmatrix}, \quad u_0 = 138 \qquad (5.193)$$

Figure 5.55 shows the resulting transmission torque, the control signal, the engine speed, and the wheel speed when a gear shift is commanded at t=1 s, with the control signal chosen according to (5.192).

This control law achieves $z = 0$ with a realizable control signal, but the oscillations introduced are not damped. Therefore, the time needed to obtain zero transmission torque is not optimized. The performance of this approach is worse if the driveline is oscillating at the time for the gear shift, or if there are disturbances present.

Final Control Criterion

The final cost criterion for the transmission-torque controller is obtained by including (5.192) in the cost criterion (5.186)

$$\lim_{T\to\infty} \int_0^T z^2 + \eta(u - u_{shift}(\dot{\alpha}_w, l))^2 \qquad (5.194)$$

$$= \lim_{T\to\infty} \int_0^T (\underline{\mathbf{M}}\,\mathbf{x} + Du)^2 + \eta(u - \mu_x\dot{\alpha}_w - \mu_l l)^2$$

If the driveline is stiff, there is no difference between the two terms in the cost function (5.194). Furthermore, the point at which the cost function is zero is no stationary point, since the speed of the vehicle will decrease despite $z = 0$ and $u = u_{shift}$.

5.5.3   Transmission-Torque Control Design

The gear-shift control is in this section given efficient treatment by solving (5.194) for a control law by using LQG technique, and available software. This is done by linearizing the driveline model and rewriting (5.194) in terms of the linearized variables. A state-feedback matrix is derived that minimizes (5.194) by solving a Riccati equation. The derived feedback law is a function of η, which is chosen such that high bandwidth together with a feasible control signal is obtained.

The linearized driveline model is given by (5.108) and (5.109) in Section 5.4.3. The cost function is expressed in terms of $\Delta\mathbf{x}$ and Δu by using (5.109)

$$\lim_{T\to\infty} \int_0^T (\underline{\mathbf{M}}\,\Delta\mathbf{x} + D\Delta u + \underline{\mathbf{M}}\,\mathbf{x}_0 + Du_0)^2$$

$$+ \quad \eta(\Delta u - \mu_x\Delta x_3 + u_0 - \mu_x x_{30} - \mu_l l)^2$$

$$= \lim_{T\to\infty} \int_0^T (\underline{\mathbf{M}}\,\Delta\mathbf{x} + D\Delta u + r_1)^2 + \eta(\Delta u - \mu_x\Delta x_3 + r_2) \quad (5.195)$$

with

$$r_1 = \underline{\mathbf{M}}\,\mathbf{x}_0 + Du_0 \qquad (5.196)$$
$$r_2 = u_0 - \mu_x x_{30} - \mu_l l$$

The constants r_1 and r_2 are expressed as state variables, by augmenting the plant model (A, B) with models of the constants r_1 and r_2. This was done in (5.113) to (5.116).

By using these equations, the cost function (5.195) can be written in the form

$$\lim_{T\to\infty} \int_0^T \mathbf{x}_r^T \underline{\mathbf{Q}}\,\mathbf{x}_r + R\Delta u^2 + 2\underline{\mathbf{x}}_r^T N\Delta u \qquad (5.197)$$

with

$$\underline{\mathbf{Q}} = (\underline{\mathbf{M}}\ 1\ 0)^T(\underline{\mathbf{M}}\ 1\ 0) + \eta(0\ 0\ -\mu_x\ 0\ 1)^T(0\ 0\ -\mu_x\ 0\ 1)$$
$$\underline{\mathbf{N}} = (\underline{\mathbf{M}}\ 1\ 0)^T D + \eta(0\ 0\ -\mu_x\ 0\ 1)^T \qquad (5.198)$$
$$R = D^2 + \eta$$

The cost function (5.197) is minimized by the state-feedback gain

$$\underline{\mathbf{K}}_c = \underline{\mathbf{Q}}^{-1}(\underline{\mathbf{B}}_r^T \underline{\mathbf{P}}_c + \underline{\mathbf{N}}^T) \tag{5.199}$$

where $\underline{\mathbf{P}}_c$ is the stabilizing solution to the Riccati equation (5.121). The resulting control law is

$$\Delta u = -\underline{\mathbf{K}}_c \underline{\mathbf{x}}_r = -\begin{pmatrix} K_{c1} & K_{c2} & K_{c3} \end{pmatrix} \Delta \underline{\mathbf{x}} - K_{c4} r_1 - K_{c5} r_2 \tag{5.200}$$

which by using (5.196) gives

$$u = K_0 x_{30} + K_l l - \begin{pmatrix} K_{c1} & K_{c2} & K_{c3} \end{pmatrix} \underline{\mathbf{x}} \tag{5.201}$$

with

$$\begin{aligned} K_0 &= \begin{pmatrix} \lambda_x & \delta_x & \mu_x \end{pmatrix} \underline{\Gamma} \\ K_l &= \begin{pmatrix} \lambda_l & \delta_l & \mu_l \end{pmatrix} \underline{\Gamma} \end{aligned} \tag{5.202}$$

where $\underline{\Gamma}$ is given by

$$\underline{\Gamma} = \begin{pmatrix} 1 - K_{c4} D - K_{c5} \\ \begin{pmatrix} K_{c1} & K_{c2} & K_{c3} \end{pmatrix} - K_{c4} M \\ K_{c5} \end{pmatrix} \tag{5.203}$$

with λ, δ, and μ given by (5.103), (5.104), and (5.192).

The solution to the gear-shift criterion (5.194) is the transmission-torque controller (5.201), which obtains active damping with a realizable control signal. The parameter η is tuned to balance the behavior of the unconstrained active damping solution (5.187) and the gear-shift condition (5.192). The transmission-torque controller with tuned η is studied in the following example.

Example 5.5 *Consider the 144L truck in the same driving situation as in Example 5.3. The transmission-torque controller (5.201) then becomes*

$$u = 2.37 \cdot 10^{-4} x_{30} - 0.0327 l - \begin{pmatrix} 4.2123 & 0.0207 & -1.2521 \end{pmatrix} \underline{\mathbf{x}} \tag{5.204}$$

where $\eta = 0.03$ and $\sigma = 0.0001$ are used. With this controller the phase margin is guaranteed to be at least $60°$ and the amplitude margin is infinite [48].

Figure 5.56 shows the resulting transmission torque, the control signal, the engine speed, and the wheel speed when a gear shift is commanded at $t=1$ s, with the control signal chosen according to (5.204).

The transmission-torque controller achieves $z = 0$ with a realizable control signal. The oscillations in the driveline are damped, since the controller forces the engine inertia to work in the opposite direction of the oscillations. Therefore, the time needed for the torque control phase and the speed synchronization phase is minimized, since resonances are damped and engagement of neutral gear is commanded at a torque level giving no oscillations in the transmission speed.

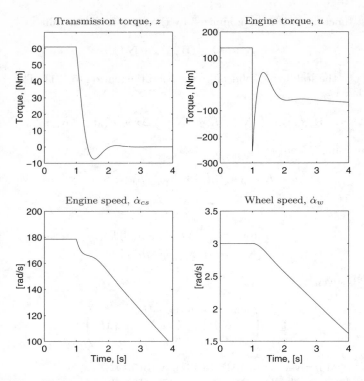

Figure 5.56 The Drive-shaft model controlled with the transmission-torque controller (5.204), solving the gear-shift criterion (5.194). At t=1 s, a gear shift is commanded. A realizable control signal is used such that the transmission torque is driven to zero, while oscillations are actively damped.

5.5.4   Influence from Sensor Location

The transmission-torque controller investigated in the previous section uses feedback from all states $(x_1 = \alpha_{cs}/i_t i_f - \alpha_w$, $x_2 = \dot{\alpha}_{cs}$, and $x_3 = \dot{\alpha}_w)$. A sensor measuring shaft torsion (e.g., x_1) is not used, and therefore an observer is needed to estimate the unknown states. In this work, either the engine speed or the wheel speed is used as input to the observer. This results in different control problems depending on sensor location. Especially the difference in disturbance rejection is investigated.

The observer gain is calculated using Loop-Transfer Recovery (LTR) [48]. The unknown load can be estimated as in Section 5.4.4.

The transmission-torque control law (5.201) becomes

$$u = K_0 x_{30} + K_l l - \begin{pmatrix} K_{c1} & K_{c2} & K_{c3} \end{pmatrix} \hat{\underline{x}} \qquad (5.205)$$

with K_0 and K_l given by (5.202). The estimated state $\hat{\underline{x}}$ is given by the Kalman filter

$$\Delta\dot{\hat{\underline{x}}} = \underline{A}\,\Delta\hat{\underline{x}} + \underline{B}\,\Delta u + \underline{K}_f(\Delta y - \underline{C}\,\Delta\hat{\underline{x}}) \qquad (5.206)$$

$$\underline{K}_f = \underline{P}_f\underline{C}^T\underline{V}^{-1} \qquad (5.207)$$

where $\underline{P}_f$ is found by solving the Riccati equation (5.130).

When using a LQG-controller with feedback from all states, the phase margin, φ, is at least $60°$, and the amplitude margin, a, is infinite, as stated before. This is obtained also when using the observer by increasing ρ towards infinity. For Example 5.5 the following values are used

$$\rho_m = 10^4 \Rightarrow \varphi_m = 77.3°, \quad a_m = 2.82 \qquad (5.208)$$

$$\rho_w = 10^{11} \Rightarrow \varphi_w = 74.3°, \quad a_w = 2.84 \qquad (5.209)$$

where the aim has been to have at least $60°$ phase margin.

The observer dynamics is cancelled in the transfer functions from reference value, r, to performance output, z, and to control signal, u. Hence, these transfer functions are not affected by the sensor location. However, the dynamics will be included in the transfer functions from disturbances to both z and u.

Influence from Load Disturbances

Figure 5.57 shows how the performance output and the control signal are affected by load disturbances, v. In Section 5.4.4 it was shown that for the speed controller, the resonant open-loop zeros become poles of the closed-loop system when feedback from the engine-speed sensor is used. The same equations are valid for the transmission-torque controller with the minor difference that the D matrix in the performance output, (5.161), is not equal to zero, as for the speed controller. Hence, also the transfer function DG_{vu} should be added to (5.133). The closed-loop transfer function G_{vu} is given by

$$(G_{vu})_{cl} = -\frac{F_yG_{vy}}{1 + F_yG_{uy}} \qquad (5.210)$$

according to (5.82) and the matrix inversion lemma. Thus, the closed-loop transfer function from v to u also has the controller F_y in the numerator. Hence, the closed-loop transfer function from v to z has the open-loop zeros as poles. For $\dot{\alpha}_{cs}$-feedback, this means that a resonance peak is present in the transfer functions from v to performance output and to control signal.

Influence from Measurement Disturbances

The influence from measurement disturbances e are shown in Figure 5.58. According to (5.139) the closed-loop transfer function from e to z is

$$(G_{ez})_{cl} = -\frac{G_{uz}F_y}{1 + G_{uy}F_y} \qquad (5.211)$$

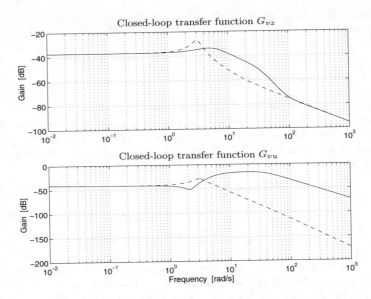

Figure 5.57 Closed-loop transfer functions from load disturbance, v, to performance output, z, and to control signal, u. Feedback from $\dot{\alpha}_w$ is shown in solid and feedback from $\dot{\alpha}_{cs}$ is shown in dashed lines. With $\dot{\alpha}_{cs}$-feedback the transfer functions have a resonance peak, resulting from the open-loop zeros.

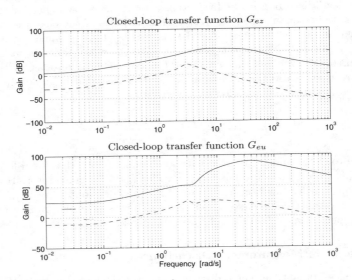

Figure 5.58 Closed-loop transfer functions from measurement noise, e, to performance output, z, and control signal, u. Feedback from $\dot{\alpha}_w$ is shown in solid and feedback from $\dot{\alpha}_{cs}$ is shown in dashed. The difference between the two feedback principles are described by the dynamic output ratio. The effect increases with lower gears.

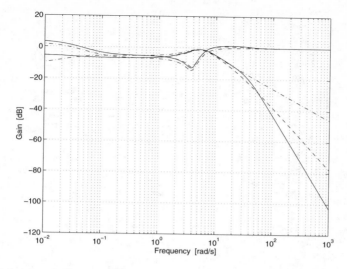

Figure 5.59 Sensitivity function S and complementary sensitivity function T. The dash-dotted lines correspond to the case with all states known. When only one velocity is measured, the solid lines correspond to $\dot{\alpha}_w$-feedback, and the dashed lines correspond to $\dot{\alpha}_{cs}$-feedback.

Then

$$(G_{ez})_{cl} = -T_w \frac{G_{uz}}{G_{uw}} \quad \text{with} \quad \dot{\alpha}_w-\text{feedback} \qquad (5.212)$$

$$(G_{ez})_{cl} = -T_m \frac{G_{uz}}{G_{um}} \quad \text{with} \quad \dot{\alpha}_{cs}-\text{feedback} \qquad (5.213)$$

with the transfer functions T_w and T_m given by (5.140).

When ρ in (5.131) is increased towards infinity, $T_m = T_w$, as was discussed in Section 5.4.4. Then (5.212) and (5.213) give

$$(G_{ez})_{cl,m} = (G_{ez})_{cl,w} G_{w/m} \qquad (5.214)$$

where cl, m and cl, w denote closed loop with feedback from $\dot{\alpha}_{cs}$ and $\dot{\alpha}_w$ respectively. The dynamic output ratio $G_{w/m}$ was defined in Definition 5.1, and is given by (5.143).

The frequency range in which the relation $T_m = T_w$ is valid depends on how large ρ in (5.131) is made, as discussed in Section 5.4.4. Figure 5.59 shows the sensitivity functions (5.145) and the complementary sensitivity functions T_w and T_m (5.140) for the two cases of feedback. It is seen that $T_m = T_w$ is valid up to about 10 rad/s (≈ 1.6 Hz). The roll-off rate at higher frequencies differ between the two feedback principles. This is due to that the open-loop transfer functions G_{uw} and G_{um} have different relative degrees. T_w has a steeper roll-off rate than T_m, because that G_{uw} has a relative degree of two, and G_{um} has a relative degree of only one.

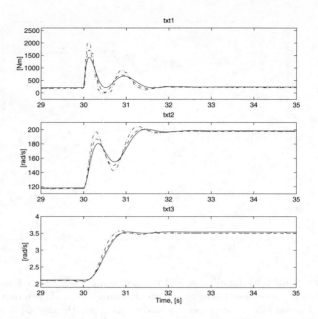

Figure 5.60 Simulation configuration. As a step for demonstrating feasibility for real implementation, the Nonlinear clutch and drive-shaft model is simulated with the controller based on the Drive-shaft model.

Hence, the difference in G_{ez} depending on sensor location is described by the dynamic output ratio $G_{w/m}$. The difference in low-frequency level is equal to the conversion ratio of the driveline. Therefore, this effect increases with lower gears.

5.5.5   Simulations

As in the case of the speed controller in Section 5.4.5, the feasibility of the gear-shift controller is studied by simulating a more complicated vehicle model than it was designed for. Also here, the disturbances that are difficult to systematically generate in real experiments are treated in the simulations. The control design is simulated with the Nonlinear clutch and drive-shaft model, according to Figure 5.60. The effects from different sensor locations are also studied in accordance with the discussion made in Section 5.5.4.

The Nonlinear clutch and drive-shaft model is given by Equations (5.59) to (5.61). The steady-state level for the Nonlinear clutch and drive-shaft model is calculated by solving the model equations for the equilibrium point when the load and speed are known. By using the parameter relationship (5.166), the equation for the transmission torque is computed by (5.8).

The transmission-torque controller used is based on the Drive-shaft model, and was developed in the previous sections. The wheel speed or the engine speed is input to the observer (5.206), and the control law (5.205) generates the control signal.

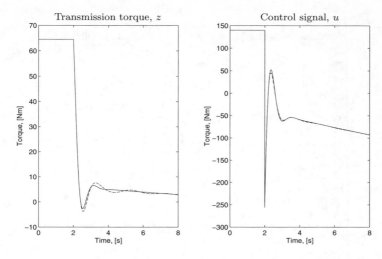

Figure 5.61 Simulation of the Nonlinear clutch and drive-shaft model with observer and control law based on the Drive-shaft model. A gear shift is commanded at t=2 s. Feedback from the wheel-speed sensor is shown in solid lines, and feedback from the engine-speed sensor is shown in dashed lines. The design still works when simulated with extra clutch dynamics.

Three simulations are performed with the driving situation as in Example 5.5, (i.e., with wheel speed $\dot{\alpha}_w = 3$ rad/s, and load $l = 3000$ Nm). In the simulations, a gear shift is commanded at $t = 2$ s. The first simulation is without disturbances. In the second simulation, the driveline is oscillating prior to the gear shift. The oscillations are a result of a sinusoid disturbance acting on the control signal. The third gear shift is simulated with a load impulse at $t = 3$ s. The disturbance is generated as a square pulse with 0.1 s width and 1200 Nm height.

In order to simulate the nonlinear model, the differential equations (5.59) to (5.61) are scaled such that the five differential equations (one for each state) have about the same magnitude. The model is simulated using the Runge Kutta (45) method [72] with a low step size to catch the effect of the nonlinearity.

Figure 5.61 shows the simulation without any disturbances. This plot should be compared to Figure 5.56 in Example 5.5, where the design is tested on the Drive-shaft model. The result is that the performance does not critically depend on the simplified model structure. The design still works if the extra nonlinear clutch dynamics is added. In the simulation, there are different results depending on which sensor that is used. The model errors between the Drive-shaft model and the Nonlinear clutch and drive-shaft model are better handled when using the wheel-speed sensor. However, neither of the sensor alternatives reaches $z = 0$. This is due to the low-frequency model errors discussed in Section 5.5.1. In Figure 5.62 the simulation with driveline oscillations prior to the gear shift is shown. The result is that the performance of the controller is not affected by the oscillations. Figure 5.63 shows the simulation with a load disturbance. The disturbance is better damped when using feedback from the wheel-speed sensor,

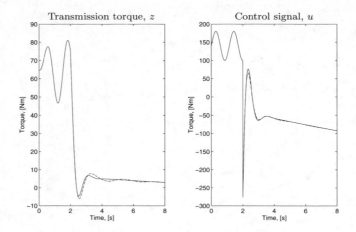

Figure 5.62 Same simulation case as in Figure 5.61, but with driveline oscillations at the start of the transmission-torque controller. Feedback from the wheel-speed sensor is shown in solid lines, and feedback from the engine-speed sensor is shown in dashed lines. The conclusion is that the control law works well despite initial driveline oscillations.

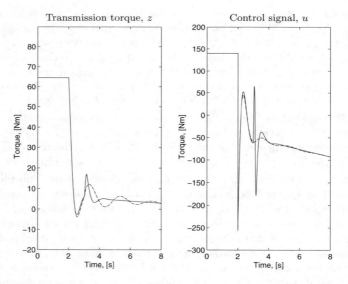

Figure 5.63 Same simulation case as in Figure 5.61, but with a load disturbance at t=3 s. Feedback from the wheel-speed sensor is shown in solid lines, and feedback from the engine-speed sensor is shown in dashed lines. The conclusion is that the load disturbance is better attenuated when using feedback from the wheel-speed sensor.

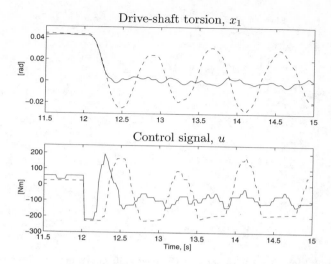

Figure 5.64 Control signal and drive-shaft torsion when using the gear-shift controller that controls the drive-shaft torsion to zero, started at 12.0 s. Prior to that, the engine has the stationary speed 1900 RPM with gear 1 engaged. In dashed lines, a PI controller is used that gives $x_1 = 0$, but with undamped driveline resonances. The solid lines are extension with the active damping controller.

than from the engine-speed sensor, which is a verification of the discussion in Section 5.5.4.

5.5.6 Gear-Shift Controller Experiments

Some experiments are briefly presented to demonstrate the performance in real field tests. Internal driveline torque control is used to drive the drive-shaft torsion to zero. This is motivated by the fact that the drive shaft is the main flexibility of the driveline, according to Chapter 5.1. If this torsion is small it is reasonable to believe that the transmission torque also is small, if the dynamical effects in the transmission are neglected.

Demonstration of Active Damping in Field Trials

For reason of comparison, Figure 5.64 shows a first trial with a PI controller in dashed lines. The proportional part of the controller gives the speed of the controller, but is not sufficient for damping out the oscillations in the driveline. The result of active damping is seen in Figure 5.64 in solid lines.

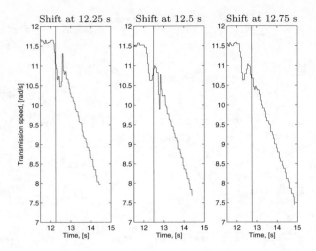

Figure 5.65 Field trials with start of the gear-shift controller at 12.0 s, all with the same controller controlling the drive-shaft torsion to zero. Engagement of neutral gear is commanded every 0.25 s after the start of the controller, indicated by the vertical lines. The transmission speed is seen when neutral gear is engaged after a delay time. The amplitudes of the transmission speed oscillations after the gear shift are less than 1 rad/s with different signs, which is an acceptable level.

Hence, active damping is obtained in field trials with a virtual sensor measuring the drive-shaft torsion. This gives additional support to the **Drive-shaft model** structure and parameters, derived in Chapter 5.1.

Validation of Controller Goal

The drive-shaft torsion is controlled to zero with damped driveline resonances, which was the goal of the controller. However, it is not yet proved that this actually is sufficient for engaging neutral gear with sufficient quality (short delay and no oscillations). The way to prove this is to use the controller demonstrated in Figure 5.64, and engage neutral gear and measure the oscillations in the transmission speed. This is done in Figures 5.65 to 5.67, where the controller is started at 12.0 s and gear shifts are commanded every 0.25 s, starting at 12.25 s.

From these figures, it is clear that controlling the drive-shaft torsion to zero is sufficient for obtaining gear shifts with short delay time. Oscillations in transmission speed are minimized to under 1 rad/s in amplitude with different signs, which is well in the range for giving no disturbance to the driver. Furthermore, the speed synchronization phase, where the engine speed is controlled to match the propeller shaft speed, can be done fast, since there are only minor oscillations in the transmission speed.

Figure 5.65 also shows that a gear shift can be commanded after only 0.25 s after the controller has started, and an acceptable shift quality is obtained. These results are for gear 1, where the problems with oscillations are largest. The time to a commanded engagement of neutral gear can be decreased further for higher gears.

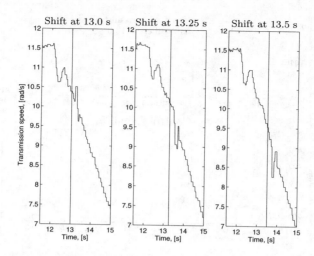

Figure 5.66 Same type of field experiment as in Figure 5.65, but with commanded engagement of neutral gear at 13.0, 13.25, and 13.5 s. The amplitudes of the transmission speed oscillations after the gear shift are less than 1 rad/s with different signs, which is an acceptable level.

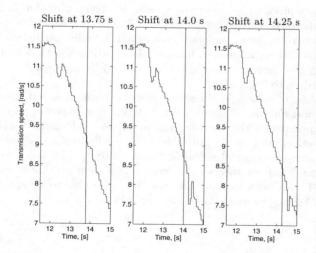

Figure 5.67 Same type of field experiment as in Figure 5.65, but with commanded engagement of neutral gear at 13.75, 14.0, and 14.25 s. The amplitudes of the transmission speed oscillations after the gear shift are less than 1 rad/s with different signs, which is an acceptable level.

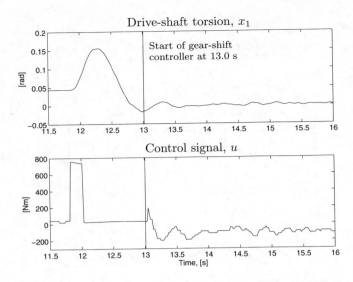

Figure 5.68 Control signal and drive-shaft torsion during field trials with start of the gear-shift controller at 13.0 s. The driveline is oscillating prior to the gear shift due to an engine torque pulse at 11.7 s. The controller controls the drive-shaft torsion to zero with damped resonances despite initial driveline oscillations.

Gear Shifts with Initial Driveline Oscillations

One important problem, necessary to handle, is when a gear shift is commanded at a state where the driveline is oscillating. This was discussed in Section 5.5.5 where the controller was simulated with initial driveline oscillations. To verify that the controller structure can handle this situation and that it also works in real experiments, driveline resonances are excited by an engine torque pulse at 11.7 s, according to Figure 5.68.

Figures 5.68 to 5.70 show the same type of experiments, but the controller is started at different time delays after the engine torque pulse has occured. For all three experiments, the resulting engine torque, calculated by the feedback controller, actively damps the initial driveline oscillations and obtains $x_1 = 0$.

The difference in control signal in Figures 5.68 to 5.70 is a strong evidence that driveline dynamics affects shift performance so much that feedback control is motivated. An open-loop scheme would not be able to handle these initial oscillations, leading to longer time for gear shifts.

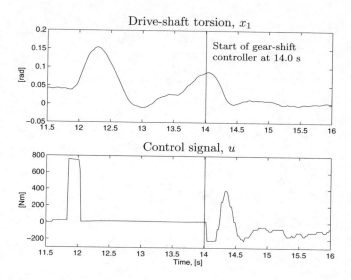

Figure 5.69 Control signal and drive-shaft torsion during field trials with start of the gear-shift controller at 14.0 s. The controller controls the drive-shaft torsion to zero with damped resonances despite initial driveline oscillations.

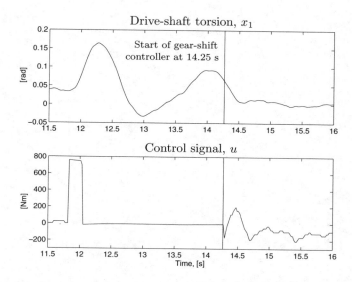

Figure 5.70 Control signal and drive-shaft torsion during field trials with start of the gear-shift controller at 14.25 s. The controller controls the drive-shaft torsion to zero with damped resonances despite initial driveline oscillations.

6 Vehicle Modelling

6.1 Introduction

The last few years have seen scientific and technical competition within the automobile industry become increasingly intense. Because of this it is important for individual manufacturers to ensure that new designs are brought to the market as quickly as possible. In the future it must be possible to carry out the design of a new model, from conception to production, in as little as eighteen months.

These days the equipment within a motor vehicle includes a myriad of electrical and electronic subsystems. Many of these subsystems serve to improve driving comfort, i.e. electric windows, air conditioning systems etc. On top of this there are safety relevant vehicle subsystems, such as drive dynamics control and anti-lock brake systems.

An ever decreasing design effort for such systems, coupled with increasing amounts of equipment, is only possible due to the far-reaching use of computer simulations in the design of new vehicles. The aim of computer models, such as the one shown schematically in Figure 6.1 is to reveal, as early as possible in the design phase, the effect on the dynamic behaviour of the vehicle of new components operating in conjunction with the existing subsystems. With such an approach the effect of a new component can be analysed in the definition phase, long before the prototype is complete.

To date, modelling efforts have concentrated on reproducing as exactly as possible the behaviour of individual components. This approach has yielded, for example, exact descriptions of the wheel dynamics using the finite element method. Simulations of such models are computationally expensive and time consuming. Due to the fact that there is a huge difference between different vehicles in terms of structure and kinematics, such models are very specific, and special know-how is required to alter a model for use with a different vehicle type.

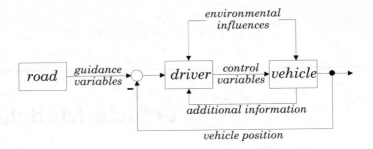

Figure 6.1 The standard vehicle-driver-road control loop

The modelling approach described in this chapter has the following aims:

- reduction of model complexity to a level sufficient for vehicle dynamics

- implementation on a PC in a common programming language, so that usage is widely spread instead of being constrained to a few specialised departments.

- interaction between submodels, whereby the design time is concentrated upon the subsystem currently under investigation.

- only necessary accuracy, so that time consuming tests with experimental vehicles can be reduced.

In order to obtain these aims, the system will be decomposed into its individual components. When carrying out such a partitioning, it is important to ensure that meaningful variables are chosen for the interfaces between the different submodels. It is thus sensible to choose, insofar as it is possible, torques or forces and angular or longitudinal velocities.

6.2 Co-ordinate Systems

For the theoretical analysis of vehicle dynamics, and for the design of observer- or control-algorithms, the equations of motion must be known and the physical interactions between the various subsystems must be written in the form of mathematical equations. For the construction of a vehicle model there are two main approaches. If the aim is to produce a model which is as exact as possible, the methods of theoretical physics such as Lagrange or Euler are used. The resultant models are very precise, however the individual equations lose their reference to physical quantities as the calculations are carried out for generalised co-ordinate systems. The alternative approach, as used in many publications, is to attempt to model the vehicle as simply as possible and with as little computing-time as possible. To this end emphasis is placed here on the classical *single-track model*, which gives good results for many driving situations. The first publication of this

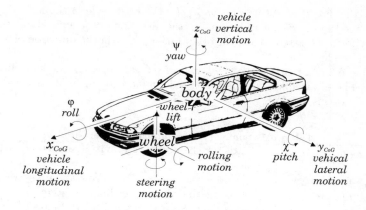

Figure 6.2 Degrees of freedom of the vehicle

method dates back to 1940 [69]. When dealing with simplified models a distinction is often made between models for drive dynamics and models for vertical dynamics analysis, and the interactions between the two are ignored. The approach detailed in this chapter follows a middle road between the two modelling methods. The vertical dynamics and the drive dynamics are modelled together and all important non-linearities are included. In contrast to the Lagrange or Euler methods the calculations are limited to 4 co-ordinate systems.

In order to differentiate, indices are introduced for the individual co-ordinate systems:

- "CoG" for the chassis (Center of gravity) co-ordinate system,

- "Un" for the undercarriage system,

- "W" for the wheel co-ordinate system,

- "In" for the fixed inertial system.

With the exception of the fixed inertial system, all co-ordinates move during travel. Figure 6.2 shows the 6 degrees of freedom of the vehicle as well as the Centre of Gravity (CoG) co-ordinate system.

The *Centre of Gravity co-ordinate system*, which has its origin at the vehicle centre-of-gravity is of the most importance. All movements of the vehicle body are given with reference to this co-ordinate system. The *undercarriage co-ordinates* differ from this only in the pitch and roll angle. The origin of the undercarriage co-ordinate system lies at road-level in the middle of the perpendicular projection of the rear axle.

Finally, the *wheel co-ordinate system* is required. To be precise there is a co-ordinate system for each individual wheel. In this book, the co-ordinate directions for the rear wheels are the same as for the undercarriage co-ordinate system and for the front wheels only the wheel turn angle (the angle between the longitudinal vehicle axis and the wheel plane) is different.

For the direction of the *rotation angles* there is a rule of thumb:
Orient the thumb of your right hand in the direction of the axis, about which the vehicle body is rotated. Then the other fingers show in the direction of a positive rotation angle.

Table 6.2 summarises the most important variables for the co-ordinate systems. These variables will be discussed in more detail and used extensively throughout this chapter.

Table 6.1 Summary of co-ordinate system variables

$x_{CoG}, y_{CoG}, z_{CoG}$	-	Axis for the centre of gravity (chassis) co-ordinate system
x_{Un}, y_{Un}, z_{Un}	-	Axis for the undercarriage co-ordinate system
x_W, y_W, z_W	-	Axis for the wheel co-ordinate system[1]
x_{In}, y_{In}, z_{In}	-	Axis for the inertial (fixed) co-ordinate system
ψ	-	Yaw angle (rotation about z_{CoG})
χ	-	Pitch angle (rotation about y_{CoG})
φ	-	Roll angle (rotation about x_{CoG})
α	-	Tire side slip angle (angle between x_W and v_W, the wheel ground contact point velocity)
δ_W	-	Wheel turn angle[2] (angle between x_{CoG} and x_W)
β	-	Vehicle body side slip angle (angle between x_{CoG} and v_{CoG}, the vehicle (CoG) velocity)

6.3   Wheel Model

The most important point for the creation of a simulation model for a motor vehicle is the exact observation of the horizontal forces on the wheel. The task of the wheel model is to derive these forces. In order to calculate the wheel forces it is necessary to know wheel slip, tire side slip angle and friction co-efficients, as these are inputs for the force equations. For the derivation of the wheel slip it is necessary to determine the individual wheel velocities. For the tire side slip angle calculation, the wheel caster has to be taken into consideration and the curve radii of the individual wheels calculated. The order of the necessary calculations is shown in Figure 6.3.

6.3.1   Wheel Ground Contact Point Velocities

This section is concerned with the velocity of the wheels with reference to some fixed reference point - the so-called *wheel ground contact point velocity* or *wheel velocity v_W*. Here, the rotation of the wheels is not considered. This is in contrast to the derivation of the *rotational equivalent velocity v_R* of the wheels, which will be considered later.

---

[1]The suffixes F and R are used to denote front and rear wheels, and R and L to denote right and left wheels. Thus x_{WFR} refers to the x-direction of the front right wheel.

[2]This angle should not be confused with the steering wheel angle, which is denoted by δ_S.

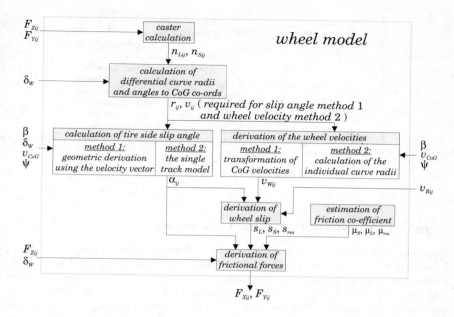

Figure 6.3 The wheel model

There are two main methods for the derivation of the velocities at the wheel-ground contact points. One approach uses the method of calculating the four wheel velocities via a transformation of the CoG velocity to a two-track (as opposed to the single-track) model. With the two-track model the additional wheel velocity component caused by the yaw rate is no longer orthogonal to the vehicle longitudinal axis and the calculation is significantly more complex. The second approach is to obtain the vehicle movement as an orbit around the instantaneous centre with angular velocity $\dot{\psi}$ and $\dot{\beta}$ and then calculate the curve radius to each individual wheel. This is made possible by the orthogonal arrangement between the wheel ground contact point velocity and the line between the wheel-ground contact point and the instantaneous centre. Both methods are equivalent and the choice depends on complexity and the opportunity for simplification. For both methods the exact knowledge of the distance from the CoG to the wheel-ground contact point is required. This is dependant upon the dynamic wheel caster. The point of action of the wheel force does not lie in the center of the wheels, but (due to the caster) towards the rear. Caster is the tilting of the steering axis either forward (negative caster) or backwards (positive caster) from the vertical wheel axis. The wheel caster is a measure of the shift of the pressure distribution in the tire contact area. Positive caster provides directional stability and helps the wheels to return to a forward-pointing direction after a turn.

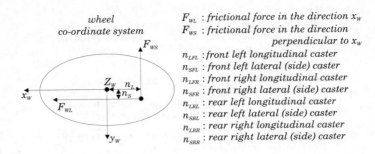

Figure 6.4 View from above of the tire contact area

Method 1: Transformation of the CoG Velocity

The velocities of the wheel ground contact points are determined via a transformation of the CoG velocity to the contact point between tire and road. The magnitude and direction of the chassis (CoG) velocity, the yaw rate, the tire side slip angle and the wheel turn angle must be known, as well as the caster dependant distances r_{ij} between the CoG and the wheel ground contact points (see Figure 6.5). To calculate these distances r_{ij} from the CoG to the wheel ground contact points, it is necessary to know the casters n_L and n_S. These can be obtained using the approximation formula [8]:

$$n_L = \frac{1}{2}\left(l_0 + l_1\frac{F_Z}{F_{Z0}}\right) \quad \text{and} \quad n_S = 3n_L\tan(\alpha) + \frac{F_Y}{c_{press}} \qquad (6.1)$$

n_L is known as the "dynamic caster", n_S takes into consideration the lateral force influence of the pressure distribution on the CoG. F_Z is the force acting vertically at the wheel ground contact point, and F_Y the lateral wheel force. The parameters of Eq. 6.1 are given in Table 6.2.

Table 6.2 Parameters for the wheel model

F_{Z0}	$5000\,N$	Nominal vertical force at wheel contact
c_{press}	$230000\,N/m$	Parameter to correct for tire pressure distribution
l_0	$-0.03\,m$	caster parameter
l_1	$0.12\,m$	caster parameter

Figure 6.4 shows an ariel view of the tire contact area, including the wheel ground contact point.

The middle point of the contact area migrates outwards and creates a torque with the longitudinal force, which during acceleration increases the self aligning torque and during braking decreases it. Whereas the caster is generally assumed to be constant and only the component in the direction of the wheel plane is considered [52], using the above method the caster can be calculated dynamically and in vector form (i.e. direction information included). The frictional forces F_L and F_S act in the direction of the wheel velocity v_W and perpendicular to it. The forces F_{WL} and F_{WS} are obtained by transformation into the wheel co-ordinate system (Eqs 6.24 and 6.25).

The derivation of the wheel ground contact point velocities is carried out in the undercarriage co-ordinate system. One proceeds with the assumption that the vehicle velocity can be described as a superposition of pure translatory motion with magnitude v_{CoG} and angle β to the vehicle longitudinal axis, and a purely rotational motion with yaw rate $\dot{\psi}$ around the CoG, as shown in Fig 6.5.

The wheel ground contact point velocities are given by the geometric super-position of the CoG velocity and a part of the magnitude $\left| r_{ij} \cdot \dot{\psi} \right|$ in the direction specified in Figure 6.5. Both the distances r_{ij} and the angles ϑ_{ij} between the wheel-ground contact points and the undercarriage axis are dependant upon the casters.

Geometric calculations (see Figure 6.6) result in the following equations for the distances:

$$
\begin{aligned}
r_{FL} &= \Big(\big(l_F - n_{LFL} \cos \delta_W + n_{SFL} \sin \delta_W \big)^2 \\
&\quad + \big(\tfrac{b_F}{2} - n_{SFL} \cos \delta_W - n_{LFL} \sin \delta_W \big)^2 \Big)^{1/2} \\
r_{FR} &= \Big(\big(l_F - n_{LFR} \cos \delta_W + n_{SFR} \sin \delta_W \big)^2 \\
&\quad + \big(\tfrac{b_F}{2} + n_{SFR} \cos \delta_W + n_{LFR} \sin \delta_W \big)^2 \Big)^{1/2} \\
r_{RL} &= \Big(\big(l_R + n_{LRL} \big)^2 + \big(\tfrac{b_R}{2} - n_{SRL} \big)^2 \Big)^{1/2} \\
r_{RR} &= \Big(\big(l_R + n_{LRR} \big)^2 + \big(\tfrac{b_R}{2} + n_{SRR} \big)^2 \Big)^{1/2}
\end{aligned}
\tag{6.2}
$$

and for the angles:

$$
\begin{aligned}
\vartheta_{FL} &= \arctan \left(\frac{\tfrac{b_F}{2} - n_{SFL} \cos \delta_W - n_{LFL} \sin \delta_W}{l_F - n_{LFL} \cos \delta_W + n_{SFL} \sin \delta_W} \right) \\
\vartheta_{FR} &= \arctan \left(\frac{l_F - n_{LFR} \cos \delta_W + n_{SFR} \sin \delta_W}{\tfrac{b_F}{2} + n_{SFR} \cos \delta_W + n_{LFR} \sin \delta_W} \right) \\
\vartheta_{RL} &= \arctan \left(\frac{l_R + n_{LRL}}{\tfrac{b_R}{2} - n_{SRL}} \right) \\
\vartheta_{RR} &= \arctan \left(\frac{\tfrac{b_R}{2} + n_{SRR}}{l_R + n_{LRR}} \right)
\end{aligned}
\tag{6.3}
$$

The caster n_{Lij} is always defined positive in the direction $-x_W$, n_{Sij} always in the direction of $-y_W$, hence n_{Lij}, n_{Sij} can be negative.

Whereas the course angle changes with the angular velocity ($\dot{\psi} + \dot{\beta}$), the chassis only turns with velocity $\dot{\psi}$ about the vertical axis, as shown in Figure 6.5.

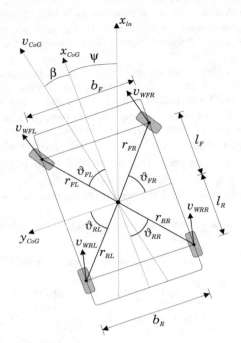

v_{WFL} : *front left wheel velocity*
v_{WFR} : *front right wheel velocity*
v_{WRL} : *rear left wheel velocity*
v_{WRR} : *rear right wheel velocity*
r_{FL} : *distance from CoG to front left wheel ground contact point*
r_{FR} : *distance from CoG to front right wheel ground contact point*
r_{RL} : *distance from CoG to rear left wheel ground contact point*
r_{RR} : *distance from CoG to rear right wheel ground contact point*
ϑ_{FL} : *angle between chassis (CoG) coordinate system and front left*
    wheel ground contact point
ϑ_{FR} : *angle between chassis (CoG) coordinate system and front right*
    wheel ground contact point
ϑ_{RL} : *angle between chassis (CoG) coordinate system and rear left*
    wheel ground contact point
ϑ_{RR} : *angle between chassis (CoG) coordinate system and rear right*
    wheel ground contact point
l_F : *distance from CoG to front axle*
l_R : *distance from CoG to rear axle*
b_F : *distance between wheels on front axle*
b_R : *distance between wheels on rear axle*

Figure 6.5 Velocity components throughout the vehicle

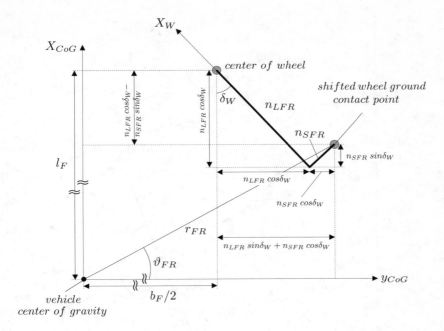

Figure 6.6 Geometric calculation of the distance r_{FR}

The wheel ground contact point velocities consist of two components: the component due to the CoG velocity and the component due to the motion about the vertical vehicle axis, $\dot{\psi}$. A division into longitudinal and lateral vehicle directions gives the following equations, where $\vec{e_X}$ denotes the longitudinal CoG co-ordinate direction and $\vec{e_Y}$ the lateral CoG co-ordinate direction:

$$\underline{v}_{WFL} = \left(v_{CoG}\cos\beta - \dot{\psi}r_{FL}\sin\vartheta_{FL}\right)\vec{e_X} + \left(v_{CoG}\sin\beta + \dot{\psi}r_{FL}\cos\vartheta_{FL}\right)\vec{e_Y}$$

$$\underline{v}_{WFR} = \left(v_{CoG}\cos\beta + \dot{\psi}r_{FR}\cos\vartheta_{FR}\right)\vec{e_X} + \left(v_{CoG}\sin\beta + \dot{\psi}r_{FR}\sin\vartheta_{FR}\right)\vec{e_Y}$$

$$\underline{v}_{WRL} = \left(v_{CoG}\cos\beta - \dot{\psi}r_{RL}\cos\vartheta_{RL}\right)\vec{e_X} + \left(v_{CoG}\sin\beta - \dot{\psi}r_{RL}\sin\vartheta_{RL}\right)\vec{e_Y}$$

$$\underline{v}_{WRR} = \left(v_{CoG}\cos\beta + \dot{\psi}r_{RR}\sin\vartheta_{RR}\right)\vec{e_X} + \left(v_{CoG}\sin\beta - \dot{\psi}r_{RR}\cos\vartheta_{RR}\right)\vec{e_Y}$$

$$(6.4)$$

Eqs. 6.4 are then the basis for the calculation of the tire side slip angle using the velocity balances (method 1) given in Section 6.3.2. In practice, the calculation variables ϑ_{ij} and r_{ij}, are time dependant because of the time dependant casters. The presented approach is an approximation and enables the direct calculation of both the magnitude and the direction of the wheel ground contact point velocities. The magnitudes of the wheel speeds are calculated by taking the square root of the sum of the squares of the two components $\vec{e_X}$ and $\vec{e_Y}$.

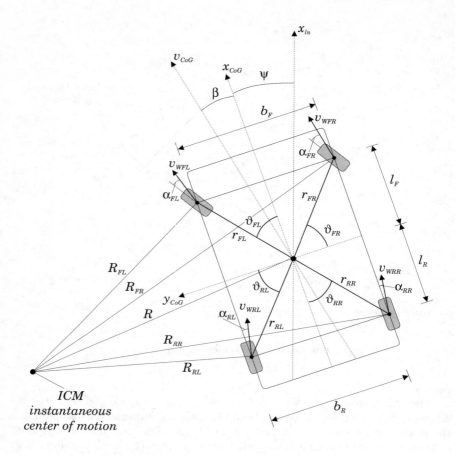

Figure 6.7 Individual curve-radii of the wheels when cornering

Approximation of the Velocities at the Wheel-Ground Contact Points

As mentioned earlier it is assumed that the caster has no dynamics of its own. The caster component perpendicular to the wheel plane is also neglected. This is allowable because the caster effect is very small compared to the distances l_F, l_R and $b_F/2$, $b_R/2$. The angles ϑ_{ij} and the radii r_{ij} can be calculated in advance, so that the evaluation of Eqs. 6.4 requires only a few calculation steps. Moreover, $\sin\beta$ and $\cos\beta$ can be approximated with first order Taylor polynomials; with the assumption that the vehicle body side slip angle β is limited to a value which is less than $10°$, the error will be less than 0.5% . To calculate the wheel ground contact point velocities the following approximations are substituted into Eqs. 6.4:

$$\sin\beta = \beta$$
$$\cos\beta = 1 \qquad\qquad (6.5)$$

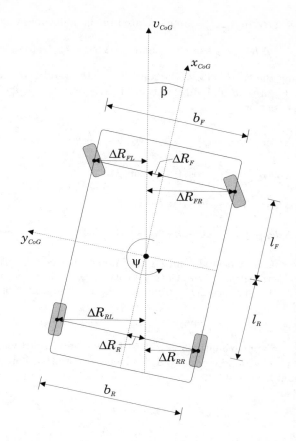

Figure 6.8 Differential curve radii of the individual wheels

Method 2: Calculating the Individual Curve Radii

If one considers the vehicle during a turn from a birds eye view, one realises that each wheel follows an individual curve. The velocities of the CoG and the wheel-ground contact points are perpendicular to the connecting lines to the instantaneous center of motion (ICM), as shown in Figure 6.7.

An exact method for calculating the individual curve radii R_{ij} exists, but has the disadvantage that the distance from the CoG to the instantaneous centre (ICM) must be known.

Under the assumption that the distance R from the vehicle CoG to the instantaneous centre (ICM) is much larger than the distances r_{ij}, one can consider the differential radii ΔR_{ij} as parallel lines, as shown in Figure 6.8.

With the differential radii approach one has the possibility to determine the velocities of the wheel-ground contact points v_{Wij}, without knowing the absolute turn radius R of the CoG.

The values ΔR_F and ΔR_R are calculated in the following way:

$$\Delta R_F = l_F \cdot \tan\beta \quad\text{and}\quad \Delta R_R = l_R \cdot \tan\beta$$

By disregarding the caster effect, the four differential radii ΔR_{ij} are found from inspection of Figure 6.8 and substitution of ΔR_F and ΔR_R, and are given by the following equations:

$$\Delta R_{FL} = \left(\frac{b_F}{2} - \Delta R_F\right)\cos\beta = \frac{b_F}{2}\cos\beta - l_F \cdot \sin\beta$$

$$\Delta R_{FR} = \frac{b_F}{2}\cos\beta + l_F \cdot \sin\beta$$

$$\Delta R_{RL} = \frac{b_R}{2}\cos\beta + l_R \cdot \sin\beta$$

$$\Delta R_{RR} = \frac{b_R}{2}\cos\beta - l_R \cdot \sin\beta \tag{6.6}$$

The velocities of the wheel ground contact points can now be calculated using an additive superposition of the CoG velocity v_{CoG} and the additional angular velocity due to the distance ΔR_{ij} from the wheel to the centre of gravity, i.e.:

$$v_{Wij} = v_{CoG} \mp \dot\psi \Delta R_{ij} \tag{6.7}$$

Substituting the approximations (Eq. 6.5) for $cos\beta$ and $sin\beta$ yields the magnitudes of the wheel ground contact point velocities (note that here no information about direction is available):

$$v_{WFL} = v_{CoG} - \dot\psi\left(\frac{b_F}{2} - l_F\beta\right)$$

$$v_{WFR} = v_{CoG} + \dot\psi\left(\frac{b_F}{2} + l_F\beta\right)$$

$$v_{WRL} = v_{CoG} - \dot\psi\left(\frac{b_R}{2} + l_R\beta\right)$$

$$v_{WRR} = v_{CoG} + \dot\psi\left(\frac{b_R}{2} - l_R\beta\right) \tag{6.8}$$

Comparison of the Two Methods for the Calculation of Wheel Velocities

The question now arises whether the methods satisfy the requirements in terms of low computational expense and high accuracy within the area of driving stability. To determine this a simulation run in the limiting range under exact calculation of the wheel-ground contact point velocities is carried out. Figure 6.9 shows the inputs in the form of the wheel turn angles δ_W and the individual state variables a_y, v_{CoG}, β and $\dot\psi$.

The test drive is carried out on dry road conditions with a maximum adhesion coefficient of approximately 1.2. The wheel turn angle δ_W has a sinewave form with an amplitude of $7°$ and a frequency of approximately $0.7\,Hz$. The lateral

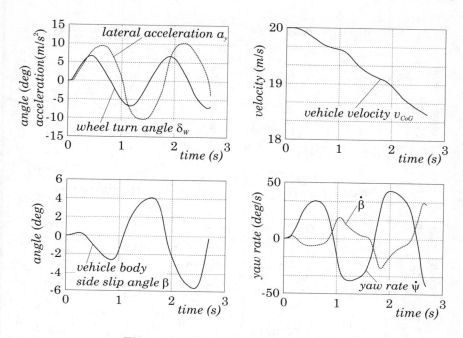

Figure 6.9 Simulation of stable driving

acceleration a_Y takes values up to $10\,m/s^2$ with which the wheels are well into the nonlinear region. The vehicle velocity v_{CoG} drops because of the turn resistance. The vehicle body side slip angle β takes values up to approximately $6°$, and the plot shows increasing oscillatory behaviour, indicating the onset of an unstable driving situation. Additionally the rate of change of vehicle body side slip angle $\dot{\beta}$ and the yaw rate $\dot{\psi}$ are shown, to give an impression of the turning motion of the chassis. a_Y, δ_W and $\dot{\psi}$ are measured on the experimental vehicle. v_{CoG}, β and $\dot{\beta}$ are estimated values (see Chapter 7).

In Figure 6.10 the velocities of the wheel ground contact points are calculated from the states from Figure 6.9. The solid lines marked with ①show the calculation from Eq. 6.4 and the corresponding approximation using Eqs. 6.5 (Method 1). Method 2 of calculation using differential radii ΔR_{ij} and parallelisation of the turn radii is marked with ②. The wheel velocity errors are very small.

Method 2, because of its simplicity, is preferable if only the magnitude of the wheel velocities is required. Method 1 must be used when the wheel side slip angle is to be derived individually for all four wheels (See Section 6.3.2, Method 1: Calculation of the tire side slip angle for the two-track model).

6.3.2   Wheel Slip and Tire Side Slip Angle

The wheel slip must be very accurately calculated. Due to the extremely high gradient of the cohesion coefficient characteristics, errors in the per-thousand

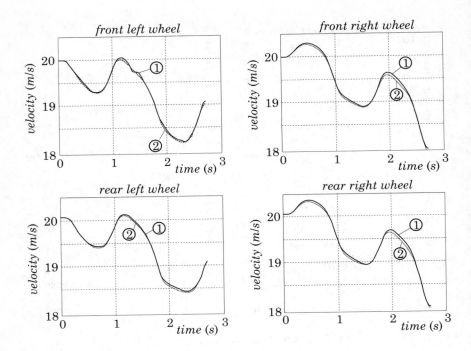

Figure 6.10 Comparison of the two methods for the derivation of the wheel ground contact point velocities

range can result in force reactions of considerable dimensions. A typical value for the gradient at the origin is 30, this means that a per-thousand wheel slip change causes an adhesion coefficient change of 3 % i.e. a horizontal force of 3 % of the wheel ground contact force.

The calculation of the wheel slip s_L, s_S requires the tire side slip angle α, as the wheel slip is a vector and thus the velocities in the slip direction must be transformed. Two methods for the calculation of the tire side slip angle α are then compared.

Wheel Slip Calculation

If the vehicle drives without tire side slip, the wheel slip is simply the difference between the rotational equivalent wheel velocity and the CoG velocity. By simultaneous appearance of longitudinal and lateral wheel slip there are various definitions in the literature. Burckhardt calculates the longitudinal wheel slip in the direction of motion of the wheel, as well as the force [13]. In contrast to this Reimpell specifies the longitudinal wheel slip in the direction of the wheel plane [67].

Here, the Burckhardt approach is chosen. The longitudinal slip s_L is defined in the direction of the wheel ground contact point velocity v_{Wij}, and the lateral

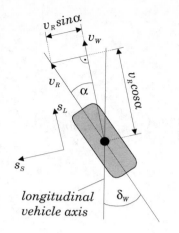

v_R : *rotational equivalent wheel velocity*
v_W : *wheel ground contact point velocity*

Figure 6.11 Wheel slip calculation

slip s_s at right angles to this (Eq. 6.9). The rotational equivalent wheel velocity v_{Rij} is multiplied with the cosine of the tire side slip angle to obtain the projection in the direction of the wheel velocity v_W.

	Braking $v_R \cos \alpha \leq v_W$	**Driving** $v_R \cos \alpha > v_W$	
Longitudinal slip	$s_L = \frac{v_R \cos \alpha - v_W}{v_W}$	$s_L = \frac{v_R \cos \alpha - v_W}{v_R \cos \alpha}$	(6.9)
Side slip	$s_S = \frac{v_R \cdot \sin \alpha}{v_W}$	$s_S = \tan \alpha$	

The resultant slip s_L must always be smaller than 1. Therefore, the speed difference is divided by the respective larger speed, i.e. v_W for braking and v_R when accelerating. With these definitions the limiting of s_L is ensured. The resultant wheel slip is the geometrical sum of the longitudinal and side slip:

$$s_{Res} = \sqrt{s_L^2 + s_S^2} \tag{6.10}$$

Tire Side Slip Angle Calculation

Method 1: Geometric Derivation Using Wheel Velocity Vector

If the directions of the wheel ground contact point velocities v_W are known (Eq. 6.4) the four tire side slip angles α can easily be derived geometrically. The tire side slip angle α is, as shown in Figure 6.11, the angle between the wheel plane and the velocity of the wheel ground contact point. For the calculation of the tire-slip angle based on the simplified versions of Eqs 6.4 the following are obtained (see Figure 6.12):

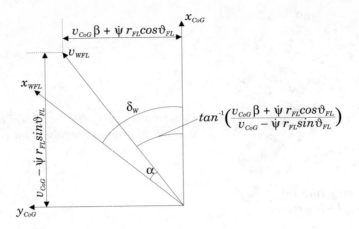

Figure 6.12 Calculation of the front left tire side slip angle

$$\alpha_{FL} = \delta_W - \arctan\left(\frac{v_{CoG}\beta + \dot{\psi}r_{FL}\cos\vartheta_{FL}}{v_{CoG} - \dot{\psi}r_{FL}\sin\vartheta_{FL}}\right)$$

$$\alpha_{FR} = \delta_W - \arctan\left(\frac{v_{CoG}\beta + \dot{\psi}r_{FR}\sin\vartheta_{FR}}{v_{CoG} + \dot{\psi}r_{FR}\cos\vartheta_{FR}}\right)$$

$$\alpha_{RL} = -\arctan\left(\frac{v_{CoG}\beta - \dot{\psi}r_{RL}\sin\vartheta_{RL}}{v_{CoG} - \dot{\psi}r_{RL}\sin\vartheta_{RL}}\right)$$

$$\alpha_{RR} = -\arctan\left(\frac{v_{CoG}\beta - \dot{\psi}r_{RR}\cos\vartheta_{RR}}{v_{CoG} + \dot{\psi}r_{RR}\sin\vartheta_{RR}}\right) \qquad (6.11)$$

Method 2: The Single-Track Model

In the single-track model, the wheels on each axis are considered as a single unit, as shown in Figure 6.13. Because of this, it is only possible to derive one single tire side slip angle for the left and right wheels on the front axle, and one for the wheels on the rear axle.

The instantaneous centre of motion (ICM) is such that the velocity vectors of the CoG and the wheels are perpendicular to the lines connecting these points to the instantaneous centre. For a known vehicle body side slip angle β the tire side slip angles α can be calculated.

The definition of the tire side slip angles α_F and α_R can be taken from Figure 6.14, and are calculated in accordance with Mitschke [53] by forming the velocity balance equations in the vehicle longitudinal and lateral directions.

The chassis and the wheels have identical velocities at the wheel ground contact points. For the front wheel in the lateral direction (from Figs 6.13 and 6.14):

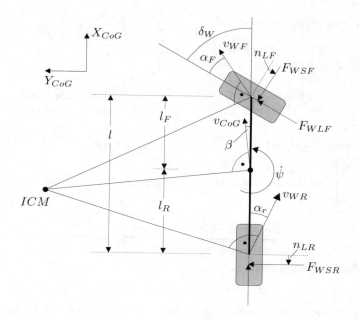

F_{WLF}	:	longitudinal front wheel force
F_{WLR}	:	longitudinal rear wheel force
F_{WSF}	:	lateral (side) front wheel force
F_{WSR}	:	lateral (side) rear wheel force
$\dot{\psi}$	:	yaw rate
δ_W	:	wheel turn angle
α_F	:	tyre side slip angle front
α_R	:	tyre side slip angle rear
β	:	vehicle body side slip angle
l	:	wheel base
l_F	:	distance from CoG to front axle
l_R	:	distance from CoG to front axle
n_{LF}	:	Caster effect front
n_{LR}	:	Caster effect rear
ICM	:	instaneous center(of motion)
v_{WF}	:	direction of front wheel velocity
v_{WR}	:	direction of rear wheel velocity
v_{CoG}	:	direction of CoG velocity

Figure 6.13 Variables for the single-track model

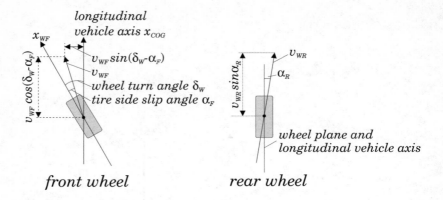

Figure 6.14   Definition of the tire side slip angle α for the single-track model

$$\underbrace{v_{WF}\sin(\delta_W - \alpha_F)}_{wheel\ velocity} = \underbrace{l_F \cdot \dot\psi + v_{CoG}\sin\beta}_{chassis\ velocity} \tag{6.12}$$

and in the longitudinal direction:

$$v_{WF}\cos(\delta_W - \alpha_F) = v_{CoG}\cos\beta \tag{6.13}$$

Dividing the two equations gives the equation for the calculation of the tire side slip angle for the front axle:

$$\tan(\delta_W - \alpha_F) = \frac{l_F \cdot \dot\psi + v_{CoG}\sin\beta}{v_{CoG}\cos\beta} \tag{6.14}$$

Similarly, for the rear axle:

$$\tan\alpha_R = \frac{l_R \cdot \dot\psi - v_{CoG}\sin\beta}{v_{CoG}\cos\beta} \tag{6.15}$$

At stable driving conditions, the tire side slip angle α is normally no larger than 5° and the above equation can be simplified by substituting $\sin\beta \approx \beta$ and $\cos\beta \approx 1$. The classic equations for the tire side slip angles are then given as:

$$\alpha_F = -\beta + \delta_W - \frac{l_F \cdot \dot\psi}{v_{CoG}} \quad \text{and} \quad \alpha_R = -\beta + \frac{l_R \cdot \dot\psi}{v_{CoG}} \tag{6.16}$$

Figure 6.15 shows the relationships of the simplified tire side slip angle calculations for the single-track model. To compare the two methods the extreme driving shown in Figure 6.9 is once more used. Figure 6.16 shows the results for the derivation of the tire-slip angle. The tire side slip angles calculated using the transformation of the CoG method (Eq. 6.11) are marked with ①. Curve ②, calculated using the single-track model (Eq. 6.16) can not be differentiated.

Important to note is that the extremely simple equations for the calculation of the tire-slip angle based on the single-track model give good results for driving in the limiting range. Thus this simple method can be later used for observer design.

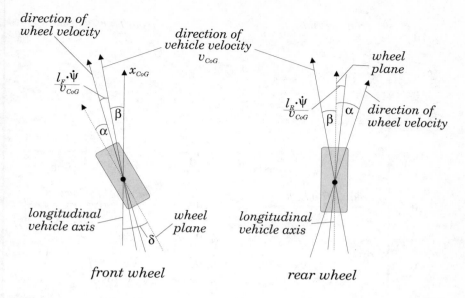

Figure 6.15 Simplified tire side slip angle calculation for the single-track model

6.3.3 Friction Co-efficient Calculation

The friction behaviour of the wheels can be approximated with parametric characteristics, as shown in Figure 6.17. The friction, or cohesion co-efficient μ is defined as the ratio of the frictional force acting in the wheel plane F_{fric} and the wheel ground contact force F_Z:

$$\mu = \frac{F_{fric}}{F_Z} \tag{6.17}$$

The calculation of friction forces can be carried out using the method of Burckhardt [13]:

$$\mu(s_{Res}) = c_1 \cdot \left(1 - e^{-c2 \cdot s_{Res}}\right) - c_3 s_{Res} \tag{6.18}$$

The Burckhardt approach, Eq. 6.18, can be extended via a pair of factors, where c_4 describes the influence of a higher drive velocity and c_5 the influence of a higher wheel load. Both factors have a maximum value of 1, i.e. they lead to a reduction of the friction co-efficient. Incorrect tire pressure can also lead to a reduction of the friction co-efficient. This effect however can be disregarded for variations in pressure of less than $0.3\,bar$. The resulting friction co-efficient is then given by:

$$\mu_{Res}(s_{Res}) = \left(c_1 \cdot \left(1 - e^{-c2 \cdot s_{Res}}\right) - c_3 s_{Res}\right) \cdot e^{-c4 \cdot s_{Res} \cdot v_{CoG}} \cdot \left(1 - c_5 F_Z^2\right) \tag{6.19}$$

The parameters c_1, c_2, and c_3 are given for various road surfaces in Table 6.3. Parameter c_4 lies in the range $0.02\,s/m$ to $0.04\,s/m$. This results, for a slip of

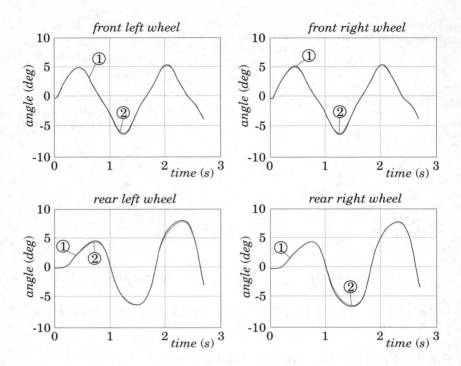

Figure 6.16 Results of the two methods of calculating the tire side slip angle

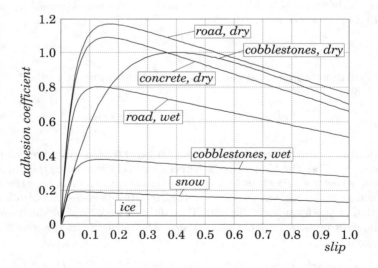

Figure 6.17 Typical cohesion coefficient characteristics

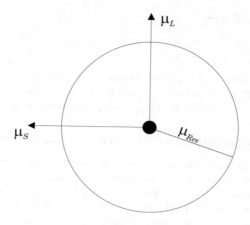

Figure 6.18 Kamm circle

10 % and velocity of $20\,m/s$, in a friction co-efficient change of almost 8 %. As a first estimate, a homogeneous axle load distribution with static values for the wheel contact force of $F_Z = 4500\,N$ per wheel is assumed. At extreme cornering the wheel contact force can fall almost to zero, or can rise to almost double the normal value. With parameter $c_5 = 0.0015\,1/(kN^2)$ and a dynamic wheel force of $8\,kN$, a reduction in the friction coefficient of 9.6 % results.

The friction co-efficient values shown in Figure 6.17 are only valid for quasi-static operating points, and not for quickly changing dynamic transition states. For fast changes of the tire side slip angle, an analysis of the time dependency of the cornering forces is given in [1].

The resultant slip s_{Res} is directed in the same direction as the resultant friction co-efficient μ_{Res}. This gives the following equations for the friction co-efficients in the longitudinal and lateral directions:

$$\mu_L = \mu_{Res} \frac{s_L}{s_{Res}} \quad and \quad \mu_S = \mu_{Res} \frac{s_S}{s_{Res}} \tag{6.20}$$

Assuming that the friction behaviour of the tire is independent of the direction of the slip, the behaviour in Eq. 6.20 can be described using a Kamm circle. This gives information about the directional distribution of the friction co-efficients, as shown in Figure 6.18. The contact between the tire and the road, together with the vehicle velocity and the wheel load, determines the level of the maximum resultant friction co-efficient $\mu_{Res,Max}$, which can then be split into longitudinal and lateral friction co-efficients.

In the presence of tread profile the friction behaviour can also be dependant on direction. The maximum friction co-efficient in the lateral direction is smaller than in the longitudinal direction. In this case the Kamm circle degenerates to an ellipse. Formula-wise this is expressed using an attenuation factor k_S for the lateral friction co-efficient:

$$\mu_L = \mu_{Res} \frac{s_L}{s_{Res}} \quad and \quad \mu_S = k_s \mu_{Res} \frac{s_S}{s_{Res}} \tag{6.21}$$

For $k_S = 1$ Eqs. 6.20 and 6.21 are identical. Common low profile tires have an attenuation factor of between 0.9 and 0.95. The behaviour can be different during braking and acceleration. This effect is not considered here.

Friction Value Characteristics for Various Road Surfaces

Table 6.3 gives a list of the parameter sets for various road surfaces [13].

With the exception of wet cobblestones the Burckhardt characteristics correspond very precisely to measured characteristics [52]. A measured friction co-efficient characteristic for cobblestones exhibits a higher initial gradient, however this levels out at friction values of about 0.4, and then runs with a smaller gradient to the maximum value, where it can then again be well approximated.

Table 6.3 Parameter sets for friction co-efficient characteristics (Burckhardt)

	c_1	c_2	c_3
Asphalt, dry	1.2801	23.99	0.52
Asphalt, wet	0.857	33.822	0.347
Concrete, dry	1.1973	25.168	0.5373
Cobblestones, dry	1.3713	6.4565	0.6691
Cobblestones, wet	0.4004	33.7080	0.1204
Snow	0.1946	94.129	0.0646
Ice	0.05	306.39	0

6.3.4   Calculation of Friction Forces

The friction co-efficients in the direction of the wheel velocity v_W and orthogonal to it can be calculated using Eqs 6.10, 6.19 and 6.21. The frictional forces can then be calculated from the friction co-efficients using Eq. 6.17. This then gives the frictional forces F_L and F_S in the direction of the wheel ground contact velocity v_W, and at right angles to it (see Figure 6.19):

In the direction v_W :

$$\begin{aligned} F_L &= \mu_L F_Z \\ &= \mu_{Res} \cdot \frac{s_L}{s_{Res}} \cdot F_Z \end{aligned} \tag{6.22}$$

In the direction at right angles to v_W

$$\begin{aligned} F_S &= \mu_S F_Z \\ &= \mu_{Res} \cdot k_S \cdot \frac{s_S}{s_{Res}} \cdot F_Z \end{aligned} \tag{6.23}$$

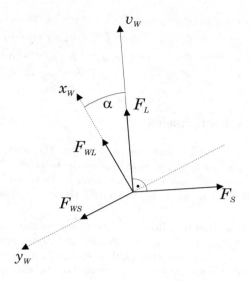

Figure 6.19 Direction of frictional forces

Transforming into the wheel co-ordinate system (x_W, y_W):

In the direction x_W :
$$F_{WL} = F_L \cos\alpha - F_S \sin\alpha \tag{6.24}$$

In the direction y_W :
$$F_{WS} = -F_S \cos\alpha - F_L \sin\alpha \tag{6.25}$$

Substituting Eq. 6.22 into Eq. 6.24, and Eq. 6.23 into Eq. 6.25 then yields:

$$F_{WL} = \mu_{Res} \cdot \frac{s_L}{s_{Res}} \cdot F_Z \cdot \cos\alpha - \mu_{Res} \cdot k_S \cdot \frac{s_S}{s_{Res}} F_Z \cdot \sin\alpha$$

$$= \left(\mu_{Res} \cdot \frac{s_L}{s_{Res}} \cdot \cos\alpha - \mu_{Res} \cdot k_S \cdot \frac{s_S}{s_{Res}} \cdot \sin\alpha \right) \cdot F_Z \tag{6.26}$$

$$F_{WS} = -\mu_{Res} \cdot k_S \cdot \frac{s_S}{s_{Res}} \cdot F_Z \cdot \cos\alpha - \mu_{Res} \frac{s_L}{s_{Res}} \cdot F_Z \cdot \sin\alpha$$

$$= -\left(\mu_{Res} \cdot k_S \cdot \frac{s_S}{s_{Res}} \cdot \cos\alpha + \mu_{Res} \cdot \frac{s_L}{s_{Res}} \cdot \sin\alpha \right) \cdot F_Z \tag{6.27}$$

The longitudinal F_{WL} and side F_{WS} friction forces are now transformed from the wheel co-ordinate system to the undercarriage co-ordinate system. For the wheels on the rear axle no transformation is necessary as the wheel plane lies parallel to the longitudinal vehicle axis:

$$F_{XRL} = F_{WL,RL} \quad , \quad F_{YRL} = F_{WS,RL}$$
$$F_{XRR} = F_{WL,RR} \quad , \quad F_{YRR} = F_{WS,RR} \tag{6.28}$$

For the wheels on the front axle the forces are transformed by the wheel turn angle δ_W:

$$
\begin{aligned}
F_{XFL} &= F_{WL,FL}\cos\delta_{WL} - F_{WS,FL}\sin\delta_{WL} \\
F_{YFL} &= F_{WS,FL}\cos\delta_{WL} + F_{WL,FL}\sin\delta_{WL} \\
F_{XFR} &= F_{WL,FR}\cos\delta_{WR} - F_{WS,FR}\sin\delta_{WR} \\
F_{YFR} &= F_{WS,FR}\cos\delta_{WR} + F_{WL,FR}\sin\delta_{WR} \qquad (6.29)
\end{aligned}
$$

6.3.5   Tire Characteristics

In the previous section the frictional forces as well as the wheel slip and tire side slip angle have been derived; this section illustrates the effect of the tire slip. The tire slip is derived geometrically from the vehicle state variables. For control of the tire side slip angle it is necessary to control the rotation around the vehicle vertical axis.

The following three figures show the tire characteristics dependant on tire side slip angle for dry asphalt. The tire characteristics are normally given with the tire side slip angle as a parameter. This does not mean however that the tire side slip angle remains constant during a braking or steering manoeuvre.

Figure 6.20 shows the plot of lateral friction co-efficients against longitudinal friction co-efficients. Without tire side slip angle there is no side force possible, hence a branch of the group of curves lies along the axis. For a 2° tire side slip angle there is already the possibility of lateral friction co-efficients of up to $\mu_S = 0.7$. The cause of this is the fact that the side slip at $\alpha = 2°$ can already lie at $s_S = 3.5\,\%$ and this produces this high friction value for dry road surfaces. If the tangent to the curves is constructed, the Kamm circle of Figure 6.18 is produced. The tendency of the group of curves is easy to understand: the larger the tire side slip angle α, the smaller the longitudinal force F_L. For a tire side slip angle of 16° a friction value of almost $\mu_L = 1$ is possible in the longitudinal direction. Figs. 6.21 and 6.22 show the influence of the tire side slip angle in more detail.

Figure 6.21 shows a plot of longitudinal friction co-efficient μ_L against longitudinal slip s_L. It illustrates the reduction in braking force when braking in a curve. If the driver turns during full braking the result is a tire side slip angle together with a side force. This causes a reduction in the longitudinal force and the braking distance is increased. The maximum wheel turn angle, which is dependant on the vehicle type, is approximately $\delta_W = 30°$. For stable driving situations no tire side slip angle greater than $\alpha = 16°$ can occur, as the vehicle body side slip angle β lies in a similar value range. The shift of the maximum of the longitudinal friction co-efficient μ_L to higher slip values s_L for increasing tire side slip angle α is clear.

Figure 6.22 shows a plot of lateral friction co-efficient μ_S against longitudinal slip s_L. During non-braking turning the lateral friction co-efficient μ_S makes available the whole traction (adhesion) potential, so that the curves begin with the maximum value. With a tire side slip angle of about $\alpha = 8°$ the lateral friction co-efficient μ_S assumes its maximum value. If the longitudinal slip μ_L increases, the side force sinks rapidly. This can be only partly compensated by an increase in the tire side slip angle.

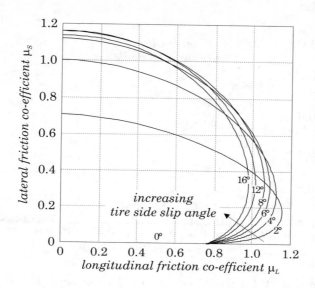

Figure 6.20 Lateral friction coefficient μ_S over longitudinal friction coefficient μ_L

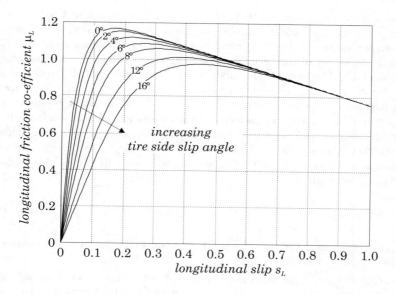

Figure 6.21 Longitudinal friction coefficient μ_L over longitudinal slip s_L

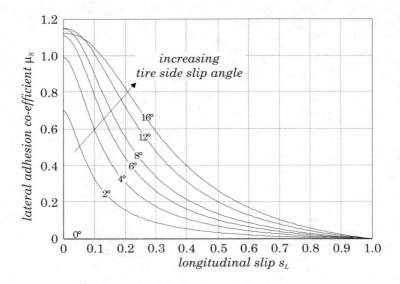

Figure 6.22 Lateral friction coefficient μ_S over longitudinal slip s_L

Effect of the Camber Angle on the Tire Side Slip Angle

Till now it has been assumed that the wheel stands perpendicular to the road. In practice the wheel stands at a camber angle γ to the vertical axis. The direction of the camber angle is defined according to [53]: γ is negative when the wheel leans towards the center of the turning curve. This corresponds to a *leaning-into-the-turn* of a bike. The tire side slip angle α is made smaller by this. Approximating $s_S = \tan \alpha$ by $s_S \approx \alpha$, the characteristic friction curve $\mu_S(\alpha)$ is shifted upwards with negative γ. Using the curves from [67] and [53] linear approximations are developed for the calculation of forces in the presence of camber angle. Using the approximately parallel shift of the lateral tire slip curves, the camber angle can be interpreted as a shifting of the tire side slip angle α. With this, a negative camber angle γ means a shifting to smaller tire side slip angles. The following approximation is used:

$$\alpha^* = \alpha + k_{camb}\gamma \tag{6.30}$$

k_{camb} is chosen as 0.1. With this a 10° camber angle gives the same effect as a 1° tire side slip angle.

For an exact calculation of the tire camber, one must observe the axle geometry. A camber angle of $\gamma = 0.5°$ is set for the neutral position of the chassis suspension. On top of this a camber angle change of $\gamma = 0.3°$ is generated per cm of spring displacement Δz_W. In cornering, this results in a stabilising turning motion of the rear wheels. The maximum camber angle is approximately $\gamma = 3°$.

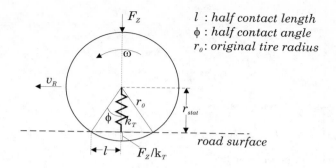

Figure 6.23 Static and dynamic wheel radius

6.3.6 Definition of the Wheel Radius

To calculate the angular wheel velocity ω, a torque balance is formed for each wheel. The accelerating torque is the drive torque T_{Drive} of the driveline. The decelerating effects come from the braking torque T_{Br} and tire friction torque $r_{eff}F_{WL}$. With the moment of inertia of the wheel, J_W, one obtains:

$$J_W\dot{\omega} = T_{Drive} - T_{Br} - r_{eff}F_{LW} \tag{6.31}$$

The effective dynamic rolling radius r_{eff} is different from the static tyre radius r_{stat}.

Static Tire Radius

The static tire radius r_{stat} relates the stationary wheel ground contact force F_Z to the tire spring stiffness k_T, as shown in Figure 6.23:

$$r_{stat} = r_0 - \frac{F_Z}{k_T} \tag{6.32}$$

Dynamic Tire Radius

The dynamic tire radius r_{eff} relates the angular wheel velocity ω to the rotational equivalent velocity v_R (Figure 6.23). The rotational equivalent velocity v_R may be calculated as:

$$
\begin{aligned}
v_R &= \text{(effective tire circumference)} \times \text{(tire rotations per time)} \\
&= 2 \cdot \pi \cdot r_{eff} \times n_T \\
&= r_{eff} \cdot \omega
\end{aligned}
$$

The rotational equivalent velocity v_R can also be calculated, along with the angular rotation ω, by running through length l and corresponding angle ϕ in the same reference time t:

$$v_R = \frac{l}{t} \quad ; \quad \omega = \frac{\phi}{t} \tag{6.33}$$

$$\frac{l}{t} = r_{eff} \cdot \frac{\phi}{t} \quad ; \quad r_{eff} = \frac{l}{\phi} \tag{6.34}$$

From the geometric relationships;

$$r_{stat} = r_0 \cdot \cos \phi \quad ; \quad l = r_0 \cdot \sin \phi \quad , \tag{6.35}$$

the following can be obtained:

$$r_{eff} = r_0 \cdot \frac{\sin \left(\arccos \left(\frac{r_{stat}}{r_0} \right) \right)}{\arccos \left(\frac{r_{stat}}{r_0} \right)} \tag{6.36}$$

6.4   The Complete Vehicle Model

If the chassis is considered as a body with 6 degrees of freedom (x_{CoG}, y_{CoG}, z_{CoG}, ψ, χ, φ), with forces from road, gravitation and wind acting upon the chassis, then the structure of Figure 6.24 results. The chassis itself is divided into a rotary part for the calculation of yaw rate $\dot{\psi}$, roll rate $\dot{\varphi}$, pitch rate $\dot{\chi}$ and their integrals, and a translatory part for the calculation of displacement, velocity and acceleration in the direction of the three co-ordinate axis. Wind strength is considered in the longitudinal and lateral velocity directions, and the gravitational force in the chassis co-ordinate directions. The wheels together with the chassis are modelled as a vertical spring-damper system. For the vehicle suspension a linear and a nonlinear method are carried out and compared.

6.4.1   Chassis Translatory Motion

The translatory variables are calculated in the inertial co-ordinate system and then transformed into the undercarriage co-ordinate system. As well as the horizontally acting wheel forces and the vertically acting chassis forces, the gravitational forces and the wind strength are calculated in the three undercarriage co-ordinate directions. Because all of the forces relevant for the translatory motion are contact forces to the environment, it is sensible to carry out the integration in the inertial system, as otherwise forces would appear by the transformation between two accelerating co-ordinate systems. The calculation equations are force balances for the three co-ordinate directions of the inertial co-ordinate system:

$$m_{CoG} \begin{bmatrix} \ddot{x}_{In} \\ \ddot{y}_{In} \\ \ddot{z}_{In} \end{bmatrix} = \underline{T}_{UIn} \underbrace{\begin{bmatrix} F_{XFL} + F_{XFR} + F_{XRL} + F_{XRR} + F_{windX} + F_{GX} + F_R \\ F_{YFL} + F_{YFR} + F_{YRL} + F_{YRR} + F_{windY} + F_{GY} \\ F_{ZCFL} + F_{ZCFR} + F_{ZCRL} + F_{ZCRR} + F_{windZ} + F_{GZ} \end{bmatrix}}_{\text{Forces in the undercarriage co-ordinate system}} \tag{6.37}$$

Where, F_{Xij}, F_{Yij} are the wheel forces, F_{ZCij} the vertical chassis forces, F_{wind} are the wind forces, F_G the gravitational forces and F_R is the rolling resistance.

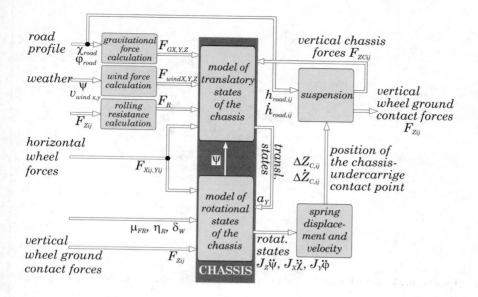

Figure 6.24 Structure and signal flows for the Complete Vehicle Model

The wheel forces F_{Xij} and F_{Yij} are calculated using the tire characteristics, as shown in Section 6.3.4. The vertical chassis forces F_{ZCij} are approximated in Section 7.4.1. The derivation of the wind forces, gravitational forces and rolling resistance is given in this section. $\underline{T}_{UIn}$ is a transformation matrix for rotating the vector from the undercarriage to the inertial co-ordinate system.

Transformation between Co-ordinate Systems

To begin with, the transformation from the CoG co-ordinate system to the inertial co-ordinate system will be considered. Figure 6.25 shows how the transformation is calculated for a rotation of the CoG co-ordinate system by a yaw angle ψ about the vertical axis.

Consider the point p, whose co-ordinates in the CoG co-ordinate system are p_{xCoG}, p_{yCoG}. The z-co-ordinate is not affected in the rotation. The projections of these points into the inertial co-ordinate system are shown in Figure 6.25 and yield the following:

$$p = (p_{xCoG} \cos \psi - p_{yCoG} \sin \psi) \, \vec{x}_{In} + (p_{xCoG} \sin \psi + p_{yCoG} \cos \psi) \, \vec{y}_{In}$$
$$+ (p_{zCoG}) \, \vec{z}_{In} \tag{6.38}$$

In matrix form this can be written as

$$\begin{bmatrix} x_{In} \\ y_{In} \\ z_{In} \end{bmatrix} = \underline{T}_{RotZ} \begin{bmatrix} x_{CoG} \\ y_{CoG} \\ z_{CoG} \end{bmatrix} \quad , \tag{6.39}$$

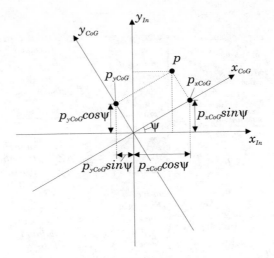

Figure 6.25 Rotation of the CoG co-ordinate system relative to the Inertial system

where $\underline{T}_{RotZ}$, the matrix which carries out the transformation T_{CoGIn} required due to rotation about the z axis is given by

$$\underline{T}_{RotZ} = \begin{bmatrix} \cos(\psi) & -\sin(\psi) & 0 \\ \sin(\psi) & \cos(\psi) & 0 \\ 0 & 0 & 1 \end{bmatrix} . \qquad (6.40)$$

To rotate in the opposite direction (i.e. from inertial to CoG) $\underline{T}_{RotZ}$ must be inverted. Due to the special structure of this matrix this corresponds to a rotation with a negative yaw angle ψ or a transposition of the matrix:

$$\underline{T}_{RotZ}^{-1} = \underline{T}_{RotZ}^{T} = \underline{T}_{RotZ}(-\psi) \qquad (6.41)$$

The above then describes a transformation due to a yaw angle (rotation about the vertical z axis). Similar transformation matrices can be derived for the roll and pitch angles:

- **Pitch angle**

$$\underline{T}_{RotY} = \begin{bmatrix} \cos(\chi) & 0 & \sin(\chi) \\ 0 & 1 & 0 \\ -\sin(\chi) & 0 & \cos(\chi) \end{bmatrix} \qquad (6.42)$$

- **Roll angle**

$$\underline{T}_{RotX} = \begin{bmatrix} 1 & 0 & 0 \\ 0 & \cos(\varphi) & -\sin(\varphi) \\ 0 & \sin(\varphi) & \cos(\varphi) \end{bmatrix} \tag{6.43}$$

A rotation about several axes corresponds to a multiplication of the rotation matrices. This presents the problem that the sequence of matrix multiplication affects the results. The standard order in the literature is: yaw-pitch-roll.

Transformation from CoG to Undercarriage Co-ordinate System

$$\underline{T}_{CoGU} = \underline{T}_{RotY} \cdot \underline{T}_{RotX} = \begin{bmatrix} \cos(\chi) & \sin(\chi)\sin(\varphi) & \sin(\chi)\cos(\varphi) \\ 0 & \cos(\varphi) & -\sin(\varphi) \\ -\sin(\chi) & \cos(\chi)\sin(\varphi) & \sin(\chi)\cos(\varphi) \end{bmatrix} \tag{6.44}$$

The inverse transformation can be used to calculate the transformation from undercarriage to CoG co-ordinate systems. This gives:

$$\underline{T}_{UCoG} = \underline{T}_{CoGU}^{-1} = \underline{T}_{RotX}^{-1} \cdot \underline{T}_{RotY}^{-1} = \underline{T}_{RotX}^{T} \cdot \underline{T}_{RotY}^{T} = \underline{T}_{CoGU}^{T} \tag{6.45}$$

Thus for a rotation around all three axis:

$$\begin{aligned} \underline{T}_{CoGIn} &= \underline{T}_{RotZYX} = \underline{T}_{RotZ} \cdot \underline{T}_{RotY} \cdot \underline{T}_{RotX} \\[2mm] &= \begin{bmatrix} \cos\psi\cos\chi & -\sin\psi\cos\varphi-\cos\psi\sin\chi\sin\varphi & \sin\psi\sin\varphi+\cos\psi\sin\chi\cos\varphi \\ \sin\psi\cos\chi & \cos\psi\cos\varphi+\sin\psi\sin\chi\sin\varphi & -\cos\psi\sin\varphi-\sin\psi\sin\chi\cos\varphi \\ \sin\chi & \cos\chi\sin\varphi & \cos\chi\cos\varphi \end{bmatrix} \end{aligned}$$

$$\begin{aligned} \underline{T}_{InCoG} &= \underline{T}_{RotXYZ} = \\ &= \underline{T}_{RotZYX}^{-1} = \underline{T}_{RotZYX}^{T} = \underline{T}_{RotZYX}\big|_{\psi=-\psi,\ \chi=-\chi,\ \varphi=-\varphi} \end{aligned} \tag{6.46}$$

Eq. 6.46 can be used to rotate from the CoG to the inertial systems. If however the road is not level, this must be taken into consideration by modifying the angles in $\underline{T}_{RotZYX}$:

$$\underline{T}_{CoGIn} = \underline{T}_{RotZYX}\big|_{\psi=\psi,\ \chi=\chi-\chi_{road},\ \varphi=\varphi-\varphi_{road}} \tag{6.47}$$

Similarly the transformation matrix for a rotation from undercarriage to inertial co-ordinates is:

$$\underline{T}_{UIn} = \underline{T}_{RotZYX}\big|_{\psi=\psi,\ \chi=-\chi_{road},\ \varphi=-\varphi_{road}} \tag{6.48}$$

Wind Force Calculation

The wind velocity is directed against the vehicle. To calculate the wind force, firstly the external wind velocity is transformed into the undercarriage co-ordinate system, then subtracted from the vehicle velocity, and finally the wind force calculated. The vehicle lift is disregarded.

$$
\begin{bmatrix} F_{windX} \\ F_{windY} \\ F_{windZ} \end{bmatrix} = \begin{bmatrix} -c_{aerX} A_L \frac{\rho}{2} \left(v_{CoGX} - v_{windX} \cos\psi - v_{windY} \sin\psi \right)^2 \\ -c_{aerY} A_S \frac{\rho}{2} \left(v_{CoGY} - v_{wind}^* \right)^2 \cdot \text{sign}\left(-v_{wind}^* \right) \\ 0 \end{bmatrix}
$$
(6.49)

with the abbreviation

$$
v_{wind}^* = -v_{windX} \sin\psi + v_{windY} \cos\psi
$$

$c_{aerX,Y}$ are the co-efficients of aerodynamic drag, $A_{L,S}$ the front and side vehicle areas, and $v_{windX,Y}$ the wind velocities.

Gravitational Force Calculation

The undercarriage co-ordinate system is at angle χ_{road} (due to road inclination) and φ_{road} (due to road camber) to the inertial system. A positive inclination χ_{road} means an upwards inclined road and a positive camber φ_{road} means a road which raises the right hand side of the vehicle. The transformation of the gravitational forces into the undercarriage co-ordinate system corresponds to a multiplication with the rotation matrix from the previous section, with yaw angle $\psi = 0$:

$$
\begin{bmatrix} F_{GX} \\ F_{GY} \\ F_{GZ} \end{bmatrix} =
$$

$$
= \begin{bmatrix} \cos(\chi_{road}) & \sin(\chi_{road})\sin(\varphi_{road}) & \sin(\chi_{road})\cos(\varphi_{road}) \\ 0 & \cos(\varphi_{road}) & -\sin(\varphi_{road}) \\ -\sin(\chi_{road}) & \cos(\chi_{road})\sin(\varphi_{road}) & \cos(\chi_{road})\cos(\varphi_{road}) \end{bmatrix} \cdot \begin{bmatrix} 0 \\ 0 \\ mg \end{bmatrix}
$$
(6.50)

Rolling Resistance Calculation

The tire rolling resistance force F_R is calculated according to [52]:

$$
F_R = -f_{R0} F_Z - f_{R1} F_Z \frac{v}{30} - f_{R2} F_Z \frac{v^4}{30^4}
$$
(6.51)

The dependence of the tire rolling resistance on the tire pressure is not regarded here.

Vehicle Body Side Slip Angle Calculation

For the direct calculation of the vehicle body side slip angle β the CoG (chassis) velocity must be given in inertial co-ordinates $v_{CoG,X}$ and $v_{CoG,Y}$, and the yaw angle subtracted from the chassis direction (Figure 6.7):

$$
\beta = \arctan\left(\frac{v_{CoG,Y}}{v_{CoG,X}} \right) - \psi
$$
(6.52)

In Section 7.3.2, a nonlinear observer for the estimation of the vehicle body side slip angle β is presented.

6.4.2 Chassis Rotational Motion

The rotational variables can be calculated directly in the undercarriage co-ordinate system since the roll and pitch axis are assumed to lie at the road level. For this the torque equations are used:

- **Torque balance around the vertical vehicle axis (yaw rate):**

$$
\begin{aligned}
J_Z \ddot{\psi} = {} & (F_{YFR} + F_{YFL}) \cdot (l_F - n_{LF}) - (F_{YRR} + F_{YRL}) \cdot (l_R + n_{LR}) \\
& + (F_{XRR} - F_{XRL}) \cdot \frac{b_R}{2} + F_{XFR} \cdot \left(\frac{b_F}{2} - n_{SFR} \sin \delta_W \right) \\
& - F_{XFL} \cdot \left(\frac{b_F}{2} + n_{SFL} \sin \delta_W \right)
\end{aligned}
\tag{6.53}
$$

In the following equations the vertical chassis forces F_{ZCij} are set equal to the wheel ground contact forces F_{Zij}, i.e. neglecting the suspension dynamics. This is justified, since roll and pitch motions are slower than vertical wheel motions on a rough road.

- **Torque balance around the vehicle longitudinal axis (roll rate):**

$$
J_X \ddot{\varphi} = (F_{ZFL} - F_{ZFR}) \cdot \frac{b_F}{2} + (F_{ZRL} - F_{ZRR}) \cdot \frac{b_R}{2} + m_{CoG} a_Y h_{CoG}
\tag{6.54}
$$

- **Torque balance around the lateral vehicle axis (pitch rate):**

$$
J_Y \ddot{\chi} = (F_{ZFL} + F_{ZFR}) \cdot l_F - (F_{ZRL} + F_{ZRR}) \cdot l_R + m_{CoG} a_X h_{CoG}
\tag{6.55}
$$

The distances $n_{F,R}$ are due to the longitudinal casters:

$$
n_{LF} = \frac{n_{LFL} + n_{LFR}}{2} \qquad\qquad n_{LR} = \frac{n_{LRL} + n_{LRR}}{2}
\tag{6.56}
$$

6.4.3 Suspension

A quarter-vehicle model is used for each wheel (Figure 6.26).

In contrast to Figure 6.26 however, the mass portion m_q is not constant as the load within the vehicle varies. The normal forces F_Z of the four quarter masses are determined in Section 7.4.1.

Each wheel has an individual mass m_W, which is connected via wheel spring k_W and wheel damping d_W to the ground, and via a spring-damper system (k_U, d_U) to the chassis. All four wheel suspensions are assumed to be vertically directed. The indices ij are front/rear and left/right.

The forces which act upon the wheel are:

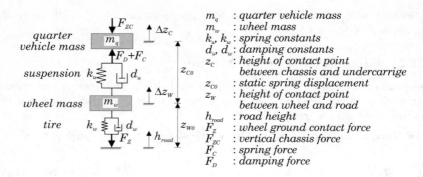

m_q : quarter vehicle mass
m_w : wheel mass
k_u, k_w : spring constants
d_u, d_w : damping constants
z_C : height of contact point
         between chassis and undercarrige
z_{C0} : static spring displacement
z_W : height of contact point
         between wheel and road
h_{road} : road height
F_Z : wheel ground contact force
F_{ZC} : vertical chassis force
F_C : spring force
F_D : damping force

Figure 6.26 Forces and displacements in the quarter vehicle model

- Wheel ground contact forces

$$
\begin{aligned}
F_{Zij} &= \Delta F_{Zij} + F_{ZCij0} \\
&= k_W \left(h_{road} - \Delta z_{Wij} - z_{Wij0} \right) + d_W \left(\dot{h}_{road} - \dot{z}_{Wij} \right) \quad (6.57)
\end{aligned}
$$

- Suspension spring forces:

$$
F_{Cij} = k_U \left(\Delta z_{Wij} + z_{Wij0} - \Delta z_{Cij} - z_{Cij0} \right) \tag{6.58}
$$

- Suspension damping forces:

$$
F_{Dij} \tag{6.59}
$$

The constants k_W, k_U, d_U and d_W are equal for wheels on the same axle. The wheel damping constant d_W is set equal to zero. The reference road level (flat road) is $h_{road,0} = 0$. The static spring displacements z_{Wij0} and z_{Cij0} are so chosen that they balance the static forces F_{ZCij0} by exact horizontal positioning of the unloaded vehicle.

$$
F_{ZCij0} = -k_W z_{Wij0} \overset{!}{=} -k_U \left(z_{Wij0} - z_{Cij0} \right) \tag{6.60}
$$

The force balances at the quarter chassis and the wheels are:

$$
\begin{aligned}
m_q \ddot{z}_{Cij} &= k_U \left(\Delta z_{Wij} - \Delta z_{Cij} + z_{Wij0} - z_{Cij0} \right) + F_{ZCij0} + F_{Dij} \\
&= k_U \left(\Delta z_{Wij} - \Delta z_{Cij} \right) + F_{Dij} \tag{6.61}
\end{aligned}
$$

and,

$$
\begin{aligned}
m_W \ddot{z}_{Wij} &= k_W \left(h_{road} - \Delta z_{Wij} - z_{Wij0} \right) + d_W \left(\dot{h}_{road} - \dot{z}_{Wij} \right) - \\
&\quad - k_U \left(\Delta z_{Wij} + z_{Wij0} - \Delta z_{Cij} - z_{Cij0} \right) - F_{Dij} \\
&= k_W \left(h_{road} - \Delta z_{Wij} \right) + d_W \left(\dot{h}_{road} - \dot{z}_{Wij} \right) - \\
&\quad - k_U \left(\Delta z_{Wij} - \Delta z_{Cij} \right) + F_{Dij} \tag{6.62}
\end{aligned}
$$

Linear Suspension Model

The suspension damping force is proportional to the resulting displacement speed $\dot{z}_W - \dot{z}_C$.

$$F_{Dij} = d_U \left(\dot{z}_W - \dot{z}_C \right) \tag{6.63}$$

The damping of the wheel d_W is neglected. The quarter vehicle can then be described by a fourth order state space model of the form,

$$\dot{\underline{x}} = \underline{A}\,\underline{x} + \underline{b}u$$
$$\dot{\underline{y}} = \underline{C}\,\underline{x} + \underline{d}u$$

The state vector is

$$\underline{\dot{x}} = [\Delta z_W, \quad \dot{z}_W, \quad \Delta z_C, \quad \dot{z}_C]^T \quad , \tag{6.64}$$

the input variable is

$$u(t) = h_{road}(t) \quad , \tag{6.65}$$

and the output vector is

$$\underline{y} = [\ddot{z}_W, \quad \ddot{z}_C, \quad (\Delta z_C - \Delta z_W)]^T \quad . \tag{6.66}$$

The road profile h_{road} may be approximated by a randomly distributed Gaussian noise with an assumed covariance

$$c_{hh} = 2\pi A v_{X,CoG} \quad . \tag{6.67}$$

The amplitude factor A is dependent upon the road profile, and $v_{X,CoG}$ is the longitudinal vehicle velocity [28]. For a dynamic analysis, the linear model can be used to define a transfer function between the vertical acceleration $\ddot{z}_C$ and the road profile h_{road}:

$$\begin{aligned}
G(s) &= \frac{s^2 z_C(s)}{h_{road}(s)} \\
&= \frac{k_W d_U s^3 + k_W k_U s^2}{m_W m_q s^4 + d_U \left(m_W + m_q(k_W + k_U) \right) s^2 + d_U k_W s + k_W k_U}
\end{aligned} \tag{6.68}$$

Effect of Parameter Variations on the Linear Suspension Model

The influence of the spring stiffness k_U, damping d_U and quarter vehicle mass m_q parameters is investigated by simulating an example. For this, the following representative parameter values are substituted into Eq. 6.68:

$$\begin{aligned}
m_q &= 350\,kg, \quad m_W = 31\,kg, \quad k_U = 20900\,N/m, \\
k_W &= 10800\,N/m, \quad d_U = 1140\,Ns/m
\end{aligned}$$

Simulations are carried out to show how strongly the amplitude and phase of $G(s)$ are affected by changes in the parameters. The following changes are considered: $m_q = 200 - 400\,kg$, $d_U = 500 - 2000\,Ns/m$ and $k_U = 10000 - 30000\,N/m$.

Figure 6.27 shows that a change in the quarter vehicle mass m_q only has effects at frequencies under the resonant frequency. The spring constant k_U has a significant influence on the amplitude of $G(s)$ for frequencies around $1\,Hz$, and the resonant frequency also changes slightly.

The variation of the damping constant d_U has a similar effect for frequencies around $6\,Hz$, however the amplitude at the resonant frequency varies much more strongly than with the parameters m_q and k_U. This means a strong dependency of driving comfort on shock absorber characteristics.

Nonlinear Suspension Model

Suspension systems have a nonlinear damping characteristic. When moving upwards the wheel generates a smaller damping force F_D than when moving downwards. The nonlinearity allows an upward bump from the road profile to have a small impact on the chassis, while vertical wheel oscillations are still effectively damped during the downward movement of the wheel. The damping force is approximated by:

$$F_{Dij} \approx d_{U,l}\left(\dot{z}_{Wij} - \dot{z}_{Cij}\right) + d_{U,nl}\sqrt{|\dot{z}_{Wij} - \dot{z}_{Cij}|}\,sign\left(\dot{z}_{Wij} - \dot{z}_{Cij}\right) \qquad (6.69)$$

Inserting this into Eq. 6.61 yields:

$$\begin{aligned} m_q\ddot{z}_{Cij} &= k_U\left(\Delta z_{Wij} - \Delta z_{Cij}\right) + d_{U,l}\left(\dot{z}_{Wij} - \dot{z}_{Cij}\right) + \\ &\quad + d_{U,nl}\sqrt{|\dot{z}_{Wij} - \dot{z}_{Cij}|}\,sign\left(\dot{z}_{Wij} - \dot{z}_{Cij}\right) \end{aligned} \qquad (6.70)$$

Figure 6.28 shows a plot of the damping force F_D over the relative velocity $\dot{z}_W - \dot{z}_C$.

It is necessary to measure the required inputs (undercarriage vertical acceleration $\ddot{z}_C$ and relative spring-damper displacement ($\Delta z_W - \Delta z_C$). The relative spring velocity ($\dot{z}_W - \dot{z}_C$) is then determined by numerical differentiation from the measured relative spring-damper displacement:

$$\dot{y}(k) \approx \frac{y(k) - y(k-1)}{T_s} \qquad (6.71)$$

Here, $y(k)$ is the measured signal at time k and T_s the sampling time of the process.

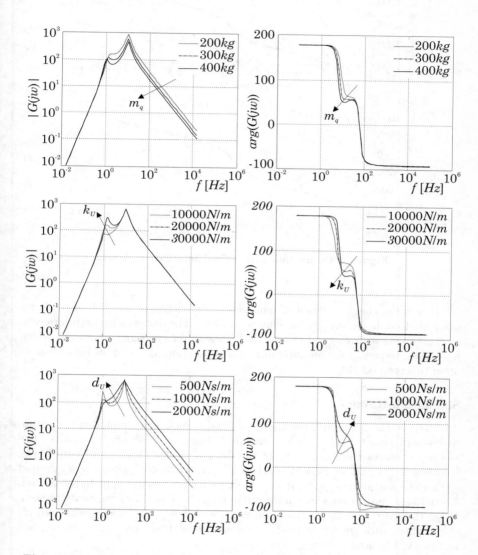

Figure 6.27 Magnitude and phase characteristics for parameter variations of $G(s)$

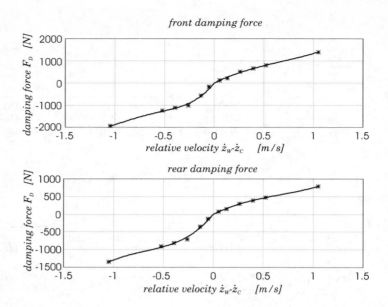

Figure 6.28 Interpolation of the damping characteristic

This is the classic method of numerical differentiation, which is suitable for linear and nonlinear estimation equations alike. For disturbance and noise-free measurements it gives good results. Noisy measurement signals however, which have high frequency signals superimposed upon them, demand an improvement upon this method [49].

Simulation Results

To compare the linear and nonlinear suspension models a simulation with stepwise steering angle excitation is carried out. Figure 6.29 shows the results. The top figure shows the assessment of the drive situation, i.e. wheel turn angle, vehicle velocity and lateral acceleration. The test drive took place on dry ground so that the unstable range begins at about 1 g lateral acceleration. In the bottom figure the advantages of the nonlinear damping characteristics can easily be seen. Using the more realistic nonlinear model, a well damped transient behaviour results, whilst with the linear model roll angle oscillations appear, which can not be observed in actual driving situations.

6.4.4   Reduced Nonlinear Two-track Model

The reduced model should contain only those state variables which are essential for vehicle dynamic control and ABS control. These are the vehicle speed v_{CoG}, the vehicle body side slip angle β and the yaw rate $\dot{\psi}$. Starting from the left portion of Eq. 6.37, only the $x-$ and $y-$ components are considered, i.e. the

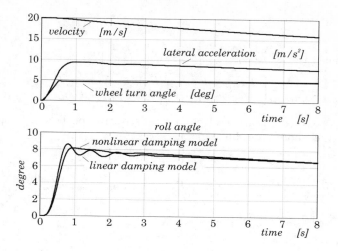

Figure 6.29 Roll angle from linear and nonlinear suspension models

z-component is disregarded. In this case, the forces F_{Xij} and F_{Yij} are identical in the undercarriage and the CoG co-ordinate systems. From Figure 6.7, the vehicle speed v_{CoG} can be transformed into the fixed inertial co-ordinate system by:

$$\left[\begin{array}{c} \dot{x}_{In} \\ \dot{y}_{In} \end{array} \right] = v_{CoG} \cdot \left[\begin{array}{c} \cos{(\beta + \psi)} \\ \sin{(\beta + \psi)} \end{array} \right] \tag{6.72}$$

By differentiation, the accelerations in Eq. 6.37 are obtained:

$$\left[\begin{array}{c} \ddot{x}_{In} \\ \ddot{y}_{In} \end{array} \right] = v_{CoG} \cdot \left(\dot{\beta} + \dot{\psi} \right) \left[\begin{array}{c} -\sin{(\beta + \psi)} \\ \cos{(\beta + \psi)} \end{array} \right] + \dot{v}_{CoG} \left[\begin{array}{c} \cos{(\beta + \psi)} \\ \sin{(\beta + \psi)} \end{array} \right] \tag{6.73}$$

These accelerations are now transformed from the inertial into the undercarriage system (which is identical to the CoG system for x- and y- directions). The required transformation matrix $\underline{T}_{RotZ}^{-1}$ (Eq. 6.41) is reduced to the order 2, and multiplied into the above equation.

$$\begin{aligned} \left[\begin{array}{c} \ddot{x}_{CoG} \\ \ddot{y}_{CoG} \end{array} \right] &= \left[\begin{array}{cc} \cos{\psi} & \sin{\psi} \\ -\sin{\psi} & \cos{\psi} \end{array} \right] \cdot \left[\begin{array}{c} \ddot{x}_{In} \\ \ddot{y}_{In} \end{array} \right] = \\ &= v_{CoG} \cdot \left(\dot{\beta} + \dot{\psi} \right) \left[\begin{array}{c} -\sin{\beta} \\ \cos{\beta} \end{array} \right] + \dot{v}_{CoG} \left[\begin{array}{c} \cos{\beta} \\ \sin{\beta} \end{array} \right] \end{aligned} \tag{6.74}$$

If gravitational forces F_{GX} and F_{GY}, rolling resistance force F_R, lateral wind force F_{windY}, and the wind velocity v_{wind} are neglected, the complete Eqs 6.37 for horizontal translatory motion are then given in the CoG co-ordinate system by

$$
v_{CoG} \cdot \left(\dot{\beta} + \dot{\psi} \right) \begin{bmatrix} -\sin\beta \\ \cos\beta \end{bmatrix} + \dot{v}_{CoG} \begin{bmatrix} \cos\beta \\ \sin\beta \end{bmatrix} =
$$

$$
= \frac{1}{m_{CoG}} \begin{bmatrix} F_{XFL} + F_{XFR} + F_{XRL} + F_{XRR} + F_{windX} \\ F_{YFL} + F_{YFR} + F_{YRL} + F_{YRR} \end{bmatrix} . \quad (6.75)
$$

The two state equations are resolved for the derivatives of the vehicle speed $\dot{v}_{CoG}$ and the vehicle body side slip angle $\dot{\beta}$:

$$
\dot{v}_{CoG} =
$$

$$
\frac{1}{m_{CoG} \cdot \cos\beta} \left[F_{XFL} + F_{XFR} + F_{XRL} + F_{XRR} - c_{aerX} A_L \frac{\rho}{2} \cdot v_{CoG}^2 \right] +
$$

$$
+ v_{CoG} \left(\dot{\beta} + \dot{\psi} \right) \tan\beta \quad (6.76)
$$

$$
\dot{\beta} =
$$

$$
\frac{1}{m_{CoG} \cdot v_{CoG} \cdot \cos\beta} [F_{YFL} + F_{YFR} + F_{YRL} + F_{YRR} - m_{CoG} \dot{v}_{CoG} \sin\beta] - \dot{\psi} \quad (6.77)
$$

In a last step, the mutual interdependance on $\dot{v}_{CoG}$ and $\dot{\beta}$ is eliminated.

(I) $\dot{v}_{CoG} =$

$$
\frac{\cos\beta}{m_{CoG}} \left[F_{XFL} + F_{XFR} + F_{XRL} + F_{XRR} - c_{aerX} A_L \frac{\rho}{2} \cdot v_{CoG}^2 \right] +
$$

$$
+ \frac{1}{m_{CoG}} (F_{YFL} + F_{YFR} + F_{YRL} + F_{YRR}) \sin\beta \quad (6.78)
$$

(II) $\dot{\beta} =$

$$
\frac{\cos\beta}{m_{CoG} \cdot v_{CoG}} [F_{YFL} + F_{YFR} + F_{YRL} + F_{YRR}] -
$$

$$
- \frac{\sin\beta}{m_{CoG} \cdot v_{CoG}} \left(F_{XFL} + F_{XFR} + F_{XRL} + F_{XRR} - c_{aer} A_L \frac{\rho}{2} \cdot v_{CoG}^2 \right) - \dot{\psi} \quad (6.79)
$$

The rotational yaw movement is described by Eq. 6.53.

(III) $J_Z \ddot{\psi} =$

$$
(F_{YFR} + F_{YFL}) \cdot (l_F - n_{LF}) -
$$

$$
- (F_{YRR} + F_{YRL}) \cdot (l_R + n_{LR}) + (F_{XRR} - F_{XRL}) \cdot \frac{b_R}{2} +
$$

$$
+ F_{XFR} \left(\frac{b_F}{2} - n_{SFR} \sin\delta_W \right) - F_{XFL} \left(\frac{b_F}{2} + n_{SFL} \sin\delta_W \right) \quad (6.80)
$$

The Eqs. (I), (II) and (III) represent the nonlinear two-track model. The wheel forces are taken from Eqs. 6.28 and 6.29. By neglecting the tire side slip angle

α, i.e. the different directions of x_W and v_W, the wheel forces can be stated as:

$$
\begin{aligned}
F_{XFL} &\approx F_{LFL} \cos \delta_{WL} - F_{SFL} \sin \delta_{WL} \quad, \\
F_{YFL} &\approx F_{SFL} \cos \delta_{WL} + F_{LFL} \sin \delta_{WL} \quad, \\
F_{XFR} &\approx F_{LFR} \cos \delta_{WR} - F_{SFR} \sin \delta_{WR} \quad, \\
F_{YFR} &\approx F_{SFR} \cos \delta_{WR} + F_{LFR} \sin \delta_{WR} \quad, \\
F_{XRL} &\approx F_{LRL} \quad, \quad F_{YRL} \approx F_{SRL} \quad, \\
F_{XRR} &\approx F_{LRR} \quad, \quad F_{YRR} \approx F_{SRR} \quad.
\end{aligned}
\tag{6.81}
$$

These forces are inserted into the three nonlinear model equations. The wheel side forces F_S are now approximated to be proportional to the tire side slip angles α.

$$
\begin{aligned}
F_{SFL} &= c_{FL} \cdot \alpha_{FL} = c_{FL} \cdot \left(\delta_{WL} - \beta - \frac{l_F \dot\psi}{v_{CoG}} \right) \\[2mm]
F_{SFR} &= c_{FR} \cdot \alpha_{FR} = c_{FR} \cdot \left(\delta_{WR} - \beta - \frac{l_F \dot\psi}{v_{CoG}} \right) \\[2mm]
F_{SRL} &= c_{RL} \cdot \alpha_{RL} = c_{RL} \cdot \left(-\beta + \frac{l_R \dot\psi}{v_{CoG}} \right) \\[2mm]
F_{SRR} &= c_{RR} \cdot \alpha_{RR} = c_{RR} \cdot \left(-\beta + \frac{l_R \dot\psi}{v_{CoG}} \right)
\end{aligned}
\tag{6.82}
$$

c_{ij} are the tire side slip constants. They must be adapted (Section 7.4.2). It is assumed that the left and right wheel turn angles are the same, i.e. $\delta_{WL} \approx \delta_{WR} \approx \delta_W$.

The wheel turn angle and the longitudinal wheel forces F_{Lij} are utilised as control inputs for vehicle dynamic control by steering and by applying an appropriate brake pressure. The reduced nonlinear two-track model becomes

$$
\begin{aligned}
\text{(I)} \quad f_1 &= \dot{v}_{CoG} = \\
&= \frac{1}{m_{CoG}} \Big\{ F_{LFL} \cos(\beta - \delta_W) F_{LFR} \cos(\delta_W - \beta) + \\
&\quad + \left[F_{LRL} + F_{LRR} - c_{aer} A_L \frac{\rho}{2} \cdot v_{CoG}^2 \right] \cos\beta + \\
&\quad + \left[c_{FL}\delta_W - c_{FL}\beta - \frac{1}{v_{CoG}} c_{FL} l_F \dot\psi \right] \sin(\beta - \delta_W) + \\
&\quad + \left[c_{FR}\beta - c_{FR}\delta_W + \frac{1}{v_{CoG}} c_{FR} l_F \dot\psi \right] \sin(\delta_W - \beta) + \\
&\quad + \left[\frac{1}{v_{CoG}} c_{RL} l_R \dot\psi - c_{RL}\beta - c_{RR}\beta + \frac{1}{v_{CoG}} c_{RR} l_R \dot\psi \right] \sin\beta \Big\}
\end{aligned}
\tag{6.83}
$$

(II) $\quad f_2 \;\; = \;\; \dot\beta =$

$$= \frac{1}{m_{CoG} v_{CoG}} \Big\{ -F_{LFL}\sin(\beta - \delta_W) + F_{LFR}\sin(\delta_W - \beta)+$$

$$+ \Big[c_{FL}\delta_W - c_{FL}\beta - \frac{1}{v_{CoG}}c_{FL}l_F\dot\psi \Big]\cos(\beta - \delta_W) +$$

$$+ \Big[c_{FR}\delta_W - c_{FR}\beta - \frac{1}{v_{CoG}}c_{FR}l_F\dot\psi \Big]\cos(\delta_W - \beta) +$$

$$+ \Big[\frac{1}{v_{CoG}}c_{RL}l_R\dot\psi - c_{RL}\beta + \frac{1}{v_{CoG}}c_{RR}l_R\dot\psi - c_{RR}\beta \Big]\cos\beta +$$

$$+ \Big[c_{aer}A_L\frac{\rho}{2}v_{CoG}^2 - F_{LRL} - F_{LRR} \Big]\sin\beta \Big\} - \dot\psi \qquad (6.84)$$

(III) $\quad f_3 \;\; = \;\; \ddot\psi =$

$$= \frac{1}{2J_Z v_{CoG}} \Big\{ \big[c_{FL}\delta_W v_{CoG}b_F - c_{FL}\beta v_{CoG}b_F+$$

$$- c_{FL}l_F\dot\psi b_F + 2F_{LFL}v_{CoG}l_F \big]\sin\delta_W +$$

$$+ \big[2c_{FL}\delta_W v_{CoG}l_F - 2c_{FL}\beta v_{CoG}l_F - 2c_{FL}l_F\dot\psi l_F - F_{LFL}v_{CoG}b_F \big]\cos\delta_W +$$

$$+ \big[c_{FR}\beta v_{CoG}b_F - c_{FR}\delta_W v_{CoG}b_F + c_{FR}l_F\dot\psi b_F + 2F_{LFR}v_{CoG}l_F \big]\sin\delta_W +$$

$$+ \big[2c_{FR}\delta_W v_{CoG}l_F - 2c_{FR}\beta v_{CoG}l_F - 2c_{FR}l_F\dot\psi l_F + F_{LFR}v_{CoG}b_F \big]\cos\delta_W +$$

$$+ [2c_{FL} + 2c_{FR}]l_F\dot\psi n_{LF} + [-2c_{RL}l_R - 2c_{RL}n_{LR} - 2c_{RR}n_{LR} - 2c_{RR}l_R]l_R\dot\psi +$$

$$+ [2c_{FL}v_{CoG}n_{LF} + 2c_{FR}v_{CoG}n_F + 2c_{RL}v_{CoG}n_{LR}+$$

$$+ 2c_{RL}v_{CoG}l_R + 2c_{RR}v_{CoG}n_{LR} + 2c_{RR}v_{CoG}l_R]\beta +$$

$$+ [-2c_{FL}v_{CoG}n_{LF} - 2c_{FR}v_{CoG}n_{LF}]\delta_W - F_{LRL}b_R v_{CoG} + F_{LRR}b_H v_{CoG} \Big\}$$

$$(6.85)$$

In state space form, the reduced nonlinear two-track model can be written as:

$$\dot{\underline{x}} \;\; = \;\; \underline{A}\,(\underline{x},\underline{u})\,\underline{x} + \underline{B}\,(\underline{x},\underline{u})\,\underline{u}$$
$$\underline{y} \;\; = \;\; \underline{C}\,(\underline{x},\underline{u})\,\underline{x}$$

The state vector is:

$$\underline{x} = \Big[v_{CoG}\; \beta\; \dot\psi \Big]^T \qquad (6.86)$$

the control input;

$$\underline{u} = [F_{LFL}\; F_{LFR}\; F_{LRL}\; F_{LRR}\; \delta_W]^T \qquad (6.87)$$

and the measurement vector:

$$\underline{y} = \Big[v_{CoG}\; \dot\psi \Big]^T \qquad (6.88)$$

The equations are:

$$\underline{\dot{x}} = \begin{bmatrix} \dot{v}_{CoG} \\ \dot{\beta} \\ \ddot{\psi} \end{bmatrix} = \underline{f}(\underline{x}, \underline{u}) = \begin{bmatrix} f_1(\underline{x}, \underline{u}) \\ f_2(\underline{x}, \underline{u}) \\ f_3(\underline{x}, \underline{u}) \end{bmatrix} \tag{6.89}$$

$$\underline{y} = \underline{C}(\underline{x}, \underline{u})\,\underline{x} = \begin{bmatrix} 1 & 0 & 0 \\ 0 & 0 & 1 \end{bmatrix} \underline{x} \tag{6.90}$$

The nonlinear model can be linearised around the actual operating point.

$$\underline{f}(\underline{x}, \underline{u}) \approx \underline{f}(\underline{x}_0, \underline{u}_0) + \underbrace{\left.\frac{\partial \underline{f}(\underline{x}, \underline{u})}{\partial \underline{x}}\right|_{\substack{\underline{x} = \underline{x}_0 \\ \underline{u} = \underline{u}_0}} \cdot (\underline{x} - \underline{x}_0)}_{\text{Jacobian}} + \underbrace{\left.\frac{\partial \underline{f}(\underline{x}, \underline{u})}{\partial \underline{u}}\right|_{\substack{\underline{x} = \underline{x}_0 \\ \underline{u} = \underline{u}_0}} \cdot (\underline{u} - \underline{u}_0)}_{\text{Jacobian}}$$

$$\tag{6.91}$$

The two Jacobians can be found in Appendix A.2.

6.4.5 Vehicle Stability Analysis

Analytical stability criteria are not available for nonlinear systems. Therefore, the nonlinear two-track model is further reduced to a linear single-track model of second order.

Reduced Linear Single-track Model

No differences are made between the left and right track.

$$F_{LF} = \tfrac{1}{2}\left(F_{LFL} + F_{LFR}\right) \quad F_{LR} = \tfrac{1}{2}\left(F_{LRL} + F_{LRR}\right) \tag{6.92}$$

$$c_F = \tfrac{1}{2}\left(c_{FL} + c_{FR}\right) \quad c_R = \tfrac{1}{2}\left(c_{RL} + c_{RR}\right) \tag{6.93}$$

For small vehicle body side slip angles, the trigonometric functions can be linearised using $\sin\beta \approx 0$ and $\cos\beta \approx 1$.

In addition, it is assumed that the vehicle body speed v_{CoG} is constant over a limited time period, i.e. the derivative $\dot{v}_{CoG} = 0$. The wind force F_{windX} is also neglected, as well as force terms $F_S \sin\delta_W$. Eq. 6.75 for the translatory motion then simplifies to

$$
\begin{aligned}
m_{CoG} \cdot v_{CoG} \cdot \left(\dot{\beta} + \dot{\psi}\right) &= F_{SF} + F_{SR} \\
&= c_F\left(\delta_W - \beta - \frac{l_F\dot{\psi}}{v_{CoG}}\right) + c_R\left(-\beta + \frac{l_R\dot{\psi}}{v_{CoG}}\right)
\end{aligned}
\tag{6.94}
$$

and the rotational yaw movement to

$$J_Z \ddot{\psi} = F_{SF} l_F - \underbrace{F_{SF} n_{LF}}_{\approx 0} - F_{SR} l_R - \underbrace{F_{SR} n_{LR}}_{\approx 0} + \underbrace{F_{LR} \frac{b_R}{2} + F_{LF} \frac{b_R}{2}}_{\approx 0}$$

$$= c_F l_F \left(\delta_W - \beta - \frac{l_F \dot{\psi}}{v_{CoG}} \right) - c_R l_R \left(-\beta + \frac{l_R \dot{\psi}}{v_{CoG}} \right) \quad . \tag{6.95}$$

The state variables are the vehicle body side slip angle β and the yaw rate $\dot{\psi}$. The vehicle speed v_{CoG} is considered as a parameter. As control input, only the wheel turn angle δ_W remains and as measurement variable the yaw rate $\dot{\psi}$. Thus the linear single-track model is not suited for vehicle dynamic control. The state equations are:

$$\begin{bmatrix} \dot{\beta} \\ \dot{\psi} \end{bmatrix} = \begin{bmatrix} -\dfrac{c_F + c_R}{m_{CoG} v_{CoG}} & \dfrac{c_R l_R - c_F l_F}{m_{CoG} v_{CoG}^2} - 1 \\[3mm] \dfrac{c_R l_R - c_F l_F}{J_Z} & \dfrac{c_R l_R^2 - c_F l_F^2}{J_Z v_{CoG}} \end{bmatrix} \cdot \begin{bmatrix} \beta \\ \dot{\psi} \end{bmatrix} + \begin{bmatrix} \dfrac{c_F}{m_{CoG} v_{CoG}} \\[3mm] \dfrac{c_F l_F}{J_Z} \end{bmatrix} \delta_W$$

$$\dot{\psi} = \begin{bmatrix} 0 & 1 \end{bmatrix} \cdot \begin{bmatrix} \beta \\ \dot{\psi} \end{bmatrix}$$

According to [54], this linear single-track model is only valid for lateral accelerations below $0.4\,g$. By adaptation of the side force constants c_F and c_R (see Section 7.4.2), the validity range may be extended. For stationary operation, $\ddot{\psi} = 0$, $\dot{\beta} = 0$, $\dot{v}_{CoG} = 0$, the vehicle moves on a circular path at constant speed.

Position of Eigenvalues During Test Drives

The transfer function between yaw rate $\dot{\psi}$ and wheel turn angle δ_W is

$$\dot{\psi} = \frac{1}{l} \cdot \frac{v_{CoG}}{1 + v_{CoG}^2 / v_{char}^2} \cdot \delta_W \tag{6.96}$$

with characteristic speed

$$v_{char}^2 = \frac{c_F c_R l^2}{m_{CoG} (c_R l_R - c_F l_F)} \tag{6.97}$$

and vehicle length $l = l_F + l_R$. For production cars, the characteristic speed varies between 68 and $112\,km/h$. A small characteristic speed means that the car is understeering. The characteristic equation of the linear single-track model is:

$$s^2 + \frac{\left(J_Z + m_{CoG} l_F^2 \right) c_F + \left(J_Z + m_{CoG} l_R^2 \right) c_R}{J_Z m_{CoG} v_{CoG}} s +$$

$$+ \frac{c_F c_R l^2 + m_{CoG} v_{CoG}^2 (c_R l_R - c_F l_F)}{J_Z m_{CoG} v_{CoG}^2} = 0 \tag{6.98}$$

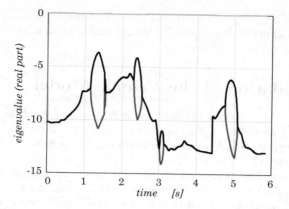

Figure 6.30 Real part of the eigenvalues during evasive action manoeuvre

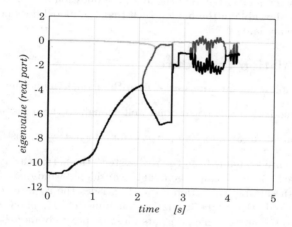

Figure 6.31 Real part of the eigenvalues during braking manoeuvre in a curve

Asymptotic stability requires both terms to be positive. The term associated with s always meets this requirement. The absolute term is only positive if

$$c_R l_R > c_F l_F \quad , \tag{6.99}$$

which is true for all production vehicles.

In Figs 6.30 and 6.31 the position of the real part of the time variant eigenvalues is shown for two driving manoeuvres. Figure 6.30 belongs to an evasive action manoeuvre, and Figure 6.31 to an ABS braking in a curve.

For the evasive action manoeuvre, both eigenvalues show stable behaviour, with a satisfactory distance from the instability limit. When the two real parts coincide, there exists a complex- conjugate pair of eigenvalues.

During ABS braking in a curve, stability can become an issue (Figure 6.31). During ABS braking on stretches with low maximum friction values, the steering response of the vehicle is poor.

6.5   Validation of the Vehicle Model

Once the model is constructed it must be verified with as much information from the real system as possible. This process is known as *validation*. The necessary information consists of *a-priori* knowledge, measured data and experience of the user with the model [47] [32].

The most common method of model validation is to evaluate the reaction of the model to measured data and compare it with actual values. The data used for this should be different from that used for training of the model.

The construction of a model often involves many simplifications through which the outputs of the model deviate to a greater or lesser extent from the real values. By model construction the following question arises: Where are such simplifications allowable in the model, such that the model does not deviate too much from the actual system.

6.5.1   Validation Procedure

From [47] the following questions arise with the model validation:

1. Do the model outputs correspond well enough to the measured data?

2. Is the model suitable for the purpose for which it was constructed?

The more data are available from the real system, the better the above questions can be answered. A model can in general be considered validated when, following evaluation with suitable validation data, it satisfies the requirements for which it was constructed. Before the validation, one must clearly know which purpose the model is to be put to, which outputs must be precisely modelled, and where certain errors can be accepted.

The following can be stated as tasks of the validation:

- If simplifications have been carried out during the modelling process which are too large, or not suitable, these must be found out and suitable corrections made.

- If faults have been made during the implementation of the model, these should be detected and remedied.

- The physical parameters of the model should be checked and if necessary adjusted.

If the model behaves as expected with successful validation, then a lot of faith can be placed in the model.

The **validation of the vehicle model** is carried out as follows:

According to the dynamic variables to be validated, suitable driving manoeuvres are defined, during which the data are recorded. The chosen manoeuvres should reproduce the behaviour of the vehicle in characteristic situations in such a way that an interpretation can follow without requiring computationally intensive processing. If for example the behaviour of the longitudinal vehicle dynamics are to be validated, then,

- Straight ahead braking and accelerating driving

would be suitable, as this would stimulate pitch oscillations, whilst at the same time coupled roll and yaw movements would scarcely appear. If on the other hand the lateral dynamics vehicle variables are to be verified, the following driving manoeuvre would especially stimulate the corresponding dynamics:

- Step changes in the steering angle

- Sine-wave form steering input

The recorded measured variables are compared with the corresponding outputs from the model in order to determine where the model is sufficiently accurate and where tuning of the model structure or its parameters is necessary. Via repeated tuning and comparison of measured and simulated data, one arrives at a version of the model which reproduces the desired drive dynamics with sufficient accuracy.

In order to carry out validation, test drives were carried out with an experimental vehicle, and the following variables recorded:

Model input variables		
	δ_S	steering wheel angle
	ω_{ij}	wheel angular velocities

Model output variables		
	a_x	acceleration in x-direction (at CoG)
	a_y	acceleration in y-direction (at CoG)
	v_{CoG}	velocity of the CoG
	$\dot{\psi}$	yaw rate
	$\dot{\chi}$	pitch rate
	$\dot{\varphi}$	roll rate

The data recording is carried out using a real driver to provide the steering angle and the desired acceleration, hence the driver model, and the motor/drive/brake model are not applicable here. The outputs produced by driver models, δ_S and ω_{ij}, are replaced by the measured values. These then act as the inputs for the validation model. Also, the road model is replaced by actual road data for the validation.

The validation model calculates, from the inputs δ_S and ω_{ij}, among other things the outputs a_x, a_y, a_z, v_{CoG}, $\dot{\psi}$, $\dot{\chi}$ and $\dot{\varphi}$, which according to the above list are also available as measured outputs, so that a direct comparison can be carried out between the model and actual outputs.

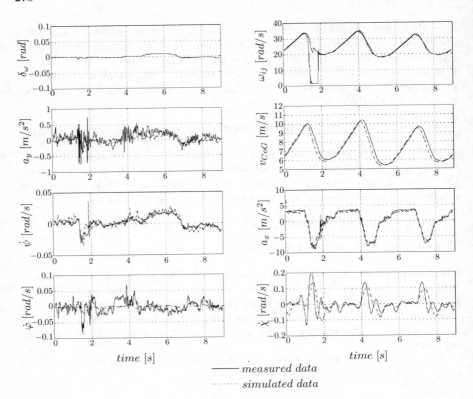

measured data

········ simulated data

Figure 6.32 Model validation: straight ahead braking and acceleration

6.5.2 Validation Results

From the multitude of driving situations used to validate the model, the above mentioned three driving manoeuvres will be used as examples in each case.

Figure 6.32 shows the results of a straight ahead braking and acceleration manoeuvre, in order to analyse the estimation quality of the longitudinal variables.

The simulated longitudinal dynamics correspond very well to the measured data. Even with the scarcely stimulated lateral dynamics the simulation results show only small errors for the roll motion. The short-term locking of the front wheels at $1.8 - 2\,s$ leads to small disturbances in this range, however these do not negatively influence the simulation.

Similarly good results are given for the test drive with step changes in steering angle, as shown in Figure 6.33. The change in steering angle with a velocity of $50\,km/h$ amounts to a steering wheel angle of almost $100°$, which corresponds to wheel turn angles of $0.1\,rad$. Again the calculated values follow the measured data very well. The roll rate is also well reproduced. The pitch rate, which according to the measured data is to some extent dynamic, is simulated in the

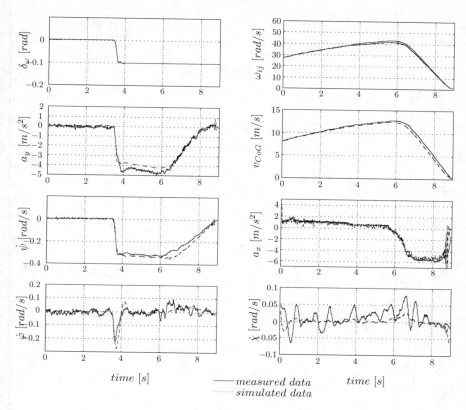

Figure 6.33 Model validation: step change in steering angle

model as semi-constant at zero. This can result in differences if the measured data are affected by coupling, which has been disregarded in the model.

As the last example, the sine-wave form driving is considered (Figure 6.34).

For this test drive the same can be said as with the step change in steering angle: the simulated values track the measured variables well. Whilst the yaw rate is almost exactly modelled, the modelled roll rate shows too large a peak value compared to the actual data. This can be an indication that the moment of inertia J_x around the roll axis has been set too small.

In summary one can say that **with sufficient excitation of the respective dynamics, the longitudinal and lateral dynamics were very well reproduced.** Problems appeared in the simulation of the roll rate during straight ahead driving and the pitch rate during a step change in steering angle and sine-wave form steering, as these dynamic variables are scarcely excited. The yaw rate, which is required for many dynamic control operations, was modelled very well for all drive situations investigated.

The simulation model has proved itself suitable for calculation of the relevant drive dynamics variables given steering angle and angular wheel velocity. The

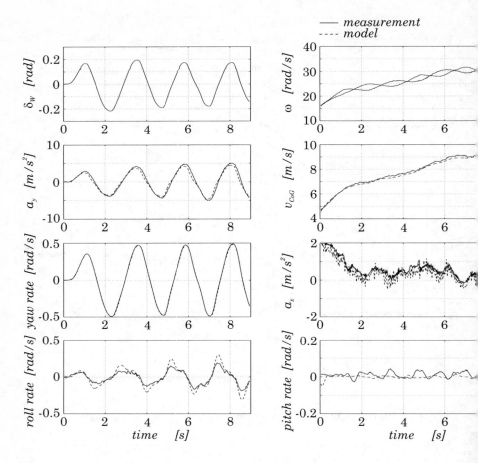

Figure 6.34 Model validation: sine wave form steering

same can also be said about the vehicle body side slip angle β and the wheel forces; because the measurements were so well simulated, one can also assume that the non-measurable variables will give good results. Hence the wheel forces calculated by the model are used for the identification of the mass moments of inertia (see Section 7.2.2).

7 Vehicle Parameters and States

This Chapter describes various approaches for the estimation and observation of variables which are not directly measurable. Section 7.1 presents two methods of obtaining the vehicle velocity in the inertial co-ordinate system, a Kalman filter approach and a fuzzy estimator. In Section 7.2, various approaches for estimating the friction characteristics, the mass moments of inertia and the road gradient are given. In Section 7.3 the vehicle body side slip angle is estimated using a nonlinear observer. In Section 7.4, approximation formulas are given for the wheel ground contact forces, the tire side slip constants and the roll and pitch angles.

7.1 Vehicle Velocity Estimation

The vehicle velocity v_{CoG} is obtained via a fusion of the data from all rotational wheel velocity v_R and longitudinal acceleration sensors. Via integration of the acceleration a fifth estimate for the vehicle velocity is made available. The estimation must be very accurate, as a basis for the wheel slip calculation (see Section 6.3.2). Some systems only select the maximum rotational wheel speed as the estimate for the vehicle velocity. When all four wheels happen to lock simultaneously, this approach is very inaccurate.

Two alternative estimation methods for the vehicle velocity are regarded, the Kalman filter and the fuzzy estimator.

7.1.1 Sensor Data Pre-processing

All sensors contain systematic errors which must be corrected. The signals are first low-pass filtered. During normal driving conditions, the offset of the longitudinal acceleration a_x sensor signal is compensated by the rotational wheel speed information. Wheel speed differences are due to driving in curves. Wheel speed measurements are therefore corrected by transformation to the CoG. Only for extreme curves must the vehicle body side slip angle β be known. Otherwise the yaw rate $\dot{\psi}$ is sufficient. The wheel ground contact point velocities v_{Wij} are approximated by the measureable wheel rotational equivalent velocities v_{Rij}. The transformation of Eq. 6.8 considers the different directions of the wheel and the vehicle velocities. The wheel speeds are inversely corrected from the wheel ground contact points to the center of gravity.

$$
\begin{aligned}
v_{RFL,C} &= \left[v_{RFL} + \dot{\psi} \left(\frac{b_F}{2} - l_F\beta \right) \right] \cdot \frac{1}{\cos\left(\delta_W - \beta\right)} \\
v_{RFR,C} &= \left[v_{RFR} - \dot{\psi} \left(\frac{b_F}{2} + l_F\beta \right) \right] \cdot \frac{1}{\cos\left(\delta_W - \beta\right)} \\
v_{RRL,C} &= \left[v_{RRL} + \dot{\psi} \left(\frac{b_R}{2} + l_R\beta \right) \right] \cdot \frac{1}{\cos\beta} \\
v_{RRR,C} &= \left[v_{RRR} - \dot{\psi} \left(\frac{b_R}{2} - l_R\beta \right) \right] \cdot \frac{1}{\cos\beta}
\end{aligned}
$$

$$(7.1)$$

All four corrected rotational equivalent wheel speeds $v_{Rij,C}$ are now effective estimates for the vehicle velocity $\hat{v}_{CoG}$. In order to obtain the desired accuracy an equalisation of the radii of the wheels must be carried out. For this, scaling factors for the radii are determined during driving with small steering angles and low accelerations.

The signals from the acceleration sensor are corrupted by several systematic errors, which all arise from the fixed installation on the vehicle body. The sensor is adjusted in the direction of the vehicle longitudinal axis, whilst the acceleration affects the vehicle in the direction of travel. The appearing angular offset is however sufficiently small, so that the cosine of it can be set to 1. If the vehicle drives on an incline, the sensor direction is correct with respect to the vehicle body. Because of the tilted position of the sensor in relation to the inertial co-ordinate system however, a component of the gravitational acceleration g is measured, which must be corrected by $(\chi - \chi_{road})$. Pitch angle changes result in a cosine component of the angle offset which can be neglected. Another error source is caused by the vehicle body side slip angle β. The centripetal force which acts orthogonal to the vehicle velocity yields a lateral acceleration component in the sensor signal. Altogether, the pre-processing of the acceleration sensor is:

$$a_{X,C} = \hat{\ddot{x}} = a_X - g\sin\left(\chi - \chi_{road}\right) + a_Y\sin\beta \qquad (7.2)$$

7.1.2   Kalman Filter Approach

The Kalman filter can determine state variables in a similar way as the Luenberger observer. The difference is that the Kalman Filter is designed for stochastic or time varying processes. An important pre-requisite is that the system

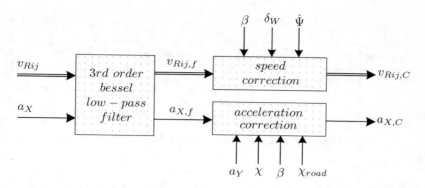

Figure 7.1 Structure of the sensor data pre-processing

input and the measurement noise must be white. The Kalman filter has advantages especially in cases where the stochastic properties of the noise processes are known.

If a Kalman filter is used for the data fusion then it is necessary to formulate the system model in discrete state-space form (see Section 4.4.4). The state vector (longitudinal acceleration a_X, vehicle speed v_{CoG}) is:

$$
\begin{aligned}
\underline{x}(k+1) &= \underline{A}(k)\underline{x}(k) + \underline{B}(k)\underline{u}(k) \\
&= \begin{bmatrix} 1 & 0 \\ T_s & 1 \end{bmatrix} \begin{bmatrix} a_X(k) \\ v_{CoG}(k) \end{bmatrix} + \begin{bmatrix} 1 & 0 \\ 0 & 1 \end{bmatrix} \begin{bmatrix} u_1(k) \\ u_2(k) \end{bmatrix}
\end{aligned} \tag{7.3}
$$

The measurement vector is:

$$
\begin{aligned}
\underline{y}(k) &= \underline{C}(k)\underline{x}(k) + \underline{e}(k) = \begin{bmatrix} a_{X,C}(k) \\ v_{RFL,C}(k) \\ v_{RFR,C}(k) \\ v_{RRL,C}(k) \\ v_{RRR,C}(k) \end{bmatrix} \\
&= \begin{bmatrix} 1 & 0 \\ 0 & 1 \\ 0 & 1 \\ 0 & 1 \\ 0 & 1 \end{bmatrix} \begin{bmatrix} a_X(k) \\ v_{CoG}(k) \end{bmatrix} + \begin{bmatrix} e_a(k) \\ e_1(k) \\ e_2(k) \\ e_3(k) \\ e_4(k) \end{bmatrix}
\end{aligned} \tag{7.4}
$$

The input noise $\underline{u}$ serves as an excitation to the system. $\underline{e}$ is the vector of measurement noise. Figure 7.2 shows the structure of the Kalman Filter.

The Kalman filter approach assumes the measurement noise to be white. The wheel ground contact point velocities v_{Wij} were approximated by the rotational equivalent wheel speeds v_{Rij}; these signals contain however systematic, slip-dependant offsets (Section 6.3.2), which contradicts the assumption of the measurement noise to be white. For the corrected acceleration sensor signals, one can assume a white noise error with constant power density. This is achieved by the pre-processing in Section 7.1.1.

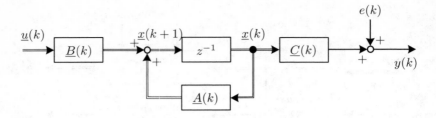

Figure 7.2 Velocity estimation using a Kalman Filter

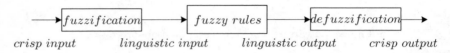

Figure 7.3 Processing steps of a fuzzy system

In order to apply a Kalman Filter in spite of systematic errors, four different covariance matrices could be defined. The proper matrix is then selected according to the current driving situation.

- **Large positive acceleration:** the covariance of the non-driven wheel noise is small and that of the driven wheel and acceleration noise is large.

- **Small positive acceleration:** the covariance of all wheels is small and that of the acceleration sensor is large.

- **Small negative acceleration:** the covariance of all wheels and of the acceleration is small.

- **Large negative acceleration:** the covariance of all wheels is large and that of the acceleration sensor is small.

With such an approach, the Kalman filter produces good results. It requires however intensive calculations for the gain matrix. The idea is now to replace the Kalman Filter by a fuzzy logic estimator which also classifies the driving situations in order to determine suitable weighting factors for the sensor signals. The available heuristic knowledge about the vehicle behaviour can be included in the fuzzy estimator by the formulation of the rules.

7.1.3   Short Introduction to Fuzzy Logic

A fuzzy system [1] can be divided into three parts, as shown in Figure 7.3.

Crisp, continuous inputs are transformed into linguistic variables with membership grades between 0 and 1. This process is known as fuzzification. The linguistic inputs are then evaluated using fuzzy rules and formed into fuzzy outputs. Continuous crisp outputs are then obtained via the process of defuzzification.

---

[1]Here, only a brief introduction to Fuzzy logic is given. For a more detailed explanation see [81]

A MIN-MAX inference scheme is chosen in this book; AND-operations are carried out using the minimum operator and OR-operations using the maximum operator. The defuzzification is carried out using the centroid method:

$$y_{Def} = \frac{\displaystyle\int_{-\infty}^{+\infty} y \cdot \mu_{res}(y) \cdot dy}{\displaystyle\int_{-\infty}^{+\infty} \mu_{res}(y) \cdot dy} \tag{7.5}$$

The rule base contains only premises which are combined using the AND-operator. The individual processing levels will now be further explained by an example.

Example

The rule base shall consists of two rules:

IF $\quad T=low \quad$ AND $\quad P=large \quad$ THEN $\quad y=middle$
IF $\quad T=middle \quad$ AND $\quad P=large \quad$ THEN $\quad y=small$

The two crisp inputs, T_o and P_o are first fuzzified. One then determines the truth value of the premises w_1 ($T = \ldots$) and w_2 ($P = \ldots$), from which the activations μ_{B1} and μ_{B2} of the rules can be determined, i.e. the membership function of the conclusion can be determined. If more rules exist then the resulting membership function μ_{RES} of the conclusion is formed from the aggregation of the outputs of all rules. From the area under the final resulting membership function, the crisp output value is determined using Eq. 7.5.

The complete process is shown schematically in Figure 7.4.

7.1.4 Fuzzy Estimator

Figure 7.5 shows the structure of the fuzzy estimator.

From the estimated vehicle velocity and the corrected wheel speeds, slip values are calculated which are more suited for the classification of driving situations than the wheel speeds themselves.

$$\hat{s}_L = \frac{v_{R,C}(k-1) - \hat{v}_{CoG}(k-1)}{\hat{v}_{CoG}(k-1)} \tag{7.6}$$

Eq. 7.6 corresponds to the definition of longitudinal slip for braking wheels transformed into the CoG co-ordinates. Differences in brake and drive slip must not be considered, as slip values beyond 2.5 % trigger a fuzzy rule which excludes the respective wheel speed.

In addition, the maximum difference between all corrected wheel speeds is a further input to the fuzzy estimator:

$$\max\{\Delta v_R\} = v_{R,C,max} - v_{R,C,min} \tag{7.7}$$

The corrected longitudinal acceleration can be used directly as an input for the fuzzy estimator.

evaluation of the first rule

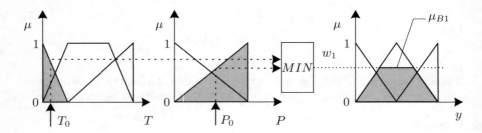

evaluation of the second rule

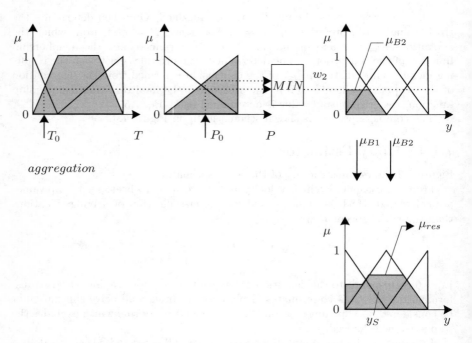

aggregation

Figure 7.4 Example of the evaluation of a rule base

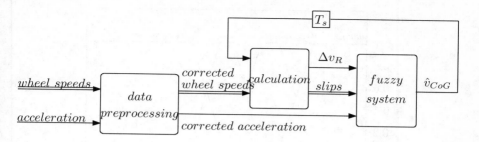

Figure 7.5 Structure of the Fuzzy Estimator

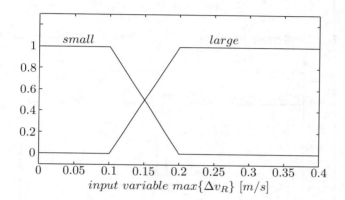

Figure 7.6 Membership functions for max $\{\Delta v_R\}$

The fuzzy estimator contains a the feedback structure, since the estimated vehicle velocity $\hat{v}_{CoG}$ is used for the slip calculation. Therefore the stability of the system must be checked.

The fuzzy velocity estimator has six inputs:

$$u = [\max\{\Delta v_R\} \quad \hat{s}_{LFL} \quad \hat{s}_{LFR} \quad \hat{s}_{LRL} \quad \hat{s}_{LRR} \quad a_{X,C}] \tag{7.8}$$

For the fuzzification of the six inputs, three different membership functions are used. For max $\{\Delta v_R\}$, two attributes are possible, as shown in Figure 7.6. The linguistic variables average all wheel speeds when they are close together. The robustness of the estimator is improved. The new estimate $\hat{v}_{CoG}$ is calculated from the four wheel speeds, the previous velocity estimate and the current longitudinal acceleration.

Figure 7.7 shows the membership functions for the corrected longitudinal acceleration. For acceleration one class is used, *positive*, whilst for braking two classes, *negative* and *very_negative* are used.

Figure 7.8 shows the membership functions for slip. The variables are chosen to correspond to those of the longitudinal acceleration. In order to get an error of 0.2 %, the linguistic variable *zero* is only assigned a range of ±0.2 %.

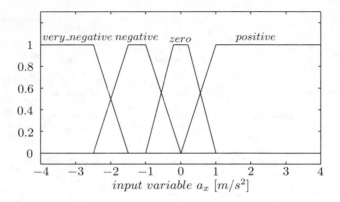

Figure 7.7 Membership functions for the corrected longitudinal acceleration a_x

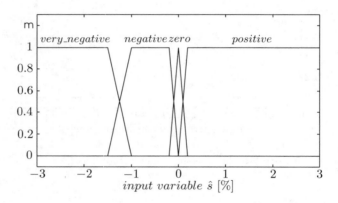

Figure 7.8 Membership functions for the estimated slip value $\hat{s}$

Uniform membership functions are used for the defuzzification of all five weighting factors (Figure 7.9).

A rule base of 68 rules is sufficient to describe the different driving situations [17]. The classification of the driving situations depends heavily on the acceleration. The rule base can be divided as follows:

- $\max\{\Delta v_R\}$ is small (Figure 7.6), which results in equal weighting factors for the wheel velocities.

All other rules are activated only if $\max\{\Delta v_R\}$ is large.

- $a_{X,C}$ positive:
  With rear-wheel driven cars, the rear wheel speeds show a large slip when accelerating. Thus the weighting factors are selected to be small. The front wheels are weighted according to their slip. $a_{X,C}$ is always slightly

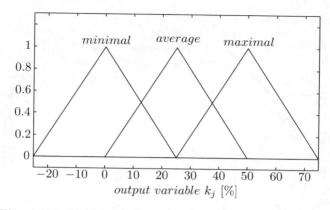

Figure 7.9 Membership functions for the output weightings k_j

weighted. If a measurement error occurs on both front wheels, leading to a negative slip, the estimation is based only upon $a_{X,C}$.

- $a_{X,C}$ zero:
  The front or rear wheel velocities are maximally weighted for constant velocity driving. $a_{X,C}$ is then minimally weighted to allow for the acceleration sensor compensation and the road gradient estimation. If an unexpectedly large slip value appears on any wheel than it is minimally weighted.

- $a_{X,C}$ negative:
  All wheels begin to slip and are minimally weighted. $a_{X,C}$ is slightly weighted. If any wheel has a zero slip then it is slightly weighted. In the case of a positive slip at one wheel, the wheel speed is maximally and the acceleration minimally weighted.

- $a_{X,C}$ very negative:
  The rules are similar to those for $a_{X,C}$ negative. When the brake pressure is reduced, wheels begin to run freely again, then the wheels and the acceleration are maximally weighted, as long as none of the wheels show a positive slip.

It is necessary to plan for the case where the four weighting factors are equal to zero. In this case the vehicle velocity is derived from the last estimate of the vehicle velocity $\hat{v}_{CoG}(k-1)$ and the product of the longitudinal acceleration and the sampling time $T_s \cdot a_{X,C}$.

In order to suppress estimation errors, the reliability of the wheel velocities is checked. For this the wheel velocities are differentiated and the derivative moving-average filtered over ten values. If the average differential exceeds a given threshold then the respective wheel is considered to be unreliable and the corresponding weighting factor set to zero. A threshold of $25\,m/s^2$ has turned out to be suitable for small vehicle accelerations, and $50\,m/s^2$ for large accelerations. This separate check keeps the number of required fuzzy rules low.

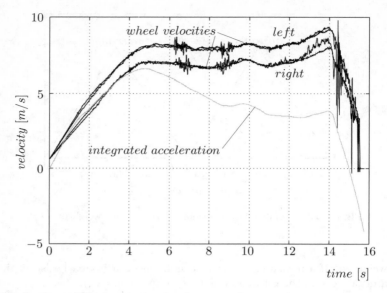

Figure 7.10 Vehicle velocity estimation without sensor data pre-processing

The fuzzy logic outputs are the weighting factors k_i. The vehicle velocity is then estimated as the weighted average:

$$\hat{v}_{CoG}(k) = \frac{\sum_{i=1}^{4} k_i v_{RiC}(k) + k_5 \left(\hat{v}_{CoG}(k-1) + T_s a_{X,C}\right)}{\sum_{i=1}^{5} k_i} \tag{7.9}$$

7.1.5   Results of Velocity Estimators

In a test drive, a cornering manoeuvre with ABS braking was carried out. Figure 7.10 shows the results of the velocity estimator without data preprocessing.

Because the vehicle body side slip angle goes up to $10°$ the integral of the longitudinal acceleration is very imprecise. The sensor data pre-processing is very important in this case. Between $t = 7\,s$ and $t = 9\,s$, the rotational wheel velocities are disturbed because of ground waves. The left and right wheel speeds show a similar behaviour. There is however a large difference between left and right wheel speeds.

Figure 7.11 shows the corrected wheel speeds and the velocity estimate from the fuzzy estimator. The disturbances and the large drive slip are very well smoothed out. For ABS braking, the estimated fuzzy velocity is slightly above the largest wheel velocity.

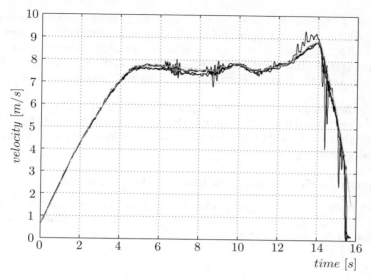

Figure 7.11 Fuzzy estimation of vehicle velocity based on pre-processed sensor data

7.2 Identification of Vehicle Parameters

Using theoretical modelling methods such as those of Chapter 6 a so-called *parametric model* can be obtained, which gives the relationship between the physical data of the system and its parameters. Static parameters can be obtained via measurements or from data sheets. Some parameters are however subject to change over time, and so to improve model quality they must be periodically estimated and replaced within the model. The derivation of these parameters is carried out using measured input and output signals together with a suitable parameter estimation method.

Depending upon the model structure, a-priori knowledge, knowledge about disturbances, available computing time (on-line / off-line) and required estimation quality, an estimation method is chosen from multitude of available methods [10]. Because of the relatively low computation requirements and its real-time applicability, the least squares method is considered here in more detail.

Parameter estimation is applied to the estimation of the friction co-efficients, the mass moments of inertia, the road gradient and the shock absorber characteristics.

In Appendix A.5 the basic theory of least squares estimation is reviewed, followed by a description of the recursive least squares algorithm and the discrete root filter method in covariant form.

7.2.1 Friction Characteristics

The identification of the friction characteristics consists of two processing steps. Firstly the current friction values μ_L are obtained and then the complete friction characteristic is estimated using pairs of (μ_{Res}, s_{Res}) values. In order to calculate the friction values the forces on the wheels must be known. During cornering the friction values can only be averaged over all wheels, based on the lateral acceleration. However, if a wheel brakes at straight ahead driving, the actual friction value, and thus the friction characteristics, can be obtained in the presence of slip.

Both the estimation of the friction co-efficients and that of the friction characteristic are carried out with a recursive least squares (RLS) algorithm. Outliers must be eliminated via data processing, as they can lead to large inaccuracies in RLS-estimation.

Estimation of the Friction Co-efficients During Braking

In order to estimate the friction value μ, the wheel load F_Z and the horizontal force $F_{fric} = \sqrt{F_L^2 + F_S^2}$ are necessary [40], [24]. The longitudinal friction value is defined as the ratio:

$$\mu_L = \frac{F_L}{F_Z} \tag{7.10}$$

During straight ahead driving, a friction co-efficient estimation can be carried out using a torque balance about the wheel axis (single wheel model). This gives the longitudinal frictional force F_L, from which the friction co-efficient μ_L can be calculated:

$$\mu_L(s_L) = \frac{J_W \dot{\omega} + T_{Br} - T_{Drive}}{F_Z \cdot r_{eff}} \tag{7.11}$$

The different directions of the wheel ground contact point velocity v_W and the rotational equivalent wheel velocity v_R are neglected. To obtain the friction co-efficient from Eq. 7.11, the wheel angular acceleration $\dot{\omega}$, the brake and drive torques T_{Br}, T_{Drive} and the wheel ground contact force F_Z are required.

- The wheel angular acceleration is derived from the difference between two consecutive wheel angular velocity measurements:

$$\dot{\omega}(n) = \frac{\omega(n) - \omega(n-1)}{T_s} \tag{7.12}$$

  Where T_s is the sampling time.

- The wheel ground contact force F_Z is calculated according to Section 7.4.1.

- The drive torque T_{Drive} is derived from the engine torque.

- The brake torque T_{Br} is derived from the measured brake pressure or from the motor current in electric brakes.

Using Eq. 7.11 the influence of the two torques on the friction characteristics can be estimated. For dry road surfaces, the brake torque dominates by a factor of at least 10. At the other extreme, on an icy road where large accelerations can appear for small brake torques, the values are of the same order.

The friction co-efficient is estimated by a recursive least squares estimator. A forgetting factor λ_{RLS} and an additive term α_{RLS} are introduced because the friction co-efficients vary during the estimation.

The normalised model equation is:

$$y(n) = u(n) \cdot a(n) \qquad (7.13)$$

Comparing Eq. 7.13 with 7.11 gives the measurement value:

$$y(n) = \frac{J_W \dot{\omega} + T_{Br} - T_{Drive}}{F_Z \cdot r_{eff}} \quad , \qquad u(n) = 1 \quad , \qquad a(n) = \mu(n) \quad . \qquad (7.14)$$

The estimated parameter $\hat{a}$ is obtained by [32]:

$$\hat{a}(n) = \hat{a}(n-1) + k(n) \cdot [y(n) - u(n) \cdot \hat{a}(n-1)] \qquad (7.15)$$

$$k(n) = [\lambda_{RLS} + u_n \cdot p(n-1) \cdot u(n)]^{-1} \cdot p(n-1) \cdot u(n) \qquad (7.16)$$

$$p(n) = \frac{1}{\lambda_{RLS}} \cdot [1 - k(n) \cdot u(n)] \cdot p(n-1) + \alpha_{RLS} \qquad (7.17)$$

The following values are suitable for the estimation constants λ_{RLS} and α_{RLS}:

$$\lambda_{RLS} = 0.9$$
$$\alpha_{RLS} = 1000 \cdot [y(n) - u(n) \cdot \hat{a}(n)]^2$$

The brake torques $T_{BrF,R}$ are calculated from the measured brake pressures $p_{BrF,R}$ using the brake transmission factors k_{BrF} and k_{BrR} (see Eq. 8.1):

$$T_{BrF} = r_{eff} k_{BrF} p_{BrF} \qquad T_{BrR} = r_{eff} k_{BrR} p_{BrR} \qquad (7.18)$$

The brake transmission factors vary between $\frac{k_{Br}}{A_{Br}} = 0.3$ and 0.4. Figure 7.12 shows the estimated friction co-efficients for a test drive. The front left wheel runs on wet grass and the front right one on dry asphalt. The anti-locking control begins to reduce the brake torque at about $200\,ms$. The left wheel shows the typical slip control cycles of an ABS-controlled braking. The right wheel displays only a very small brake slip.

Calculation of the Brake Transmission Factors

A probable cause for error in using the single wheel model (Eq. 7.11) lies in the inaccurate knowledge of the brake transmission factors. The brake transmission factors represent the relationship between brake pressure and brake torque at the wheel ground contact. They are obtained via the formula:

$$k_{BrF,R} = \frac{\mu_{Br} \cdot A_{Br} \cdot r_{Br}}{r_{eff}} \qquad (7.19)$$

where μ_{Br} is the friction co-efficient between brake pad and brake disc, A_{Br} the area of the wheel brake cylinder and r_{Br} the effective frictional radius of the brake disc. A_{Br} and r_{Br} are known. The friction co-efficient μ_{Br} can however

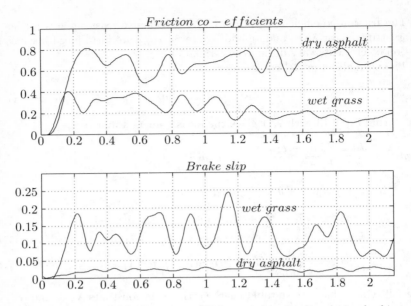

Figure 7.12 Estimated friction co-efficients and brake slips during braking

change due to ageing of the brakes, moisture on the contact area of the brakes or heating during extended braking manoeuvres.

At equal temperatures, the brake transmission factors on the individual wheels have a fixed relationship to one another. The factors for the right and left wheels are equal, and the factor for the rear wheels is smaller by the brake force distribution factor DB:

$$k_{BrR} = DB \cdot k_{BrF} \quad , \qquad DB < 1 \tag{7.20}$$

If the torque balance equations are constructed for the four wheels, the following system of equations results:

$$
\begin{aligned}
J_W \cdot \dot{\omega}_{FL} &= (F_{LFL} - k_{BrF} \cdot p_{BrFL})\, r_{eff} \\
J_W \cdot \dot{\omega}_{FR} &= (F_{LFR} - k_{BrF} \cdot p_{BrFR})\, r_{eff} \\
J_W \cdot \dot{\omega}_{RL} &= (F_{LRL} - k_{BrF} \cdot DB \cdot p_{BrR})\, r_{eff} \\
J_W \cdot \dot{\omega}_{RR} &= (F_{LRR} - k_{BrF} \cdot DB \cdot p_{BrR})\, r_{eff} \\
m_{CoG} \cdot a_X &= F_{XFL} + F_{XFR} + F_{XRL} + F_{XRR} + F_W
\end{aligned}
\tag{7.21}
$$

In the rear brakes, the pressures are identical. By this, the vehicle is stabilised during braking. The forces F_X can be approximated by the forces F_L for small wheel turn angles and small tire slip angles. If this system of equations is solved for k_{BrF}, the following formula for the brake transmission factor results:

$$k_{BrF} = \frac{m_{CoG} \cdot a_X - J_W \cdot \dfrac{[\dot{\omega}_{FL} + \dot{\omega}_{FR} + \dot{\omega}_{RL} + \dot{\omega}_{RR}]}{r_{eff}}}{p_{BrFL} + p_{BrFR} + DB \cdot p_{BrR} + DB p_{BrR}} \tag{7.22}$$

Estimation of Friction Co-efficients During Acceleration

Slip and the friction co-efficients do not appear only during braking, but also during acceleration. The forces which act on the wheels during acceleration are much smaller than those during braking. When braking on a rough road surface, vehicle decelerations of up to $1\,g$ are possible. Contrary to this, vehicle accelerations are much smaller. Large slips can only occur on slippery road surfaces. Because of this it is only possible to determine the friction co-efficients during acceleration when the vehicle is driving on very low friction surfaces. The torque balances for the driven wheels and the motion equation in the longitudinal direction are given by:

$$
\begin{aligned}
J_W \cdot \dot{\omega}_L &= T_{Drive} - r_{eff} \cdot F_{LL} \\
J_W \cdot \dot{\omega}_R &= T_{Drive} - r_{eff} \cdot F_{LR} \\
m_{CoG} \cdot a_X &= F_{LL} + F_{LR}
\end{aligned}
\tag{7.23}
$$

ω_R and ω_L are the rotational wheel speeds and F_{LL} and F_{LR} are the longitudinal forces of the driven right and left wheels.

This system of equations can be solved for the friction co-efficients. E.g. for rear wheel drive:

$$
\begin{aligned}
\mu_{LL} &= \frac{m_{CoG} \cdot a_X \cdot r_{eff} + J_W \cdot (\dot{\omega}_R - \dot{\omega}_L)}{r_{eff} \cdot 2 \cdot F_{ZRL}} \\
\mu_{LR} &= \frac{m_{CoG} \cdot a_X \cdot r_{eff} + J_W \cdot (\dot{\omega}_L - \dot{\omega}_R)}{r_{eff} \cdot 2 \cdot F_{ZRR}}
\end{aligned}
\tag{7.24}
$$

Estimation of Friction Co-efficients During Cornering

For the estimation of friction co-efficients during cornering, one must differentiate between braking and non-braking driving situations. For **braking situations**, the longitudinal friction co-efficient μ_L can be calculated using the single wheel model (Eq. 7.11). The tire side slip angles $\alpha_{F,R}$ can be derived from Eq. 6.16 when the observed vehicle side slip angle β is known. The slips s_L and s_S are calculated from Eq. 6.9. The resultant slip and friction co-efficients are derived using Eqs 6.10 and 6.20:

$$
\begin{aligned}
s_{Res} &= \sqrt{s_L^2 + s_S^2} \\
\mu_{Res} &= \mu_L \cdot \frac{s_{Res}}{s_L}
\end{aligned}
\tag{7.25}
$$

For **non-braking cornering** the friction co-efficients cannot be derived at the individual wheels with the above approach. A global approximation of μ_{Res} is thus carried out. The resulting friction force can be derived from Eq. 6.37 for translatory vehicle motion. The forces F_{GX}, F_{GY}, F_R and F_{wind} are neglected.

$$
\begin{aligned}
m_{CoG}\ddot{x} &= F_{XFL} + F_{XFR} + F_{XRL} + F_{XRR} + F_{wind} \\
m_{CoG}\ddot{y} &= F_{YFL} + F_{YFR} + F_{YRL} + F_{YRR}
\end{aligned}
\tag{7.26}
$$

The resultant friction force is:

$$
\begin{aligned}
F_{fric} &= \left((F_{XFL} + F_{XFR} + F_{XRL} + F_{XRR})^2 + \right. \\
&\quad \left. + (F_{YFL} + F_{YFR} + F_{YRL} + F_{YRR})^2 \right)^{1/2} \\
&= \left((m_{CoG}\ddot{x} - F_{wind})^2 + (m_{CoG}\ddot{y})^2 \right)^{1/2}
\end{aligned}
$$

The resulting normal force is:

$$
F_Z = m_{CoG}\, g \tag{7.27}
$$

When measuring or observing the longitudinal and lateral accelerations a_X and a_Y, the resulting friction co-efficient can be approximated as:

$$
\begin{aligned}
\mu_{Res} &= \frac{F_{fric}}{F_Z} \\
&= \frac{1}{g}\sqrt{\left(a_X - \frac{F_{wind}}{m_{CoG}} \right)^2 + a_Y^2}
\end{aligned}
$$

The resultant slip is approximated by the average

$$
s_{Res} \approx \frac{1}{2}\left(\sin(\alpha_F) + \sin(\alpha_R) \right) \tag{7.28}
$$

Estimation of the Friction Characteristic over Slip

The above methods allow the estimation of the actual friction co-efficients at any instant. It is however useful to know the entire friction characteristic over slip. At braking, the slip and with it the friction co-efficient are constantly changing with the ABS control cycles. Individually estimated friction values would always lag behind by the estimator dynamics. Assuming a constant road surface, instantaneous values of μ may be taken from the estimated friction characteristic without any time delays. Of particular interest is the point of maximum friction.

The friction characteristic over slip is estimated, based on individual friction co-efficient - slip pairs (μ_{Res}, s_{Res}) estimated before. The parameter estimation is again carried out using an RLS algorithm. The following formulation [39] of the friction characteristic results in a linear estimation problem:

$$
\mu_{Res}(s_{Res}) = \frac{\mu'(0) \cdot s_{Res}}{1 + c_1 s_{Res} + c_2 s_{Res}^2} \tag{7.29}
$$

The above is therefore utilised as a model, rather than the Burckhardt approach of Eq. 6.19. The initial gradient $\mu'(0)$ has a value around 30 for almost all road surface conditions and is fixed beforehand. Thus the number of parameters to be estimated is two.

The model must now be brought into a suitable form for linear estimation. The linearised model is:

$$
\begin{aligned}
y(n) &= \mu'(0) \cdot s_{Res}(n) - \mu_{Res}(n) \\
&= \left[\mu_{Res}(n) \cdot s_{Res}(n)\, ,\ \mu_{Res}(n) \cdot s_{Res}^2(n) \right] \cdot \begin{bmatrix} c_1 \\ c_2 \end{bmatrix} \tag{7.30}
\end{aligned}
$$

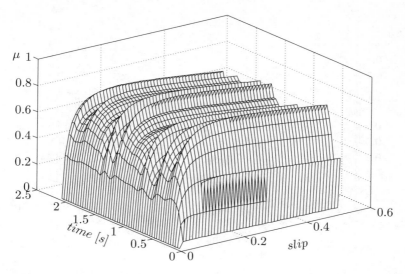

Figure 7.13 Estimated friction characteristic for the front right wheel (dry asphalt)

The parameters c_1 and c_2 can now be derived using a recursive least squares algorithm (Eqs A.75 to A.77).

The parameters were estimated for the example of Figure 7.12. The transient behaviour of the estimator can be seen in Figs 7.13 and 7.14. For both wheels, the initial characteristic curve used was that for wet asphalt. Figure 7.13 shows the plot of the friction characteristic for the front right wheel. During a braking manoeuvre the friction characteristic is reliably estimated.

Figure 7.14 shows the estimation results for the front left wheel. After approximately $200\,ms$ a friction characteristic with low maximum is estimated, which is plausible for wet grass.

7.2.2 Mass Moments of Inertia

For the calculation of the translatory vehicle motions, good results can normally be obtained by assuming a single mass at the CoG. The rotational motion on the other hand depends upon the mass distribution around the relevant axis.

The following mass moments of inertia occur on the vehicle:

- J_X moment of inertia with respect to the roll (longitudinal) axis

- J_Y moment of inertia with respect to the pitch (lateral) axis

- J_Z moment of inertia with respect to the yaw (vertical) axis

For the pitch and roll only the vehicle body moves, and not the so-called "unsprung" vehicle parts (wheels, axles). For yaw motion on the other hand the whole vehicle turns around the axis.

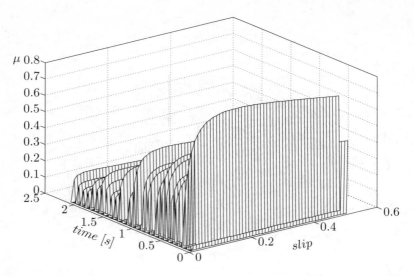

Figure 7.14 Estimated friction characteristic for the front left wheel (wet grass)

An analytical derivation of these mass moments of inertia is very complex. According to [68] there are at present neither simple measurement techniques nor universally applicable calculation methods available. Part of the identification task is thus the derivation of the mass moments of inertia.

Method 1 : Approximate Calculation of Mass Moments of Inertia

[68] describes an approximate method using the so-called radii of gyration $i_{X,Y,Z}$, which are recorded in tables for particular vehicle types and loading conditions. Table 7.1 lists values for a limousine in the middle class [68]. The radii of gyration

Table 7.1 Radii of gyration (in m) for a middle-class limousine

Loading	i_X	i_Y	i_Z
Empty	0.65	1.21	1.20
2 People	0.64	1.13	1.15
4 People	0.60	1.10	1.14
4 People + luggage	0.56	1.13	1.18

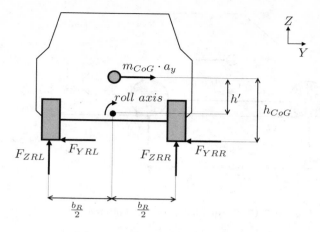

Figure 7.15 Torque balance at the roll axis

i_X and i_Y relate to the vehicle body, and i_Z to the whole vehicle:

$$\begin{aligned}
J_X &= (m_{CoG} - m_{Un}) \cdot i_X^2 \\
J_Y &= (m_{CoG} - m_{Un}) \cdot i_Y^2 \\
J_Z &= m_{CoG} \cdot i_Z^2
\end{aligned} \tag{7.31}$$

m_{CoG} is the complete vehicle mass and m_{Un} the unsprung vehicle mass (Axles and wheels). For the experimental vehicle the values $80\,kg$ (front) and $130\,kg$ (back) are used for the unsprung masses.

Because in this method a whole vehicle class is treated the same way, the results which are obtained are not precise. The results should be considered as an indication of the variation of the mass moments of inertia dependant upon the loading conditions.

Method 2: RLS-estimation of the Mass Moments of Inertia

The starting point for the derivation of the estimation equations for the mass moments of inertia comes from the vehicle model of Chapter 6. In Chapter 6 the roll and pitch axis were assumed to lie at the road level. The torque equations about the roll and pitch axis must now be extended to cover the real torques due to longitudinal and lateral tire forces.

The forces for the roll motion are shown in Figure 7.15.

Constructing the torque balance equations according to Figure 7.15 yields:

$$\begin{aligned}
J_X \cdot \ddot{\varphi} &= (F_{ZFL} - F_{ZFR}) \cdot \frac{b_F}{2} + (F_{ZRL} - F_{ZRR}) \cdot \frac{b_R}{2} \\
&\quad + (F_{YFL} + F_{YFR} + F_{YRL} + F_{YRR}) \cdot (h_{CoG} - h') + m_{CoG} \cdot a_Y \cdot h'
\end{aligned} \tag{7.32}$$

Similarly, Figure 7.16 shows the situation for the pitch axis, where the longitudinal tire forces are also included.

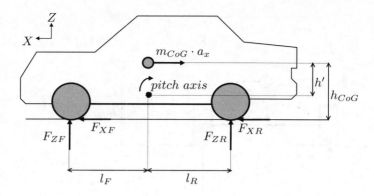

Figure 7.16 Torque balance at the pitch axis

The pitch torque balance is:

$$J_Y \cdot \ddot{\chi} = (F_{ZFL} + F_{ZFR}) \cdot l_F - (F_{ZRL} + F_{ZRR}) \cdot l_R$$
$$+ (F_{XFL} + F_{XFR} + F_{XRL} + F_{XRR}) \cdot (h_{CoG} - h') + m_{CoG} \cdot a_X \cdot h'$$

$$(7.33)$$

As already mentioned, the height of the CoG has no effect on the torque balance equations for yaw, as long as the yaw axis passes through the CoG of the vehicle. Thus the equations can be taken directly from the vehicle model (Eq. 6.53):

$$J_Z \cdot \ddot{\psi} = (F_{YFR} + F_{YFL}) \cdot (l_F - n_{LF}) - (F_{YRR} + F_{YRL}) \cdot (l_R + n_{LR})$$
$$+ (F_{XRR} - F_{XRL}) \cdot \frac{b_R}{2} + F_{XFR} \cdot \left(\frac{b_F}{2} - n_{SFR} \sin \delta_W \right)$$
$$- F_{XFL} \cdot \left(\frac{b_F}{2} + n_{SFL} \sin \delta_W \right)$$

$$(7.34)$$

Eqs. 7.32 to 7.34 form the basis for the estimation of the mass moments of inertia. They are re-written with measured terms $y(k)$ on the left hand side and parameter terms $\underline{\Theta}(k)$ on the right hand side of the model equation:

$$y(k) = \underline{\Psi}^T(k) \cdot \underline{\Theta}(k) \tag{7.35}$$

The following parameters are assumed to be constant and known:

l_F	Front wheel base
l_R	Rear wheel base
b_F	Front track width
b_R	Rear track width
h_{CoG}	height of CoG above the road
$h_{CoG} - h'$	height of the pitch and roll axis above the road

The following variables are measured:

ω_{ij}	Rotational wheel speeds
a_x, a_y	longitudinal and lateral acceleration
δ_W	wheel turn angle
$\dot{\psi}$	yaw rate
Δz_{cij}	relative displacement of contact points between chassis and undercarriage

The following variables and parameters are calculated or estimated:

m_{CoG}	vehicle mass (Section 7.4.4)
F_{Zij}	vertical wheel ground contact forces (Section 7.4.1)
$n_L F$, $n_L R$	front and rear casters (Equation 6.1)
c_{ij}	tire side slip constants (Section 7.4.2)
χ, φ	pitch and roll angles (Section 7.4.3)
v_{CoG}	vehicle speed (Section 7.1)
β	vehicle body side slip angle (Section 7.3)
α_F, α_R	front and rear side slip angle (Equation 6.16)
v_{Rij}	rotational equivalent wheel speeds (Section 6.3.6)
v_{Wij}	wheel ground contact point velocities (Equation 6.8)
s_{Lij}, s_{Sij}	longitudinal and lateral slip values (Equation 6.9)
μ_{Res}	friction coefficient (Section 7.2.1)
F_{Xij}, F_{Yij}	longitudinal and lateral wheel forces (Section 6.3.4)

The angular accelerations are obtained via numerical differentiation. As an alternative to the calculation of F_{Xij}, F_{Yij} as in Section 6.3.4, the sum of forces could also be derived from the respective acceleration Equ. 7.26.

From the above, the following three estimation equations result:

$$
\underbrace{(F_{ZFL} - F_{ZFR}) \cdot \frac{b_F}{2} + (F_{ZRL} - F_{ZRR}) \cdot \frac{b_R}{2} + \left(\sum_{i=FL}^{RR} F_{Yi} \right) \cdot (h_{CoG} - h')}_{y(k)}
$$

$$
= \underbrace{[\ddot{\varphi}, -a_Y]}_{\underline{\Psi}^T(k)} \cdot \underbrace{\begin{bmatrix} J_X \\ m_{CoG} \cdot h' \end{bmatrix}}_{\Theta(k)} \qquad (7.36)
$$

$$
\underbrace{(F_{ZFL} + F_{ZFR}) \cdot l_F - (F_{ZRL} + F_{ZRR}) \cdot l_R + \left(\sum_{i=FL}^{RR} F_{Xi} \right) \cdot (h_{CoG} - h')}_{y(k)}
$$

$$
= \underbrace{[\ddot{\chi}, -a_X]}_{\underline{\Psi}^T(k)} \cdot \underbrace{\begin{bmatrix} J_Y \\ m_{CoG} \cdot h' \end{bmatrix}}_{\Theta(k)} \qquad (7.37)
$$

$$\underbrace{\begin{array}{c}(F_{YFR} + F_{YFL})\,(l_F - n_{LF}) - (F_{YRR} + F_{YRL})\,(l_R + n_{LR}) + \\ F_{XFR}\left(\frac{b_F}{2} - n_{SFR}\sin\delta_W\right) - F_{XFL}\left(\frac{b_F}{2} + n_{SFL}\sin\delta_W\right)\end{array}}_{y(k)}$$

$$= \underbrace{\left[\begin{array}{cc} \ddot{\psi} & -\frac{F_{XRR} - F_{XRL}}{2} \end{array}\right]}_{\underline{\Psi}^T(k)} \cdot \underbrace{\left[\begin{array}{c} J_Z \\ b_R \end{array}\right]}_{\underline{\Theta}(k)}$$

$$(7.38)$$

The estimation approach for the yaw moment of inertia J_Z (Eq. 7.38) is formulated to include the estimation of the rear track width b_R. As b_R is already known, a comparison of the estimated and actual b_R will give an indication as to the quality of the estimation.

Results for the Estimated Mass Moments of Inertia

Good identification results, according to [47], can only be obtained if there is sufficient excitation of the system by the inputs. Thus, for the estimation of the three mass moments of inertia J_X, J_Y and J_Z, suitable driving manoeuvres must be chosen.

For each of the three mass moments of inertia, test drives with loading conditions of 2 and 5 persons are compared. By comparing the results for the different loading conditions, the extent to which the estimator detects the variations in the moments of inertia can be seen. The results are given in Figs 7.17 and 7.18. The reference values are in each case indicated with dashed lines and each figure contains the results of two test drives.

As seen from Eqs. 7.36 and 7.37, the product $m_{CoG} \cdot h'$ is estimated as well as the moments of inertia J_X and J_Y. If constant and known h' is assumed, the vehicle mass m_{CoG} can also be estimated.

While the estimator very closely approximates the reference values for J_X, the estimated values for J_Y have significantly larger oscillations around the expected final value, as shown in the example of Figure 7.18.

The results show that the moment of inertia J_X can be determined quite accurately for suitably chosen test drives. The vehicle mass lies in the expected range, as does the moment of inertia J_Y. A reliable detection of the loading conditions, e.g. in this case whether there are 2 or 5 people in the vehicle, is however not always possible. The value of the moment of inertia itself only varies from approximately $2300\,kgm^2$ to $2500\,kgm^2$, i.e. less than $10\,\%$. Complications arise because the vehicle pitch is stimulated to a lesser degree than the roll and yaw, hence the RLS - estimator is excited to a lesser extent and degraded transient oscillations result.

Figure 7.19 shows the results for the moment of inertia J_Z around the vertical vehicle axis.

Here, in accordance with Eq. 7.38, the track width b_R is identified as well as the moment of inertia J_Z. The reference value for the track width is $1.4\,m$. Essentially the same results as for the other two moments of inertia are obtained,

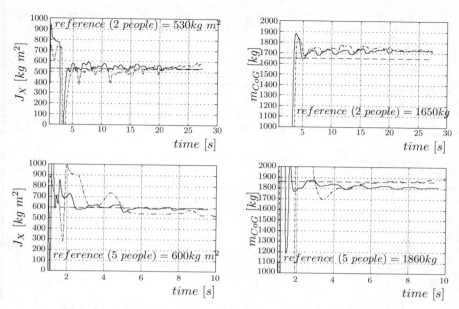

Figure 7.17 Estimation results for J_X and m_{CoG} with 2 and 5 people

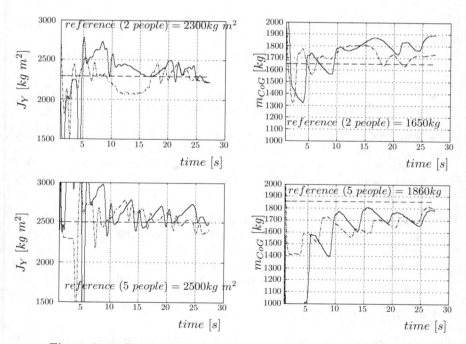

Figure 7.18 Estimation results for J_Y and m_{CoG} with 2 and 5 people

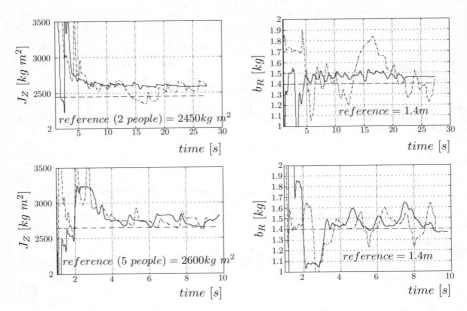

Figure 7.19 Estimation results for J_Z and b_R with 2 and 5 people

namely that the estimated values are of the same order of magnitude as the reference values.

To summarise the results of all three mass moments of inertia, J_X, J_Y and J_Z:

- The wheel forces required for the estimation can be calculated from the wheel ground contact forces and the wheel model.

- The mass moments of inertia depend upon the loading conditions. They vary less than 10 %. On one hand, this makes the detection of the loading conditions from the mass moments of inertia very difficult. On the other hand, the mass moments of inertia can be applied with reasonable accuracy for different loading conditions.

- The vehicle mass m_{CoG} is derived from the product $m_{CoG} \cdot h'$, whereby h' (the distance of the CoG from the rotation centre) is assumed constant and known. The disregarding of the dependence of h' on the loading conditions leads to inaccuracies in the mass calculations. If however the mass is measured separately before the test drive, then one can infer h'.

7.2.3 Road Gradient

The model accuracy for real driving with road gradient (positive or negative) is strongly influenced by the actual road gradient angle χ_{road}, which is also required for transmission control.

Here, the method of estimating the road gradient from [17] is given, and the accuracy investigated. The starting point of this method is an offset error in the longitudinal acceleration signal a_X. This offset value is dependant upon the gravitational acceleration g and the road gradient χ_{road}:

$$a_X = \ddot{x} - g \cdot \sin \chi_{road} \tag{7.39}$$

For upward driving, i.e. a positive pitch angle χ_{road}, the measured longitudinal acceleration a_X is reduced by the component $g \sin\chi_{road}$ which has the opposite direction as $\ddot{x}$. The acceleration of the vehicle can be calculated using the angular wheel velocity ω:

$$\ddot{x} = r_{eff} \cdot \dot{\omega} \tag{7.40}$$

To avoid errors due to excessive wheel slip, only the angular velocity of the non-driven wheels should be used.

Solving Eq. 7.39 for the road gradient angle χ_{road}, and substituting $\sin(\chi) \approx \chi$ for small angles, the equation for the calculation of the road gradient is obtained:

$$\chi_{road} = \frac{r_{eff} \cdot \dot{\omega} - a_X}{g} \tag{7.41}$$

With this equation the road gradient can be quickly obtained from the measured variables a_X and ω. The results are shown in Figure 7.20. The vehicle drives through a "valley", first a negative and then a positive road gradient.

When the bottom of the valley is reached in the left hand plots of Figure 7.20, the sign of the expression $(\ddot{x} - a_X)$ changes. The right hand plots show the estimated road gradients.

The road gradient can be determined with a resolution of under 5 %.

7.2.4 Shock Absorber Characteristics

The design of suspension systems for automobiles has gained importance in the last few years, due to their influence on the vehicle characteristics [25]. Also, much effort has been directed towards the design of active and semi-active control algorithms with the purpose of reducing the dynamic wheel forces [14], [39], [13]. Many of these studies however have been carried out in the laboratory, where the shock absorber characteristics are already known.

Basic to the design of a new suspension controller is the reliable estimation of the shock absorber characteristics. In this section the nonlinear suspension model of Section 6.4.3 is taken to estimate its parameters d_{Ul} and d_{Unl}.

Re-arranging Eq. 6.70 yields:

$$
\begin{aligned}
(\Delta z_{Wij} - \Delta z_{Cij}) = \quad & - \frac{d_{Ul}}{k_U} (\dot{z}_{Wij} - \dot{z}_{Cij}) \\
& - \frac{d_{Unl}}{k_U} \sqrt{|\dot{z}_{Wij} - \dot{z}_{Cij}|} \, \mathrm{sign} (\dot{z}_{Wij} - \dot{z}_{Cij}) + \frac{m_q}{k_U} \ddot{z}_{Cij}
\end{aligned}
\tag{7.42}
$$

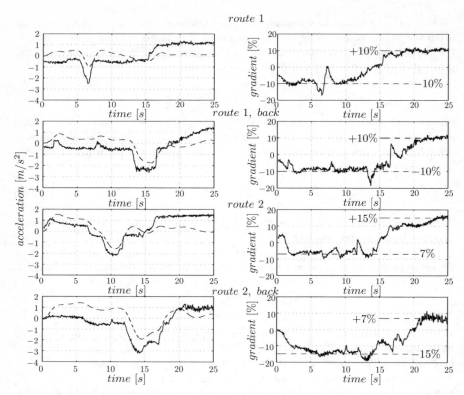

Figure 7.20 Acceleration signals (left) and estimated road gradients (right)

With the measured variable $y(t) = \Delta z_{Wij}(t) - \Delta z_{Cij}(t)$, the general form of the linear RLS estimation problem is:

$$
\begin{aligned}
y(k) &= a_1 \dot{y}(k) + a_2 \sqrt{|\dot{y}(k)|}\,\text{sign}(\dot{y}(k)) + b_0 u(k) \\
&= \underline{\psi}^T(k) \cdot \underline{\Theta}
\end{aligned}
\tag{7.43}
$$

The observation vector is:

$$
\underline{\Psi}(k) = \begin{bmatrix} -\dot{y}(k) & \sqrt{|\dot{y}(k)|}\,\text{sign}(\dot{y}(k)) & u(k) \end{bmatrix}^T
\tag{7.44}
$$

and the estimated parameter vector:

$$
\begin{aligned}
\underline{\Theta} &= \begin{bmatrix} a_1 & a_2 & b_0 \end{bmatrix}^T \\
&= \begin{bmatrix} -\dfrac{d_{ul}}{k_U} & \dfrac{d_{Unl}}{k_U} & \dfrac{m_q}{k_U} \end{bmatrix}^T
\end{aligned}
\tag{7.45}
$$

Figure 7.21 shows the results for the shock absorber characteristics estimation.

For upward bumps $\dot{z}_C - \dot{z}_W < 0$, the damping force is estimated too high. During downward movements $\dot{z}_C - \dot{z}_W > 0$, the estimate is very precise. Alternative approaches for improving the numerical differentiation are presented in [49].

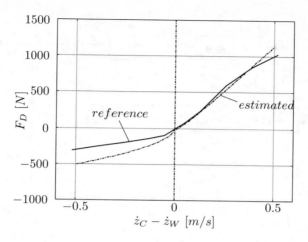

Figure 7.21 Damping force F_D as a function of velocity $\dot{z}_C - \dot{z}_W$

7.3 Vehicle Body Side Slip Angle Observer

7.3.1 Basic Theory of a Nonlinear Observer

In general, observers are implemented when certain state variables cannot be measured without unacceptable expense. If, as is here the case, the system is in nonlinear form, the direct application of a Luenberger observer is not possible. To overcome this problem, Zeitz [82] proposes an observer design using linearisation which is modelled on the Luenberger observer. Figure 7.22 shows the structure of the nonlinear observer from Zeitz.

The following nonlinear system is the starting point for the design:

$$
\begin{aligned}
\underline{\dot{x}} &= \underline{f}(\underline{x}, \underline{u}) \\
\underline{y} &= \underline{c}(\underline{x})
\end{aligned}
\tag{7.46}
$$

As in the linear case the state observation follows:

$$
\begin{aligned}
\underline{\dot{\hat{x}}} &= \underline{f}(\underline{\hat{x}}, \underline{u}) + \underline{L}(\underline{\hat{x}}, \underline{u}) \cdot (\underline{y} - \underline{\hat{y}}) \\
\underline{\hat{y}} &= \underline{c}(\underline{\hat{x}})
\end{aligned}
\tag{7.47}
$$

The observer gain matrix $\underline{L}$ must now be specified such that the estimation error $\underline{\tilde{x}}(t)$ tends to zero for $t \to \infty$:

$$
\lim_{t \to \infty} \underline{\tilde{x}}(t) = \lim_{t \to \infty} \underline{x}(t) - \underline{\hat{x}}(t) = 0
\tag{7.48}
$$

The error differential equation is formed, the solution of which can be used to determine whether or not the condition of Eq. 7.48 is satisfied:

$$
\underline{\dot{\tilde{x}}}(t) = \underline{\dot{x}}(t) - \underline{\dot{\hat{x}}}(t) = \underline{f}(\underline{x}, \underline{u}) - \underline{f}(\underline{\hat{x}}, \underline{u}) - \underline{L}(\underline{\hat{x}}, \underline{u}) \cdot \underbrace{(\underline{c}(\underline{x}) - \underline{c}(\underline{\hat{x}}))}_{\underline{y} - \underline{\hat{y}}}
\tag{7.49}
$$

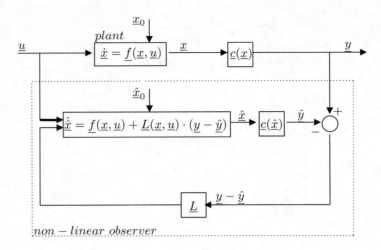

Figure 7.22 Structure of the nonlinear observer

$\underline{f}(\underline{x}, \underline{u})$ and $\underline{c}(\underline{x})$ are then expanded around $\underline{\hat{x}}$ using the Taylor series expansion, whereby each is curtailed after the linear term:

$$\underline{f}(\underline{x}, \underline{u}) \approx \underline{f}(\underline{\hat{x}}, \underline{u}) + \frac{\partial \underline{f}}{\partial \underline{x}}(\underline{\hat{x}}, \underline{u}) \cdot (\underline{x} - \underline{\hat{x}}) \tag{7.50}$$

$$\underline{c}(\underline{x}) \approx \underline{c}(\underline{\hat{x}}) + \frac{\partial \underline{c}}{\partial \underline{x}}(\underline{\hat{x}}) \cdot (\underline{x} - \underline{\hat{x}}) \tag{7.51}$$

The Jacobian matrix

$$\frac{\partial \underline{f}}{\partial \underline{x}} = \begin{bmatrix} \frac{\partial f1}{\partial x1} & \frac{\partial f1}{\partial x2} & \cdots & \frac{\partial f1}{\partial xn} \\ \vdots & \vdots & \ddots & \vdots \\ \frac{\partial fn}{\partial x1} & \frac{\partial fn}{\partial x2} & \cdots & \frac{\partial fn}{\partial xn} \end{bmatrix} \tag{7.52}$$

is given in Appendix A.2. Using this linearisation approach, one obtains a formal linear error differential equation whose solution can be reduced to zero with suitable choice of the observer gain matrix $\underline{L}$.

Substitution of Eqs. 7.50 and 7.51 in Eq. 7.49 leads to the following linearised estimation error differential equation:

$$
\begin{aligned}
\dot{\tilde{x}}(t) &= \dot{x}(t) - \dot{\hat{x}}(t) \\
&= \underline{f}(\underline{x}, \underline{u}) - \underline{f}(\hat{\underline{x}}, \underline{u}) - \underline{L}(\hat{\underline{x}}, \underline{u}) \cdot (\underline{c}(\underline{x}) - \underline{c}(\hat{\underline{x}})) \\
&= \underline{f}(\hat{\underline{x}}, \underline{u}) + \frac{\partial \underline{f}}{\partial \underline{x}}(\hat{\underline{x}}, \underline{u}) \cdot (\underline{x} - \hat{\underline{x}}) - \underline{f}(\hat{\underline{x}}, \underline{u}) \\
&\quad - \underline{L}(\hat{\underline{x}}, \underline{u}) \cdot \left(\underline{c}(\hat{\underline{x}}) + \frac{\partial \underline{c}}{\partial \underline{x}}(\hat{\underline{x}}) \cdot (\underline{x} - \hat{\underline{x}}) - \underline{c}(\hat{\underline{x}}) \right) \\
&= \frac{\partial \underline{f}}{\partial \underline{x}}(\hat{\underline{x}}, \underline{u}) \cdot \tilde{\underline{x}} - \underline{L}(\hat{\underline{x}}, \underline{u}) \cdot \frac{\partial \underline{c}}{\partial \underline{x}}(\hat{\underline{x}}) \cdot \tilde{\underline{x}} \\
&= \underbrace{\left[\frac{\partial \underline{f}}{\partial \underline{x}}(\hat{\underline{x}}, \underline{u}) - \underline{L}(\hat{\underline{x}}, \underline{u}) \cdot \frac{\partial \underline{c}}{\partial \underline{x}}(\hat{\underline{x}}) \right]}_{\underline{F}(\hat{\underline{x}}, \underline{u})} \cdot \tilde{\underline{x}}
\end{aligned} \tag{7.53}
$$

An observer gain matrix $\underline{L}$ must now be found such that the observer dynamic matrix $\underline{F}(\hat{\underline{x}}, \underline{u})$ is constant and its eigenvalues lie to the left of the j - axis, so that the solution $\tilde{\underline{x}}(t)$ of the estimation error differential equation tends to zero for $t \to \infty$ for any initial conditions. The suitable choice of $\underline{L}(\hat{\underline{x}}, \underline{u})$ is given by equating $\underline{F}(\hat{\underline{x}}, \underline{u})$ with a constant matrix $\underline{G}$, whose values are predefined according to desired dynamics (pole placement).

$$
\underline{F}(\hat{\underline{x}}, \underline{u}) = \frac{\partial \underline{f}}{\partial \underline{x}}(\hat{\underline{x}}, \underline{u}) - \underline{L}(\hat{\underline{x}}, \underline{u}) \cdot \frac{\partial \underline{c}}{\partial \underline{x}}(\hat{\underline{x}}) \overset{!}{=} \underline{G} \tag{7.54}
$$

From this, the observer gain matrix $\underline{L}(\hat{\underline{x}}, \underline{u})$ can be calculated:

$$
\underline{L}(\hat{\underline{x}}, \underline{u}) = \left[\frac{\partial \underline{f}}{\partial \underline{x}}(\hat{\underline{x}}, \underline{u}) - \underline{G} \right] \cdot \left[\frac{\partial \underline{c}}{\partial \underline{x}}(\hat{\underline{x}}) \right]^{+} \tag{7.55}
$$

The matrix $\frac{\partial \underline{c}}{\partial \underline{x}}(\hat{\underline{x}})$ is in general non-square. Therefore the Moore-Penrose pseudo-inversion is used for inversion:

$$
\left[\frac{\partial \underline{c}}{\partial \underline{x}}(\hat{\underline{x}}) \right]^{+} = \left[\frac{\partial \underline{c}}{\partial \underline{x}}(\hat{\underline{x}}) \right]^{T} \cdot \left(\left[\frac{\partial \underline{c}}{\partial \underline{x}}(\hat{\underline{x}}) \right] \cdot \left[\frac{\partial \underline{c}}{\partial \underline{x}}(\hat{\underline{x}}) \right]^{T} \right)^{-1} \tag{7.56}
$$

7.3.2 Observer Design

The nonlinear observer is used for the observation of the vehicle body side slip angle β based on the reduced nonlinear two-track model (section 6.4.4).

Eqs 6.83 to 6.85 give the nonlinear state space description required for the design of the nonlinear observer according to Eq. 7.46. According to these equations, F_{LFL}, F_{LFR}, F_{LRL}, F_{LRR} and δ_W are the inputs $\underline{u}$ for the observer. The wheel forces in the L-direction are thus explicitly defined as inputs, and the wheel forces in the S-direction appear implicitly in the tire side slip constants c_F and c_R (Eq. 6.82).

The equations 6.83 to 6.85 are brought into the form:

$$\underline{\dot{x}} = \underline{f}(\underline{x}, \underline{u}) \Leftrightarrow \begin{bmatrix} v_{\dot{C}oG} \\ \dot{\beta} \\ \ddot{\psi} \end{bmatrix} = \begin{bmatrix} \underline{f}_1\left(v_{CoG}, \beta, \dot{\psi}, F_{LFL}, F_{LFR}, F_{LRL}, F_{LRR}, \delta_W\right) \\ \underline{f}_2\left(v_{CoG}, \beta, \dot{\psi}, F_{LFL}, F_{LFR}, F_{LRL}, F_{LRR}, \delta_W\right) \\ \underline{f}_3\left(v_{CoG}, \beta, \dot{\psi}, F_{LFL}, F_{LFR}, F_{LRL}, F_{LRR}, \delta_W\right) \end{bmatrix}$$

$$(7.57)$$

The states, inputs and measurements are defined as follows:

State Vector:

$$\underline{x} = \begin{bmatrix} v_{CoG} \\ \beta \\ \dot{\psi} \end{bmatrix}$$

Input Vector:

$$\underline{u} = \begin{bmatrix} F_{LFL}, F_{LFR}, F_{LRL}, F_{LRR}, \delta_W \end{bmatrix}^T$$

Measurement:

$$\underline{y} = \begin{bmatrix} v_{CoG} \\ \dot{\psi} \end{bmatrix}$$

In the input vector $\underline{u}$, the wheel turn angle δ_W is handled by the driver. By steering, the vehicle body side slip angle β is controlled. In dangerous driving situations, the driver may be supported by a vehicle dynamic control system, which uses the longitudinal wheel forces $F_{LFL}, F_{LFR}, F_{LRL}, F_{LRR}$ as additional input variables. The elements of the Jacobian matries are given in Appendix A.2.

To determine the observer gain matrix $\underline{L}(\hat{\underline{x}}, \underline{u})$ a suitable desired observer dynamic matrix $\underline{G}$ must be chosen in Eq. 7.54. The simplest way of determining the eigenvalues of the observer dynamic matrix $\underline{F}$ is to have the matrix $\underline{G}$ in diagonal form; the eigenvalues can then be directly read from the main diagonal elements. For this reason the desired matrix $\underline{G}$ is chosen as a diagonal matrix, whose main diagonal elements are the desired eigenvalues for the matrix $\underline{F}(\hat{\underline{x}}, \underline{u})$ (Eq. 7.54):

$$\underline{G} = \begin{bmatrix} \lambda_1 & 0 & 0 \\ 0 & \lambda_2 & 0 \\ 0 & 0 & \lambda_3 \end{bmatrix} \qquad (7.58)$$

The three eigenvalues λ_1, λ_2 and λ_3 must be carefully chosen in order to influence the dynamics of the observer gain matrix $\underline{L}$.

With $\underline{y} = \underline{c}(\underline{x}) = \begin{bmatrix} v_{CoG} \\ \dot{\psi} \end{bmatrix}$, $\underline{c}$ is a constant 2×3 matrix. The pseudo-inverse can be obtained using Eq. 7.56 as:

$$\left[\frac{d\underline{c}}{d\underline{x}}(\hat{\underline{x}})\right]^+ = \begin{bmatrix} 1 & 0 \\ 0 & 0 \\ 0 & 1 \end{bmatrix} \qquad (7.59)$$

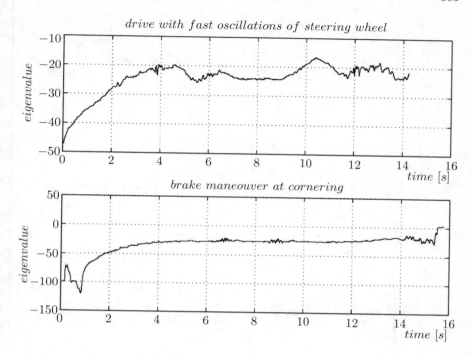

Figure 7.23 Position of time-variant eigenvalue λ_2 during test drives

The Jacobian matrix $\partial \underline{f}/\partial \underline{x}$, the matrix $\underline{G}$ and the pseudo inverse are substituted into Eq. 7.55. The elements of the observer gain matrix $\underline{L}(\hat{\underline{x}}, \underline{u})$ are obtained as functions of the Jacobian matrix and the desired eigenvalues:

$$\underline{L}(\hat{\underline{x}}, \underline{u}, \lambda_1, \lambda_3) = \begin{bmatrix} \dfrac{\partial f1}{\partial x1} - \lambda_1 & \dfrac{\partial f1}{\partial x3} \\[2mm] \dfrac{\partial f2}{\partial x1} & \dfrac{\partial f2}{\partial x3} \\[2mm] \dfrac{\partial f3}{\partial x1} & \dfrac{\partial f3}{\partial x3} - \lambda_3 \end{bmatrix} \qquad (7.60)$$

Note that only two of the chosen eigenvalues appear in the above calculation, thus only two of the desired eigenvalues of the matrix $\underline{F}(\hat{\underline{x}}, \underline{u})$ can be placed in the chosen positions. There remains a time-variant eigenvalue λ_2, which is shown during test drives in Figure 7.23. It can be seen, that also λ_2 remains in the stable region.

Simulation Results

The Figs 7.24 and 7.25 show results of the observer based on the reduced nonlinear two-track model. As examples, two drive situations are carried out with the experimental vehicle, in which the longitudinal and the lateral dynamics are

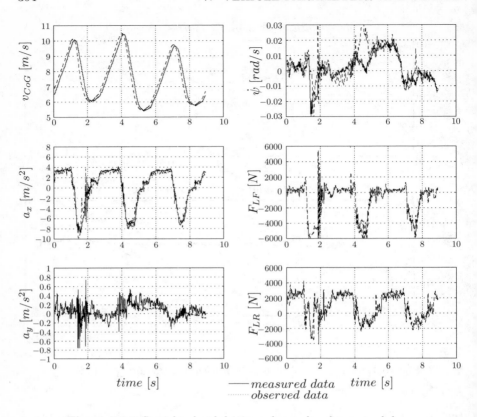

Figure 7.24 Straight ahead driving: observed and measured data

excited.   From the comparison of the measured and observed state variables
v_{CoG} and $\dot{\psi}$ the quality of the observer itself and of the input variables (the wheel
forces) can be seen.   The first test drive involves braking and accelerating during
straight ahead driving, as shown in Figure 7.24.   The lateral and longitudinal
accelerations can be used as additional comparison variables, as they can be
calculated from the observed state variables according to the following [54]:

$$\hat{a}_x = \dot{v}_{CoG} \cdot \cos \beta$$
$$\hat{a}_y = v_{CoG} \cdot \left(\dot{\beta} + \dot{\psi}\right) \tag{7.61}$$

The left and the right wheel forces are averaged at the front and at the rear
respectively.   The vehicle body side slip angle β and the averaged wheel forces
F_{LF}, F_{LR}, F_{SF}, F_{SR} cannot be measured.   For comparison, they are calculated
as shown in section 6.3.4.

The measured and observed values for v_{CoG} and $\dot{\psi}$ correspond so well that
they almost coincide.   The derived accelerations $\hat{a}_X$ and $\hat{a}_Y$ also follow the actual
measured variables very well.   Thus it can be concluded that the observed vehicle

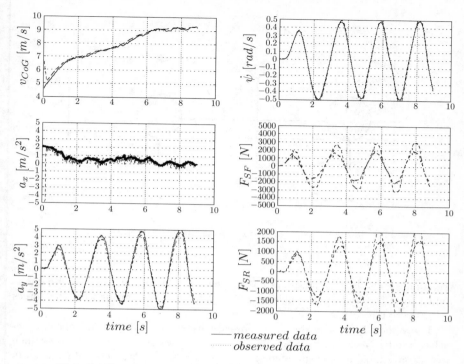

Figure 7.25 Sine wave form steering: observed and measured data

body slide slip angle β and the wheel forces F_{LF} and F_{LR} should also correspond to their unmeasureable real counterparts. If only one of the two accelerations a_x and a_Y are measured in the complete vehicle control system, the other one can be determined using the observer and equation 7.61. The second test drive corresponds to a sine wave form steering manoeuvre, with slowly increasing velocity. In this manoeuvre the lateral dynamics are excited, so the wheel forces in the y-direction as opposed to the x-direction are shown in Figure 7.25. Again, the observed variables v_{CoG} and $\dot{\psi}$ correspond extremely well to the measured variables, as do the derived accelerations.

For lateral accelerations of up to $\pm 4\,m/s^2$, which is not exceeded for either of the above test drives, one can assume reliable derivation of the horizontal wheel forces $F_{LF,R}$ and $F_{SF,R}$. Thus, a method has been found with which to derive the input variables $F_{LF,R}$ and $F_{SF,R}$. As these are derived from the vertical wheel ground contact forces F_{Zij}, the latter can also be assumed as reliable input variables.

7.4 Approximation of other Vehicle Parameters

One of the most important tasks of the identification is to obtain the forces acting upon the wheels, which are very difficult to obtain in terms of measurement

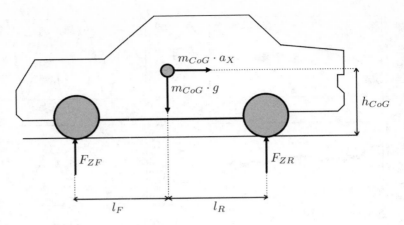

Figure 7.26 Axle load shifting during acceleration

techniques. The longitudinal and lateral wheel forces, F_X and F_Y can be determined from the friction co-efficients μ_S, μ_L and the wheel ground contact forces F_{Zij} (Section 6.3.4).

The vehicle body side slip angle observer in Section 7.3 uses the wheel forces either implicitly or explicitly as inputs, and observes additional variables which are also available as measurements. If these measured variables are sufficiently well reproduced, then it can be assumed that also the input wheel forces to the observer correspond sufficiently well to reality. In Section 7.3, the variables v_{CoG}, β and $\dot{\psi}$ in the nonlinear two-track model were observed. Of these, v_{CoG} and $\dot{\psi}$ are also measured, and hence can be used for comparison (Figure 7.24 and 7.25).

7.4.1   Calculation of Wheel Ground Contact Forces

If the coupling between roll and pitch is neglected as in [17], the dependencies of the quarter vehicle forces F_{ZCij} on the longitudinal and lateral accelerations a_X and a_Y can be determined separately. By disregarding suspension dynamics, the quarter vehicle forces F_{ZC} are identical to the wheel ground contact forces F_Z. According to this approach the common front wheel ground contact force F_{ZF} is formed as shown in Figure 7.26.

The force due to longitudinal acceleration ($m_{CoG} \cdot a_X$) at the CoG causes a pitch torque which reduces the front axle load and increases the rear axle load. The vehicle mass is estimated in Section (7.4.4).

Constructing the torque balance at the rear axis contact point yields:

$$l \cdot F_{ZF} = l_R \cdot m_{CoG} \cdot g - h_{CoG} \cdot a_X \tag{7.62}$$

Thus:

$$F_{ZF} = m_{CoG} \cdot \left(\frac{l_R}{l} g - \frac{h_{CoG}}{l} a_x \right) \tag{7.63}$$

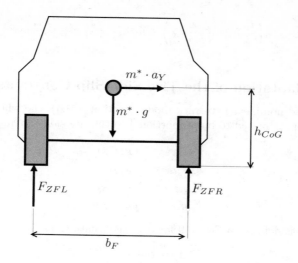

Figure 7.27 Wheel load shifting during cornering

During cornering the lateral acceleration causes a roll torque as shown in Figure 7.27, whose distribution over the front and rear axle depends on the axle load.

The two axles are considered to be decoupled from one another. In the case of the front axle load a virtual mass m^* is used:

$$m^* = \frac{F_{ZF}}{g} \tag{7.64}$$

From the torque balance equation at the ground contact point of the front left wheel:

$$F_{ZFR} \cdot b_F = F_{ZF} \cdot \frac{b_F}{2} + m^* \cdot a_Y \cdot h_{CoG} \tag{7.65}$$

Substituting the virtual mass of Eq. 7.64, and F_{ZF} from Eq. 7.63 and solving for F_{ZFR}, gives the front right dynamic wheel force (Eq. 7.67). By analogy the wheel forces for the other three wheels can then be derived:

$$F_{ZFL} = \frac{1}{2}m_{CoG} \cdot \left(\frac{l_R}{l}g - \frac{h_{CoG}}{l}a_X \right) - m_{CoG} \cdot \left(\frac{l_R}{l}g - \frac{h_{CoG}}{l}a_X \right) \cdot \frac{h_{CoG} \cdot a_Y}{b_F \cdot g} \tag{7.66}$$

$$F_{ZFR} = \frac{1}{2}m_{CoG} \cdot \left(\frac{l_R}{l}g - \frac{h_{CoG}}{l}a_X \right) + m_{CoG} \cdot \left(\frac{l_R}{l}g - \frac{h_{CoG}}{l}a_X \right) \cdot \frac{h_{CoG} \cdot a_Y}{b_F \cdot g} \tag{7.67}$$

$$F_{ZRL} = \frac{1}{2}m_{CoG} \cdot \left(\frac{l_F}{l}g + \frac{h_{CoG}}{l}a_X \right) - m_{CoG} \cdot \left(\frac{l_F}{l}g + \frac{h_{CoG}}{l}a_X \right) \cdot \frac{h_{CoG} \cdot a_Y}{b_R \cdot g} \tag{7.68}$$

$$F_{ZRR} = \frac{1}{2} m_{CoG} \cdot \left(\frac{l_F}{l} g + \frac{h_{CoG}}{l} a_X \right) + m_{CoG} \cdot \left(\frac{l_F}{l} g + \frac{h_{CoG}}{l} a_X \right) \cdot \frac{h_{CoG} \cdot a_Y}{b_R \cdot g}$$

$$(7.69)$$

7.4.2 Adaptation of the Tire Side Slip Constants

In the reduced nonlinear two-track model (section 6.4.4), the wheel side forces have been approximated to be proportional to the tire side slip angles α_{ij}:

$$
\begin{aligned}
F_{SFL} &= c_{FL} \alpha_{FL} \\
F_{SFR} &= c_{FR} \alpha_{FR} \\
F_{SRL} &= c_{RL} \alpha_{RL} \\
F_{SRR} &= c_{RR} \alpha_{RR}
\end{aligned}
$$

$$(7.70)$$

The side slip is defined in Eq. 6.9 for driving situations as

$$s_S = \tan \alpha \quad , \tag{7.71}$$

which is linearised to

$$s_S \approx \alpha \quad . \tag{7.72}$$

The wheel side forces are then

$$F_{S_{ij}} = \mu_{S_{ij}}(s_{S_{ij}}) F_{Z_{ij}} = c_{ij} \cdot s_{S_{ij}} \quad , \tag{7.73}$$

or the tire side slip constant

$$c_{ij} = \frac{\partial \mu_{S_{ij}}(s_{S_{ij}})}{\partial s_{S_{ij}}} \cdot F_{Z_{ij}} \quad . \tag{7.74}$$

This is approximated by

$$c_{ij} \approx \frac{\mu_{S_{ij}}}{\alpha_{ij}} \cdot F_{Z_{ij}} \quad . \tag{7.75}$$

From [54], the wheel turn angle is

$$\delta_W \approx \left(\frac{\delta_S}{i_S} - \frac{n_{LF} + n_C}{k_s} (F_{SFL} + F_{SFR}) \right) \quad . \tag{7.76}$$

n_{LF} is the longitudinal caster of the front wheels. n_C is the caster determined by the extrapolated intersection point of the steering column with the road surface (Figure 7.28). Side force F_{SF} results in a self righting torque at the wheels. The driver must increase the steering angle δ_S in order to compensate for this self righting torque T_{self}, which can be assumed to be proportional to the angular difference.

$$
\begin{aligned}
T_{self} &\overset{!}{=} k_s \left(\frac{\delta_S}{i_S} - \delta_W \right) \\
&\approx (F_{SFL} + F_{SFR}) \cdot (n_{LF} + n_C)
\end{aligned}
$$

$$(7.77)$$

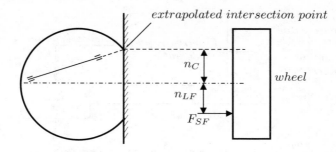

Figure 7.28 Extrapolated intersection point of the steering column

k_s is a rotational spring constant of the steering and i_S the transmission ratio of the steering angle δ_S. The effective wheel turn angle δ_W is smaller than the transformed steering angle $\frac{\delta_S}{i_S}$.

The sum of the front wheel side forces

$$
\begin{aligned}
2 \cdot F_{SF} = F_{SFL} + F_{SFR} &= (c_{FL} + c_{FR})\alpha_F \\
&= (c_{FL} + c_{FR})\left(\delta_W - \beta - \frac{l_F\dot{\psi}}{v_{CoG}}\right)
\end{aligned}
$$

are inserted into Eq. 7.76, which is resolved for δ_W.

$$
\delta_W = \frac{1}{1 + \dfrac{(n_{LF} + n_C)(c_{FL} + c_{FR})}{-k_s}}\left(\frac{\delta_S}{i_S} + \frac{(n_{LF} + n_C)(c_{FL} + c_{FR})}{-k_s}\left(\beta + \frac{l_F\dot{\psi}}{v_{CoG}}\right)\right)
$$

(7.78)

This is inserted into the front side force equation, yielding an average front side force

$$
\begin{aligned}
F_{SF} &= \underbrace{\frac{(c_{FL} + c_{FR})/2}{1 + \dfrac{(n_{LF} + n_C)(c_{FL} + c_{FR})}{-k_s}}}_{c_F^*}\underbrace{\left(\frac{\delta_S}{i_S} - \left(\beta + \frac{l_F\dot{\psi}}{v_{CoG}}\right)\right)}_{\approx \alpha_F} \\
&\approx c_F^*\alpha_F \quad .
\end{aligned}
$$

(7.79)

The average rear side force is

$$
F_{SR} = \frac{(c_{RL} + c_{RR})}{2}\alpha_R = c_R \cdot \alpha_R \quad .
$$

(7.80)

For equal tire side slip constants

$$
c_{FL} = c_{FR} = c_{RL} = c_{RR} = c \quad ,
$$

(7.81)

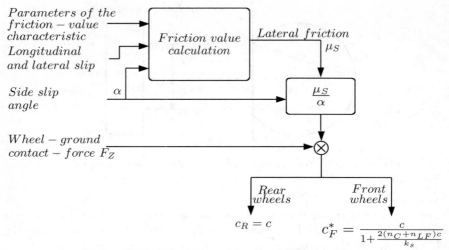

Figure 7.29 Calculation of the tire side slip constants

a new constant for the front tires can be derived

$$c_F^* = \frac{1}{1 + \dfrac{2(n_C + n_{LF})c}{k_s}} c \quad , \tag{7.82}$$

which considers the self righting torque. The average front tire side slip constants c_F^* is reduced by the influence of the side slip forces, which are self righting the front wheels. The adaptation procedure is shown in Figure 7.29.

7.4.3   Approximation of Pitch and Roll Angles

The pitch and roll angles χ, φ are calculated from the relative displacement Δz_C of the quarter vehicle on top of the suspension. In this simplified approach, the impact of a rough road surface is disregarded.

$$\hat{\chi} = \frac{1}{l} \cdot \left(\frac{\Delta z_{CRL} + \Delta z_{CRR}}{2} - \frac{\Delta z_{CFL} + \Delta z_{CFR}}{2} \right) \tag{7.83}$$

A positive pitch angle means that the vehicle is diving down at the front.

$$\hat{\varphi} = \frac{1}{b_F + b_R} \cdot \left(\frac{\Delta z_{CFL} + \Delta z_{CRL}}{2} - \frac{\Delta z_{CFR} + \Delta z_{CRR}}{2} \right) \tag{7.84}$$

A positive roll angle means that the vehicle is leaning towards the right hand side relative to the forward direction. Figure 7.30 shows a comparison between measured and approximated pitch and roll angles during a test drive. The approximated angles are ahead of the measured angles in time, and are also not accurate in amplitude. This is mainly due to the fact that the input values Δz_C are corrupted. Considering the small computational expense however, this approximation gives still good results.

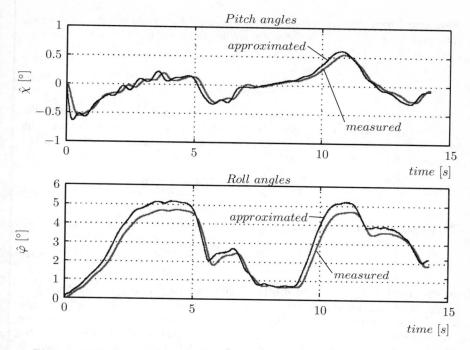

Figure 7.30 Comparison of approximated and measured pitch and roll angles

7.4.4   Approximation of Vehicle Mass

The vehicle mass m_{CoG} is a temporally slowly variable parameter. Therefore it is not necessary to estimate the vehicle mass constantly but only for certain driving conditions. The vehicle mass can be estimated out of a force-balance. The occurred errors will be analyzed and the approximation will be executed only during suitable driving conditions.

To derive the force-balance it would be needful to consider all power consumers, e.g. air-condition and radio. All these consumers reduce the available torque for the acceleration of the vehicle. To bypass all these measurements the estimation will be made only in driving conditions with a high engine torque. The engine output will then be reduced insignificantly by parasitic consumers. The result is the following force-balance:

$$F_{Acc} = F_{Drive} - F_{windx} - F_R - F_G \tag{7.85}$$

The rolling resistance between tires and road is calculated after Eq. 6.51, the wind force will be approximated to:

$$F_{windx} = c_{aer} \, A_L \, \frac{\rho_0}{2} \, v_{CoG} \tag{7.86}$$

F_G is the gravitational force and arises:

$$F_G = m_{CoG} \, g \, \sin \chi_{road} \tag{7.87}$$

The engine torque is converted with the transmission ratio of the gear and the differential, as well as with the static rolling radius of the wheel into the drive force:

$$F_{Drive} = \frac{T_e}{r_{Stat}} \, i_{gear} \, i_{diff} \qquad (7.88)$$

The acceleration force does not correspond to the vehicle mass m_{CoG} multiplied by the vehicle acceleration. This is because of the rotatory parts of the drive line and the wheels which must also be accelerated. Hence, it is necessary to add a mass factor f_{mass} to compensate the effect. According to [53] arises:

$$f_{mass} = 1 + \frac{4J_W + i_{diff}^2(J_{DT} + i_{gear}^2 J_{crank})}{m_{CoG} \, r_{Stat}^2} \qquad (7.89)$$

Thus results in the following estimation equation for the vehicle mass:

$$m_{CoG} = \frac{F_{Drive} - F_{windx} - F_R}{f_{mass}\dot{v}_{CoG} + g \cdot \chi_{road}} \qquad (7.90)$$

Input values into Eq. 7.90 are the vehicle velocity v_{CoG}, the road gradient χ_{road}, gear and differential transmission i_{gear} and i_{diff} and the engine torque T_e. For mass estimation those driving conditions are determined, whenever the engine torque is exactly known. An additional energy consuming part is the torque converter of the automatic transmission. The mass estimation is executed only if the converter bypass is closed, so that the losses of the torque converter are eliminated. Furthermore, driving conditions with small modifications of the throttle angle are determined, since in dynamic transitions errors occur in the engine map. The engine map contains only a static allocation of the engine torque dependent on the engine speed and the throttle angle. Modern engine management control units provide an estimated engine torque output signal.

Figure 7.31 shows the estimated mass during an accelerated drive. In the upper pictures the velocity and the engine torque are represented. The lower picture shows the estimated mass during the test drive. Because of a disturbance of the acceleration signal the mass is estimated to high in a short period. After calculating the average over the entire time period, the vehicle mass results to 1821 kg. The real mass of the test vehicle was measured before the test drive by 1810 kg. Thus, the estimated mass corresponds very well with the true mass. For mass estimation a constantly accelerated drive suits perfectly. Since the time period used for the estimation of the vehicle mass can also be assembled, several short accelerated driving conditions are sufficient for the mass estimation.

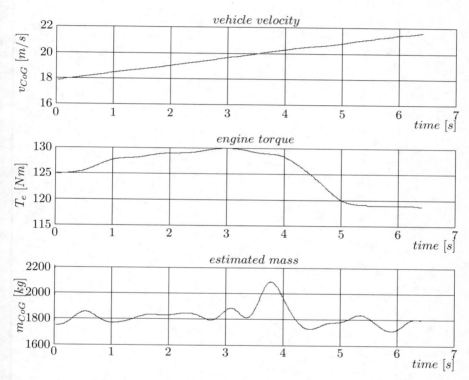

Figure 7.31 Approximation results of the vehicle mass

8 Vehicle Control Systems

8.1 ABS Control Systems

The ABS system aims to minimise the braking distance while retaining steerability during braking. The shortest braking distance can be reached when the wheels operate at the slip of maximum adhesion co-efficient μ_L (Figure 6.17).

8.1.1 Torque Balance at wheel-road contact

By modelling the torque balance at the wheel-road contact a better understanding of how ABS systems are able to operate around maximum friction can be obtained. Figure 8.1 shows the forces acting on the wheel.

In hydraulic brakes, the brake torque at the wheel base depends on the applied braking pressure p_{Br}:

$$T_{Br} = F_{Br} \cdot r_{eff} = r_{Br} \cdot \mu_{Br} \cdot A_{Br} \cdot p_{Br} = r_{eff} \cdot k_{Br} \cdot p_{Br} \qquad (8.1)$$

Disregarding the drive torque, the torque balance is (Eq. 7.11):

$$J_W \dot{\omega} = r_{eff} \cdot \mu_L(s_L) \cdot F_Z - r_{eff} \cdot k_{Br} \cdot p_{Br} \qquad (8.2)$$

This is shown schematically in Figure 8.2.

On applying the braking pressure p_{Br}, the brake torque T_{Br} increases. The difference between friction torque T_{WL} and brake torque T_{Br} is negative, resulting in a wheel deceleration. The wheel rotational equivalent velocity v_R (after the integrator in Figure 8.2) starts to decrease and yields an increasing slip s_L. At first the friction co-efficient $\mu_L(s_L)$ increases as well, building up the friction torque T_{WL} which narrows the torque difference.

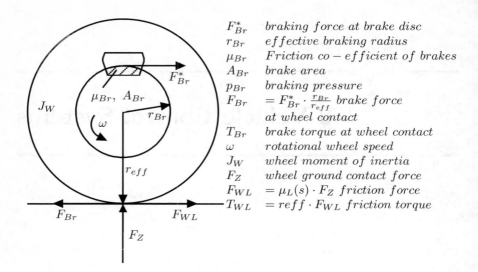

F_{Br}^*	$braking\ force\ at\ brake\ disc$
r_{Br}	$effective\ braking\ radius$
μ_{Br}	$Friction\ co-efficient\ of\ brakes$
A_{Br}	$brake\ area$
p_{Br}	$braking\ pressure$
F_{Br}	$= F_{Br}^* \cdot \frac{r_{Br}}{r_{eff}}\ brake\ force$
	$at\ wheel\ contact$
T_{Br}	$brake\ torque\ at\ wheel\ contact$
ω	$rotational\ wheel\ speed$
J_W	$wheel\ moment\ of\ inertia$
F_Z	$wheel\ ground\ contact\ force$
F_{WL}	$= \mu_L(s) \cdot F_Z\ friction\ force$
T_{WL}	$= reff \cdot F_{WL}\ friction\ torque$

Figure 8.1 Torque balance at the wheel-road surface contact

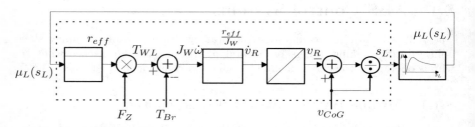

Figure 8.2 Block diagram of torque balance at wheel base

After passing the maximum friction co-efficient, the friction curve changes the sign of its gradient. Thus the loop becomes *unstable*, resulting, in the absence of control, in extremely high rotational wheel deccelerations: blocking of wheel.

8.1.2   Control Cycles of the ABS System

The control cycles are shown in Figure 8.3 [5]. At braking the driver increases the braking pressure (Phase 1).

The rotational equivalent wheel speeds v_{Rij} are measured and differentiated to give the wheel accelerations $\dot{v}_{Rij}$. The point of maximum friction is passed when the wheel speed derivative is below a given threshold a_1:

$$\dot{v}_R < -a_1 \tag{8.3}$$

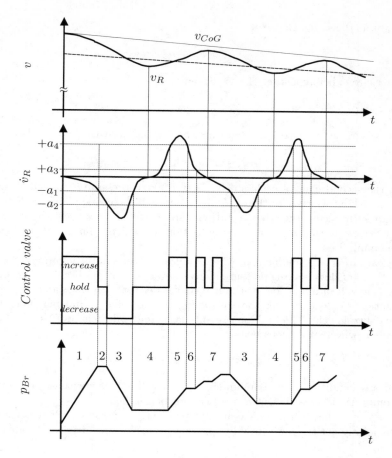

Figure 8.3 Control cycles of the ABS system with hydraulic brakes

In the very first control cycle, an even lower threshold a_2 is applied. Between a_1 and a_2, braking pressure is held (Phase 2). The introduction of the additional threshold a_2 serves to suppress eventual noise influences.

For

$$\dot{v}_R < -a_2 \tag{8.4}$$

braking pressure is decreased (Phase 3). The wheel gains speed again. When threshold a_1 is reached again, the pressure drop is stopped (Phase 4). When the wheel speed derivative passes beyond

$$\dot{v}_R > a_4 \tag{8.5}$$

braking pressure is increased in order to prevent the wheel returning to too small slip values (Phase 5). Between

$$a_4 > \dot{v}_R > a_3 \qquad (8.6)$$

the pressure is held constant (Phase 6), and below

$$\dot{v}_R < a_3 \qquad (8.7)$$

it is slowly raised (Phase 7). When the wheel speed derivative goes below

$$\dot{v}_R < -a_1 \qquad (8.8)$$

again the second control cycle starts. Now braking pressure is immediately decreased without waiting for threshold a_2 to be reached (second phase 3). Running through such cycles, the wheel rotational speed is kept in an area where wheel slip s_L is close to that of the maximum friction co-efficient. Thus *braking distance* can be minimised.

In case of a large moment of wheel inertia J_W, of small friction co-efficients $\mu_L(s_L)$ and of slow braking pressure increase (due to cautious braking, e.g. on icy roads), the wheel might lock without reaching deceleration threshold $-a_1$. Such a situation would endanger the *steerability* of the vehicle. Independant of the above control cycles, the braking pressure is therefore decreased if the rotational equivalent wheel speed goes below:

$$v_R < (1 - s_{L,max})v_{CoG} \qquad (8.9)$$

Under any conditions, a maximum slip $s_{L,max}$ will not be surpassed, even if the maximum friction co-efficient $\mu_L(s_L)$ cannot be reached.

The front wheels of a vehicle are independently controlled, whereas the rear wheels jointly get the lower braking pressure. This ensures driving stability.

8.2   Control of the Yaw Dynamics

The control of the yaw dynamics detailed here is based on the reduced nonlinear two-track model of Section 6.4.4. In linearised form the model is given by the following equation (Eq. 6.91):

$$\underline{f}(\underline{x}, \underline{u}) \approx \underline{f}(\underline{x}_0, \underline{u}_0) + \underbrace{\frac{\partial \underline{f}(\underline{x}, \underline{u})}{\partial \underline{x}}\bigg|_{\substack{\underline{x} = \underline{x}_0 \\ \underline{u} = \underline{u}_0}}}_{\text{Jacobian}} \cdot (\underline{x} - \underline{x}_0) + \underbrace{\frac{\partial \underline{f}(\underline{x}, \underline{u})}{\partial \underline{u}}\bigg|_{\substack{\underline{x} = \underline{x}_0 \\ \underline{u} = \underline{u}_0}}}_{\text{Jacobian}} \cdot (\underline{u} - \underline{u}_0)$$

$$(8.10)$$

The three state variables are $\dot{\psi}$, which is measured, and v_{CoG} and β, which are estimated (Sections 7.1 and 7.3). The control inputs are:

$$\underline{u} = [F_{LFL} \ F_{LFR} \ F_{LRL} \ F_{LRR} \ \delta_W]^T \qquad (8.11)$$

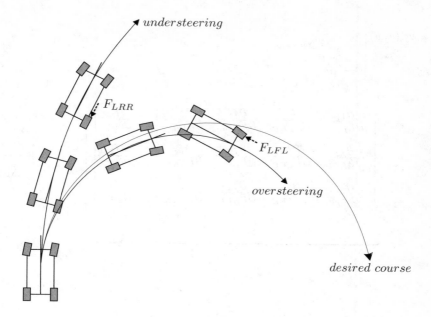

Figure 8.4 Under- and oversteering

Note that, when only the brakes are available as actuators, then only braking forces F_{LFL}, F_{LFR}, F_{LRL}, and F_{LRR} can be generated. In the case when each wheel were driven individually, e.g. by electrical motors, accelerating forces F_{LFL}, F_{LFR}, F_{LRL}, and F_{LRR} could also be generated.

The wheel turn angle δ_W is influenced by the driver using the steering wheel. In the event of an unappropiate vehicle body side slip angle β, the driver attempts to correct the error using steering. When the driver is overloaded, i.e. in critical driving situations, the inputs F_{Lij} can be used to correct the vehicle body side slip angle, via short term braking of the individual wheels.

Figure 8.4 shows the cases where the braking forces could be used to correct the angular position of the vehicle relative to the desired course.

In the case of understeering, braking can be applied to the rear right wheel, causing a yaw torque about the CoG which corrects for the understeering. This is applied until the error in β falls below a given threshold, at which point the driver can once more control the yaw motion using the steering. A respective correction is applied at oversteering.

8.2.1   Derivation of Simplified Control Law

Note that the driver influences the steering (i.e. δ_W), and the controller affects the brake forces F_{Lij}, thus the effect of the two can be separated. The Jakobian is:

$$\frac{\partial \underline{f}(\underline{x},\underline{u})}{\partial \underline{u}}\Bigg|_{\substack{\underline{x}=\underline{x}_0 \\ \underline{u}=\underline{u}_0}} \cdot \Delta \underline{u} =$$

$$= \underbrace{\begin{bmatrix} \dfrac{\partial f_1}{\partial F_{LFL}} & \dfrac{\partial f_1}{\partial F_{LFR}} & \dfrac{\partial f_1}{\partial F_{LRL}} & \dfrac{\partial f_1}{\partial F_{LRR}} & \left| \; \dfrac{\partial f_1}{\partial \delta_W} \right. \\[2mm] \dfrac{\partial f_2}{\partial F_{LFL}} & \dfrac{\partial f_2}{\partial F_{LFR}} & \dfrac{\partial f_2}{\partial F_{LRL}} & \dfrac{\partial f_2}{\partial F_{LRR}} & \left| \; \dfrac{\partial f_2}{\partial \delta_W} \right. \\[2mm] \dfrac{\partial f_3}{\partial F_{LFL}} & \dfrac{\partial f_3}{\partial F_{LFR}} & \dfrac{\partial f_3}{\partial F_{LRL}} & \dfrac{\partial f_3}{\partial F_{LRR}} & \left| \; \dfrac{\partial f_3}{\partial \delta_W} \right. \end{bmatrix}}_{\substack{\underline{M}_F\big|_{\substack{\underline{x}=\underline{x}_0 \\ \underline{u}=\underline{u}_0}} \qquad \underline{m}_\delta\big|_{\substack{\underline{x}=\underline{x}_0 \\ \underline{u}=\underline{u}_0}}}}\Bigg|_{\substack{\underline{x}=\underline{x}_0 \\ \underline{u}=\underline{u}_0}} \cdot \begin{bmatrix} \Delta \underline{u}_F \\[2mm] \hline \Delta u_\delta \end{bmatrix}$$

(8.12)

$$= \underline{M}_F\Big|_{\substack{\underline{x}=\underline{x}_0 \\ \underline{u}=\underline{u}_0}} \cdot (\underline{u}_F - \underline{u}_{F0}) + \underline{m}_\delta\Big|_{\substack{\underline{x}=\underline{x}_0 \\ \underline{u}=\underline{u}_0}} \cdot (\delta_W - \delta_{W0}) \qquad (8.13)$$

Where,

$$\Delta \underline{u}_F = (\underline{u}_F - \underline{u}_{F0})$$

$$\Delta \underline{u}_F = \begin{bmatrix} F_{LFL} - F_{LFL0} \\[2mm] F_{LFR} - F_{LFR0} \\[2mm] F_{LRL} - F_{LRL0} \\[2mm] F_{LRR} - F_{LRR0} \end{bmatrix}$$

$$\Delta u_\delta = \delta_W - \delta_{W0}$$

Substituting this in Eq. 8.10 gives:

$$\dot{\underline{x}} = \underbrace{\underline{f}(\underline{x}_0,\underline{u}_0) + \frac{\partial \underline{f}(\underline{x},\underline{u})}{\partial \underline{x}}\Bigg|_{\substack{\underline{x}=\underline{x}_0 \\ \underline{u}=\underline{u}_0}} \cdot (\underline{x} - \underline{x}_0) + \underline{m}_\delta\Big|_{\substack{\underline{x}=\underline{x}_0 \\ \underline{u}=\underline{u}_0}} \cdot (\delta_W - \delta_{W0})}_{\text{Vehicle dynamics + driver input}}$$

$$\underbrace{+ \, \underline{M}_F\Big|_{\substack{\underline{x}=\underline{x}_0 \\ \underline{u}=\underline{u}_0}} \cdot (\underline{u}_F - \underline{u}_{F0})}_{\text{Yaw control input}} \qquad (8.14)$$

To allow a good physical interpretation of the control parameters, the controller will be designed using a pole placement approach. Normally, the output vector $\underline{y}$ is fed back. This output vector however does not contain β, which is the main variable to be controlled. Because of this, the state vector $\underline{x}$ is obtained using an observer (Section 7.3). The controller design can then be based on the feedback of the state vector $\underline{x}$, where v_{CoG} is estimated (Section 7.1), $\dot{\psi}$ measured and β observed (Section 7.3).

A control law is then defined for small deviations from the operating point $\underline{x} - \underline{x}_0$. This is justified because under normal, non-critical cornering, $\underline{x} - \underline{x}_0$ is equal to zero. Only when pre-determined thresholds are exceeded, in critical situations, is there a difference between the desired and actual state vectors which must be controlled.

The following control law is used:

$$\Delta \underline{u}_F = -\underline{K}_C \cdot \Delta \underline{x} \quad , \tag{8.15}$$

where $\underline{K}_C$ is the feedback matrix.

Substituting into the linearised state space description Eq. 8.14 gives:

$$\Delta \underline{\dot{x}} = \left. \frac{\partial \underline{f}}{\partial \underline{x}} \right|_{\substack{\underline{x} = \underline{x}_0 \\ \underline{u} = \underline{u}_0}} \cdot \Delta \underline{x} - \left. \underline{M}_F \right|_{\substack{\underline{x} = \underline{x}_0 \\ \underline{u} = \underline{u}_0}} \cdot \underline{K}_C \cdot \Delta \underline{x} + \left. \underline{m}_\delta \right|_{\substack{\underline{x} = \underline{x}_0 \\ \underline{u} = \underline{u}_0}} \cdot \Delta \delta_W \quad ,$$

$$\Delta \underline{\dot{x}} = \left(\left. \frac{\partial \underline{f}}{\partial \underline{x}} \right|_{\substack{\underline{x} = \underline{x}_0 \\ \underline{u} = \underline{u}_0}} - \left. \underline{M}_F \right|_{\substack{\underline{x} = \underline{x}_0 \\ \underline{u} = \underline{u}_0}} \cdot \underline{K}_C \right) \cdot \Delta \underline{x} + \left. \underline{m}_\delta \right|_{\substack{\underline{x} = \underline{x}_0 \\ \underline{u} = \underline{u}_0}} \cdot \Delta \delta_W \quad ,$$

$$\tag{8.16}$$

where the term inside the brackets represents the system matrix for the closed loop. The driver input shall be regarded as superimposed noise. The dynamic characteristics of this system can then be set using pole placement. A desired matrix $\underline{G}$ is defined, which has the desired system characteristics, i.e. the desired pole positions:

$$\left. \frac{\partial \underline{f}}{\partial \underline{x}} \right|_{\substack{\underline{x} = \underline{x}_0 \\ \underline{u} = \underline{u}_0}} - \underline{M}_F \cdot \underline{K}_C \overset{!}{=} \underline{G} \tag{8.17}$$

Solving for $\underline{K}_C$ gives the control law:

$$\underline{K}_C = [\underline{M}_F]^+ \cdot \left(\left. \frac{\partial \underline{f}}{\partial \underline{x}} \right|_{\substack{\underline{x} = \underline{x}_0 \\ \underline{u} = \underline{u}_0}} - \underline{G} \right) \quad , \tag{8.18}$$

where $[\underline{M}_F]^+$ is the Moore-Penrose pseudo inverse of $\underline{M}_F$.

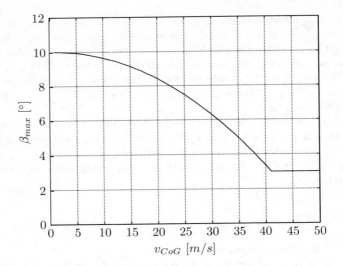

Figure 8.5 Dependence of maximum vehicle body side slip angle on speed

Note that the above gives the feedback matrix $\underline{K}_C$ for the operating point x_0, u_0. Thus, $\underline{K}_C$ must be re-calculated for each new operating point. This involves:

- Calculation of the tire side slip constants (Section 7.4.2),

- Estimation of the vehicle velocity (Section 7.1),

- Observation of the vehicle body side slip angle (Section 7.3),

8.2.2   Derivation of Reference Values

The lateral acceleration a_y is limited by the friction co-efficient μ_S. Theoretically, a vehicle can turn with a lateral acceleration of 9.81 times the maximum lateral friction co-efficient, i.e. for $\mu_S = 1$, the lateral vehicle acceleration could be $9.81\,m/s^2$, if the vehicle body side slip angle were zero. For vehicle body side slip angles greater than zero, a maximum acceleration of $8\,m/s^2$ is adopted. For friction coefficients below 1, the maximum lateral acceleration is given by:

$$a_{Ymax} = \mu_S \cdot 8\,m/s^2 \tag{8.19}$$

The vehicle body side slip angle β is also limited. The predominant variable affecting this is the vehicle speed v_{CoG} (see Figure 8.5):

$$\beta_{max} = 10° - 7° \cdot \frac{v_{CoG}^2}{(40\,m/s)^2} \tag{8.20}$$

The reference vehicle body side slip angle is thus given by:

$$\beta_{ref} = \begin{cases} \beta & , \quad |\beta| \le |\beta_{max}| \\ \pm\beta_{max} & , \quad \text{otherwise} \end{cases} \tag{8.21}$$

Note that $(\beta_{ref} - \beta) = \Delta x_2 = 0$ when the vehicle body side slip angle is below it's maximum limit.

In the case of **oversteering**, the yaw rate $\dot\psi$ must also be limited by means of the yaw dynamic control. If the derivative of the vehicle body side slip angle $\dot\beta$ is approximated to zero, Eq. 6.77 yields:

$$\dot\psi \approx \frac{1}{v_{CoG} \cdot \cos\beta} \cdot \left(\underbrace{\frac{F_{YFL} + F_{YFR} + F_{YRL} + F_{YRR}}{m_{CoG}} - \dot v_{CoG} \cdot \sin\beta}_{a_Y} \right) \tag{8.22}$$

$$\dot\psi_{max} = \frac{1}{v_{CoG} \cdot \cos\beta} (a_{Ymax} - \dot v_{CoG} \cdot \sin\beta_{ref}) \tag{8.23}$$

The reference yaw rate in the case of **oversteering** is then,

$$\dot\psi_{ref} = \begin{cases} \dot\psi & , \quad |\dot\psi| \le |\dot\psi_{max}| \\ \pm\dot\psi_{max} & , \quad \text{otherwise} \end{cases} \tag{8.24}$$

When the yaw rate is below it's maximum limit, the difference $\dot\psi_{ref} - \dot\psi = \Delta x_3 = 0$.

In the case of **understeering**, the vehicle body side slip angle β and the yaw rate $\dot\psi$ are well below their maximum allowable values. The driver tries to maintain the vehicle on the desired course by increasing the steering angle. If the tire side slip angle α and therefore the lateral wheel slip s_S become too large, the lateral friction coefficient exceeds the maximum. The vehicle would then leave the set course. In order to prevent such situations, the vehicle body must turn into the curve at a yaw rate greater than the actual one.

The rear tire side slip angles α_R shall be used as a reference to determine when the front tire side slip angles α_F reach a critical value. A critical ratio of $|\alpha_F/\alpha_R| = 1.5$ is adopted here.

The reference yaw rate in the case of **understeering** is:

$$\dot\psi_{ref} = \begin{cases} \pm\dot\psi_{max} & , \quad |\alpha_F/\alpha_R| \ge 1.5 \\ \dot\psi & , \quad \text{otherwise} \end{cases} \tag{8.25}$$

In **non-critical** driving situations, the differences between reference and actual values are zero:

$$\begin{aligned} \Delta x_1 &= v_{CoGref} - v_{CoG} = 0 \\ \Delta x_2 &= \beta_{ref} - \beta = 0 \\ \Delta x_3 &= \dot\psi_{ref} - \dot\psi = 0 \end{aligned} \tag{8.26}$$

In these cases the control input is equal to zero. Only for $|\beta| > |\beta_{max}|$, $|\dot\psi| > |\dot\psi_{max}|$ or $|\alpha_F/\alpha_R| > 1.5$, the control becomes active.

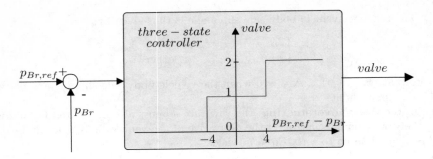

Figure 8.6 Underlying brake pressure control loop

The vehicle speed v_{CoG} has not been considered up to now. In an enhanced approach, a maximum vehicle velocity could be derived e.g. from an image processing of the future highway course. If the vehicle speed would exceed this maximum, a corresponding braking force would be generated by the above control law.

Electrical brake systems can generate directly a braking force F_{Br}. Hydraulic brakes have a nonlinear characteristic. The brake force F_{Br} must then be converted into corresponding drive signals for the hydraulic brake valves. If $\dot{\omega}$ is neglected, Eq. 8.2 becomes:

$$F_{WL} = \mu_L \cdot F_Z = k_{Br} \cdot p_{Br} \qquad (8.27)$$

The hydraulic brake pressure is generated by an underlying control loop, as shown in Figure 8.6.

As a simulation example, the case is considered where the driver must carry out an evasive action manoeuvre at high speed. Figure 8.7 shows the uncontrolled behaviour of the vehicle. After the first steering action, the vehicle starts to turn around and is no longer steerable.

Figure 8.8 shows the behaviour of the controlled state variables. The vehicle body side slip angle cannot be limited to the desired value, however the states remain stable and the vehicle steerable. The deviation of the yaw angle from the desired maximum value is smaller than the deviation of the vehicle body side slip angle.

Figure 8.9 shows the wheel rotational equivalent velocities and the brake pressures. Because the vehicle is concerned in a non-braking drive situation, hence no braking pressure can be reduced, only one wheel is controlled at a time. During the first steering action, the brake pressure on the front right wheel is increased, and during the reverse steering the front left brake pressure is increased. In the second control cycle, the pulsating of the brake pressure shows that the underlying ABS system is activated, to ensure that the maximum value of the friction co-efficient is not exceeded.

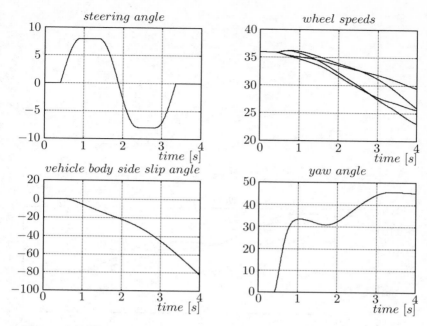

Figure 8.7 Uncontrolled behaviour of the vehicle at an evasive manoeuvre

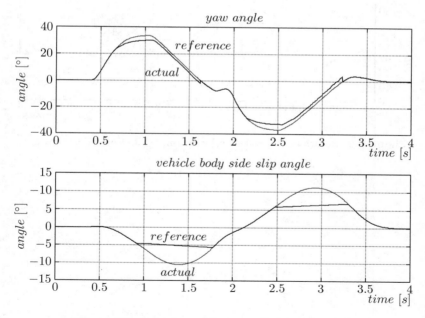

Figure 8.8 Behaviour of the controlled state variables

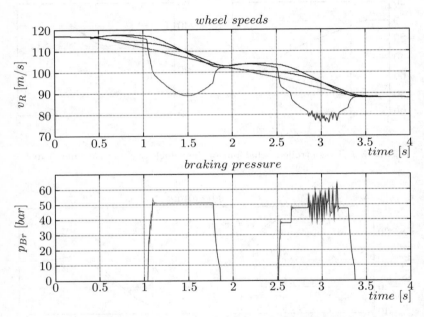

Figure 8.9 Rotational equivalent velocities and stabilising brake pressure

9 Road and Driver Models

9.1 Road Model

9.1.1 Requirements of the Road Model

The construction of a course is a fundamental prerequisite for all simulations with driver-vehicle models. In order for practically relevant applications to be carried out, the course must first be defined and then must be connected to the complete model in a meaningful manner.

Naturally, as detailed a reproduction of the road is required as possible, i.e. environmental influences such as wind and weather should be reproduced as realistically as is necessary and possible. Furthermore, the road data under different road gradients in the longitudinal and lateral directions, and different road surfaces, on top of the actual course co-ordinates must not be forgotten. The most important criteria to be considered however is that the course must be one which can, in reality, actually be driven. The planned desired course must therefore satisfy the following criteria [36]:

- **Continuity of the path**
  No car can move instantaneously from one point to another. Thus the continuity of the course is an elementary criterion. The path must be complete (without gaps) in order that the vehicle can travel from the start to the end point.

- **Continuity of the curvature**
  The physical relationship between the rotational equivalent wheel velocity v_R and the rotational velocity of the vehicle in a curve ω_C is given by

$$\omega_C = \frac{v_R}{\rho} \quad , \tag{9.1}$$

where ρ corresponds to the curve radius. From this it can be seen that a step-wise change in curve radius ρ would have to result in a step-wise change in the curve rotational velocity ω_C; this is not possible in a real moving vehicle.

- **Differentiability of the set course**
  If a course path is carried out without steps, it is essential that the course path is differentiable, because vehicles cannot in general move in a zigzag fashion. A sharp bend in the set course corresponds to a point with infinitely large curvature $1/\rho$, which again cannot be carried out by a real vehicle.

Essential Data

The important values which a road model must provide are:

- Co-ordinates in the x- and y directions
- Curve radius ρ
- Desired yaw angle ψ_{road} and yaw rate $\dot{\psi}_{road}$
- Recommended speed, which must be given for guidance v_{ref}
- Road gradient in longitudinal and lateral directions χ_{road}, φ_{road}
- Road surface information $\mu(s)$
- Wind velocity v_{wind}

These values are calculated during the simulation using the previously defined set course, and made available both to the driver model and, partially, to the vehicle model. The driver takes in the road information with help of his sensory organs, judges them, and uses them as guidance and system measurements for the steering and control. The vehicle model uses the available values to derive the dynamic changes of the drive states.

9.1.2   Definition of the Course Path

A relatively simple and easy to understand method of producing a course path is the division of the whole road path into separate sections. It is possible to reproduce all road courses which occur in real road systems using only three different path forms, namely straight line s, spirals, and circular arc segments. As many individual segments as required can be strung together to form a complete course. Each segment is defined using a parameter set. As well as the start and end-positions of each segment, additional parameters such as wind strength and recommended velocity can be defined. Care must be taken however, to ensure that the criteria given in the previous section for a realistic course are satisfied, i.e. the endpoint of one segment must correspond to the beginning point of the next. In order to simplify matters, it is assumed that the given parameters such as recommended velocity, road inclination and road surface remain constant

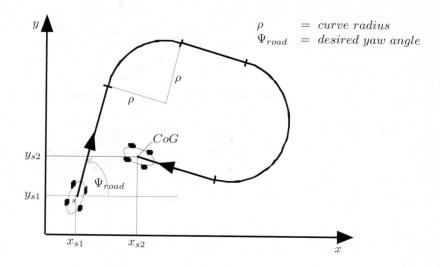

Figure 9.1 Course definition using segmentation

within the individual segments. This simplification does not put any limits on course design, as a change in parameters is possible via the division of the course into smaller segments.

Figure 9.1 shows an example course constructed from 5 segments. The straight-line segments are at an angle ψ_{road} to the fixed co-ordinate system. The circular arc segments have radius ρ, which corresponds to curvature $\kappa = 1/\rho$.

In the following the various forms will be considered in more detail, and the parameters necessary for the definition of the segments given.

Straight line segments

Straight line segments form the simplest section of the road path. Formally they are described in the following way:

The curvature is equal to zero and the curve radius correspondingly infinite. The following parameters are necessary to define the segment:

Straight line segment parameters	
s_0	initial value of arc (m)
s_end	final value of arc (m)
v_{ref}	recommended speed in current segment (m/s)
ψ_0	initial yaw angle $(degrees)$
ψ_end	final yaw angle $(degrees)$

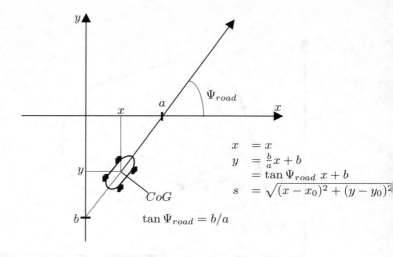

$$x = x$$
$$y = \frac{b}{a}x + b$$
$$= \tan \Psi_{road}\, x + b$$
$$s = \sqrt{(x-x_0)^2 + (y-y_0)^2}$$

$$\tan \Psi_{road} = b/a$$

Figure 9.2 Straight line segments

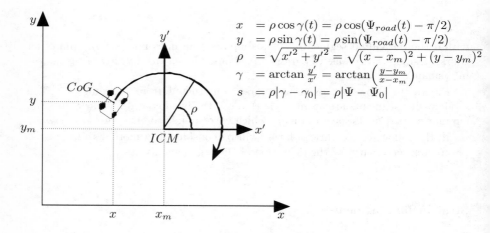

$$x = \rho \cos \gamma(t) = \rho \cos(\Psi_{road}(t) - \pi/2)$$
$$y = \rho \sin \gamma(t) = \rho \sin(\Psi_{road}(t) - \pi/2)$$
$$\rho = \sqrt{x'^2 + y'^2} = \sqrt{(x-x_m)^2 + (y-y_m)^2}$$
$$\gamma = \arctan \frac{y'}{x'} = \arctan\left(\frac{y-y_m}{x-x_m}\right)$$
$$s = \rho|\gamma - \gamma_0| = \rho|\Psi - \Psi_0|$$

Figure 9.3 Circular arc segment

Circular arc segment

Here the radius ρ is constant. The mathematical representation is given in polar co-ordinates in Figure 9.3.

The required parameters for a circular arc segment are:

Circular arc segment parameters	
a/c	Direction (*anticlockwise/clockwise*)
s_0	initial value of arc (m)
s_end	final value of arc (m)
v_{ref}	recommended speed in current segment (m/s)
ψ_0	initial yaw angle (*degrees*)
ψ_end	final yaw angle (*degrees*)
ρ	curve radius (m)

Spiral

The curves of roads built today are generally made up of entrance curves, a section of constant radius and an exit curve. The transition between straight line and circular arc segments is made possible by clotoide spirals, as in this way the demanded condition of continually variable curvature can be satisfied. Clotoide spirals are curves where the radius decreases inversely proportional to increasing curve length s:

$$\rho(s) = \frac{v_{ref}^2}{\pi s} T^2 \tag{9.2}$$

a_N : Normal acceleration of the CoG trajectory
T : Spiral co-efficient (unit: time)
v_{ref} : Vehicle velocity
$\rho(s)$: Curve radius

The normal acceleration of the CoG increases with the curve length s:

$$a_N(s) = \frac{v_{ref}^2}{\rho(s)} = \frac{\pi s}{T^2} \tag{9.3}$$

The distance of the asymptotic points from the center point $(x_m,\ y_m)$ is determined by the spiral coefficient T.

$$x(s) = x_m + \int_0^s \cos\left(\frac{\pi s^2}{2T^2 v_{ref}^2}\right) ds \quad ; \quad y(s) = y_m + \int_0^s \sin\left(\frac{\pi s^2}{2T^2 v_{ref}^2}\right) ds \tag{9.4}$$

One problem when dealing with spirals is the calculation of the Cartesian coordinates of the individual path points from Eq. 9.4, as the integrals are not closed solutions. The derivation of the curve radius $\rho(s)$ is thus only numerically possible; for this reason observance of the criteria from Section 9.1.1 becomes difficult.

9.1.3 Road Surfaces and Wind Strength

It has already been stated that as exact a reproduction as possible of real roads with different road surface qualities such as weather behaviour should be considered. Thus for a complete definition of the course some additional parameters are required.

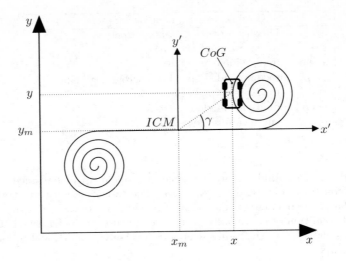

Figure 9.4 Spiral

The separate definition of road surface and weather is not meaningful here, because for the vehicle model, and in particular the wheel model, only a friction co-efficient μ_{Res} resulting from a combination of the two factors is relevant. Another important factor for the reconstruction of real environmental conditions is the wind force. The wind force is derived during the simulation from the previously defined wind velocities. Thus the wind velocities for the individual x, y and z directions should be defined separately for each segment.

9.2   PID Driver Model

In order to close the loop in a simulation, knowledge about human control behaviour is required. To date, descriptions of driver behaviour have not been sufficiently realistic. The main problem lies in the fact that the behaviour is dependant upon physical and psychological factors, as well as the demands of the driving situation. Despite these difficulties, many attempts have been made. The driving behaviour of humans can, for example, be modelled using classical control theory or fuzzy theory. In the classical approach taken in this section, the driver is modelled as a continuous PID controller. The PID controller reduces the lateral errors very well, but does not behave like a human driver. For a closed loop vehicle-driver simulation this is often sufficient.

The PID controller consists of two almost independent sub-controllers for the longitudinal and lateral dynamics. Coupling occurs only during critical driving situations, if the longitudinal controller reduces the throttle angle. Fig 9.5 shows the structure of the longitudinal controller. As the driver knows the engine characteristics he can set either the desired acceleration $a_{x,des}$ or the corresponding throttle angle $\alpha_{t,des}$.

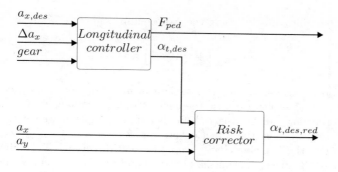

Figure 9.5 Structure of the longitudinal controller

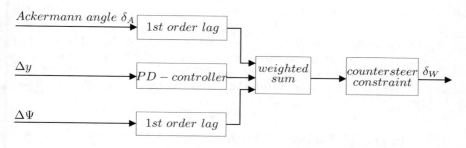

Figure 9.6 Structure of the lateral controller

A proportional controller compensates for errors between the desired and actual acceleration, which occur for example during hill driving. If the engine torque is still too small, despite an open throttle, the transmission control moves down a gear to increase the torque. If the desired acceleration is zero, the longitudinal controller does not accelerate even in the event of a negative actual acceleration. Thus, during cornering a throttle angle of zero is stipulated. This is mainly important for simulating critical driving situations, where the curve resistance and hence the brake deceleration can become relatively large. The risk corrector (Figure 9.5) mirrors the behaviour of the driver, in that no acceleration is carried out when driving quickly and cornering at the same time. The risk corrector comes into play between 60 and 90 % of the exploited traction potential, and reduces the drive torque proportionally. In this approach the stipulation of suitable speed is not the task of the driver (dependant on road geometry), but of the course designer. The longitudinal dynamics driver within the model has just the task to maintain the previously defined acceleration and speed.

The lateral controller is more complex. It consists of three parts, as shown in Figure 9.6.

The inputs are three pre-processed variables. Under the assumption that no vehicle body side slip angle β or tire side slip angle α is present, the wheel turn angle can be approximated using the Ackermann angle (see [52]):

$$\delta_A \approx \frac{l}{\rho}\left(1 + \frac{v_{CoG}^2}{v_{char}^2}\right) \approx \frac{l_R + l_F}{\rho} \tag{9.5}$$

The first order lag has a time constant of $30\,ms$ and represents the driver behaviour during steering. Because the curve radius $\rho(s)$ changes only slowly, this
fast first order lag can be used. A further input, implemented with an equivalent first order lag, is the direction error $\Delta\psi = \psi + \beta - \psi_{road}$, which is the
angle between the vehicle velocity and the road direction. This simulates the
experience of the driver, in that he identifies and prevents a vehicle "drift". The
PD controller reduces the lateral displacement Δy with the following transfer
function:

$$G_{\Delta y}(s) = \frac{0.3s + 1}{0.15s + 1} \tag{9.6}$$

All three controller outputs are weighted and summed together. The resulting
steering angle is constrained against counter-steering, which is important for the
vehicle stability during changing curve conditions. Here, the driver should not
steer to the right during a left turn. The PID driver model is capable of holding
the vehicle on the road in critical driving situations.

9.3   Hybrid Driver Model

In this section a more realistic hybrid driver model is presented which describes
the complete cognitive process of the human operator [49]. From a behavioural
psychology point of view driver behaviour can be modelled as a *situation-cognition-
action* reaction chain [31]. Basic to this is the situation-action model designed
by [12], which is based on the following assumptions:

- The course of travel can be stated as a sequence of situations,

- Every driver has several alternative actions at his disposal for any given
  situation, each of which will result in alternative consequential situations,

- Each driver chooses one of the possible actions, giving consideration to
  individual intentions.

9.3.1   Vehicle Control Tasks

In human vehicle control tasks can be divided into approximately 65 main tasks
and 1799 elementary tasks which a vehicle guidance system must carry out.
In [70] and [71] the functions are split into six different task groups.

- Strategical tasks (choice of route, time of departure)

- Navigational tasks (adherence to the chosen route during travel)

- Tasks relating to the road (chosen position within traffic, course)

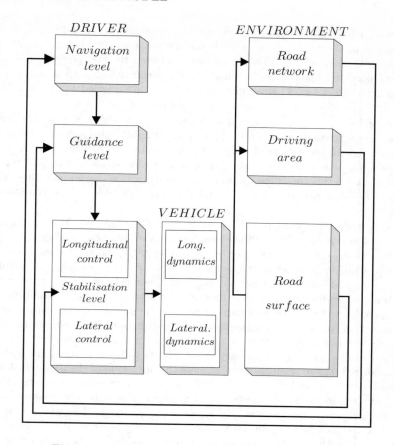

Figure 9.7 The three level hierarchy of vehicle control

- Speed control (choice of speed according to situation)

- Traffic related tasks (interacting with other road users in such a way that the traffic is not obstructed and collisions with other road users are avoided)

- Adherence to rules (traffic signs, signals etc.)

In general drivers have to cope with all of these tasks. The importance of the different tasks changes according to the driver type. An experienced driver for instance will weight the tasks differently than a learner. The six driving task groups above can be further compressed into three main activities, as shown in Fig. 9.7. These are:

1. *Navigational level* - Macro-activities (way finding)

2. *Guidance level* - Situation dependant activities (collision avoidance)

3. *Stabilisation level* - Micro-activities (manoeuvring the vehicle)

The navigation level involves the choice of an optimal route from A to B from a range of alternative routes. This is normally carried out before the start of the journey, and depending on the distance between the two points, can involve forward planning for a long time period. For frequently travelled routes (such as the daily trip to work) the choice of a route is only carried out once, and the chosen route is then stored in memory for future trips.

The guidance level is concerned with ensuring that the driver fits his driving to the existing road-condition and the traffic. At this level the driving behaviour of the next 5-10 seconds is planned. To do this the driver observes the traffic situation, the course of the road, and possible traffic signs. As well as this the driver must control the three motion variables (position, speed and direction of the vehicle). The desired velocity is calculated at this level and passed onto the stability level.

The stabilisation level is the lowest level in the hierarchy, but at the same time has the highest priority. This level has the task of transforming the desired variables, as specified by the other levels, into suitable control values. As well as this, the stability level must compensate for disturbances, such as side-winds or changes in gradients. The time constants at this level are given by the vehicle dynamics. The processes of the three hierarchical levels occur simultaneously during a trip, and thus conflicts can occur. If the traffic situation requires intense concentration at the stabilisation level, it may happen that the tasks of the guidance level are not dealt with. For example, a road sign is overlooked. In addition to this, and to the primary driving tasks today's drivers have a myriad of secondary tasks to contend with, such as the operation of the air conditioning, the audio system, and the use of telephones etc. This division of attention is especially important when considering the human information acquisition. Here, only the guidance and the stability levels are considered. The navigation level is carried out before the journey by the road model. The two lower levels can be described with "Driver-vehicle-environment" system, as shown in Figure 9.8. Again, a division into longitudinal and lateral guidance is made. The guidance level in this figure is responsible for the calculation of the desired reference values, while the stability level carries out the control of throttle angle, brake force and steering wheel angle. It is noticeable that the guidance level does not calculate a reference value for the lateral guidance. This is because the task of the lateral controller is well defined - i.e. to keep the lateral error to zero. The instantaneous lateral error can be calculated using the current drive states. For the longitudinal control the situation is somewhat different. The task is to maintain a velocity as exactly as possible. The reference velocity is however strongly dependent upon the street course and the characteristics of the driver. The guidance values for the longitudinal controller change relatively frequently and must be calculated at the guidance level.

9.3.2   Characteristics of the Human as a Controller

The human controller is not a technical controller with mathematically determined characteristics. [76] describes a good, safe driver as follows: "The good driver ....

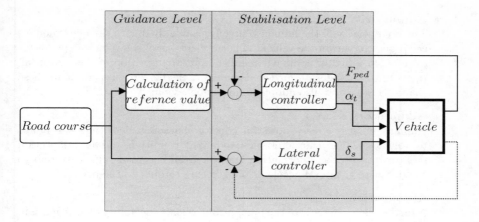

Figure 9.8 The driver-vehicle-environment system

- has complete command of the vehicle equipment

- keeps fairly well to the rules

- takes no unnecessary risks

- has good anticipation ability of the traffic situation in the immediate future

- shows consideration for the mistakes of others

- keeps his temper under control."

This is of course no scientifically correct definition of the characteristics of human control. It shows however that the control behaviour is also dependant upon psychological factors. Drivers possess characteristics which are common to all humans. These physiological and psychological factors are considered together as personal factors. These factors affect the characteristics of the human as a controller. The general characteristics of human controllers are:

- **Operating states**
  [26] studied the steering behaviour of humans and determined that there are two different states which humans switch between. The first state is the so-called *error correction mode*, in which the human acts as a classical controller and seeks to control the lateral error without interruption. If the lateral error falls below a certain threshold the driver switches to an *error ignoring mode*, whereby the driver tolerates a certain lateral offset and keeps the steering angle constant. Only when the lateral error exceeds a certain threshold will the driver return to error-correcting mode. The thresholds are driver dependent and vary greatly. The transfer from error ignoring to error correction mode can be modelled as an event. The different event rates shall later be joined at prioritised queuing systems, which model the limited human resources to cope with such events.

- **Nonlinearity**
  The nonlinearity of the human controller is mainly due to the many nonlinear processes within the vehicle. The acceleration of the vehicle depends for example in a highly nonlinear manner upon the position of the gas pedal. In order to compensate for this behaviour, the driver must adapt to these characteristics and also adopt nonlinear behaviour.

- **Adaptation**
  Humans possess a very powerful control characteristic - they can adapt to various vehicle characteristics and road conditions. This adaptation requires the precise information transfer from the road-vehicle system to the driver (e.g. lateral acceleration, steering torque) to the driver.

- **Anticipation**
  A further characteristic of the human controller is the ability of anticipation. Using the eyes and ears humans can see what is coming up in the future time and space, and react accordingly. This ability is however not instinctive, but must be learnt. Hence the extent of the anticipation grows with the experience of the driver.

- **Time variance**
  Time variance of a controller means that identical input variables at two different time instants may result in two different outputs. The change of the calculated values for the control inputs is explained by the fact that the parameters or characteristics of the controller change with time. In human controllers, the personal factors are responsible for the changes in characteristics.

Mapping of Driving Tasks to the Human Cognitive Levels

In order to model the human brain the three driving task levels must be mapped to the three human cognitive ability levels. For this, Rasmussen [65] differentiates between:

- Skill-based behaviour

- Rule-based behaviour

- Knowledge-based behaviour

These three levels are shown schematically in Figure 9.9.

In the skill level, the execution of mainly automatic and routine tasks are carried out. Sampled signals from the environment are compared with previously acquired patterns. Skill based tasks can be subject to information reduction, followed by characterisation and "discovery" of events. This stimulus-reaction mechanism is first trained in a learning process and from then on runs unconsciously. In Section 9.3.5 this is modelled using queuing theory. Examples of the action at this level are the maintenance of a course on a straight road, adherence to a particular speed, or execution of standard actions when overtaking.

Rule-based behaviour occurs in known situations. When the circumstances of a given situation have occurred previously, and it can be dealt with using

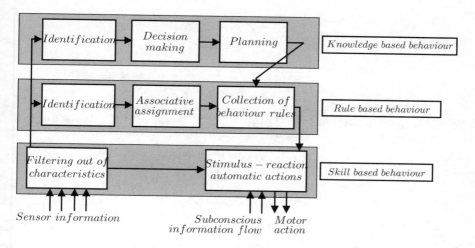

Figure 9.9 The three human behaviour categories (of Rasmussen)

previously learned rules. The incoming information is interpreted only after a process of selective information reduction. It characterises the different states of the environment. Fuzzy logic is an obvious choice for the modelling of this level, hence these states are linked to the actions to be performed by IF-THEN rules.

Knowledge based behaviour is used in previously unknown situations. Appropriate rules are derived from a modification and combination of existing rules.

Because the execution of unconscious activities takes place in the skill level, allowing the higher levels to concentrate on other matters, there is only a limited amount of processing capacity available to the higher levels. The activities at the higher level run more slowly, but have the advantage of flexibility. In contrast, the lower level has a high operating speed, but is inflexible. With increasing driver experience more and more conscious activities become unconscious ones.

9.3.3 Information Handling

The previous section discussed which tasks humans have to carry out within the driver-vehicle-environment system. Now the processing steps within the human will be discussed in more detail. These can be divided into three subsequent steps: information acquisition - information processing - control action. This is shown schematically in Figure 9.10.

Information Acquisition of Humans

The driver requires first of all information about the current drive state and the future course. The driver obtains this information via the eyes. The most important perception types are the optical (i.e. information obtained via the eyes) and the vestibular (linear and rotary motion perceived by the sense of balance). The eyes supply the main part of the information. In the literature,

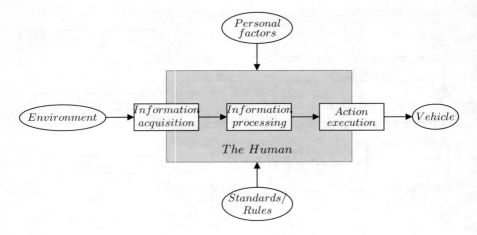

Figure 9.10 Information handling of the driver

values above 90 % are given as the amount of information the eyes supply. The visual sense is distinguished not only because of the wealth of information that it provides, but also in that it provides information about future events (in terms of time and space), which the driver must deal with. The other sensory organs only provide information about the current drive states.

Information Processing and Control Action

After the information acquisition, data reduction takes place, as not all the obtained data can be processed. This takes place partly in the sensory organs themselves and partly in the brain. Every sensory organ is equipped with a mechanism whereby physical stimuli can be stored for a short period of time. Thus a physical stimulus can be perceived even though it is no longer present. When, for example, the attention is directed on one object, the sensory short term memory allows information from other physical stimulation to be obtained, for later processing. The information from the sensory organs are selected, assessed and formed into a meaningful complete picture, so that the driver can understand the whole situation and react accordingly.

The various stages of information processing can be seen in Figure 9.11 ([77]). Each step of the processing reshapes the incoming signals in a suitable way. The individual transformations require a certain amount of time and a certain portion of the limited processing resources. Thus the speed of the processing and the amount of data which can be processed is limited. The number of alternatives is dependent upon the experience of the driver. The driver selects one course of action at a time which he considers suitable. He then implements the required changes to throttle, brake and steering wheel to carry out the chosen plan. The reactions of the vehicle and the environment can then be seen again by the driver and so the loop is complete.

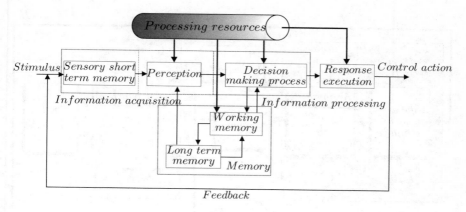

Figure 9.11 Model of the human information processing

Perception

The perception process is a mapping of many different physical stimuli to perception categories. For example the various ways of writing the letter A,a,*a*, **a** all belong to one perception category. Through this division of the many physical stimuli into fewer categories the huge quantity of data can be reduced. However, important information can be lost. For this reason the original physical stimuli are additionally saved at a higher processing level.

Decision Making Process

The process of decision making is carried out in accordance with real time requirements. On the one hand decisions are made in a very fast reflexive manner. For example, a driver approaching a traffic light which is changing from green to amber has two possibilities. He can either brake and stop before the lights or accelerate and attempt to pass the lights before they change to red. The decision however must be made in a fraction of a second. This critical situation thus requires reflexive decision making. On the other hand the planning of an overtaking manoeuvre is a comparatively longer process. Here a decision is first made as to whether the perceived information will be saved in memory, before a response is selected. If the information is saved, it enters working memory. A further decision is then made as to whether the information is only required for the short term, or if the current situation contains information which is so important that it should be saved in long term memory and thus "learnt". After a long decision period a suitable response to the current situation is chosen, using the just saved information and the various alternative actions called forth from long term memory.

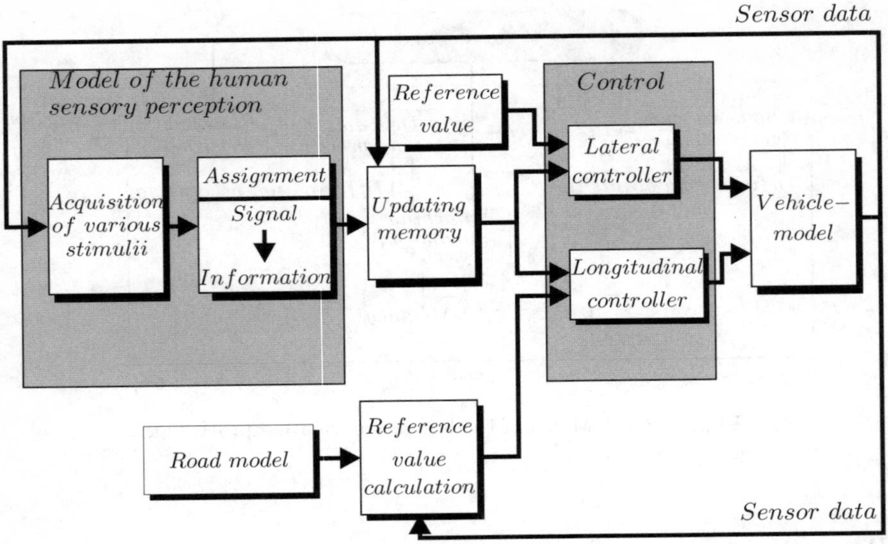

Figure 9.12 Adaptation of the cognitive process to the driver model

The Response Execution

Once a response is produced by the decision making procedure it is transformed into corresponding control outputs to the steering wheel, throttle and brake pedal.

Processing Resources

All parts of the information processing procedure, with the exception of the sensory short term memory, require processing resources in order to function effectively. The supply of resources is shown at the top in Figure 9.11. If a processing level requires more capacity, this has to be taken from the remaining processing blocks, so that their performance falls. This may result in the tasks of these blocks being incomplete or faulty.

Through constant learning and practise of recurring tasks the resources required for the execution of tasks can be reduced. Thus an experienced driver requires much less resources than a learner driver, placed in the same situation, would require.

9.3.4   Complete Driver Model

The characteristics of humans as controllers must now be transferred with suitable modelling approaches into the a driver model. The individual blocks for the representation of the human cognitive processes are replaced by suitable function blocks. The resulting driver model is shown in Figure 9.12.

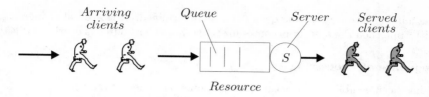

Figure 9.13 Queuing system

Basic to this driver model is that humans can only reach a high control quality when all drive-relevant information is available to them. The control quality depends upon the experience and personality of the driver. Although both the lateral and longitudinal controllers always have access to the current guidance variables, the state variables (i.e. the actual values) are taken from memory (as represented by the block "Updating memory" in Figure 9.12). The updating of the memory values is dependant upon the results of the information acquisition. Thus it is possible that the controller uses outdated rather than current values. In a situation where the precessing resources of the driver are heavily overloaded, e.g. by servicing the telephone simultaneously to driving, the control performance will significantly degrade.

9.3.5 Model of Human Information Acquisition

The information intake of humans is a very complex task and thus some simplifications are necessary in order to model the process. Two major simplifications are carried out:

- Only two perception channels are considered: the visual and the vestibular.

- Other traffic users are not considered.

Queuing Theory

Queuing systems are used for the reproduction of the acquisition processes with limited resources. In the human information acquisition, the intake and processing abilities are limited.

Queuing systems basically consist of two parts: a queue and a server. This construction is shown in Figure 9.13.

The incoming clients go first into the queue, which acts as a temporary storage for the clients and determines which client is passed into the server next. The sequence of processing is determined by priority or by the arrival order of the clients. The chosen client passes into the server and is processed. The processing lasts for a certain amount of time, the service time τ_S, which in most cases has a stochastic distribution. The time between the arrival of two clients is termed the inter-arrival time τ_A, which can also be regarded as a stochastic variable. The aim of the queuing theory is to describe analytically the waiting time τ_W which a client spends in the queue, based on the distribution of the inter-arrival time and the service time. Furthermore, from the inter-arrival times and the service time the number of clients in the queue can be determined. If this number increases with time then the system becomes unstable, i.e. the resource is overloaded [41].

Sequence of Processing

It has been established that the queuing policy is to determine which clients are served (processed) first. Normally the principle of first come, first served is used, i.e. the customers which arrive at the queue first are served first. There are however a range of other possibilities:

Priority Queuing

Each client has a predefined priority assigned to it. In this case the order of processing is dependant not upon the order in which the clients arrive in the queue, but upon the priority: higher priority clients are always served first.

Limited capacity Queuing

A limited capacity queue is one in which only a limited number of clients can be stored prior to processing. If the maximum number of clients is reached then no new clients are taken into the queue. As well as this number-based limit there are also time based limits, whereby a client which has been in the queue longer than a specified time is removed from the queue, whether it has been processed or not.

Pre-emptive / Non-pre-emptive

If a client appears in the queue with a higher priority than the client which is currently being processed, there are two possibilities. Firstly the lower priority client can be removed from the server and the higher priority client processed immediately. Only when the higher priority client has been served can the lower priority client continue being processed. Such a system is termed *pre-emptive*. If on the other hand the higher priority client has to wait until the lower priority client is finished, the system is termed *non-pre-emptive*.

The human information intake is modelled using two separate queues (Figure 9.14).

One queue is used to model the visual information intake. Every possible viewpoint on the road and within the vehicle is reproduced as a source node. A source node becomes a client or event when the driver should consider the corresponding viewpoint. A client thus represents a viewing event. The viewpoints can be divided into two groups: those on the road and those within the vehicle. This latter group are considered as disturbances as they provide no relevant driving information. Each event, as it appears, is given a number, which denotes which source node the event came from, and a priority, which depends on the source node. The level of priority represents the importance of the corresponding source node. The time of appearance of each event is also recorded. As well as deciding when a view point will be seen, it must also be decided the length of viewing time. Thus each event is assigned a service time which represents the normal time a driver must consider the corresponding viewpoint in order to obtain all the necessary information. Once these values have been assigned the clients enter

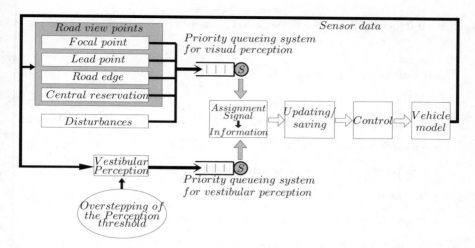

Figure 9.14 Queuing model of human information intake

the priority queuing system of the visual information intake. When a request is processed by the server this means that the driver looks at the corresponding viewpoint for the duration of the assigned service time. Once the client has been processed in this way it passes to a so-called destination node, where it is erased. The system operates in pre-emptive mode. Previously it was stated that all the sensory organs have a short term memory capability. This is reproduced in the queuing system by limiting the amount of time a client may wait in the queue. If a client has not been serviced within this time period then it is removed from the queue and erased. A further source node is necessary to prevent the case that there is no client either in the queue or in the server - this would in effect correspond to the driver having closed eyes. To prevent this there is always an event in the category "lead point", if there are no other clients in the queue.

Assignment of signals to an information category takes place in the block "Assignment Signal - Information". The assignment is necessary because a viewpoint can contain several pieces of information. The information from this is then updated in memory, and the controller has access to the current values with the event arrival rate of the "clients" (i.e. preception events).

The vestibular information acquisition is modelled with a separate queue in parallel. In the source nodes clients are created when the state values exceed the corresponding perception thresholds. The clients then land in the queue and are served, and the values assigned and updated in the same way as with the visual intake.

9.3.6   Inter-event Arrival and Service Times

In this section the time interval between the creation of customers, *the inter-event arrival time*, will be defined. The viewpoints are divided into two main groups, those outside the vehicle and those within the vehicle (disturbances). The overall viewing frequency f_{view} of a driver is in the range of 2-6 viewpoints per second, and is given by:

$$f_{view}(v_{CoG}, a_X) = \frac{1}{3}\left[\frac{s}{m}\right]|a_x| - 0.001401\left[\frac{s}{m^2}\right]v_{CoG}^2 - 0.09384\left[\frac{1}{m}\right]v_{CoG} + 7\left[\frac{1}{s}\right]$$

(9.7)

This overall viewing frequency is divided between various viewpoints on the road:

- Visual focus (point corresponding to approximately 3 seconds drive away)

- Leadpoint (furthest point of driver view)

- Road edge

- Centre of road (i.e. central reservation)

The time intervals for the individual viewpoints are given by:

Visual focus

$$\tau_f = \frac{35\left[\frac{m}{s}\right]f_1 + 6\left[\frac{m}{s^2}\right]f_2 + 17°\left[\frac{1}{s}\right]f_3 + 4.5°\left[\frac{1}{s^2}\right]f_4 + 90°f_5}{C^* \cdot \left(f_1 v_{CoG} + f_2|a_Y| + f_3|\dot{\psi}| + f_4|\ddot{\psi}| + f_5|\Delta\psi|\right) \cdot p_f}$$

(9.8)

Lead point

$$\tau_l = \frac{35\left[\frac{m}{s}\right]l_1 + 6\left[\frac{m}{s^2}\right]l_2 + 17°\left[\frac{1}{s}\right]l_3 + 4.5°\left[\frac{1}{s^2}\right]l_4 + 90°l_5}{C^* \cdot \left(l_1 v_{CoG} + l_2|a_Y| + l_3|\dot{\psi}| + l_4|\ddot{\psi}| + l_5|\Delta\psi|\right) \cdot p_l}$$

(9.9)

Road edge

$$\tau_r = \frac{0.4\,[m]\,r_1 + \left[\frac{m}{s}\right]r_2 + 17°\left[\frac{1}{s}\right]r_3 + 4.5°\left[\frac{1}{s^2}\right]r_4 + 90°r_5 + 35\left[\frac{m}{s}\right]r_6}{C^* \cdot \left(r_1|y| + r_2|\dot{y}| + r_3|\dot{\psi}| + r_4|\ddot{\psi}| + r_5|\Delta\psi| + r_6 v_{CoG}\right) \cdot p_r}$$

(9.10)

Road center

$$\tau_c = \frac{0.4\,[m]\,m_1 + \left[\frac{m}{s}\right]m_2 + 17°\left[\frac{1}{s}\right]m_3 + 4.5°\left[\frac{1}{s^2}\right]m_4 + 90°m_5 + 35\left[\frac{m}{s}\right]m_6}{C^* \cdot \left(m_1|y| + m_2|\dot{y}| + m_3|\dot{\psi}| + m_4|\ddot{\psi}| + m_5|\Delta\psi| + m_6 v_{CoG}\right) \cdot p_m}$$

(9.11)

with the abbreviation

$$C^* = \left(c_1|a_X| + c_2 v_{CoG}^2 + c_3 v_{CoG} + 7\right)\quad.$$

The variables $f_1 \ldots f_5$, $l_1 \ldots l_5$, $r_1 \ldots r_6$, $m_1 \ldots m_6$, $c_1 \ldots c_3$, p_f, p_l, p_r and p_m are weighting factors, values for which are given in Appendix A.4. Values for the constants $c_1 \ldots c_3$ are also given in Appendix A.4.

Using Eqs 9.8 to 9.11, the event inter-arrival time for viewpoints outside the vehicle can now be calculated.

The inter-arrival time of disturbances has been determined by [79], who lists mean values and standard deviations for the viewing frequencies of viewpoints within a vehicle. The viewing frequencies are assumed to have a normal distribution over time. An exception is the arrival time of the revolution counter, which is mainly used during acceleration manoeuvres:

$$\tau_{tacho} = \frac{3 \left[\frac{m}{s}\right]}{|a_X|} \tag{9.12}$$

Values for the event inter-arrival times of some common disturbances are given in Appendix A.4.

Determination of the Service Times

The service time is the amount of time which the driver spends looking at a particular point.

In the literature, the service times for the road viewpoints are given as between 0.25 and 1.8 seconds [30]. Here a middle value of 0.5 to 1 second is used. The viewing length is however dependent upon the vehicle speed; it increases with increasing speed. A linear relationship between the service time and the vehicle velocity is defined for the lead point, road edge and road center as:

$$\tau_S = \frac{1}{70} \left[\frac{s^2}{m}\right] v_{CoG} + \frac{1}{2} [s] \tag{9.13}$$

The viewing time for the visual focus lies between 1.2 and 1.9 seconds [78].

The service times of the disturbances are taken from [79], and some are listed in Appendix A.4.

Viewpoint Priorities

The order of processing is dependant upon the priorities of the customers. Each transaction is assigned a priority depending upon the importance of the corresponding view point. The higher the priority is, the more important the viewpoint is. The priorities of some common viewing points are given in Appendix A.4.

Simulation Results

Simulations were carried out using typical road courses. The event inter-arrival times and service times for view points within the car were compared with the measured values found by [79]. Figure 9.15 shows the values obtained for the event inter-arrival times for the disturbances. The average values calculated using the queuing theory model correspond very well to the measured values. Figure 9.16 shows a comparison of calculated and measured service times for the disturbances. Again, the correspondence is good.

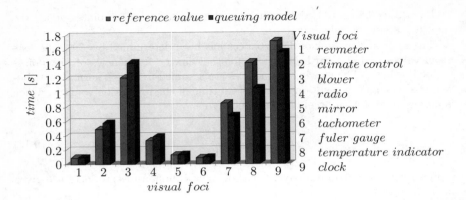

Figure 9.15 Average event inter-arrival times of disturbances

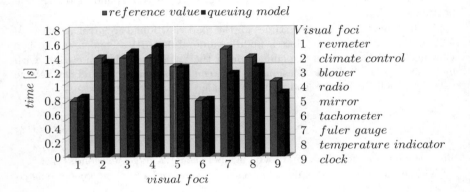

Figure 9.16 Average service times of disturbances

9.3.7   Reference Value Calculation

The longitudinal controller requires a reference value (desired velocity) which it can compare with the actual value (actual velocity). The calculation of this desired value, which is dependant upon the road layout and the individual driver, is the task of the "Reference value calculation" block of the driver model. In the following a pure acceleration controller is considered. Thus a reference acceleration must be considered, rather than a reference velocity. The task first requires the construction of a velocity profile for the upcoming road. This changes throughout the journey. Thus only the current, and short term future reference velocity can be calculated. This velocity profile must then be tuned according to the driver type.

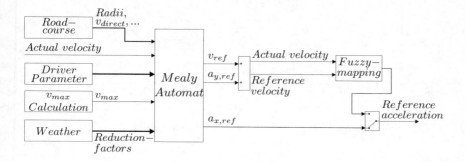

Figure 9.17 Structure of reference value calculation

A reference velocity is derived for all subsequent course segments (Section 9.1.2). For the modelling of such a system of different course segments, automata are particularly suitable.

Structure of the Desired Value Calculation

The structure of the desired value calculation is shown in Figure 9.17.

A Mealy automat forms the core of this function block. From the "Road course" block come the current and future values for the course radius, velocity etc. The automat also requires the parameters of the driver in order to fit the velocity to the driver type. It further requires the maximum possible velocity, which is calculated from the friction characteristic between the tyres and road. The weather conditions along the course path also have a strong influence on the maximum permitted velocity - this information being provided by the "weather" block. From these inputs the automat calculates its own states and the outputs v_ref, ay_ref and ax_ref. The actual and reference velocities must then be converted into reference accelerations, which are then passed to the longitudinal controller.

The Mealy Automat

All physically realisable automata react in a particular way to inputs from the environment. For each input the automat moves from its current state to a new state (state transfer on external event). The output is then calculated from the current state of the automat and the current input variables. There are various types of automata - here we are concerned with the Mealy Automat. Figure 9.18 shows the states and transitions of a finite Mealy automat for the reference value calculation.

In describing the individual states two times are used: t is the current simulation time and t_f is the so-called foresight time of the driver. This foresight time is a drive parameter and is dependent upon the driver type.

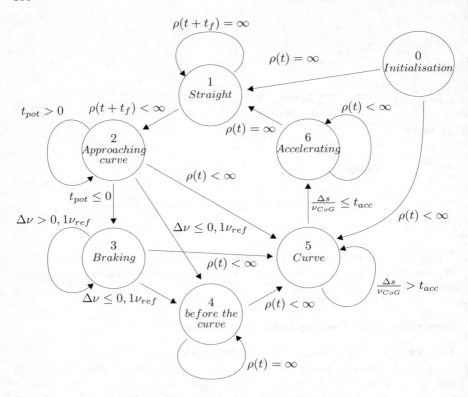

Figure 9.18 State graph of the finite automat

State 0: Initialisation

The first time the automat is called, it is in state 0. The automat does not return to state 0 during the course of travel.

State 1: Straight Line Segment

This state represents straight ahead driving with no curve in the foreseeable future (i.e. $\rho(t + t_f) = \infty$). In this stage the reference velocity for an average driver v is multiplied by a factor $fact$ which represents the driver type:

$$v_{ref} = v \cdot fact \tag{9.14}$$

If the vehicle approaches a curve, (i.e. $\rho(t + t_f) < \infty$) then the automat switches to state 2.

State 2: Approaching a Curve

The automat is in this stage when the vehicle is driving on a straight patch of road and the driver is in view of a curve. Normally a curve cannot be driven at the same speed as a straight section of road and so the driver must reduce speed before entering the curve, i.e. he must brake before he reaches the curve. The extent and time of the braking must be determined. The driver maintains the current speed until the start of the braking manoeuvre. The calculation of the curve velocity is carried out using the equations from [46]:

$$v_{ref} = \left(202.33 - 104.70 \cosh \left(\frac{\chi^*_{road} + 1}{10} \right) \right)$$
$$\cdot \tanh \left(\frac{\rho^*}{64.0 + (0.6\rho)^{0.99}} \right) \left[\frac{m}{s} \right] + 6.375 \tanh \left[1.10 (B_F - 7.70m) \right] \left[\frac{1}{s} \right] \tag{9.15}$$

$$\rho^* = \rho + (1.75 - 0.4 B_F) \frac{\sin \frac{\psi_{road}}{2}}{1 + \sin \frac{\psi_{road}}{2}} \tag{9.16}$$

$$\chi^*_{road} = \left[1 - e^{-(0.014\rho^*)^3} \right] \cdot \chi_{road} \tag{9.17}$$

The variables have the following meaning:

χ_{road} longitudinal gradient
χ^*_{road} equivalent gradient
ρ curve radius
B_F road width
ψ_{road} road yaw angle
ρ^* equivalent radius

The calculated curve velocity v_{ref} represents the velocity for optimal weather and road surface conditions for an average driver. In the calculation the actual curve radius ρ is replaced by the equivalent radius ρ^*, which considers "cutting" of the curve. In the simulations done in this book the longitudinal gradient χ_{road} was always considered to be zero. The velocity is then fitted to the driver type using a factor $fact$. To calculate the time for the start of braking, the individual driver is again important. Each driver has a "potential braking acceleration", a_{xpot}, with which they will comfortably reach the reference speed at the start of the curve. In addition to this non-critical situation (i.e. the driver has time to brake comfortably) there is a "maximum braking" situation - i.e. full brakes a_{xmax}. Thus two braking times can be calculated:

$$t_{pot} = \frac{\Delta s}{v_{CoG}} + \frac{\Delta v}{a_{xpot}} - \frac{1}{2} \left(\frac{\Delta v^2}{v_{CoG} \cdot a_{xpot}} \right) \tag{9.18}$$

$$t_{max} = \frac{\Delta s}{v_{CoG}} + \frac{\Delta v}{a_{xmax}} - \frac{1}{2} \left(\frac{\Delta v^2}{v_{CoG} \cdot a_{xmax}} \right) \tag{9.19}$$

There, Δv is the difference between the current and future reference speeds, Δs the distance to the curve. Normally the potential time is greater than the maximum time. If either of the above times reaches the value zero then the braking manoeuvre begins. If the braking manoeuvre begins because t_{pot} is equal to zero then the driver can brake with the desired "comfortable" brake force. Otherwise, a higher braking force must be used. Some drivers wish to obtain the desired curve speed before entering the curve, whilst others only reach the cornering speed within the curve itself. To allow for these driver differences a further time t_{antic} may be considered, which represents the time span where the driver already wishes to have reached the cornering velocity before entering the curve. This value must be subtracted from t_{pot} and t_{max}. Note that t_{antic} can be negative. Once braking commences the automat switches to state 3.

State 3: Braking

In this state the braking manoeuvre must be carried out. The output of this state is a reference deceleration. Firstly it must be decided if full braking is necessary or if lighter braking will suffice. If lighter braking can be used then the following equation is used:

$$ax\_ref = -\frac{v_{CoG} \cdot \Delta v - \frac{1}{2}\Delta v^2}{\Delta s_1} \tag{9.20}$$

There, $\Delta s_1 = \Delta s - v_{ref} \cdot t_{antic}$ is the distance to the point at which the driver wishes to reach the curve speed. Braking is only applied until:

$$\Delta v \leq \frac{1}{10} v_{ref} \tag{9.21}$$

If Δv falls below this threshold before the curve is reached, the automat switches to state 4, otherwise the automat enters state 5.

State 4: Before the Curve

In state 4 the vehicle is immediately before the curve, having almost reached the reference curve velocity. The necessary light braking required to obtain the reference curve speed can be calculated. Once the vehicle enters the curve, the automat enters state 5.

State 5: Curve (Circular Arc Segment or Spiral)

In this state the vehicle is travelling at the reference speed determined by the driver using his perception of the curve radius and the weather and road surface conditions. The driver can now determine from the lateral acceleration whether this speed is indeed correct or if the speed must be adjusted. The corrected reference speed is calculated based on the lateral acceleration - different drivers will tolerate different levels of lateral acceleration a_{ypot} and so again a driver factor must be included.

$$v_{ref} = \sqrt{|a_{ypot} \cdot \rho|} \tag{9.22}$$

Here, ρ is the curve radius and a_{ypot} represents the driver-dependant tolerable lateral acceleration.

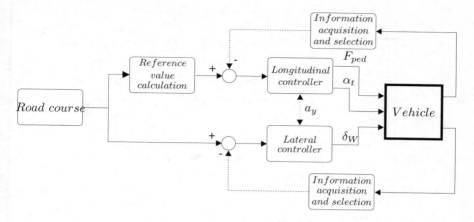

Figure 9.19 Controller structure

State 6: Accelerating

Some drivers begin to accelerate before the end of the curve. A driver dependent time t_{acc} is introduced which represents the time before the end of the curve at which the driver begins to accelerate. If the residual curve length is $\Delta s \leq v_{CoG} \cdot t_{acc}$, then state 6 is entered. The reference acceleration is calculated as:

$$a_{ref} = min \begin{cases} (v_{ref} - v_{CoG})/t_{acc} & , \\ a_{max} \end{cases} \tag{9.23}$$

9.3.8 Longitudinal and Lateral Control

The controller represents the last unit of the driver model. This block has the task of calculating the suitable control variables from the information about the actual driving state, provided by the information acquisition and information selection, the information about the future course path and the reference values. The control variables are the gas pedal position, the brake pedal force and the steering angle.

The controller consists of two connected blocks as shown in Figure 9.19. The first block serves to control the longitudinal dynamics and calculates the control variables for the gas- or brake-pedal. The second calculates the suitable steering angle and thus influences the lateral vehicle dynamics. The two controllers are coupled, since a rising vehicle speed v_{CoG} increases the lateral acceleration a_Y .

$$a_y = v_{CoG}^2 \left[\frac{\delta_W}{l(1 + K v_{CoG}^2)} \left[\frac{1}{deg} \right] - \frac{1}{\rho} \right] \tag{9.24}$$

where:

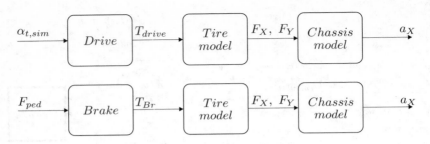

Figure 9.20 Drive and brake plants

v_{CoG} :   Vehicle velocity
δ_W :   Wheel turn angle
l :   Wheel base $l_F + l_R$
K :   Stability factor (units : $(h/km)^2$)
ρ :   Curve radius

In order to be able to design a longitudinal and lateral controller for the vehicle model described in Chapter 6.2, simplified linear longitudinal and lateral closed loop systems must be identified. The identification of the longitudinal control plant is divided into drive and brake control.

The input signals of the two systems are either the throttle angle α_t or brake pedal force F_{ped}, and the output is the longitudinal acceleration a_X (see Figure 9.20).

Identification and Validation of the Drive System

The identification is limited to the drive system of Figure 9.20, with the throttle angle as the input and the drive torque T_{Drive} as the output. For this a linear second order ARMA transfer function is assumed. For the identification a test drive on a straight dry road was carried out, whereby the initial velocity corresponds to $24\,m/s$. The transmission ratio was $i_{gear} = 1.41$. The test signals were a minimum throttle angle $\alpha_{t,sim,1} = 1\,°$ and a maximum $\alpha_{t,sim,2} = 10\,°$ (Figure 9.21). An average driver produces frequencies of between 0 and $2\,Hz$ by acceleration. The considered bandwidth of the system is therefore $5\,Hz$ and the settling time lies at approximately $0.3\,s$. Thus a sampling frequency of $100\,Hz$ will suffice. Figure 9.21 shows the behaviour of the throttle angle with time and the resulting drive torque, which are required as inputs and outputs for the identification.

The transfer function for the drive system was estimated as:

$$G_D(z^{-1}) = \frac{0.112295 + 0.112314\,z^{-1}}{1 - 1.7713\,z^{-1} + 0.810704\,z^{-2}} \qquad (9.25)$$

When the outputs of the real system and of the identified linear second order ARMA model are plotted the signals are almost identical, thus the system behaviour was very well reproduced (Figure 9.22).

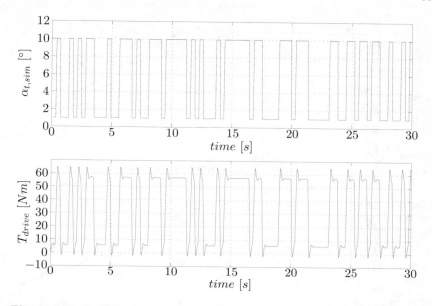

Figure 9.21 Input and output signals for the identification of the drive system

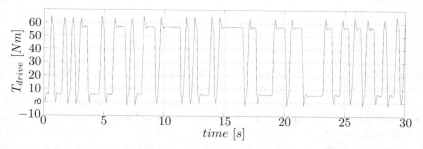

Figure 9.22 Results of the validation of the 2nd order drive model in the frequency range

Figure 9.24 shows the validation of the estimated 2nd order drive model in the frequency range. There is a good correspondence in terms of both amplitude and frequency between the estimated model (dashed line) and the real drive system (solid line).

Identification and Validation of the Brake System

Again in the case of the brake system a model is identified only for a part of the system. This reduced system takes as its input the brake pedal force F_{ped} and outputs the brake torque T_{Br}. Again a test drive on a straight dry road was carried out, this time with initial velocity of $35\,m/s$. The reason for the

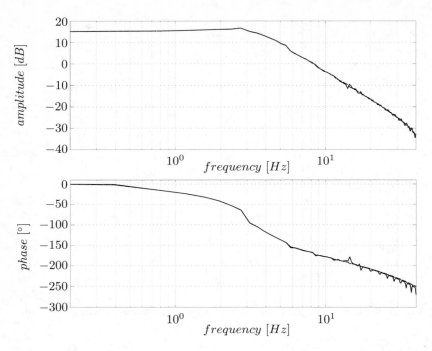

Figure 9.23 Validation of estimated 2nd order drive model

higher initial speed is to avoid the speed falling below $5\,m/s$. A linear third order ARMA model is assumed for the brake control system.

Figure 9.23 shows the input and output signals used for the identification. For upper and lower values of the PRBS (pseudo random binary sequence) test signal the following were used: $F_{ped,1} = 30\,N$, $F_{ped,2} = 80\,N$. The impulse width of the input signals was chosen as before, as the braking system has approximately the same bandwidth as the drive system. The sampling time was again chosen as $10\,ms$. Also, the sampling time for the brake system should not differ from that of the drive system.

The 3rd order transfer function for the brake system was identified as:

$$G_B(z^{-1}) = \frac{0.0909361 - 0.0861402\,z^{-1} + 0.0502816\,z^{-2}}{1 - 2.06324\,z^{-1} + 1.44986\,z^{-2} - 0.34446\,z^{-3}} \qquad (9.26)$$

A plot of the output of the real break system and the output of the 3rd order identified model in response to a PRBS input signal shows the two to be almost identical.

The frequency responses of the real system and the identified 3rd order model are shown in Figure 9.25. The plots cannot be differentiated for the main part. Hence the real brake system is well described in the frequency range of interest.

As already stated, the entire longitudinal control system cannot be identified because of the nonlinearities in the tire model. In order to design a controller for

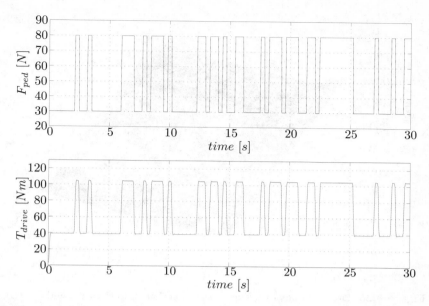

Figure 9.24 Input and output signals used for the identification of the brake system

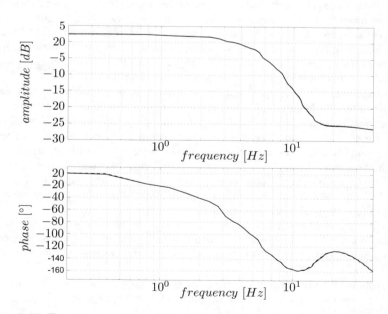

Figure 9.25 Frequency response of the real brake system (solid line) and the identified 3rd order model (dashed line)

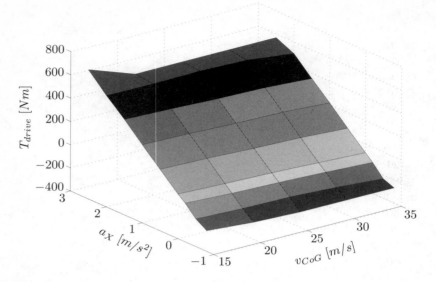

Figure 9.26 Drive torque of the engine as a function of acceleration and velocity

the entire system, these nonlinearities must be approximated. The two already obtained drive and brake models allow controllers to be designed for the brake and drive torques. The task of the longitudinal controller however is to control the longitudinal acceleration. Thus nonlinear maps are required which produce a drive or brake torque from a pre-given acceleration. The stationary acceleration properties of a vehicle are in the first place dependent upon the current velocity. This means that for each speed a different drive torque is required to obtain the same acceleration. Figure 9.26 shows the drive torque of a vehicle dependant upon the acceleration and the velocity. Using this mapping, the required desired drive torque for the drive controller can be found from a given desired acceleration.

The velocity has a similar effect on the braking. The braking properties of the vehicle are determined by the friction co-efficient between tire and road. To obtain a particular delay a different brake torque must be applied according to the level of the speed. The brake torque is obtained as a function of the acceleration and the velocity from the mapping of Figure 9.27.

The updating of the memory value is limited by the processing resources. In case of overload the waiting times in the queues will increase, respectively decreasing memory update rates. This increases the sampling time of the controllers.

It is therefore advantageous to design a controller for a wide application spectrum. The control algorithm should fulfil the following requirements:

- The controller concept must be applicable to non-minimal phase systems

- It must be suitable for the control of unstable systems and systems with poorly damped poles

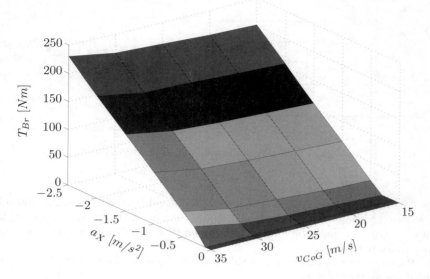

Figure 9.27 Brake torque as a function of acceleration and velocity

- It must be capable of controlling systems with unknown and variable dead-times

- It must be applicable to systems with unknown order.

These requirements are fulfilled by the General predictive controller (GPC) [15]. An introduction can be found in appendix A.3.

Drive Controller

The control of the longitudinal dynamics is divided into two parts, the drive and the brake control. Both controllers are acceleration controllers, i.e. they take as inputs the desired and actual acceleration and as output the throttle angle or brake pedal force. It is important to note that the two controllers are never active both at the same time. The most important parts of the drive controller, as shown in Figure 9.28 are the velocity dependant map, a switch which chooses the controller input, and the GPC controller itself (R-, S-, T-polynomials).

The velocity dependant map derives the drive torque T_{ref} from the desired acceleration a_{ref} and the actual velocity v_{CoG}. This is required by the GPC controller as a setpoint. In the switch a choice is made between this desired drive torque and the maximum engine brake torque which can be delivered by the vehicle given the current transmission ratio. If the desired drive torque is larger than the maximum brake torque then this desired value is passed to the controller (this is the situation depicted in Figure 9.28). If this is not the case then the maximum brake torque is passed. This has the advantage that small decelerations can appear exclusively via the braking action of the engine.

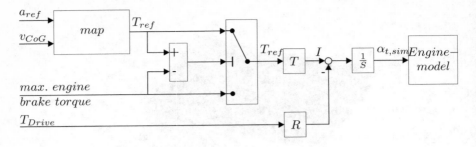

Figure 9.28 Block diagram of the drive controller

The GPC controller is implemented in the usual RST-structure and controls the drive torque via the throttle angle $\alpha_{t,sim}$. It should be remembered that the throttle angle α_t must be limited to between $0°$ and $90°$ and only this range is physically realisable.

Based on the identification of this Section the following transfer function of the drive system is given:

$$G_D(z^{-1}) = \frac{B(z^{-1})}{A(z^{-1})} = \frac{0.112295 + 0.112314\,z^{-1}}{1 - 1.7713\,z^{-1} + 0.810704\,z^{-2}} \qquad (9.27)$$

Based on this transfer function and consideration of the tuning rules, the control parameters are chosen as:

- $N_1 = 1$

- $N_2 = 40$

- $N_u = 3$

- $\lambda_u = 10$

The poles of the T-polynomial filter lie between 0.5 and 0.6 so that a better damping of the poles of the estimated model is obtained. This gives for the polynomials $R(z^{-1})$, $S(z^{-1})$ and $T(z^{-1})$ of the drive controller:

$$
\begin{aligned}
R_D(z^{-1}) &= 1.14153 - 1.90449\,z^{-1} + 0.811293\,z^{-2} & (9.28)\\
S_D(z^{-1}) &= 1 - 0.50317\,z^{-1} + 0.140577\,z^{-2} & (9.29)\\
T_D(z^{-1}) &= 0.0483358 & (9.30)
\end{aligned}
$$

Brake Controller

The structure of the brake controller is similar to that of the drive controller, and is shown in Figure 9.29.

The uppermost of the two maps in Figure 9.29 produces a desired brake torque T_{ref} as a function of the velocity v_{CoG} and a predefined desired acceleration a_{ref}, which in the case of the brake controller is negative. Map 2 has the task of giving

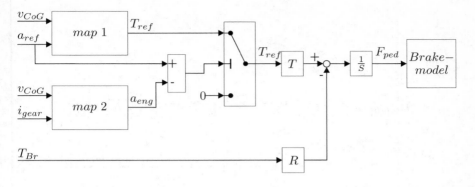

Figure 9.29 Simplified block diagram of the brake controller

the negative acceleration a_{eng} due to the braking action of the engine. This negative acceleration is dependant upon the velocity v_{CoG} and the transmission ratio i_{gear}. In the switch a comparison takes place between the desired acceleration a_{ref} and the acceleration a_{eng}. If the brake action of the engine is sufficient to achieve the desired deceleration then $T_{ref} = 0$ is taken as the control value, and the brake control remains inactive. If the required deceleration exceeds a_{eng} then the brakes must be activated, i.e. the desired brake torque from the uppermost map of Figure 9.29 is passed on.

The transfer function of the brake control system is:

$$G_B(z^{-1}) = \frac{A(z^{-1})}{B(z^{-1})} = \frac{0.0909361 - 0.0861402\,z^{-1} + 0.0502816\,z^{-2}}{1 - 2.06324\,z^{-1} + 1.44986\,z^{-2} - 0.34446\,z^{-3}} \quad (9.31)$$

The tuning parameters are chosen as the following:

- $N_1 = 1$

- $N_2 = 40$

- $N_u = 3$

- $\lambda_u = 10$

This gives the following polynomials for the brake controller in RST structure:

$$
\begin{aligned}
R_B(z^{-1}) &= 6.51905 - 13.1809\,z^{-1} + 9.1206\,z^{-2} - 2.13962\,z^{-3} \quad &(9.32)\\
S_B(z^{-1}) &= 1 - 0.239487\,z^{-1} + 0.312326\,z^{-2} \quad &(9.33)\\
T_B(z^{-1}) &= 0.319119 \quad &(9.34)
\end{aligned}
$$

Lateral Controller

The task of the lateral controller is to minimise the lateral offset of the vehicle to the ideal line. The control output is the steering angle δ_S (wheel turn angle δ_W). The GPC controller uses the offset of the centre point of the front axle.

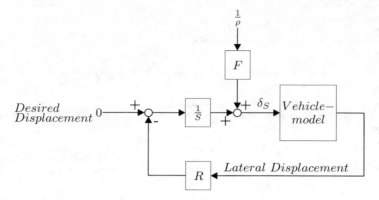

Figure 9.30 Simplified block diagram of the lateral control with feed forward

The controller has no information about the vehicle body side slip angle error, and does not control this. The controller structure is shown in Figure 9.30. Note that only R- and S-polynomials are employed.

To improve the performance of lateral the controller a static feed-forward component F is added, so that in curves the steering angle δ_S corresponds to the inverse of the curve radius ρ, using a constant factor $F = 3.6$.

An identification of the lateral control system gives the following fifth order ARMA transfer function [49]:

$$G_L(z^{-1}) = \frac{-0.0033917 + 0.0075914\, z^{-1} - 0.0037304\, z^{-2}}{1 - 4.7847z^{-1} + 9.1727z^{-2} - 8.8077z^{-3} + 4.2360z^{-4} - 0.81629z^{-5}}$$

$$(9.35)$$

The tuning parameters are chosen as:

- $N_1 = 1$

- $N_2 = 60$

- $N_u = 3$

- $\lambda_u = 50$

The poles of the S-polynomial filter are 0.5, 0.6, 0.7, 0.8, 0.9 and 0.95.
This gives the following polynomials for the lateral controller:

$$
\begin{aligned}
R_L(z^{-1}) = \;& -0.737212 + 2.42144\, z^{-1} - 1 - 64676\, z^{-2} - 2.65418\, z^{-3} \\
& + 4.17551\, z^{-4} - 0.78585\, z^{-5} - 1.66839\, z^{-6} + 1.09109\, z^{-7} \\
& - 0.195652\, z^{-8}
\end{aligned}
$$

$$(9.36)$$

$$
\begin{aligned}
S_L(z^{-1}) = \;& 1 - 4.42949\, z^{-1} + 8.36477\, z^{-2} - 8.73042\, z^{-3} + 5.43316\, z^{-4} \\
& - 2.01127\, z^{-5} + 0.409556\, z^{-6} - 0.0353928\, z^{-7}
\end{aligned}
$$

$$(9.37)$$

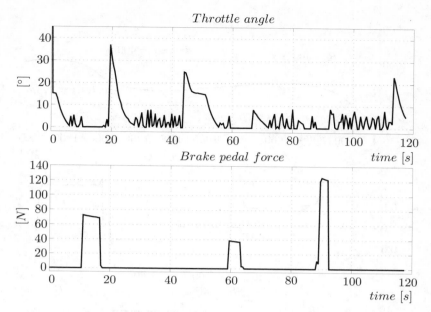

Figure 9.31 Simulation results for the longitudinal controller

Simulation Results

In order to prove the robustness and performance of the longitudinal and lateral controllers, various drive situations are simulated. Various curve radii from $\rho = 275\,m$ to $\rho = 400\,m$ are included, and the road conditions change from dry to wet. This course is then used as the reference for the following simulations.

The reference velocity of Figure 9.33 is calculated at each time instant dependent upon the weather conditions and the curve of the road. On top of this, according to the drive state (entering or leaving the curve) a suitable velocity profile is determined, which approximates the human acceleration behaviour.

The first three plots in Figure 9.33 show reference and actual values for drive and brake torques and the acceleration. In all three plots it can be seen that the actual value tracks the reference value very well, even in the case of high acceleration or deceleration. The large spread of velocities (over $30\,km/h$) also had no negative effect on the controller performances. The desired velocity is also very closely tracked after transients.

Figure 9.31 shows the throttle angle and the brake pedal force of the longitudinal controller. It can be seen that small decelerations are obtained just by engine braking, without activating the brakes (i.e. when the throttle angle and the brake pedal force are both equal to zero).

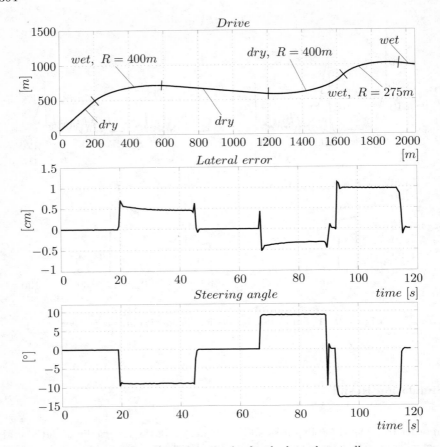

Figure 9.32 Simulation results for the lateral controller

Figure 9.32 shows the results of the lateral controller, as well as the course travelled by the vehicle, which due to the low lateral error is identical to the desired course. The second plot of Figure 9.34 shows the lateral offset of the vehicle. Despite large variations in speed, different curve radii and road surfaces, the maximum offset throughout the whole simulation is only approximately 1.2 cm. It shows no oscillating behaviour and does not need to be corrected.

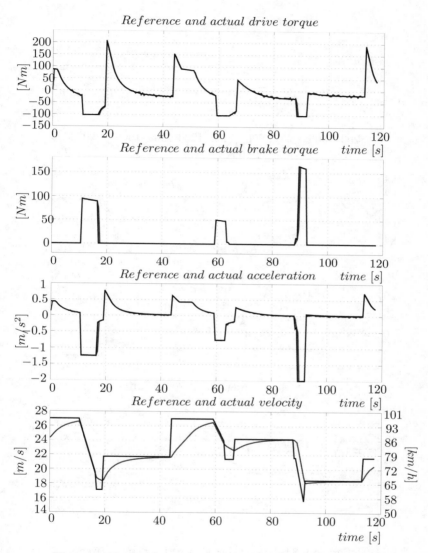

Figure 9.33 Simulation results for the longitudinal controller

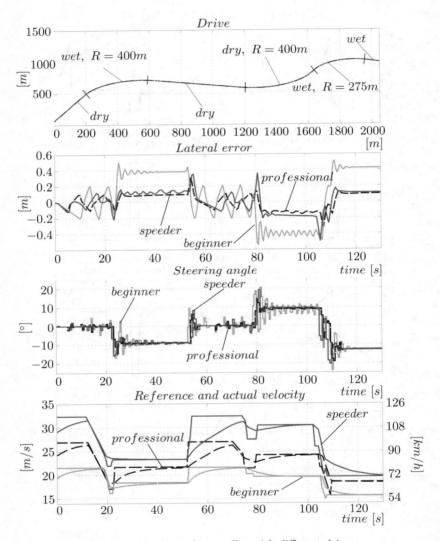

Figure 9.34 Lateral controller with different drivers

A Appendix

A.1 Introduction to Thermodynamics

A short introduction to thermodynamics is given in this appendix. It is essential to understand the thermodynamic processes for the different types of engines explained in this book.

A.1.1 First Thermodynamic Law

Ideal gases are always in a gaseous state and they behave according to the *ideal gas equation*:

$$p V = m R \vartheta \qquad (A.1)$$

where:

p is the pressure in N/m^2
V is the volume in m^3
m is the mass in kg
R is the gas constant $R = 287.4\,m^2/(s^2\,{}^\circ K)$
ϑ is the absolute temperature in ${}^\circ K$

The expression $p V$ has the unit *Joule* and it depends on the mass and temperature of the gas.

The thermal energy is defined as:

$$q = c m \vartheta \qquad (A.2)$$

where:

q is the thermal energy in J
c is the specific heat constant in $J/(kg\ °K)$

This equation is valid for all kind of materials in solid, liquid and gaseous state. The specific heat constant is material depending. In gases, different state changes have to be distinguished which will be discussed in the next section.

First Thermodynamic Law

$$dq = du + dw \qquad (A.3)$$

dq is the differential change of thermal energy. Energy which is brought into the gas is **positive**.

du is the differential change of internal energy. Internal energy which is brought into the gas **is positive**.

dw is the differential change of mechanical work. Mechanical work which is brought into the gas is **negative**.
     Please note, that this may be defined differently in other books.

The thermal energy dq brought into a gas of constant mass results in a rise in it's internal energy du and/or is transformed into mechanical work outside the gas. Thus, energy is neither created nor destroyed. This equation is solved by integration to compute the energies in state changes.

Volume Change

There are two basic principles how mechanical work can be delivered to or from the system: By a change of volume or a change of pressure.

In engines, a limited amount of compressed gas expands in a cylinder. The differential mechanical work dw_v depends on the force F upon the piston and the differential piston stroke ds:

$$dw_v = F\ ds = p\,A\ ds$$

where A is the cross-section of the cylinder and p the pressure. More general, this yields to:

$$dw_v = p\ dV \qquad (A.4)$$

The work dw_v is equivalent to the kinetic energy brought into the mechanical system due to the expansion of the gas in the cylinder. Mechanical energy brought into the gas is negative: $dp > 0$, $dV < 0$ (compression) and therefore $dw_v < 0$. Output of mechanical work from the gas is positive. This can also be seen in Figure A.1.

Pressure Change

In turbines, kinetic energy is transmitted by a continuous gas flow between two locations of different pressure:

$$dw_p = -V\ dp \qquad (A.5)$$

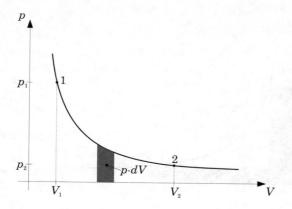

Figure A.1 Mechanical work due to volume change.

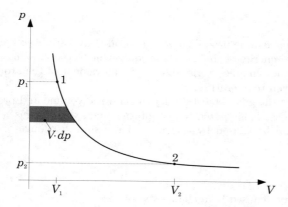

Figure A.2 Mechanical work due to pressure change

The work dw_p is equivalent to the loss of potential energy of the gas. Figure A.2 graphically explains the state change in the pV-diagram. In this case, the mechanical work is positive because the pressure change is negative: $dp < 0$.

The two different types of work are graphically explained in Figure A.3 and they are linked by the following equation:

$$w_v = \int_1^2 p \, dV = - \int_1^2 V \, dp - p_1 V_1 + p_2 V_2 \tag{A.6}$$

Assuming a constant mass and a constant temperature, the two energies are equivalent as $p_1 V_1 = p_2 V_2$ according to the ideal gas equation.

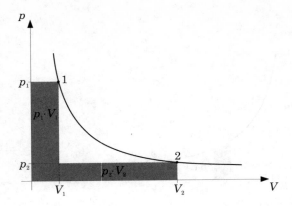

Figure A.3 Relationship between the two mechanical works.

Enthalpy

The state of the gas can be described with several state variables:

u Internal energy of the gas. It is equivalent to the amount of thermodynamic energy due to the movement of the atoms at a given temperature.

pV State of the gas. The state depends on the volume and pressure of the gas. It is related to the internal energy of the gas.

A state change can be caused by a change of pressure, a change of volume or both:

$$d(pV) = p \, dV + V \, dp \tag{A.7}$$

$p \, dV$ Kinetic energy caused by a change of volume.

$V \, dp$ Potential energy caused by a change of pressure.

The enthalpy is another state variable of the gas:

$$h = u + pV \tag{A.8}$$

The differential is:

$$dh = du + p \, dV + V \, dp \tag{A.9}$$

Compared to the first thermodynamic law in Equation A.3

$$dq = du + dw$$

the thermal energy can be written as:

$$dq = dh - V \, dp = du + p \, dV \tag{A.10}$$

For isobaric expansion, we have $dw_v = p\,dV$ and $V\,dp = 0$ and therefore $dq = dh$. This yields to:

$$dq = du + p\,dV \qquad (A.11)$$

For isochoric pressure drop, we have $dw_p = -V\,dp$ and $p\,dV = 0$ and therefore $dq = du$. This results in:

$$dq = dh - V\,dp \qquad (A.12)$$

The enthalpy h can be very useful as a state variable when dealing with gas turbine engines. The internal energy u is useful when dealing with piston engines.

A.1.2 Specific Heat Constant

Input of Thermal Energy at Constant Volume

A temperature rise can be observed when increasing the thermal energy q of a constant mass of gas at a **constant volume**. The specific heat constant c_v is defined as:

$$c_v = \frac{1}{m}\left(\frac{dq}{d\vartheta}\right)_V \qquad (A.13)$$

The differential of the internal energy is

$$du = \left(\frac{\partial u}{\partial V}\right)_\vartheta dV + \left(\frac{\partial u}{\partial \vartheta}\right)_V d\vartheta \quad,$$

Inserting this into the first thermodynamic law A.11 yields:

$$
\begin{aligned}
dq &= \left(\frac{\partial u}{\partial V}\right)_\vartheta dV + \left(\frac{\partial u}{\partial \vartheta}\right)_V d\vartheta + p\,dV \\
&= \left(\frac{\partial u}{\partial \vartheta}\right)_V d\vartheta + \left(\left(\frac{\partial u}{\partial V}\right)_\vartheta + p\right) dV \\
&= \left(\frac{\partial u}{\partial \vartheta}\right)_V d\vartheta
\end{aligned}
$$

At a constant volume we have $dV = 0$. After division by $d\vartheta$:

$$\left(\frac{dq}{d\vartheta}\right)_V = \left(\frac{\partial u}{\partial \vartheta}\right)_V$$

Equation A.13 can be written as:

$$c_v = \frac{1}{m}\left(\frac{\partial u}{\partial \vartheta}\right)_V \qquad (A.14)$$

We have shown that a change in the thermal energy dq at constant volume is equivalent to a change in the internal energy du of the gas.

Input of Thermal Energy at Constant Pressure

A temperature rise can also be observed when increasing the thermal energy of a constant mass of gas at a **constant pressure**. Please note the difference to the previous section, as the specific heat constant c_p is now defined as:

$$c_p = \frac{1}{m} \left(\frac{dq}{d\vartheta} \right)_p \qquad (A.15)$$

The differential of the enthalpy is:

$$dh = \left(\frac{\partial h}{\partial \vartheta} \right)_p d\vartheta + \left(\frac{\partial h}{\partial p} \right)_\vartheta dp$$

This relationship can be inserted into A.12 and then be simplified because $dp = 0$:

$$
\begin{aligned}
dq &= \left(\frac{\partial h}{\partial \vartheta} \right)_p d\vartheta + \left(\frac{\partial h}{\partial p} \right)_\vartheta dp - V\, dp \\
&= \left(\frac{\partial h}{\partial \vartheta} \right)_p d\vartheta + \left(\left(\frac{\partial h}{\partial p} \right)_\vartheta - V \right) dp \\
&= \left(\frac{\partial h}{\partial \vartheta} \right)_p d\vartheta
\end{aligned}
$$

The last equation is divided by $d\vartheta$:

$$\left(\frac{dq}{d\vartheta} \right)_p = \left(\frac{\partial h}{\partial \vartheta} \right)_p$$

Similar to the above section, Equation A.15 can also be written as:

$$c_p = \frac{1}{m} \left(\frac{\partial h}{\partial \vartheta} \right)_p \qquad (A.16)$$

The enthalpy of the system is changed. The input of thermal energy dq at constant pressure not only increases the internal energy du, but also produces an output of work $p\, dV$.

Gas Constant and Adiabatic Coefficient

The relationship between c_p and c_v can be seen by using the enthalpy (Equation A.8) and the ideal gas equation (Equation A.1):

$$
\begin{aligned}
h &= u + pV \\
dh &= du + d(pV) \\
m\, c_p\, d\vartheta &= m\, c_v\, d\vartheta + m\, R\, d\vartheta \\
c_p &= c_v + R
\end{aligned}
$$

The ideal gas constant R is equal to the difference between c_p and c_v:

$$R = c_p - c_v \qquad (A.17)$$

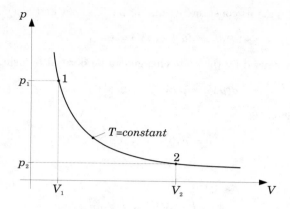

Figure A.4 Isothermic state change

The ratio of c_p to c_v is called the **adiabatic exponent**:

$$\kappa = \frac{c_p}{c_v} \tag{A.18}$$

Under normal conditions its value for air is $\kappa_{air} = \frac{3.5}{2.5} = 1.4$.

A.1.3 State Changes of Ideal Gases

Isothermal Change: $\vartheta = const$

Assuming a constant temperature, the ideal gas equation $pV = mR\vartheta$ yields:

$$p = \frac{mR\vartheta}{V} = \frac{const}{V}$$

where $pV = const$. The state change is equivalent to a hyperbolic curve in the pV-diagram which can be seen in Figure A.4. The isothermal state change is characterised by using the ideal gas equation:

$$p_1 V_1 = p_2 V_2 \tag{A.19}$$

The slope of the curve in the pV-diagram is:

$$\frac{dp}{dV} = -\frac{p}{V} \tag{A.20}$$

The internal energy of the gas remains constant:

$$du = m\,c_v\,d\vartheta = 0$$

Hence, the first thermodynamic law can be written as:

$$dq = du + dw = dw$$

The enthalpy also remains constant because of $pV = const$ and $d(pV) = 0$:

$$dh = du + d(pV) = 0$$

The kinetic energy caused by the state change can be derived by using:

$$d(pV) = p\,dV + V\,dp = 0$$

Hence, it is simplified to:

$$dw = p\,dV = -V\,dp$$

and integrated:

$$w_{1,2} = \int_1^2 p\,dV = -\int_1^2 V\,dp$$

Finally, by using the ideal gas equation:

$$w_{1,2} = q_{1,2} = m\,R\,\vartheta \int_1^2 \frac{1}{V}\,dV = m\,R\,\vartheta \ln \frac{V_2}{V_1}$$

Work $w_{1,2}$ is generated from the system by expanding the gas. The same amount of thermal energy $q_{1,2}$ must be brought into the system in order to compensate for the work and to maintain the constant temperature.

Isobaric Change: $p = const$

A state change at constant pressure is described by the ideal gas equation:

$$p = \frac{m\,R\,\vartheta}{V} = const$$

and therefore:

$$\frac{\vartheta_1}{\vartheta_2} = \frac{V_1}{V_2} \tag{A.21}$$

The state change is equivalent to a horizontal line in the pV-diagram which can be seen in Figure A.5. The isobaric state change $1 \rightarrow 2$ results in an output of mechanical work $w_{1,2}$ due to the expansion of the gas, and at the same time it results in an increased internal energy u due to the temperature rise. The input of thermal energy q is equivalent to the increase of the enthalpy h.

In this case, the first thermodynamic law can be written as:

$$dq = dh - V\,dp = dh$$

since pressure change vanishes: $dp = 0$. The differential change of thermal energy is given by:

$$dq = m\,c_p\,d\vartheta$$

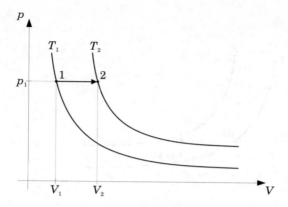

Figure A.5 Isobaric state change

Integration leads to:

$$q_{1,2} = m\,c_p \int\limits_1^2 d\vartheta = m\,c_p(\vartheta_2 - \vartheta_1) \tag{A.22}$$

The mechanical work can be derived by using the fact that $dq = dh$ and $dh = du + p\,dV$:

$$dq = du + p\,dV$$

Because of $dw_v = p\,dV$, the change of kinetic energy is:

$$
\begin{aligned}
dw_v &= p\,dV = dh - du \\
&= m\,c_p\,d\vartheta - m\,c_v\,d\vartheta \\
&= m\,R\,d\vartheta
\end{aligned}
$$

Integration leads to:

$$w_{1,2} = m\,R\vartheta \int\limits_1^2 d\vartheta = m\,R(\vartheta_2 - \vartheta_1)$$

Please note that only a small portion of thermal energy q is converted into kinetic energy w. The ratio of the input of thermal energy to the output of mechanical work can be expressed:

$$\frac{dw}{dq} = \frac{m(c_p - c_v)\,d\vartheta}{m\,c_p\,d\vartheta} = \frac{c_p - c_v}{c_p} = \frac{\kappa - 1}{\kappa}$$

which is 0.29 for air.

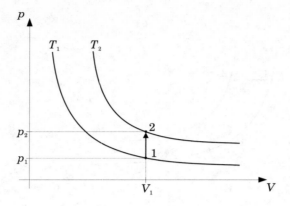

Figure A.6 Isochoric state change

Isochoric Change: $V = const$

In this case, the ideal gas equation is:

$$V = \frac{m\,R\,\vartheta}{p} = const$$

and therefore:

$$\frac{\vartheta_1}{\vartheta_2} = \frac{p_1}{p_2} \tag{A.23}$$

The state change is equivalent to a vertical line in the pV-diagram illustrated in figure A.6. The mechanical work vanishes for an isochoric state change $1 \to 2$. The input of thermal energy dq is equivalent to the increased internal energy du.

As $dq = du + p\,dV = du$, the thermal energy is given by:

$$dq \;=\; m\,c_v\,d\vartheta \tag{A.24}$$

$$q_{1,2} \;=\; m\,c_v \int_1^2 d\vartheta = m\,c_v(\vartheta_2 - \vartheta_1) \tag{A.25}$$

The enthalpy is increased more than the internal energy:

$$dh = du + p\,dV + V\,dp$$

where $p\,dV = 0$ and $V\,dp = m\,R\,d\vartheta$. The change of enthalpy is therefore:

$$dh = m\,c_v\,d\vartheta + m\,R\,d\vartheta = m\,c_p\,d\vartheta$$

The internal energy is $du = dh - V\,dp$. It has the same value as the thermal energy:

$$du = m(c_p - R)\,d\vartheta = m\,c_v\,d\vartheta = dq$$

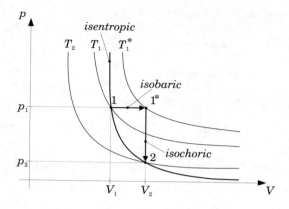

Figure A.7 Isentropic state change

Isentropic or Adiabatic Change: $q = const$

Assuming an insulated gas volume, the thermal energy of the gas remains constant. In an isentropic state change $1 \rightarrow 2$, the gas expands and mechanical work is delivered from the gas while its internal energy is reduced. The gradient of the adiabatic change in the pV-diagram is steeper than the hyperbolic curve of the isothermic change. This is due to the fact that no thermal energy is brought into the gas.

$$dq = du + p\, dV = 0$$

Hence, the first thermodynamic law can be written as:

$$-du = p\, dV$$

This means that the mechanical work is equivalent to the loss of internal energy. The change of enthalpy is:

$$dh = du + p\, dV + V\, dp = V\, dp$$

because of $dq = du + p\, dV = 0$. The isentropic change can be considered as the sequence of two state changes:

- An isobaric change where $dq_p = m\, c_p\, d\vartheta_p = dh$.

- An isochoric change where $dq_v = m\, c_v\, d\vartheta_v = du$.

The summation of exchanged thermal energies is supposed to be zero:

$$\begin{aligned} dq = dq_p + dq_v &= 0 & \text{(A.26)} \\ c_p\, d\vartheta_p + c_v\, d\vartheta_v &= 0 & \text{(A.27)} \end{aligned}$$

From the isobaric and the isochoric state changes we get:

$$isobaric : d\vartheta_p \quad = \quad \frac{p\,dV}{mR} \tag{A.28}$$

$$isochoric : d\vartheta_v \quad = \quad \frac{V\,dp}{mR} \tag{A.29}$$

This can be inserted into Equation A.27

$$c_p\frac{p\,dV}{m\,R} + c_v\frac{V\,dp}{m\,R} = 0 \quad,$$

which can be rearranged to obtain the gradient in the pV-diagram:

$$\frac{dp}{dV} = -\frac{c_p}{c_v}\frac{p}{V} = -\kappa\frac{p}{V} \tag{A.30}$$

The differential pressure change for isentropic state change is increased by the factor of κ compared to the isothermic state change (see equation A.20).

Equation A.30 can be integrated:

$$\ln p = -\kappa \ln V + const$$

This yields:

$$p\,V^\kappa = const \tag{A.31}$$

An isentropic change $1 \to 2$ is characterised by:

$$p_1V_1^\kappa = p_2V_2^\kappa$$

The kinetic energy $w_{1,2}$ is obtained by integration:

$$w_{1,2} = \int\limits_1^2 p\,dV$$

Exchanging p with $p = const\,V^{-\kappa}$ leads to:

$$w_{1,2} = const\int\limits_1^2 V^{-\kappa}\,dV = \frac{const}{1-\kappa}(V_2^{1-\kappa} - V_1^{1-\kappa})$$

Replacing $const = p_1V_1^\kappa$:

$$w_{1,2} = p_1V_1^\kappa\frac{1}{1-\kappa}(V_2^{1-\kappa} - V_1^{1-\kappa}) = p_1V_1\frac{1}{1-\kappa}\left(\left(\frac{V_1}{V_2}\right)^{\kappa-1} - 1\right)$$

Further simplifications:

$$\left(\frac{V_1}{V_2}\right)^{\kappa-1} = \frac{p_1V_1^\kappa}{p_2V_2^\kappa}\frac{p_2V_2}{p_1V_1} = \frac{p_2V_2}{p_1V_1} = \frac{\vartheta_2}{\vartheta_1}$$

The work is given by:

$$w_{1,2} = p_1 V_1 \frac{1}{1-\kappa} \left(\frac{\vartheta_2}{\vartheta_1} - 1 \right)$$

By inserting the ideal gas equation $p_1 V_1 = m R \vartheta_1 = m(c_p - c_v)\vartheta_1$ and the fact that $\kappa = c_p/c_v$, which yields:

$$
\begin{aligned}
w_{1,2} &= m(c_p - c_v)\vartheta_1 \frac{1}{\kappa - 1} \left(1 - \frac{\vartheta_2}{\vartheta_1} \right) \\
&= m(c_p - c_v)\frac{1}{\frac{c_p}{c_v} - 1}(\vartheta_1 - \vartheta_2)
\end{aligned}
$$

and finally, the mechanical work for an isentropic state change is given by:

$$w_{1,2} = m\, c_v (\vartheta_1 - \vartheta_2) \tag{A.32}$$

Polytropic Change

Polytropic state changes are necessary to model a realistic isentropic process with insufficient insulation. Therefore, the polytropic exponent n has values smaller than the isentropic exponent κ:

$$p\, V^n = const$$

with $n < \kappa$.

A.1.4 Thermodynamic Cycles

Entropy

Two different types of state changes have to be distinguished: reversible and irreversible state changes. They can be described by the following characteristics.
Reversible state changes:

- enable the system to return to the initial state

- do not need energy from outside the system when restored to their initial state.

- do not leave a permanent state change in a closed system after restoration.

Irreversible state changes:

- go into **one** direction. For example, expansion of molecules when a larger volume is available to them

- need energy from outside which is transformed into thermal energy. For example, a falling stone.

- do not return to the initial state.

The entropy is defined as:

$$S = \frac{q}{\vartheta} \tag{A.33}$$

An example is given to explain the entropy:

There are two bodies at two different temperatures ϑ. Thermal energy q is exchanged by conduction from the hot body at temperature ϑ_1 to the cold body at temperature ϑ_2. The change of entropy within the system after the transfer of thermal energy can be described by:

$$\Delta S = \frac{q_2}{\vartheta_2} - \frac{q_1}{\vartheta_1} \tag{A.34}$$

Even when $q_1 = q_2$ there is a positive change of entropy ΔS due to the irreversible process of energy flow from the hot to the cold body. Thermal energy can only be transfered from hot to cold media and not in the opposite direction. The entropy of the cold body 2 is larger than the entropy of the hot body 1 as the entropy is inversely proportional to the temperature.

A reversible state change is characterised by:

$$\Delta S = 0 \tag{A.35}$$

and an irreversible state change is characterised by:

$$\Delta S > 0 \tag{A.36}$$

which is also called the second thermodynamic law. It means that the entropy within the system always increases for real state changes.

Ideal Cycle Process

Assuming reversible state changes, the following ideal cycle process can be described: The gas absorbs thermal energy q_1 in an isothermal and reversible state change at high temperature ϑ_1. The gas then loses the thermal energy q_2 in an isothermal and reversible state change at low temperature ϑ_2. Kinetic energy $w_{1,2}$ is delivered by such an ideal engine which is equivalent to the difference of the thermal energies: $w_{1,2} = q_1 - q_2$. The entropy change shall be zero:

$$\Delta S = \frac{q_2}{\vartheta_2} - \frac{q_1}{\vartheta_1} = 0$$

and therefore:

$$\frac{q_1}{\vartheta_1} = \frac{q_2}{\vartheta_2} \tag{A.37}$$

The thermal efficiency of this ideal cycle process is equivalent to the ratio of mechanical work $w_{1,2}$ to the absorbed thermal energy q_1:

$$\eta = \frac{w_{1,2}}{q_1} = \frac{q_1 - q_2}{q_1} = \frac{\vartheta_1 - \vartheta_2}{\vartheta_1} = 1 - \frac{\vartheta_2}{\vartheta_1} \tag{A.38}$$

It can be seen that the thermal efficiency η only depends on the ratio of the absolute temperatures ϑ_1 to ϑ_2. η is always smaller than 1.

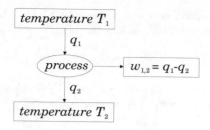

Figure A.8 Ideal cycle process

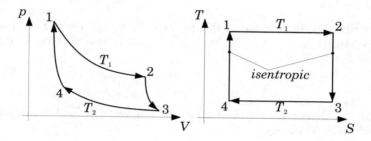

Figure A.9 pV-diagram and TS-diagram of Carnot Cycle.

Carnot Cycle

The Carnot cycle is characterised by four state changes. At the end of the process, the initial state is reached again which is the case for all periodic processes in engines. Two different cycles have to be distinguished:

Reaction within a closed combustion chamber: Engines with periodic combustion cycles and emission of mechanical work.

Gas flow through an open combustion chamber: Turbines with continuous combustion and emission of mechanical work.

The Carnot cycle is used as reference model for an ideal process. It is illustrated in the pV-diagram of figure A.9:

$1 \rightarrow 2$ Isothermal expansion of the gas from V_1 to V_2 while the temperature remains constant $\vartheta_1 = \vartheta_2$.

$$w_{1,2} = q_{1,2} = m\,R\,\vartheta_1 \ln \frac{V_2}{V_1}$$

The mechanical work $w_{1,2}$ is delivered since the gas expands. Thermal energy $q_{1,2}$ of the same amount has to be brought into the system in order to keep the temperature constant.

$2 \rightarrow 3$ Isentropic expansion of the gas from V_2 to V_3. No thermal energy is exchanged $q_{2,3} = 0$. Output of kinetic energy:

$$w_{2,3} = m\, c_v(\vartheta_2 - \vartheta_3)$$

$3 \rightarrow 4$ Isothermal compression of the gas from V_3 to V_4 while the temperature remains constant $\vartheta_3 = \vartheta_4$. The mechanical work

$$w_{3,4} = q_{3,4} = m\, R\, \vartheta_3 \ln \frac{V_4}{V_3}$$

is needed which is negative in this case because it is delivered into the gas $(V_4 < V_3)$.

$4 \rightarrow 1$ Isentropic compression of the gas from V_4 to V_1. No thermal energy is exchanged $q_{2,3} = 0$. The mechanical work is also negative in this case $(\vartheta_1 > \vartheta_4)$:

$$w_{4,1} = m\, c_v(\vartheta_4 - \vartheta_1)$$

Now, all kinetic energies of the Carnot cycle have to be added to derive the thermodynamic efficiency:

$$
\begin{aligned}
w &= w_{1,2} + w_{2,3} + w_{3,4} + w_{4,1} \\
&= m\, R\, \vartheta_1 \ln \frac{V_2}{V_1} + m\, c_v(\vartheta_2 - \vartheta_3) + m\, R\, \vartheta_3 \ln \frac{V_4}{V_3} + m\, c_v(\vartheta_4 - \vartheta_1)
\end{aligned}
$$

The work $w_{2,3}$ and $w_{4,1}$ of the isentropic state changes compensate each other because of $\vartheta_1 = \vartheta_2$ and $\vartheta_3 = \vartheta_4$:

$$w = m\, R(\vartheta_1 \ln \frac{V_2}{V_1} + \vartheta_3 \ln \frac{V_4}{V_3})$$

To simplify this equation, the characteristic equations of the isentropic process $1 \rightarrow 2$ and $3 \rightarrow 4$ are used:

$$
\begin{aligned}
p V^\kappa = p V \cdot V^{\kappa-1} &= m\, R\, \vartheta \cdot V^{\kappa-1} = const. \\
\vartheta_2 V_2^{\kappa-1} = \vartheta_3 V_3^{\kappa-1} \quad &, \quad \vartheta_1 V_1^{\kappa-1} = \vartheta_4 V_4^{\kappa-1} \\
\left(\frac{V_4}{V_1}\right)^{\kappa-1} &= \frac{\vartheta_1}{\vartheta_4}
\end{aligned}
$$

Because of $\vartheta_1 = \vartheta_2$ and $\vartheta_3 = \vartheta_4$ we get

$$
\begin{aligned}
\left(\frac{V_2}{V_1}\right)^{\kappa-1} &= \left(\frac{V_3}{V_4}\right)^{\kappa-1} \\
\frac{V_2}{V_1} &= \frac{V_3}{V_4} \\
\ln \frac{V_4}{V_3} &= -\ln \frac{V_2}{V_1}
\end{aligned}
$$

and therefore:

$$w = m R(\vartheta_1 - \vartheta_3) \ln \frac{V_2}{V_1}$$

This result is now used for the thermodynamic efficiency:

$$\eta = \frac{w}{q_{1,2}} = \frac{m R(\vartheta_1 - \vartheta_3) \ln \frac{V_2}{V_1}}{m R \vartheta_1 \ln \frac{V_2}{V_1}}$$

$$= \frac{\vartheta_1 - \vartheta_3}{\vartheta_1} = 1 - \frac{\vartheta_3}{\vartheta_1}$$

The efficiency depends only on the temperature ratio of ϑ_3 to ϑ_1. Using the compression ratio ε :

$$\varepsilon = \frac{V_4}{V_1} \tag{A.39}$$

the efficiency is ($\vartheta_3 = \vartheta_4$):

$$\eta = 1 - \frac{\vartheta_4}{\vartheta_1} = 1 - \left(\frac{V_1}{V_4}\right)^{\kappa-1}$$

$$= 1 - \frac{1}{\varepsilon^{\kappa-1}}$$

The thermal efficiency can be explained graphically in the pV-diagram in figure A.9: It is equivalent to the ratio of the integral within the cycle to the area which is produced by integrating $q_{1,2}$. The efficiency is improved by increasing the area within the cycle. This can only be achieved by a rise of the compression ratio ε or the temperature ratio.

To give an example: Assuming absolute temperatures:

$$\vartheta_1 = 2800\,^\circ K$$
$$\vartheta_3 = 300\,^\circ K$$

the thermal efficiency would be:

$$\eta = 0.89$$

and the compression ratio:

$$\varepsilon = 266$$

supposing a $\kappa = 1.4$. Such a compression ratio can hardly be produced by real engines. Typical compression ratios are at least ten times smaller.

A.2 Jacobian Matrices / Nonlinear Two-track Model

The elements of the jacobian matrices for the nonlinear reduced 3rd order model in Section 6.4.4 are:

$$\frac{\partial \dot{v}_{CoG}}{\partial v_{CoG}} = \frac{1}{m_{CoG}v_{CoG}^2}\Big(-2 \cdot constl \cdot v_{CoG}^3 \cos\beta - c_{RL} \cdot l_R \cdot \dot\psi \cdot \sin\beta -$$
$$- c_{RR} \cdot l_R \cdot \dot\psi \sin\beta + c_{FL} \cdot l_F \dot\psi \cdot \sin(\beta - \delta_W) +$$
$$+ c_{FR} \cdot l_F \cdot \dot\psi \cdot \sin(\beta - \delta_W)\Big)$$

$$\frac{\partial \dot{v}_{CoG}}{\partial \beta} = \frac{1}{m_{CoG}v_{CoG}}\Big(c_{RL} \cdot l_R \cdot \dot\psi \cdot \cos\beta + c_{RR} \cdot l_R \cdot \dot\psi \cdot \cos\beta -$$
$$- \beta \cdot c_{RL} \cdot v_{CoG} \cdot \cos\beta - \beta \cdot c_{RR} \cdot v_{CoG} \cdot \cos\beta -$$
$$- c_{FL} \cdot l_F \dot\psi \cdot \cos\beta \cdot \cos\delta_W - \beta \cdot c_{FL} \cdot v_{CoG} \cdot \cos\beta \cdot \cos\delta_W +$$
$$+ c_{FL} \cdot \delta_W \cdot v_{CoG} \cdot \cos\beta \cdot \cos\delta_W - c_{FR} \cdot l_F \cdot \dot\psi \cdot \cos\beta \cos\delta_W -$$
$$- \beta \cdot c_{FR} \cdot v_{CoG} \cdot \cos\beta \cdot \cos\delta_W + c_{FR} \cdot \delta_W \cdot v_{CoG} \cdot \cos\beta \cdot \cos\delta_W -$$
$$- c_{RL} \cdot v_{CoG} \cdot \sin\beta - c_{RR} \cdot v_{CoG} \cdot \sin\beta - F_{LRL} \cdot v_{CoG} \cdot \sin\beta -$$
$$- F_{LRR} \cdot v_{CoG} \cdot \sin\beta + constl \cdot v^3 \cdot \sin\beta -$$
$$- c_{FL} \cdot v_{CoG} \cdot \cos\delta_W \cdot \sin\beta - F_{LFL} \cdot v_{CoG} \cdot \cos\delta_W \cdot \sin\beta -$$
$$- c_{FR} \cdot v_{CoG} \cdot \cos\delta_W \cdot \sin\beta - F_{LFR} \cdot v_{CoG} \cdot \cos\delta_W \cdot \sin\beta +$$
$$+ c_{FL} \cdot v_{CoG} \cdot \cos\beta \cdot \sin\delta_W + F_{LFL} \cdot v_{CoG} \cdot \cos\beta \cdot \sin\delta_W -$$
$$- c_{FL} \cdot l_F \cdot \dot\psi \cdot \sin\beta \cdot \sin\delta_W - \beta \cdot c_{FL} \cdot v_{CoG} \cdot \sin\beta \cdot \sin\delta_W +$$
$$+ c_{FL} \cdot \delta_W \cdot v_{CoG} \cdot \sin\beta \cdot \sin\delta_W + c_{FR} \cdot v_{CoG} \cdot \cos\beta \cdot \sin\delta_W +$$
$$+ F_{LFR} \cdot v_{CoG} \cdot \cos\beta \cdot \sin\delta_W - c_{FR} \cdot l_F \cdot \dot\psi \cdot \sin\beta \cdot \sin\delta_W -$$
$$- \beta \cdot c_{FR} \cdot v_{CoG} \cdot \sin\beta \cdot \sin\delta_W + c_{FR} \cdot \delta_W \cdot v_{CoG} \cdot \sin\beta \cdot \sin\delta_W\Big)$$

$$\frac{\partial \dot{v}_{CoG}}{\partial \dot\psi} = \frac{1}{m_{CoG}v_{CoG}}\Big(c_{RL} \cdot l_R \cdot \sin\beta + c_{RR} \cdot l_R \cdot \sin\beta -$$
$$- c_{FL} \cdot l_F \cdot \sin(\beta - \delta_W) - c_{FR} \cdot l_F \cdot \sin(\beta - \delta_W)\Big)$$

$$\frac{\partial \dot\beta}{\partial v_{CoG}} = \frac{1}{m_{CoG}v_{CoG}^3} \cdot \Big(-2 \cdot c_{RL} \cdot l_R \cdot \dot\psi \cdot \cos\beta - 2 \cdot c_{RR} \cdot l_R \cdot \dot\psi \cdot \cos\beta +$$
$$+ \beta \cdot c_{RL} \cdot v_{CoG} \cdot \cos\beta + \beta \cdot c_{RR} \cdot v_{CoG} \cdot \cos\beta +$$
$$+ 2 \cdot c_{FL} \cdot l_F \cdot \dot\psi \cdot \cos(\beta - \delta_W) + \beta \cdot c_{FL} \cdot v_{CoG} \cdot \cos(\beta - \delta_W) -$$
$$- c_{FL} \cdot v_{CoG} \cdot \cos(\beta - \delta_W) + 2 \cdot c_{FR} \cdot l_F \cdot \dot\psi \cdot \cos(\beta - \delta_W) +$$
$$+ \beta \cdot c_{FR} \cdot v_{CoG} \cdot \cos(\beta - \delta_W) - c_{FR} \cdot \delta_W \cdot v_{CoG} \cdot \cos(\beta - \delta_W) +$$
$$+ F_{LRL} \cdot v_{CoG} \cdot \sin\beta + F_{LRR} \cdot v_{CoG} \cdot \sin\beta + constl \cdot v^3 \cdot \sin\beta +$$
$$+ F_{LFL} \cdot v_{CoG} \cdot \sin(\beta - \delta_W) + F_{LFR} \cdot v_{CoG} \cdot \sin(\beta - \delta_W)\Big)$$

$$\frac{\partial \dot\beta}{\partial \beta} = \frac{1}{m_{CoG}v_{CoG}^2} \cdot \Big(-c_{RL} \cdot v_{CoG} \cdot \cos\beta - c_{RR} \cdot v_{CoG} \cdot \cos\beta -$$

$$-F_{LRL} \cdot v_{CoG} \cdot \cos\beta - F_{LRR} \cdot v_{CoG} \cdot \cos\beta + constl \cdot v_{CoG}^3 \cdot \cos\beta -$$

$$- c_{FL} \cdot v_{CoG} \cdot \cos\beta \cdot \cos\delta_W - F_{LFL} \cdot v_{CoG} \cdot \cos\beta \cdot \cos\delta_W -$$

$$- c_{FR} \cdot v_{CoG} \cdot \cos\beta \cdot \cos\delta_W - F_{LFR} \cdot v_{CoG} \cdot \cos\beta \cdot \cos\delta_W -$$

$$- c_{RL} \cdot l_R \cdot \dot\psi \cdot \sin\beta - c_{RR} \cdot l_R \cdot \dot\psi \cdot \sin\beta +$$

$$+ \beta \cdot c_{RL} \cdot v_{CoG} \cdot \sin\beta + \beta \cdot c_{RR} \cdot v_{CoG} \cdot \sin\beta +$$

$$+ c_{FL} \cdot l_F \cdot \dot\psi \cdot \cos\delta_W \cdot \sin\beta + \beta \cdot c_{FL} \cdot v_{CoG} \cdot \cos\delta_W \cdot \sin\beta -$$

$$- c_{FL} \cdot \delta_W \cdot v_{CoG} \cdot \cos\delta_W \cdot \sin\beta + c_{FR} \cdot l_F \cdot \dot\psi \cdot \cos\delta_W \cdot \sin\beta +$$

$$+ \beta \cdot c_{FR} \cdot v_{CoG} \cdot \cos\delta_W \sin\beta - c_{FR} \cdot \delta_W \cdot v_{CoG} \cdot \cos\delta_W \cdot \sin\beta -$$

$$- c_{FL} \cdot l_F \cdot \dot\psi \cdot \cos\beta \cdot \sin\delta_W - \beta \cdot c_{FL} \cdot v_{CoG} \cdot \cos\beta \sin\delta_W +$$

$$+ c_{FL} \cdot \delta_W \cdot v_{CoG} \cdot \cos\beta \cdot \sin\delta_W - c_{FL} \cdot v_{CoG} \cdot \sin\beta \cdot \cos\delta_W -$$

$$- F_{LFL} \cdot v_{CoG} \cdot \sin\beta \cdot \sin\delta_W - c_{FR} \cdot l_F \cdot \dot\psi \cdot \cos\beta \cdot \sin\delta_W -$$

$$- \beta \cdot c_{FR} \cdot v_{CoG} \cdot \cos\beta \sin\delta_W + c_{FR} \cdot \delta_W \cdot v_{CoG} \cdot \cos\beta \cdot \sin\delta_W -$$

$$- c_{FR} \cdot v_{CoG} \cdot \sin\beta \cdot \cos\delta_W - F_{LFR} \cdot v_{CoG} \cdot \sin\beta \cdot \sin\delta_W \Big)$$

$$\frac{\partial \dot\beta}{\partial \dot\psi} = \frac{1}{m_{CoG}v_{CoG}^2} \cdot \Big(-m_{CoG} \cdot v^2 + c_{RL} \cdot l_R \cdot \cos\beta + c_{RR} \cdot l_R \cdot \cos\beta -$$

$$- c_{FL} \cdot l_F \cdot \cos(\beta - \delta_W) - c_{FR} \cdot l_F \cdot \cos(\beta - \delta_W) \Big)$$

$$\frac{\partial \ddot\psi}{\partial v_{CoG}} = \frac{1}{2 \cdot J_Z \cdot v_{CoG}^2} \cdot \Big(2 \cdot c_{RL} \cdot l_R^2 \cdot \dot\psi + 2 \cdot c_{RR} \cdot l_R^2 \cdot \dot\psi +$$

$$+ 2 \cdot c_{RL} \cdot l_R \cdot n_{LR} \cdot \dot\psi + 2 \cdot c_{RR} \cdot l_R \cdot n_{LR} \cdot \dot\psi +$$

$$+ 2 \cdot c_{FL} \cdot l_F^2 \cdot \dot\psi \cdot \cos\delta_W - 2 \cdot c_{FL} \cdot l_F \cdot n_{LF} \cdot \dot\psi \cdot \cos\delta_W +$$

$$+ 2 \cdot c_{FR} \cdot l_F^2 \cdot \dot\psi \cdot \cos\delta_W - 2 \cdot c_{FR} \cdot l_F \cdot n_{LF} \cdot \dot\psi \cdot \cos\delta_W +$$

$$+ b_F \cdot c_{FL} \cdot l_F \cdot \dot\psi \cdot \sin\delta_W + 2 \cdot c_{FL} \cdot l_F \cdot n_{LF} \cdot \dot\psi \cdot (\sin\delta_W)^2 -$$

$$- b_F \cdot c_{FR} \cdot l_F \cdot \dot\psi \cdot \sin\delta_W + 2 \cdot c_{FR} \cdot l_F \cdot n_{LF} \cdot \dot\psi \cdot (\sin\delta_W)^2 \Big)$$

$$\frac{\partial \ddot\psi}{\partial \beta} = \frac{1}{2 \cdot J_Z} \cdot \Big(2c_{RL} \cdot l_R + 2 \cdot c_{RR} \cdot l_R + 2 \cdot c_{RL} \cdot n_{LR} + 2 \cdot c_{RR} \cdot n_{LR} -$$

$$- 2 \cdot c_{FL} \cdot l_F \cdot \cos\delta_W + 2 \cdot c_{FL} \cdot n_{LF} \cdot \cos\delta_W -$$

$$- 2 \cdot c_{FR} \cdot l_F \cdot \cos\delta_W + 2 \cdot c_{FR} \cdot n_{LF} \cdot \cos\delta_W -$$

$$- b_F \cdot c_{FL} \cdot \sin\delta_W - 2 \cdot c_{FL} \cdot n_{LF} \cdot (\sin\delta_W)^2 +$$

$$+ b_F \cdot c_{FR} \cdot \sin\delta_W - 2 \cdot c_{FR} \cdot n_{LF} \cdot (\sin\delta_W)^2 \Big)$$

$$\frac{\partial \ddot{\psi}}{\partial \dot{\psi}} = \frac{1}{2 \cdot J_Z \cdot v_{CoG}} \cdot \Big(-2 \cdot c_{RL} \cdot l_R^2 - 2 \cdot c_{RR} \cdot l_R^2 -$$
$$-2 \cdot c_{RL} \cdot l_R \cdot n_{LR} - 2 \cdot c_{RR} \cdot l_R \cdot n_R - 2 \cdot c_{FL} \cdot l_F^2 \cdot \cos \delta_W +$$
$$+ 2 \cdot c_{FL} \cdot l_F \cdot n_{LF} \cdot \cos \delta_W - 2 \cdot c_{FR} \cdot l_F^2 \cdot \cos \delta_W +$$
$$+ 2 \cdot c_{FR} \cdot l_F \cdot n_{LF} \cdot \cos \delta_W - b_F \cdot c_{FL} \cdot l_F \cdot \sin \delta_W -$$
$$- 2 \cdot c_{FL} \cdot l_F \cdot n_{LF} \cdot (\sin \delta_W)^2 + b_F \cdot c_{FR} \cdot l_F \cdot \sin \delta_W -$$
$$- 2 \cdot c_{FR} \cdot l_F \cdot n_{LF} \cdot (\sin \delta_W)^2 \Big)$$

$$\frac{\partial \dot{v}_{CoG}}{\partial F_{LFL}} = \frac{1}{m_{CoG}} \cos(\beta - \delta_W)$$

$$\frac{\partial \dot{v}_{CoG}}{\partial F_{LFR}} = \frac{1}{m_{CoG}} \cos(\beta - \delta_W)$$

$$\frac{\partial \dot{v}_{CoG}}{\partial F_{LRL}} = \frac{1}{m_{CoG}} \cos \beta$$

$$\frac{\partial \dot{v}_{CoG}}{\partial F_{LRR}} = \frac{1}{m_{CoG}} \cos \beta$$

$$\frac{\partial \dot{v}_{CoG}}{\partial \delta_W} = \frac{1}{m_{CoG} \cdot v_{CoG}} \cdot \Big(F_{LFL} \cdot \sin(\beta - \delta_W) \cdot v_{CoG} +$$
$$+ F_{LFR} \cdot \sin(\beta - \delta_W) \cdot v_{CoG} + c_{FL} \cdot \sin(\beta - \delta_W) \cdot v_{CoG} -$$
$$- c_{FL} \cdot \cos(\beta - \delta_W) \cdot \delta_W \cdot v_{CoG} + c_{FL} \cdot \cos(\beta - \delta_W) \cdot \beta \cdot v_{CoG} +$$
$$+ c_{FL} \cdot \cos(\beta - \delta_W) \cdot l_F \cdot \dot{\psi} + c_{FR} \cdot \sin(\beta - \delta_W) \cdot v_{CoG} -$$
$$- c_{FR} \cdot \cos(\beta - \delta_W) \cdot \delta_W \cdot v_{CoG} + c_{FR} \cdot \cos(\beta - \delta_W) \cdot \beta \cdot v_{CoG} +$$
$$+ c_{FR} \cdot \cos(\beta - \delta_W) \cdot l_F \cdot \dot{\psi} \Big)$$

$$\frac{\partial \dot{\beta}}{\partial F_{LFL}} = \frac{-1}{m_{CoG} \cdot v_{CoG}} \sin(\beta - \delta_W)$$

$$\frac{\partial \dot{\beta}}{\partial F_{LFR}} = \frac{-1}{m_{CoG} \cdot v_{CoG}} \sin(\beta - \delta_W)$$

$$\frac{\partial \dot{\beta}}{\partial F_{LRL}} = \frac{-1}{m_{CoG} \cdot v_{CoG}} \sin \beta$$

$$\frac{\partial \dot{\beta}}{\partial F_{LRR}} = \frac{-1}{m_{CoG} \cdot v_{CoG}} \sin \beta$$

$$\frac{\partial \dot{\beta}}{\partial \delta_W} = -\frac{1}{m_{CoG} \cdot v_{CoG}^2} \cdot \Big(- F_{LFL} \cdot \cos(\beta - \delta_W) \cdot v_{CoG} -$$
$$- F_{LFR} \cdot \cos(\beta - \delta_W) \cdot v_{CoG} - c_{FL} \cdot \cos(\beta - \delta_W) \cdot v_{CoG} -$$
$$- c_{FL} \cdot \sin(\beta - \delta_W) \cdot \delta_W \cdot v_{CoG} + c_{FL} \cdot \sin(\beta - \delta_W) \cdot \beta \cdot v_{CoG} +$$
$$+ c_{FL} \cdot \sin(\beta - \delta_W) \cdot l_F \cdot \dot{\psi} - c_{FR} \cdot \cos(\beta - \delta_W) \cdot v_{CoG} -$$
$$- c_{FR} \cdot \sin(\beta - \delta_W) \cdot \delta_W \cdot v_{CoG} + c_{FR} \cdot \sin(\beta - \delta_W) \cdot \beta \cdot v_{CoG} +$$
$$+ c_{FR} \cdot \sin(\beta - \delta_W) \cdot l_F \cdot \dot{\psi} \Big)$$

$$\frac{\partial \ddot{\psi}}{\partial F_{LFL}} = \frac{1}{2 \cdot J_Z \cdot v_{CoG}} \cdot (2 \cdot v_{CoG} \cdot l_F \sin \delta_W - v_{CoG} \cdot b_F \cdot \cos \delta_W)$$

$$\frac{\partial \ddot{\psi}}{\partial F_{LFR}} = \frac{1}{2 \cdot J_Z \cdot v_{CoG}} \cdot (2 \cdot v_{CoG} \cdot l_F \sin \delta_W + v_{CoG} \cdot b_F \cdot \cos \delta_W)$$

$$\frac{\partial \ddot{\psi}}{\partial F_{LRL}} = \frac{1}{2 \cdot J_Z \cdot v_{CoG}} \cdot (b_R \cdot v_{CoG})$$

$$\frac{\partial \ddot{\psi}}{\partial F_{LRR}} = \frac{1}{2 \cdot J_Z \cdot v_{CoG}} \cdot (b_R \cdot v_{CoG})$$

$$\frac{\partial \ddot{\psi}}{\partial \delta_W} = \frac{1}{2 \cdot J_Z \cdot v_{CoG}} \cdot \Big(c_{FL} \cdot v_{CoG} \cdot b_F \cdot \sin \delta_W +$$
$$\cos \delta_W \cdot c_{FL} \cdot \delta_W \cdot v_{CoG} \cdot b_F - \cos \delta_W \cdot c_{FL} \cdot \beta \cdot v_{CoG} \cdot b_F -$$
$$- \cos \delta_W \cdot c_{FL} \cdot l_F \cdot \dot{\psi} \cdot b_F + 2 \cdot \cos \delta_W \cdot F_{LFL} \cdot v_{CoG} \cdot l_F +$$
$$+ 2 \cdot c_{FL} \cdot v_{CoG} \cdot l_F \cdot \cos \delta_W - 2 \cdot \sin \delta_W \cdot c_{FL} \cdot \delta_W \cdot v_{CoG} \cdot l_F +$$
$$+ 2 \cdot \sin \delta_W \cdot c_{FL} \cdot \beta \cdot v_{CoG} \cdot l_F + 2 \cdot \sin \delta_W \cdot c_{FL} \cdot l_F^2 \cdot \dot{\psi} +$$
$$+ \sin \delta_W \cdot F_{LFL} \cdot v_{CoG} \cdot b_F - c_{FR} \cdot v_{CoG} \cdot b_F \cdot \sin \delta_W +$$
$$+ \cos \delta_W \cdot c_{FR} \cdot \beta \cdot v_{CoG} \cdot b_F - \cos \delta_W \cdot c_{FR} \cdot \delta_W \cdot v_{CoG} \cdot b_F +$$
$$+ \cos \delta_W \cdot c_{FR} \cdot l_F \cdot \dot{\psi} \cdot b_F + +2 \cdot \cos \delta_W \cdot F_{LFR} \cdot v_{CoG} \cdot l_F +$$
$$+ 2 \cdot c_{FR} \cdot v_{CoG} \cdot l_F \cdot \cos \delta_W - 2 \cdot \sin \delta_W \cdot c_{FR} \cdot \delta_W \cdot v_{CoG} \cdot l_F +$$
$$+ 2 \cdot \sin \delta_W \cdot c_{FR} \cdot \beta \cdot v_{CoG} \cdot l_F + 2 \cdot \sin \delta_W \cdot c_{FR} \cdot l_F^2 \cdot \dot{\psi} -$$
$$- \sin \delta_W \cdot F_{LFR} \cdot v_{CoG} \cdot b_F - 2 \cdot c_{FL} \cdot v_{CoG} \cdot n_{LF} -$$
$$- 2 \cdot c_{FR} \cdot v_{CoG} \cdot n_{LF} \Big)$$

Note, in the above, $constl = c_{aer} \cdot A_L \cdot \frac{\rho}{2}$.

A.3 Design of GPC Controllers

The GPC controller specifications are formally described using the following cost function:

$$J_{GPC} = E \left\{ \sum_{j=N_1}^{N_2} [y(t+j) - r(t+j)]^2 + \lambda_u \sum_{j=0}^{N_u} [\Delta u(t+j-1)]^2 \right\} \qquad (A.40)$$

Where,

$y(t+j)$	:	future control value
$r(t+j)$	:	reference trajectory
$\Delta u(t+j-1)$	:	future change in control input ($\Delta = 1 - z^{-1}$)
N_1	:	lower prediction horizon
N_2	:	upper prediction horizon
N_u	:	control horizon
λ_u	:	weighting factor for the control input changes.

The first term in the cost function represents the predicted squared control error over a limited period of time between N_1 and N_2. The second term represents the weighted sum of the first N_u future control values. The larger the weighting factor λ_u, the more gently the control value changes. To reduce the computational load, the control vector is considered to be constant after time N_u, i.e. the changes are

$$\Delta u(t+i) = 0 \quad \text{for} \quad i \geq N_u \quad . \qquad (A.41)$$

At each sampling instant, the following calculations are carried out:

- The reference trajectory $r(t+j)$ is determined.

- The process outputs $y(t+j)$ are predicted, along with the future predicted control errors and controller input change for the time $N_2 - N_1$.

- Using the cost function, the future controller error and control input value changes are minimised over the considered time period.

- The first value in the optimised control vector $u(t+j)$, $0 \leq j \leq N_u - 1$ is now applied to the real system, and the process repeated.

A.3.1 The Process Model

Consider a model of the following form:

$$y(t) = \frac{B(z^{-1})}{A(z^{-1})} u(t-1) + \frac{C(z^{-1})}{A(z^{-1})\Delta} \xi(t) \qquad (A.42)$$

or

$$A(z^{-1})\Delta y(t) = B(z^{-1})\Delta u(t-1) + C(z^{-1})\xi(t) \qquad (A.43)$$

Where,

$$
\begin{aligned}
A(z^{-1}) &= 1 + a_1 z^{-1} + \ldots + a_{na} z^{-na} \\
B(z^{-1}) &= b_0 + b_1 z^{-1} + \ldots + b_{nb} z^{-nb} \\
C(z^{-1}) &= 1 + c_1 z^{-1} + \ldots + c_{nc} z^{-nc} \\
\Delta &= 1 - z^{-1}
\end{aligned}
$$

Variable $\xi(t)$ represents the system disturbance. For simplicity, $C(z^{-1})$ is chosen to be 1.

In order to minimise the cost function, the outputs of the system $y(t + j)$ must be predicted for $j = N_1, \ldots, N_2$. This requires the following *Diophantine Equation*:

$$
1 = E_j(z^{-1})A(z^{-1})\Delta + z^{-j}F_j(z^{-1}) \tag{A.44}
$$

where,

$$
\begin{aligned}
E_j(z^{-1}) &= e_{j,0} + e_{j,1}z^{-1} + \ldots + e_{j,j}z^{-j+1} \\
F_j(z^{-1}) &= f_{j,0} + f_{j,1}z^{-1} + \ldots + f_{j,j}z^{-j+1}
\end{aligned}
$$

$E_j(z^{-1})$ and $F_j(z^{-1})$ can be uniquely determined given $A_j(z^{-1})$ and j.

Multiplying Eq. A.43 by $E_j(z^{-1})z^j$ gives;

$$
E_j(z^{-1})A(z^{-1})\Delta y(t+j) = E_j(z^{-1})B(z^{-1})\Delta u(t+j-1) + E_j(z^{-1})\xi(t+j) \tag{A.45}
$$

Substituting $E_j(z^{-1})A(z^{-1})\Delta$ from Eq. A.44 gives,

$$
y(t+j) = F_j(z^{-1}) \cdot y(t) + E_j(z^{-1})B(z^{-1}) \cdot \Delta u(t+j-1) + E_j(z^{-1})\xi(t+j) \tag{A.46}
$$

The last term in Eq. A.46 respresents the system disturbance, and is dependant on future values which are not available at time t. Thus this term is set equal to zero, giving the following prediction:

$$
\hat{y}(t+j) = F_j(z^{-1}) \cdot y(t) + E_j(z^{-1})B(z^{-1}) \cdot \Delta u(t+j-1) \tag{A.47}
$$

This gives the predicted outputs $\hat{y}(t+j)$ dependant upon previous values of the output and previous and future values of the control change.

A.3.2 Recursion of the Diophantine Equation

The determination of the coefficients of the predictor polynomials is carried out recursively using the Diophantine equation. The solution of Eq. A.44 is obtained via the recursive calculation of the two polynomials $E_j(z^{-1})$ and $F_j(z^{-1})$ from the two previous values $E_{j-1}(z^{-1})$ and $F_{j-1}(z^{-1})$:

$$
\begin{aligned}
1 &= E_j(z^{-1})A(z^{-1})\Delta + z^{-j}F_j(z^{-1}) \tag{A.48} \\
1 &= E_{j+1}(z^{-1})A(z^{-1})\Delta + z^{-j-1}F_{j+1}(z^{-1}) \tag{A.49}
\end{aligned}
$$

Subtacting Eq. A.48 from Eq. A.49 gives:

$$0 = A(z^{-1})\Delta \left[E_{j+1}(z^{-1}) - E_j(z^{-1})\right] + z^{-j} \left[z^{-1}F_{j+1}(z^{-1}) - F_j(z^{-1})\right] \quad \text{(A.50)}$$

Substituting,

$$E_{j+1}(z^{-1}) - E_j(z^{-1}) = e_{j+1,j} \cdot z^{-1} + \tilde{E}(z^{-1}) \quad \text{(A.51)}$$

where $\tilde{E}(z^{-1})$ is a polynomial of order $(j-1)$ and $e_{j+1,j}$ is the j-th coefficient of $E_{j+1}(z^{-1})$ into Eq. A.50 gives,

$$0 = A(z^{-1})\Delta \tilde{E}_{j+1}(z^{-1}) + z^{-j} \left[z^{-1}F_{j+1}(z^{-1}) - F_j(z^{-1}) + A(z^{-1})\Delta e_{j+1,j}\right] \quad \text{(A.52)}$$

From Eq. A.52 it then follows that,

$$\begin{aligned}
\tilde{E}_{j+1}(z^{-1}) &= 0 \\
z^{-1}F_{j+1}(z^{-1}) &= F_j(z^{-1}) - A(z^{-1})\Delta e_{j+1,j}
\end{aligned} \quad \text{(A.53)}$$

The coefficients of $E_{j+1}(z^{-1})$ and $F_{j+1}(z^{-1})$ are then calculated in the following way:

$$\begin{aligned}
e_{j+1,j} &= f_{j,0} & \text{(A.54)} \\
f_{j+1,j} &= f_{j,j+1} - \tilde{a}_{j+1}e_{j+1,j} &, \quad j = 0,\dots, \text{degree of } F_j(z^{-1}) & \text{(A.55)}
\end{aligned}$$

where $\tilde{a}_{j+1}$ is the $(j+1)$-th coefficient of the polynomial $\tilde{A}(z^{-1}) = A(z^{-1})\Delta$. The polynomial $E_{j+1}(z^{-1})$ is given by,

$$E_{j+1}(z^{-1}) = E_j(z^{-1}) + z^{-1}e_{j+1,j} \quad \text{(A.56)}$$

and,

$$G_{j+1}(z^{-1}) = B(z^{-1}) \cdot E_{j+1}(z^{-1}) \quad \text{(A.57)}$$

The initial values for the recursion are found from Eq. A.48 for $j = 1$:

$$1 = E_1(z^{-1})\tilde{A}(z^{-1}) + z^{-1}F_1(z^{-1}) \quad \text{(A.58)}$$

As the leading element of $\tilde{A}(z^{-1})$ is 1, then,

$$\begin{aligned}
E_1 &= 1 \\
F_1 &= q\left(1 - \tilde{A}(z^{-1})\right)
\end{aligned} \quad \text{(A.59)}$$

Starting from the solution for $j = 1$, the later solutions can be recursively calculated using Eqs A.54 and A.55.

A.3.3 The Control Law

The minimisation of the cost function results in a predicted optimal control change vector $\underline{\tilde{u}}$,

$$\underline{\tilde{u}} = \left(\underline{G}^T\underline{G} + \lambda_u\underline{I}\right)^{-1}\underline{G}^T(\underline{r} - \underline{f}) \tag{A.60}$$

where,

$$
\begin{aligned}
\underline{\tilde{u}} &= [\Delta u(t), \Delta u(t+1), \dots, \Delta u(t+N_u-1)]^T \\
\underline{r} &= [r(t+N_1), r(t+N_1+1), \dots, r(t+N_2)]^T \\
\underline{f} &= [f(t+N_1), f(t+N_1+1), \dots, f(t+N_2)]^T
\end{aligned} \tag{A.61}
$$

$\underline{r}$ is the reference value sequence.

The following controller structure results (see Fig. 9.28),

$$S(z^{-1})\Delta u(t) = T(z^{-1})r(t+N_2) - R(z^{-1})y(t) \tag{A.62}$$

A.3.4 Choice of the Controller Parameters

- The lower prediction horizon N_1
  This is normally chosen as 1. If the deadtime of the process is known to be d sampling instants, then N_1 should be chosen to be at least as large as d.

- The upper prediction horizon N_2
  In general, N_2 should be chosen so that the result can track a controller action. Thus, N_2 should at least be larger than the order of $B(z^{-1})$. In practice, N_2 is chosen much larger than this, and corresponds to the rise time of the system.

- The control horizon N_u
  For simple systems, $N_u = 1$ can lead to good results, though higher values may be necessary for more complex systems (i.e. unstable systems). An increase in N_u (up to a certain point) leads to faster control and reduced effect of disturbances.

- The weighting factor λ_u
  This is normally chosen to be small, as larger values of λ_u leads to a slower overall system response and worse disturbance handling. In practice, λ_u is taken as zero, or a small value.

- The T-filter polynomial is the so-called disturbance filter. It is used to improve the robustness of the controller to unmodelled disturbances. For well damped stable processes, the following is suitable:

$$T(z^{-1}) = A(z^{-1})(1 - \mu z^{-1}) \quad , \quad 0 \le \mu < 1 \tag{A.63}$$

For smaller values of μ, the disturbance behaviour is improved, however the influence of the disturbance at higher frequencies increases. For higher values of μ, the stability of the control loop is affected. $\mu = 0$ is a compromise between the two extremes.

For badly damped processes however, $\mu = 0$ cannot be used, and the following is applied,

$$T(z^{-1}) = (1 - \mu z^{-1})^{na} \quad , \quad 0 \le \mu < 1 \tag{A.64}$$

where na is the order of the polynomial $A(z^{-1})$. μ of between 0.6 and 0.9 is suitable.

A.4   Driver Model: Constants and Weighting Factors

Table A.1 gives the constants required for the inter-arrival time calculations of Section 9.3.6.

Table A.1 Constants for the arrival time calculations

Constant	Value		Constant	Value
p_f	0.3		p_l	0.3
f_1	$9\,s/m$		l_1	$9\,s/m$
f_2	$20\,s^2/m$		l_2	$20\,s^2/m$
f_3	$7\,s/deg$		l_3	$7\,s/deg$
f_4	$30\,s^2/deg$		l_4	$30\,s^2/deg$
f_5	$5\ 1/deg$		l_5	$5\ 1/deg$
p_r	0.2		p_m	0.2
r_1	$40\ 1/m$		m_1	$40\ 1/m$
r_2	$0.1\,s/m$		m_2	$0.1\,s/m$
r_3	$5\,s/deg$		m_3	$5\,s/deg$
r_4	$20\,s^2/deg$		m_4	$20\,s^2/deg$
r_5	$0.1\ 1/deg$		m_5	$0.1\ 1/deg$
r_6	$2.5\,s/m$		m_6	$2.5\,s/m$
c_1	$\frac{1}{3}\,s^3/m$		c_3	$-0.09384\,1/m$
c_2	$0.001401\,s/m^2$			

Table A.2 shows the inter-arrival times, the service times (in seconds) and the priorities of the different perception categories.

A.5   Least Squares Parameter Estimation

A process with outputs $\underline{y}(t)$ and unknown process parameters Θ_1 to Θ_N is assumed. The output variables are however not directly measurable - only the measurement vector $\underline{y}_p(t)$ is available which is corrupted with the disturbance signal $n(t)$.

For parameter estimation, the model structure,

$$\underline{y}_m = F\left[\underline{\Theta}, \underline{u}(t)\right] \tag{A.65}$$

Table A.2 Priorities, inter-arrival and service times for different perception categories

Categorie	inter-arrival time	Service time	Priority
Visual focus	(see Eq. 9.8)	N(1.55 / 0.35)	9
Lead point	(see Eq. 9.9)	(see Eq. 9.13)	8
Road edge	(see Eq. 9.10)	(see Eq. 9.13)	7
Road center	(see Eq. 9.11)	(see Eq. 9.13)	7
Warning lights	100	N(0.83 / 0.3)	10
Speed indicator	N(86 / 27.3)	N(0.62 / 0.48)	5
Rev counter	(see Eq. 9.12)	N(0.62 / 0.48)	4
Mirror	N(130 / 3)	N(1 / 0.37)	6
Radio	N(331.7 / 155.4)	N(1.1 / 0.47)	2
Air conditioning control	N(493.8 / 277.3)	N(0.92 / 0.41)	2
Petrol gauge	N(855.5s / 399.6)	N(1.04 / 0.5)	3
Clock	N(1420 / 627.94)	N(0.83 / 0.38)	2
Temperature indicator	N(1025.6 / 666)	N(1.1 / 0.52)	3
Ventilation system	N(86 / 27.3)	N(1.1 / 0.48)	2

is assumed to be known, and the inputs are known or can be measured without errors.

The task of the parameter estimation is to determine the process parameters,

$$\underline{\Theta}^T = [\Theta_1, \Theta_2, \ldots, \Theta_N] \tag{A.66}$$

such that the modelled outputs $\underline{y}_m(t)$ correspond as exactly as possible with the measured outputs $\underline{y}_p(t)$ of the system. The quality of the correspondence is defined [32] in that the sum of the squares of the observed errors at a particular time instant k is minimised:

$$\sum_{k=1}^{M} e^2(k) = \sum_{k=1}^{M} \left[\underline{y}_p(k) - \underline{y}_m(k) \right]^2 \to MIN \tag{A.67}$$

A.5.1 Parameter Estimation Via the Least Squares Method

If it is assumed that the model is linear with respect to the parameters $\Theta_1...\Theta_N$, i.e.:

$$y_m(t) = \Theta_1 \cdot F_1 [u(t)] + \Theta_2 \cdot F_2 [u(t)] + \ldots + \Theta_N \cdot F_N [u(t)] \tag{A.68}$$

then a unique algebraic solution exists for the optimisation problem [32]. For M process outputs, the following solution is obtained:

$$\begin{bmatrix} \hat{\Theta}_1 \\ \hat{\Theta}_2 \\ \vdots \\ \hat{\Theta}_N \end{bmatrix} = \begin{bmatrix} \underline{\Psi}^T & \underline{\Psi} \end{bmatrix}^{-1} \cdot \underline{\Psi}^T \begin{bmatrix} y_p(t_1) \\ y_p(t_2) \\ \vdots \\ y_p(t_M) \end{bmatrix} \tag{A.69}$$

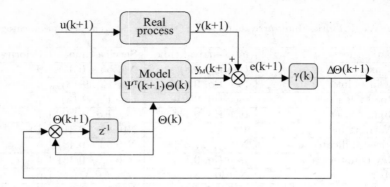

Figure A.10 The recursive least squares method

with the observation matrix:

$$\underline{\Psi} = \begin{bmatrix} F_1\left[u(t_1)\right] & F_2\left[u(t_1)\right] & \cdots & F_N\left[u(t_1)\right] \\ F_1\left[u(t_2)\right] & F_2\left[u(t_2)\right] & \cdots & F_N\left[u(t_2)\right] \\ \vdots & \vdots & \ddots & \vdots \\ F_1\left[u(t_M)\right] & F_2\left[u(t_M)\right] & \cdots & F_N\left[u(t_M)\right] \end{bmatrix} \tag{A.70}$$

A.5.2 Parameter Estimation Using Recursive Least Squares

In order to adapt the vehicle model to the current conditions and, should the occasion arise, to design adaptive controllers, changing parameters must be identified online. Whilst with non-recursive methods the estimated parameter is only available at the end of the measurement time, with dynamic parameters it is the changing parameter values after each sampling instant which are of interest. In order to prevent the saving of all past measurement values, and thus save computation time, the recursive method is used for online identification.

For the recursive least squares (RLS) the following equations apply [32]:

$$\underline{P}(k) = \left[\underline{\Psi}^T(k) \cdot \underline{\Psi}(k)\right]^{-1} \tag{A.71}$$

$$\underline{\gamma}(k) = \underline{P}(k+1) \cdot \underline{\Psi}(k+1) = \frac{\underline{P}(k) \cdot \underline{\Psi}(k+1)}{\underline{\Psi}^T(k+1)\underline{P}(k) \cdot \underline{\Psi}(k+1) + 1} \tag{A.72}$$

$$\hat{\underline{\Theta}}(k+1) = \hat{\underline{\Theta}}(k) + \underline{\gamma}(k) \cdot \left[y(k+1) - \underline{\Psi}^T(k+1) \cdot \hat{\underline{\Theta}}(k)\right] \tag{A.73}$$

$$\underline{P}(k+1) = \underline{P}(k) - \underline{\gamma}(k) \cdot \underline{\Psi}^T(k+1) \cdot \underline{P}(k) \tag{A.74}$$

Fig. A.10 shows the principle of the recursive least squares method.

The basic equations of the RLS estimator (Eqs A.71 - A.74) represent a versatile tool for online parameter identification. Further related RLS-estimators can be developed from these equations, such as RLS with weighted memory, generalised RLS, extended RLS etc. [32].

Via the introduction of a forgetting factor λ_{RLS}, which increases the elements in the covariance matrix $\underline{P}(k)$ for each iteration and thus weights the new data higher than the older data, one is able to slowly *forget* past values. This overcomes the consistency property of least squares estimators for time variant parameters. λ_{RLS} should not be chosen too small, or the influence of disturbances may not be satisfactorily removed. Good results have been obtained with values of $0.95 < \lambda_{RLS} < 0.995$. Because a large part of the identification with this RLS method is carried out with exponentially decaying memory, the corresponding equations are given. For a detailed description the reader is referred to [35], [47].

$$\gamma(k) = \frac{\underline{P}(k) \cdot \underline{\Psi}(k+1)}{\underline{\Psi}^T(k+1)\underline{P}(k) \cdot \underline{\Psi}(k+1) + \lambda_{RLS}} \tag{A.75}$$

$$\hat{\underline{\Theta}}(k+1) = \hat{\underline{\Theta}}(k) + \gamma(k) \cdot \left[y(k+1) - \underline{\Psi}^T(k+1) \cdot \hat{\underline{\Theta}}(k) \right] \tag{A.76}$$

$$\underline{P}(k+1) = \left[I - \gamma(k) \cdot \underline{\Psi}^T(k+1) \right] \cdot \underline{P}(k)\frac{1}{\lambda_{RLS}} \tag{A.77}$$

A.5.3   Discrete Root Filter Method in Covariant Form

Under certain conditions, numerical problems can appear with the above method due to an ill-conditioned covariance matrix $\underline{P}(k)$. The reasons for this can be a too high sampling rate [32] (i.e. input signals which change too slowly) or too much similarity in the signal values.

Via suitable numerically improved methods round off failures in computers with short word length ($\leq 16\,bit$) can be reduced, and the influence of initial values can be minimised.

One possible method, with which the ill conditioning of the equation system can be avoided, is the method of the discrete root filtering (DSFC), in which two triangular matrices $\underline{S}$ are used instead of the symmetric matrix $\underline{P}$:

$$\underline{P} = \underline{S} \cdot \underline{S}^T \tag{A.78}$$

As opposed to the covariance matrix, where products of the original data appear, the triangular matrices contain the roots of the products of the original data. Although the method is called the root filter method, a real construction of the roots does not occur.

Following the least squares method, substitution of the covariance matrix according to Eq. A.78 yields:

$$\underline{f}(k) = \underline{S}^T(k) \cdot \underline{\Psi}(k+1) \tag{A.79}$$

$$a(k) = \frac{1}{\underline{f}^T(k) \cdot \underline{f}(k) + \lambda_{RLS}} \tag{A.80}$$

Eqs A.75 - A.77 are now rewritten as:

$$\underline{\gamma}(k) = a(k) \cdot \underline{S}(k) \cdot \underline{f}(k) \tag{A.81}$$

$$\hat{\underline{\Theta}}(k+1) = \hat{\underline{\Theta}}(k) + \underline{\gamma}(k) \cdot \underbrace{\left[y(k+1) - \underline{\Psi}^T(k+1) \cdot \hat{\underline{\Theta}}(k) \right]}_{e(k+1)} \tag{A.82}$$

$$\underline{S}(k+1) = \left[\underline{S}(k) - \frac{1}{1 + \sqrt{\lambda_{RLS} \cdot a(k)}} \cdot \underline{\gamma}(k) \cdot \underline{f}^T(k) \right] \cdot \frac{1}{\sqrt{\lambda_{RLS}}} \tag{A.83}$$

The initial values are taken as $\underline{S}(0) = \sqrt{\lambda_{RLS}} \cdot \underline{I}$ and $\hat{\underline{\Theta}}(0) = 0$, i.e. no more thought must be given to the initial values of the parameter vectors. λ_{RLS} is the pre-defined forgetting factor.

The implementation of this method brings improvement over the RLS-estimator if microcomputers are used, as is the case in the vehicle itself.

B Nomenclature

B.1 Mathematical Definitions

Indices:

$(.)_{FL}$, $(.)_{FR}$, $(.)_{RL}$, $(.)_{RR}$ Wheel indices:
front left, front right, rear left, rear right
$(.)_F$, $(.)_R$ front and rear axle

Dimensions of vectors and matrices:

n	Number of states
m	Number of control inputs
k	Number of measurements

Vectors:

$\underline{x}$	$\in \Re^n$	State vector
$\underline{u}$	$\in \Re^m$	Input vector
$\underline{y}$	$\in \Re^k$	Measurement vector

Matrices:

$\underline{A}$	$\in \Re^{n,n}$	System matrix
$\underline{B}$	$\in \Re^{n,m}$	Input matrix
$\underline{C}$	$\in \Re^{k,n}$	Output matrix
$\underline{D}$	$\in \Re^{k,m}$	Throughput matrix
$\underline{K}_C$		feedback matrix (control law)

B.2   Physical variables

Symbol	Units	Physical variable
a_{eng}	$[m/s^2]$	negative acceleration at engine coasting
a_N	$[m/s^2]$	normal acceleration
a_X	$[m/s^2]$	longitudinal acceleration of CoG
a_{xpot}	$[m/s^2]$	potential braking acceleration of drivers
a_Y	$[m/s^2]$	lateral acceleration of CoG
a_{ypot}	$[m/s^2]$	driver-dependant tolerable lateral acceleration
a_Z	$[m/s^2]$	vertical acceleration of CoG
A_{Br}	$[m^2]$	area of wheel brake cylinder
A_{eff}	$[m^2]$	opening area of valve
$A_{L,S}$	$[m^2]$	front and side vehicle areas
b_F and b_R	$[m]$	distance between wheels on front and rear axles
B_F	$[m]$	road width
c_{aer}		coefficient of aerodynamic drag
$c_{BrF,R}$		front and rear brake transmission factors
$c_{F,R}$		front and rear tire side slip constants
c_{hh}		covariance of random road profile
c_{ij}		tire side slip constant
c_p	$[m^2/(s^2 K)]$	specific heat capacity by constant pressure
c_r		conversion ratio
c_v	$[m^2/(s^2 K)]$	specific heat capacity by constant volume
$c_{W,U}$		spring constants
c_0	$[m/s]$	sound propagation velocity at $273\,^\circ K$
$c_{1...5}$		co-efficients of Burkhard's tire equation
C	$[F]$	capacity
$\dot{CO}$	$[1/s]$	carbon monoxide emission level per time
CYL		number of cylinders
d		cylinder diameter
$d_{Fl,Fnl}$		damping constants
$d_{W,U}$		damping constants
DB		brake force distribution factor
E_{mass}	$[J]$	kinetic energy of the engine masses in motion
E_t	$[J]$	thermal energy
E_y	$[J]$	energy of signal y
$E\{\ \}$		expectation operator
f_{act}		driver dependent factor
f_{mass}		mass factor considering driveline rotation
f_p	$[Hz]$	frequency of air pulsation
F_C	$[N]$	spring force
F_{fric}	$[N]$	horizontal friction force

F_D	$[N]$	damping force
F_G	$[N]$	gravitational force
F_{Hi}		compensation factor at high engine power
F_L	$[N]$	horizontal wheel force in direction v_W
F_{Lo}		compensation factor at low engine power
F_{ped}	$[N]$	brake pedal force
F_R	$[N]$	rolling resistance force
F_S	$[N]$	horizontal wheel force in direction perpendicular to v_W
F_{wind}	$[N]$	wind force
F_{WL}	$[N]$	horizontal wheel force in direction x_W
F_{WS}	$[N]$	horizontal wheel force in direction y_W
F_X	$[N]$	longitudinal wheel force in direction x_{Un}
F_Y	$[N]$	lateral wheel force in direction y_{Un}
F_Z	$[N]$	vertical wheel force
F_{ZC}	$[N]$	vertical chassis force
F_{Z0}	$[N]$	nominal vertical wheel force
F_λ		control output factor of the lambda controller
g	$[m/s^2]$	gravitational constant
$G(s)$		transfer function
h		enthalpie of gas
h_{CoG}	$[m]$	height of CoG
h_{in}		inlet enthalpie
h_{out}		outlet enthalpie
h_{road}	$[m]$	road height
h'	$[m]$	distance from roll axis to CoG
$\dot{H}C$	$[1/s]$	hydrocarbons emission level per time
H_f	$[J/kg]$	specific energy of the fuel released in the combustion
i	$[A]$	current
i_{diff}		transmission ratio of differential
i_{gear}		transmission ratio of gear
i_s		transmission ratio of steering angle
$i_{X,Y,Z}$	$[m]$	radii of gyration
ICM		instantaneous center of motion
J	$[kg\,m^2]$	moment of inertia
J_{crank}	$[kg\,m^2]$	crankshaft moment of inertia
J_{DT}	$[kg\,m^2]$	drive-train moment of inertia
J_Z	$[kg\,m^2]$	moment of inertia about vertical axis
J_X	$[kg\,m^2]$	moment of inertia about longitudinal axis
J_Y	$[kg\,m^2]$	moment of inertia about lateral axis
J_W	$[kg\,m^2]$	moment of inertia of wheel
k		concentration ratio
k_{camb}		shifting factor of tire side slip angle by camber angle

k_i		weighting factor at fuzzy vehicle velocity estimation
k_l		adaptation factor
k_s		attenuation factor of tire tread profile
k_S	$[N/m]$	rotational spring constant of steering
k_{Br}		brake transmission factor
k_T		tire spring stiffness
k_u	$[N/m]$	spring damper stiffness
K_c		amplifier gain control parameter
$K_{l,e}$		amplifier gain
K_P, K_N		idle speed control parameters
l	$[m]$	wheel base (distance between front and rear axles)
l	$[m]$	connecting rod length
l_F	$[m]$	distance from CoG to front axle
l_R	$[m]$	distance from CoG to rear axle
L_1, L_2	$[H]$	inductances
L_{HC}, L_{CO}, L_{NO_x}		Lagrange factors
L_{st}		stochiometric ratio
m	$[kg]$	mass
m_a	$[kg]$	air mass
$\dot{m}_a$	$[kg/s]$	mass air flow
$\Delta\dot{m}_a$	$[kg/s]$	offset error air flow per time
$\dot{m}_{a,in}$	$[kg]$	mass air flow into the manifold
$\dot{m}_{a,out}$	$[kg]$	mass air flow out from the manifold
$m_{a,th}$	$[kg]$	theoretical air mass
$\dot{m}_D$	$[kg/s]$	depositing fuel flow
$\dot{m}_E$	$[kg/s]$	fuel flow from evaporation
m_f	$[kg]$	measured fuel mass per cylinder
$\dot{m}_f$	$[kg/s]$	fuel flow
$m_{f,th}$	$[kg]$	theoretical fuel mass
$\dot{m}_{f,in}$	$[kg/s]$	fuel flow injected into the manifold
$\dot{m}_{f,out}$	$[kg/s]$	fuel flow into the cylinders
m_{CoG}	$[kg]$	vehicle mass
m_{crank}	$[kg]$	crankshaft mass
m_{osc}	$[kg]$	oscillating mass
m_{piston}	$[kg]$	piston mass
m_{rod}	$[kg]$	rod mass
$m_{rod,osc}$	$[kg]$	oscillating rod mass
$m_{rod,rot}$	$[kg]$	rotational rod mass
m_{St}	$[kg]$	static wheel load
m_W	$[kg]$	wheel mass
m_W	$[kg]$	wall fuel mass
n	$[1/min]$	number of crankshaft revolutions
n_{Comb}		combustion cycles
n_L	$[m]$	longitudinal (dynamic) caster
n_S	$[m]$	lateral (side) caster

N_1		lower prediction horizon of GPC
N_2		upper prediction horizon of GPC
N_u		control horizon of GPC
$\dot{N}O_x$	$[1/s]$	nitrogen oxides emission level per time
p	$[N/m^2]$	pressure
p_{Br}	$[N/m^2]$	braking pressure
p_m	$[N/m^2]$	intake manifold pressure
p_o	$[N/m^2]$	barometric pressure
P_e	$[W]$	effective power
P_i	$[W]$	indicated power
P_{max}	$[W]$	maximum power
P_{min}	$[W]$	minimum power
$\underline{P}(k)$		covariance matrix in RLS estimation
q	$[J]$	thermal energy
$q_{hl,r}$	$[J]$	heat loss caused by incomplete combustion
$q_{hl,th}$	$[J]$	theoretical heat loss
r	$[m]$	crankshaft radius
r_{Br}	$[m]$	effective frictional radius of brake disc
r_{eff}	$[m]$	effective dynamic rolling radius
r_{ij}	$[m]$	distance from CoG to wheel ground contact point
r_{Stat}	$[m]$	static rolling radius
$r_T(t)$		rectangular time window (width T)
$r_{\Delta f}(f)$		rectangular frequency window (width Δf)
r_0	$[m]$	original wheel radius
R	$[m^2/(s^2 K)]$	gas constant
R	$[m]$	radius from wheel to instantaneous center of motion
R_i	$[\Omega]$	internal resistance
R_p	$[\Omega]$	parallel resistance
s	$[m]$	path length of road course segment
s	$[m]$	piston stroke
$\dot{s}$	$[m/s]$	piston velocity
s_j	$[m]$	piston stroke of cylinder j
s_L		longitudinal tire slip (in direction v_W)
s_{max}	$[m]$	maximum piston stroke
s_{Res}		resultant tire slip
s_S		lateral tire slip (in direction perpendicular to v_W)
S		entropy
t	$[s]$	time
t_{acc}	$[s]$	lead time for acceleration before end of curve
t_{antic}	$[s]$	time before a curve where the cornering velocity is already reduced
t_d	$[s]$	dwell time

t_f	$[s]$	foresight time
t_{inj}	$[s]$	injection time
t_i	$[s]$	ignition time
t_{pot}	$[s]$	potential lead time before braking to reach a lower speed
t_r	$[s]$	ignition release time
t_s	$[s]$	starting time
T_{Br}	$[Nm]$	braking torque
T_{burn}	$[s]$	time between opening of inlet and exhaust valve
T_c, T_i	$[s]$	time controller parameters
T_{comb}	$[Nm]$	combustion torque
$\overline{T}_{comb}$	$[Nm]$	average combustion torque
$T_{d,e}$	$[s]$	dead time (engine model)
T_{Drive}	$[Nm]$	drive torque
T_e	$[Nm]$	engine torque
T_{exh}	$[s]$	delay time between exhaust valve and lambda sensor
T_{fric}	$[Nm]$	friction torque
T_J	$[s]$	time constant
T_l	$[s]$	adaptation time constant
$T_{l,e}$	$[s]$	delay time (engine model)
T_{load}	$[Nm]$	load torque
T_{load}^*	$[Nm]$	extended load torque (with friction torque)
T_{mass}	$[Nm]$	mass torque
T_s	$[s]$	sample time
T_{self}	$[Nm]$	self righting torque at steering
$T_{U,In}$		transformation matrix (from under-carriage to inertial co-ordinate systems)
u	$[J]$	internal energy of a gas
u		control input variable
U	$[V]$	voltage
U_b	$[V]$	battery voltage
U_λ	$[V]$	output voltage lambda sensor
v_{CoG}	$[m/s]$	vehicle CoG velocity
$v_{osc,j}$	$[m/s]$	speed of oscillating mass in cylinder j
v_R	$[m/s]$	rotational equivalent wheel velocity
$v_{rot,j}$	$[m/s]$	rotational speed in cylinder j
v_W	$[m/s]$	wheel ground contact point velocity
v_{wind}	$[m/s]$	wind velocity
V	$[m^3]$	volume
V	$[kg/W]$	Fuel Consumption
$\dot{V}$	$[kg/(Ws)]$	Fuel Consumption over time
V_d	$[m^3]$	displacement volume
V_m	$[m^3]$	manifold volume
w_e	$[J/m^3]$	effective specific work per cycle

w_{fr}	$\left[J/m^3\right]$	frictional work
w_i	$\left[J/m^3\right]$	indicated specific work
$w_{i,hp}$	$\left[J/m^3\right]$	high pressure work
$w_{i,lp}$	$\left[J/m^3\right]$	low pressure work
w_{th}	$\left[J/m^3\right]$	theoretical work
x_{CoG} , y_{CoG} , z_{CoG}	$[m]$	CoG co-ordinate axis
x_{In} , y_{In} , z_{In}	$[m]$	inertial co-ordinate axis
x_{Un} , y_{Un} , z_{Un}	$[m]$	undercarriage co-ordinate axis
x_W , y_W , z_W	$[m]$	wheel co-ordinate axis
z		complex variable in z-transformation
z_C	$[m]$	chassis height
z_U	$[m]$	vertical chassis position
z_W	$[m]$	vertical wheel-chassis contact point height
α	$[rad]$	tire side slip angle
α_a	$[rad]$	fixed advance angle
α_{CS}	$[rad]$	crankshaft angle
α_e	$[rad]$	effective ignition angle
α_i	$[rad]$	ignition angle (from engine map)
α_k	$[rad]$	knock control ignition angle
α_l	$[rad]$	learned ignition angle from adaptive map
α_{RLS}		effective term in RLS estimation
α_t	$[rad]$	throttle angle
β	$[rad]$	vehicle body side slip angle
γ	$[rad]$	camber angle
δ_A	$[rad]$	Ackermann angle
δ_S	$[rad]$	steering wheel angle
δ_W	$[rad]$	wheel turn angle
ε		compression ratio
η_e		effective thermodynamic efficiency
η_{eff}		effective thermodynamic efficiency
η_{th}		theoretical thermodynamic efficiency
ϑ	$[K]$	in-cylinder temperatur
ϑ	$[K]$	temperature
ϑ_a	$[K]$	ambient air temperature
ϑ_e	$[K]$	engine temperature
ϑ_{ij}	$[m]$	angle between CoG co-ord. system and line from CoG to wheel ground contact point
ϑ_m	$[K]$	manifold air temperature
ϑ_{Sensor}	$[K]$	sensor temperature
κ		adiabatic exponent
κ	$[m]$	curvature of road
λ		air-fuel ratio
λ_a		relative air supply
λ_f		relative fuel supply
$\Delta\lambda_g$		limit cycle

λ_{RLS}		forgetting factor in RLS estimation
λ_u		weighting factor for control input changes
μ_{Br}		friction coefficient between brake pedal and brake disc
μ_L		friction co-efficient in direction of v_W
μ_{Res}		resultant friction co-efficient
μ_S		friction co-efficient in direction perpendicular to v_W
ρ_0	$[kg/m^3]$	air density
ρ		injection ratio or load
ρ	$[rad]$	road curve radius
ρ_f	$[kg/m^3]$	fuel density
τ_a	$[s]$	inter arrival time
τ_d	$[s]$	inflammation delay time
τ_s	$[s]$	self inflammation time
τ_s	$[s]$	service time
τ_w	$[s]$	waiting time
φ	$[rad]$	roll angle
φ_{road}	$[rad]$	road camber
χ		pressure ratio
χ	$[rad]$	pitch angle
χ_{road}	$[rad]$	road gradient
ψ	$[rad]$	yaw angle
ω	$[rad/s]$	wheel angular velocity
ω_c	$[rad/s]$	rotational velocity in curves

B.3 Abbreviations

CO	carbon monoxide
HC	hydrocarbons
NO_x	nitrogen oxides
O_2	oxygen
BDC	Bottom Dead Center of piston movement
CoG	Center of Gravity
ECE	Economic Commission for Europe, driving cycle in Europe
FIR	Finite Impulse Response, filter algorithm which sums weighted values of the input variable over a time interval
FTP	Federal Test Procedure, driving cycle in the USA
GPC	General Predictive Control
ICM	Instantaneous center of motion
LQG	Linear Quadratic Gaussian
LTR	Loop Transfer Recovery
PI	Proportional-Integral Controller
PID	Proportional-Integral-Differential Controller
RQ	Minimum-maximum-speed governor (mechanical)
RQV	Variable speed governor (mechanical)
TDC	Top Dead Center of piston movement

B.4 Units

$$1\,bar = 10^5\,Pa$$
$$1\,bar = 10^5\,\frac{N}{m^2}$$
$$1\,\frac{km}{h} = 0,28\,\frac{m}{s}$$
$$1\,\frac{m}{s} = 3,6\,\frac{km}{h}$$

Bibliography

[1] D. Ammon: *Radlastschwankungen, Seitenführungsvermögen und Fahrsicherheit*, VDI Berichte 1088, pp243-252, 1993.

[2] C.F. Aquino: *Transient A/F Control Characteristics of the 5 Liter Control Fuel Injection Engine*, SAE-Paper 810494, 1981.

[3] A. Björnberg and M. Pettersson and L. Nielsen: *Nonlinear driveline oscillations at low clutch torques in heavy trucks*, Presented at Reglermötet in Luleå, Sweden, 1996.

[4] B. Böning: *Improvement of Fuel Economy by Systematic Computer-Aided-Control Optimization*, Procedings of ISATA, Torino, 1980.

[5] *Automotive handbook*, Robert Bosch GmbH, Stuttgart, 1993.

[6] *Diesel fuel injection*, Robert Bosch GmbH, Stuttgart, 1994.

[7] K. Brammer and G. Siffling: *Kalman-Bucy-Filter*, R. Oldenbourg Verlag, München and Wien, 1994.

[8] W. Breuer: *State- and Parameter-Estimation for Four-Wheel-Drive Passenger-Cars*, Band II, European Control Conference , Groningen, 1993.

[9] W. Breuer: *Radmomentenregelung bei PKW*, VDI-Verlag, Fortschritt-Bericht 12/235, Düsseldorf, 1995.

[10] N. Bronstein and K. Semendjaev: *Taschenbuch der Mathematik*, Frankfurt, Verlag Harri Deutsch, 1987.

[11] D. Buck: *Der Abgaskatalysator, Aufbau, Funktion und Wirkung*, Schriftenreihe der Adam Opel AG, Nr. 42, Germany, November 1984.

[12] G. Büschges *et al*: *Systemanalyse Straßenverkehrssicherheit*, Bereich Unfallforschung, Bundesanstalt für Straßenwesen, Köln, 1972.

[13] M. Burckhardt: *Fahrwerktechnik: Radschlupf-Regelsysteme*, Würzburg, Vogel Fachbuch, 1993.

[14] J. Bußhardt, J. Führer and R. Isermann: *Ein elektronisches System zur parameteradaptiven Regelung und Diagnose von Kraftfahrzeugstoßdämpfern*, VDI Berichte 1009, Baden-Baden, pp199-217, 1992.

[15] D. W. Clarke, C. Mohtadi: *Generalized Predictive Control*, Part I and II, Automatica, Vol. 23, No. 2, 1987.

[16] S. Crisafulli, T.P. Medhurst: *Robust On-Line Digital Differentiation with an Application to Underground Coal Mining*, IFAC World Congress, Sidney, July 1993.

[17] A. Daiß: *Beobachtung fahrdynamischer Zustände und Verbesserung einer ABS- und Fahrdynamikregelung*, Dissertation Universität Karlsruhe, 1996.

[18] N. Danianoff: *Beeinflussung und Schätzung von Fahrgeschwindigkeit in Kurven*, Veröffentlichungen des Institutes für Straßenbau und Eisenbahnwesen der Universität Karlsruhe, 1981.

[19] D.J. Dobner: *A Mathematical Engine Model for Development of Dynamic Engine Control*, SAE Paper 800054, 1980

[20] H. Fehrenbach: *Model-based Combustion Pressure Computation through Crankshaft Angular Acceleration Analysis*, Proceedings of 22nd International Symposium on Automotive Technology & Automation, Vol. I, May 1990.

[21] O. Föllinger: *Regelungstechnik*, Dr. Alfred Hüthig Verlag, Heidelberg, 1990.

[22] O. Föllinger: *Nichtlineare Regelungen*, Band 1, R. Oldenbourg Verlag, München and Wien, 1987.

[23] O. Föllinger: *Nichtlineare Regelungen*, Band 2, R. Oldenbourg Verlag, München and Wien, 1993.

[24] St. Germann, M. Würtenburger and A. Daiß: *Monitoring of friction between tyre and road surface*, 3rd IEEE Conference on control Application, Glasgow, 1994.

[25] T.D. Gillespie: *Fundamentals of Vehicle Dynamics*, Society of Automotive Engineers Inc., 1992.

[26] H. Godthelp: *Studies on Human vehicle control*, Dissertation, Institute for perception TNO, NL-Soesterberg, 1984.

[27] H. Grohe: *Otto- und Dieselmotoren*, Vogel Verlag, 1989.

[28] A.J. Healy, E. Nathman and C.C. Smith: *An analytical and experimental study of automobile dynamics with random inputs*, Trans. of the ASME, pp284-292, 1977.

[29] M. Henn: *On-Board-Diagnose der Verbrennung von Ottomotoren*, Dissertation Universität Karlsruhe, 1995.

[30] K.L. Höfner and J. Hoskovec: *Registrierung der Blickbewegungen beim Autofahren - bisherige Forschungen*, Zeitschrift für Verkehrssicherheit, 19, Heft 4, pp222-241, 1973.

[31] R.D. Huguenin: *Fahrverhalten im Straßenverkehr*, Reihe Faktor Mensch im Verkehr Nr. 37, Rot- Gelb- Grün- Verlag Braunschweig, 1988.

[32] R. Isermann: *Identifikation dynamischer Systeme I und II*, Springer Verlag, 1991.

[33] R. Isermann: *Identifikation dynamischer Systeme, Band I+II*, Berlin, Springer Verlag 1992.

[34] T. Kailath: *Linear systems*, Prentice Hall, 1980.

[35] N. Kalouptsidis and S. Theodoridis: *Adaptive Signal Identification and Signal processing Algorithms*, Prentice Hall, 1993.

[36] Y. Kanayama, Y. Kimura, F. Miyazaki and T. Nogutchi: *A stable tracking control for an autonomous mobile robot*, Proc. IEEE International conference on robotics and automation, Cincinnati, OH, pp384-389, 1982.

[37] U. Kiencke, S. Dais and M. Litschel: *Automotive Serial Controller Area Network*, SAE-Paper 860391, 1986.

[38] U. Kiencke: *A View of Automotive Control Systems*, IEEE-Control Systems Volume 8 Number 4, 1988.

[39] U. Kiencke *Realtime Estimation of Adhesion Characteristic between Tyres and Road*, 12.th IFAC World Congress of Automatic Control, Vol. 1, pp15-22, Sydney, 1993.

[40] U. Kiencke and A. Daiß: *Estimation of Tyre friction for enhanced ABS-systems*, AVEC Congress, Tokio, 1994.

[41] U. Kiencke: *Ereignisdiskrete Systeme*, Modellierung und Steuerung verteilter Systeme, R. Oldenbourg Verlag, 1997.

[42] U. Kiencke and H. Kronmüller: *Meßtechnik* , Springer Verlag, Germany, 1995, Pages 183 ff.

[43] A. Kracke *Untersuchung der Gemischbildung durch Hochdruckeinspritzung bei PKW-Dieselmotoren*, VDI, Düsseldorf, 1992, Vol. 175d, series 12.

[44] O. Krämer, G. Jungbluth: *Bau und Berechnung von Verbrennungsmotoren*, Springer Verlag, 1983.

[45] K. Ledjeff: *Brennstoffzellen: Entwicklung, Technologie, Anwendung*, Müller, Heidelberg, 1995.

[46] Leins, Meewes and Gerz: *Zur Beschreibung des Verkehrsablaufes auf Straßen mit und ohne Richtungstrennung*, Forschungsbericht des Landes NRW, 1975.

[47] Ljung and Lennart: *System Identification, Theory for the user*, Prentice Hall, 1987.

[48] J. M. Maciejowski: *Multivariable feedback design*, Addison-Wesley, 1989.

[49] R. Majjad: *Hybride Modellierung und Identifikation eines Fahrer-Fahrzeug Systems*, Dissertation Universität Karlsruhe, 1997.

[50] J. L. Meriam and L. G. Kraige: *Engineering mechanics, dynamics*, John Wiley & Sons, 1987.

[51] H. Meyer: *Echtzeit Reifendrucküberwachung*, Dissertation, Universität Karlsruhe, 1995.

[52] M. Mitschke: *Dynamik der Kraftfahrzeuge*, Band A, B, C, Springer Verlag 1988.

[53] M. Mitschke: *Dynamik der Kraftfahrzeuge*, Band A, B, C, Berlin, Springer Verlag, 1990.

[54] M. Mitschke: *Dynamik der Kraftfahrzeuge*, Band A, B, C, Berlin, Springer Verlag, 1995.

[55] C. Y. Mo and A. J. Beaumount and N. N. Powell: *Active control of driveability*, SAE Paper 960046, 1996.

[56] K. Nordgård and H. Hoonhorst: *Developments in automated clutch management systems*, SAE Paper 950896, 1995.

[57] C. O. Nwagboso: *Automotive sensory systems*, Chapman & Hall, 1993.

[58] L. Orehall: *Scania OptiCruise: Mechanical gearchanging with engine control*, Truck and Commercial Vehicle International, 1995.

[59] P. Öser and W. Brandstetter: *Grundlagen zur Abgasreinigung von Ottomotoren und der Katalysator-Technik*, Motortechnische Zeitschrift 45, 1984, Germany, Page 201 − 206.

[60] M. Ostertag: *Strukturierte Optimierung technischer Prozesse am Beispiel der KFZ Crash-Erkennung*, Dissertation, Universität Karlsruhe, 1996.

[61] M. Pettersson: *Driveline modeling and principles for speed and gear-shift control*, Licentiate Thesis, University of Linsköpping, 1996.

[62] *CAN Specification*, Philips GmbH, Hamburg, Version 2.0, 1991.

[63] R. Prahbakar: *Optimisation of Automotive engine Fuel Economy and Emissions*, AMSE Publication 75 WA/Art. 19, December 1975.

[64] H-P. Preuss: *Entworf stationär perfekter Zustandsregelungen durch fiktive Ausgangsvektorrückführung*, VDI-Verlag, Fortschritt-Bericht 8/42, Düsseldorf, 1995.

[65] L. Rasmussen: *Information processing and human-machine interaction*, New York, North-Holland, 1986.

[66] J. Reimpell and P. Sponagel: *Fahrwerktechnik: Reifen und Räder*, Würzburg, Vogel Fachbuch, 1995.

[67] J. Riempell and P. Sponagel: *Fahrwerktechnik: Reifen und Räder*, Würzburg, Vogel Fachbuch, 1988.

[68] J. Riempell: *Fahrwerktechnik, Fahrzeugmechanik*, Vogel Verlag, 1992.

[69] A. Riekert and T. Schunk: *Zur Fahrmechanik des gummibereiften Kraftfahrzeuges*, Ingenieur Archiv, vol 11 (1940), pp210-224.

[70] K. Rumar: *The role of perceptual and cognitive filters in observed behaviour*, In: Evans, L., and Schwing, R.C. (Eds.), Human behaviour and traffic safety, London: Plenum, pp 151-170, 1985.

[71] K. Rumar: *In vehicle information systems*, Proc. 3rd AAVD congress on vehicle design and components, St. Helier, Jersey, Interscience Enterprises, 1986, D33-D42.

[72] Simulink: *User's Guide*, MathWorks Inc., 1993.

[73] K. Suzuki and Y. Tozawa: *Influence of powertrain torsional rigidity NVH of 6x4 trucks*, SAE Paper 922482, 1992.

[74] E.P. Todosiev: *The action point model of the driver-vehicle system*, Engineering experiment station, The Ohio State University, Columbus, report No. 202A-3, 1976.

[75] S. Witte: *Simulationsuntersuchungen zum Einfluß von Fahrverhalten und technischen Abstandsregelsystemen auf den Kolonnenverkehr*, Institut für Bauingenieur- und Vermessungswesen, Dissertation, Universität Karlsruhe, 1995.

[76] H.D. Utzelmann: *Tempowahl und -motive*, Faktor Mensch im Verkehr, Heft 24, Darmstadt 1976.

[77] C.D. Wickens: *Engineering Psychology and human performance*, Harper Collins Publishers Inc., 1992.

[78] W.W. Wierwille: *et al., Strategic use of visual resources by the driver while navigating with an in-car navigation display system*, SAE P-21, XXII FISITA Congress, Sep. 25-30, Vol. 2, Paper 885180, pp2661-2675, 1988.

[79] W.W. Wierwille and L. Tijerina: *Darstellung des Zusammenhangs zwischen der visuellen Beanspruchung des Fahrers im Fahrzeug und dem Eintreten eines Unfalls*, Zeitschrift für Verkehrssicherheit, 43, Nr. 2, pp67-74, 1997.

[80] G. Woschni: *Verbrennungsmotoren*, Skriptum zur Vorlesung, Lehrstuhl und Institut für Verbrennungskraftmaschinen und Kraftfahrzeuge, Technische Univerität München, 1980.

[81] H.J. Zimmermann: *Fuzzy set thoery and its applications*, Klawer Academic Publishers, Boston, 1991.

[82] M. Zeitz: *Nichtlineare Beobachter für chemische Reaktoren*, VDI-Verlag, Fortschritt-Bericht 8/27, Düsseldorf, 1977

Springer
and the
environment

At Springer we firmly believe that an international science publisher has a special obligation to the environment, and our corporate policies consistently reflect this conviction.

We also expect our business partners – paper mills, printers, packaging manufacturers, etc. – to commit themselves to using materials and production processes that do not harm the environment. The paper in this book is made from low- or no-chlorine pulp and is acid free, in conformance with international standards for paper permanency.

 Springer

Printing (computer to plate): Mercedes-Druck, Berlin
Binding: Buchbinderei Lüderitz & Bauer, Berlin